THE LATIN AMERICA RE
Series edited by Robin Kirk and Orin S

MW01285279

The Haiti Reader

THE

HAITI

READER

HISTORY, CULTURE, POLITICS

Laurent Dubois, Kaiama L. Glover, Nadève Ménard,
Millery Polyné, and Chantalle F. Verna, editors

DUKE UNIVERSITY PRESS   *Durham and London*   2020

© 2020 Duke University Press
All rights reserved
Printed in the United States of America on acid-free paper ∞
Typeset in Monotype Dante by BW&A Books, Inc.

Library of Congress Cataloging-in-Publication Data
Names: Glover, Kaiama L., [date] editor. | Dubois, Laurent, [date] editor. |
Ménard, Nadève, editor. | Polyné, Millery, editor. | Verna, Chantalle F.,
[date] editor.
Title: The Haiti reader : history, culture, politics / Laurent Dubois, Kaiama L.
Glover, Nadève Ménard, Millery Polyné, Chantalle F. Verna, eds.
Other titles: Latin America readers.
Description: Durham : Duke University Press 2020. | Series: The Latin America
Readers | Includes bibliographical references and index.
Identifiers: LCCN 2019016283 (print)
LCCN 2019980905 (ebook)
ISBN 9781478005162 (hardcover)
ISBN 9781478006770 (paperback)
ISBN 9781478007609 (ebook)
Subjects: LCSH: Haiti—History. | Haiti—Politics and government. |
Haiti—Civilization.
Classification: LCC F1901 .H358 2020 (print) | LCC F1901 (ebook) | DDC 972.94—dc23
LC record available at https://lccn.loc.gov/2019016283
LC ebook record available at https://lccn.loc.gov/2019980905

Cover art: Haitian schoolchildren. © Anthony Asael/Art in All of Us/
Corbis News. Courtesy of Getty Images.

For our children,
especially the youngest of the bunch,
Serenity Macaya Verna

Contents

Acknowledgments

The Haiti Reader has been a long, rich, and deeply collective endeavor. When we have explained the project to those we have reached out to for help, we've encountered great generosity and enthusiasm for the bigger project of sharing these many Haitian histories, voices, and perspectives.

Our first thanks go to Duke University Press, who came to us with the idea and have guided and collaborated with us with patience and wisdom throughout. Navigating the rights issues for both text and images across multiple countries has been exceedingly complex, and we would have been quite literally lost without the many at the press who helped us in this process. Our marvelous editors—Valerie Millholland, who first invited us to the project, and Gisela Fosado, who has accompanied us for the long journey—have been constant voices of guidance and reassurance. Lydia Rose Rappoport-Hankins was a steadfast guide for us at the press, and Emily Chilton provided a pivotal, organizing perspective at a key moment. A series of graduate students from Duke who worked as interns on the project over its many years have offered invaluable support: Lorien Olive, Casey Stegman, Anna Tybinko, Nehanda Loiseau, Ayanna Legros, and Renee Ragin. And Jenny Tan helped us profoundly in shaping the visual landscape of the book. In the early years of the project the Haiti Laboratory of the Franklin Humanities Laboratory was itself a laboratory for the reader, where we hosted meetings and also depended on the work of research assistants Julia Gaffield and Claire A. Payton in beginning to pull together our entries.

We are deeply indebted to the contributing editors who responded to our requests to join us in the project and provided introductions and in many cases translations for particular excerpts: Yveline Alexis, Alessandra Benedicty-Kokken, Christopher Bongie, Victor Bulmer-Thomas, Brandon Byrd, Lesley S. Curtis, Marlene Daut, Colin Dayan, Anne Eller, Julia Gaffield, Johnhenry Gonzalez, Allen Kim, Wynnie Lamour, Carl Lindskoog, Andrew Maginn, Christen Mucher, Graham Nessler, Rose Réjouis, Terry Rey, Grace Saunders, Matthew J. Smith, Richard Turits, and Laura Wagner. They are all important scholars of Haiti in their own work, and they took the time to share their expertise with us, making the book infinitely broader and better. They are recognized within the body of the work, which identifies the contributing editor for a given excerpt when there was one. But we are grateful to them too as a collective that embodies the best of what scholarly generosity and collaboration are about.

The field of Haitian Studies is a lovely home for us as editors, and we have found it to be a nourishing and generous space to work on this project, which we hope will be a valuable contribution to our extended network. We have received invaluable advice and support from many scholars, family, and friends, including Michel Acacia, Alice Backer, Patrick Bellegarde-Smith, Pierre Buteau, Laurence Camille, Jean Casimir, Stephanie Chancy, Michael Dash, Alex Dupuy, Robert Fatton Jr., Gerdy Gabriel, Dimmy Herard, Mireille Jérôme, Sophonie Joseph, Chelsey Kivland, Antoine Lévy, Lindja Levy, Bertin M. Louis, Ana Marie Greenidge Ménard, Guy-Gérald Ménard, Allen Morrison, Jerry Philogène, Kate Ramsey, Carline Rémy, Enrique Silva, Évelyne Trouillot, and Lyonel Trouillot. We are also grateful for the suggestions of two anonymous reviewers who read our proposal and whose comments helped shape the final work.

We depended on some of the precious libraries and collections that maintain Haitian Studies, who provided us guidance and support throughout the process. We are especially grateful to the Duke University Libraries, and particularly the Rubenstein Special Collections Library; the Library of the École Normale Supérieure in Haiti; the holders of the Sylvain Collection; and Frantz Voltaire of CIDIHCA. Voltaire was particularly generous in allowing us to use materials from his photographic collection, many of which illustrate the book. More broadly, we thank all the rights-holders who granted us permission to reproduce works here, and the authors, songwriters, and photographers who gave us permission to include their work. Special thanks to Lena Jackson, for working with us to include the works of Jerry Moïse; and to photographers Phyllis Galembo, Carl Juste, Noelle Flores Theard, and the FotoKonbit collective. We thank Elizabeth McAlister for sharing her expertise and a photograph of a rara band.

A number of dear friends and family gave of their time to read the volume, encourage us, and provide us with the space to write, and time to think and travel. Thank you to Judy C. Polyné for your attention to detail and your accounting skills, and to all our families and colleague-friends for their support all the way through this journey.

Introduction

At times it can seem as if Haiti is on everyone's mind—at least for a news cycle or two. Yet despite periods of intensive interest in Haiti, there is, overall, a surprising lack of knowledge about the specifics of the country's history and culture in the United States. And the way Haiti is viewed by natives and foreigners runs a wide gamut: for Martinican poet Aimé Césaire, Haiti is the place where "Négritude rose up for the first time and stated that it believed in its humanity," but for many in the United States the country is characterized by the endlessly repeated taglines and memes about its extreme poverty and perceived inhabitability or seen primarily as a site of political turmoil and backward cultural practices. For many Haitians, meanwhile, Haiti is a place from which to escape by any means, even at the risk of death. For many others, Haiti is the ultimate "manman cheri," the place of true home, the one to which they will always return.

Haiti's presence in both the Caribbean and global imaginary has long been colossal. Whether celebrated for its revolution and victory over Napoleon Bonaparte's army or disparaged for its poverty and political instability, Haiti is a highly symbolic nation. Yet few beyond Haitians and Haitianists, specialists of the country, venture beyond the symbols. One way to understand the limited knowledge about Haiti is as a consequence of isolating linguistic barriers. That is, while the United States is currently the most powerful external force shaping Haiti's political and economic reality, the country's literary and intellectual production since independence in 1804—along with its juridical and political life—is predominantly francophone. Yet French is in fact a minority language in Haiti, as the majority of the population speaks exclusively Haitian Creole—a language accessible to relatively few non-Haitians. As a result, even while select U.S. Americans are deeply connected to and interested in Haiti, few have more than a cursory knowledge of the country's historical and cultural realities. Those who seek to learn about Haiti find themselves almost entirely reliant on the writings of non-Haitians or Haitian writers residing in diaspora. And while a sizable portion of writing about the country by non-Haitians is certainly well informed and based on a long engagement with Haiti, an overwhelmingly negative narrative has also been constructed around the island nation. Indeed, few places have been on the receiving end of as much hostility, distortion, and fantasy on the part of outsiders.

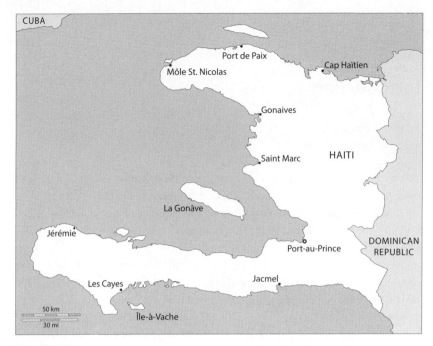

Map of Haiti

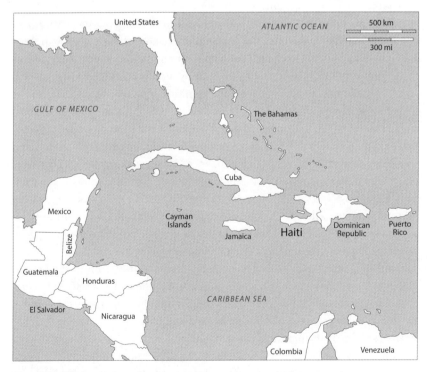

Map of Caribbean

The Haiti Reader seeks primarily to introduce a broad audience of anglophone readers to Haiti via the cultural productions of Haitians themselves. Having selected representative works from the nation's scholarly, literary, religious, visual, musical, and political culture, we hope to make plain the extent to which Haitians have long understood themselves as part of an extra-insular, progressive human community. We have sought to identify and translate key texts—poems, novels, political tracts, essays, legislation, songs, testimonies, folktales—that illuminate Haiti's history and culture. We have prioritized the presentation of material from Haitian writers and thinkers, much of it translated into English for the first time here, and have included only a very few writings by foreign observers, which are generally easier to access. Our process of selection has also been guided by a desire to offer a kind of counternarrative, highlighting some lesser-known aspects of Haitian life and culture. But overall we aim to offer as full a representation as possible of well-known as well as lesser-known periods in Haiti's past. The volume opens and closes with two transformative moments in Haitian history: the creation of the Haitian state in 1804 and the 2010 earthquake. In addition, we explore both widely known episodes in Haiti's history, such as the U.S. military occupation and Duvalier dictatorship, and such often-overlooked periods as the "long" nineteenth century and the decades immediately following Haiti's "second independence" (i.e., the end of the U.S. occupation) in 1934.

Given Haiti's far-reaching and complex entanglements with North America, Europe, other parts of the Caribbean, Latin America, and Africa, this reader is necessarily national and transnational in scope. As such, it will stand as a challenge to the way Haitians have, despite their determining role in New World political history and geography, found themselves isolated and unwelcomed outside (and often even inside) their own island—bounded and unwanted, faced with countless obstacles to inhabiting the wider world. Our collection looks closely at the extent to which regional aesthetic canons ghettoize Haiti's literary production and exacerbate the nation's sociopolitical isolation. Less widely circulated than works from other parts of the (francophone) Americas, Haitian writing has indeed had far less access to the most fundamental prerequisite for circulation: translation. *The Haiti Reader* takes steps toward addressing that exclusion by showcasing excerpts from a wide range of literary works by Haitian writers, many of them relatively unknown to anglophone audiences.

Even though Haitian thinkers have had vital engagement with issues of race and racism, nationalism, cultural formation, colonialism, postcolonialism, and political theory, Haitian thought remains largely on the margins of broader debates and canons. To take but one example among many, the pioneering work of Anténor Firmin—who in the late nineteenth century attacked the scientific racism of reigning anthropology in a work that presaged the later approach of Franz Boas—was not translated into English until 2002 and remains largely excluded from understandings of the history of anthropological thought. In effect, for the past two centuries, Haitian intellectuals like Firmin have been in dialogue with theoretical currents in Europe and the Americas and have sought to both confirm and challenge broader interpretive frameworks by drawing on their country's historical experience. Our book pays particular attention to the work of such intellectuals, providing those who read what follows with a clearer sense of Haiti's nation-building efforts and engagement with the world from the nineteenth century to the present day.

Our strategy in composing *The Haiti Reader* is premised on an acknowledgment of Haiti's marginalization and the consequent importance of situating the country and its cultural contributions squarely in the heart of the Americas. Recent scholarship on Haiti reveals its significant imbrication in cultural, ideological, and radical social movements in the Western Hemisphere and beyond—including abolitionism, Pan-Americanism, Pan-Africanism, internationalism, Indigenism, Négritude, and decolonization. The Haitian Constitution of 1816, for example, granted citizenship to all Africans and Indians seeking residence in Haiti. This proved to be a powerful legal decree given the intensification of slavery in the Caribbean and the United States, and the potential of enslaved peoples (sailors, maids, cooks, etc.) to step onto free Haitian soil. As such, the Haitian Constitution had significant implications with respect to broader New World discourses on property rights, citizenship, sovereignty, and freedom.

At the same time, *The Haiti Reader* explicitly addresses and reflects the various borders within the country. Haiti's rather ambivalent status as a "francophone" nation, for example, raises important questions concerning who "gets to" write—and so to represent—this country and its inhabitants: from the working- and middle-class Haitian diasporans who actively impart remittances and humanitarian aid through hometown associations, to the privileged border-crossing members of the intellectual and merchant elite class and the individuals and communities that are the subjects and consumers of their works and products. Our goal throughout the *Reader* is therefore to place in dialogue—and at times in tension—texts from different places within Haitian society, drawing on aspects of vernacular culture, particularly popular and religious music, to reflect the multiplicity and diversity of perspectives within the country itself.

The Haiti Reader is composed of eight chronological parts. Each section begins with a contextualizing introduction. We then present three kinds of documents in each section: visual materials; contemporary texts, including laws and political documents, essays, poems, and literary texts; and excerpts from scholarly works contextualizing the particular period and presenting broader approaches to thinking about Haitian history and culture. Unless otherwise noted, all ellipses are ours, added to indicate omitted material.

Our selections are not—could not be—exhaustive, and we have made many difficult choices while deciding what to include. Certain of these omissions were a matter of logistics: in several instances where we wished to feature certain authors or texts, the difficulty or expense of obtaining the rights to reproduce them here proved prohibitive. We have also had to be selective in fixing our temporal parameters. The *Reader* is almost exclusively focused on postindependence Haiti, offering little material on colonial Saint-Domingue or the Haitian Revolution. Readers interested in material on the Haitian Revolution can refer to Laurent Dubois and John Garrigus, *Slave Revolution in the Caribbean, 1787–1804: A History in Documents* (2006). In addition, there are fields of interest whose surface we have barely scratched. One of the more significant is queer Haitian Studies, most recently and compellingly advanced in the work of scholars like Dasha A. Chapman, Erin L. Durban-Albrecht, and Mario LaMothe in their pioneering issue of *Women and Performance: a journal of feminist theory*, "Nou Mache Ansanm (We Walk Together): Queer Haitian Performance and Affiliation." Indeed, there could be many other versions of a reader based on Haiti and its history, and we hope future scholars will continue the task of translating and publishing a broader array of works by Haitian writers and thinkers. Our hope for this text is that it will help readers discover certain topics and writers so that they can then delve into them more deeply. We offer it as an invitation into the vast corpus—an extensive archipelago—of Haitian thought, whose marvels and diversity we have sought to illuminate in the pages that follow.

We would like to add a few words on language here. We have focused particularly on making sure that the voices of Haitian writers who are not well known to anglophone readers can be made accessible, and a majority of the featured texts are translated here for the first time. We have sought to offer translations that allow anglophone readers to enjoy these texts while maintaining the style and energy of the original—including, in some cases, original terms in Creole and French. This being said, the fact that *The Haiti Reader* is presented in English somewhat obscures Haitian linguistic reality. Although Haitian Creole was only granted official language status with the 1987 Constitution, both French and Haitian Creole have been integral parts of the country's linguistic fabric dating from the colonial period, even if historically they have followed different paths. While French was brought to the island by European colonizers and imposed as the language of authority, Haitian Creole was forged by the merging of various languages and peoples within the new society. Both languages underwent many internal transformations as well as shifts in their relationship to each other over the centuries. Today, in addition to the two official languages, English and Spanish are also widely spoken within certain segments of Haitian society, and in various regions of the country. It is impossible for us to render such linguistic complexity with translations into one target language. Nonetheless, we want to remind our readers that the majority of texts presented here were translated either from Haitian Creole or from French. Several creative texts make use of both languages. Traditional distinctions that view Creole as an oral language mainly used by the poor and disenfranchised, and French as a written language mainly used in formal situations or by the elite, require nuance today more than ever. We have done our best to communicate this linguistic complexity through our introductions and translations, and we urge those who are able to read the texts in their original languages to seek out the originals and do so where possible as a next step to a greater understanding of Haiti's languages and culture.

In addition to the five main editors, we also worked with contributing editors who generously offered us selections and translations from their own work. In this sense *The Haiti Reader* is the result of a true *konbit* (cooperative, communal labor). It channels the much larger and energetic field of Haitian studies, and we hope, contributes to ever-expanding research and discussion about Haiti and its many connections to the human experience worldwide.

I

Foundations

Haiti was born as a nation in 1804, but its foundations lie in the colonial society of French Saint-Domingue and in the remarkable revolution that began
there with a massive uprising of the enslaved in 1791. The excerpts in this
section offer a few pathways through this complex and layered history. They
highlight part of the challenge of understanding and recounting Haitian
history—the fact that relatively few were able to leave behind written traces
of their lives, thoughts, and projects. For this reason, among the excerpts
here are alternative ways of accessing the colonial and revolutionary past,
including songs, contemporary novels, and images.

At the core of the events of this period were the efforts of the enslaved, who
made up the vast majority of the colony's population, to resist and ultimately
overthrow slavery and to create a different social order on the ashes of the
plantation world. From the beginning, the Haitian revolutionaries were performing on a world stage, their actions observed, commented on, dissected,
critiqued, and recounted throughout Europe, the Americas, and beyond. The
revolutionaries in Haiti understood this well, as did those who followed them,
and some—including many of the authors featured in this section—actively
sought to shape the way the broader world viewed their struggle.

There also was—and in some respects, continues to be—profound disagreement within Haiti over precisely what the revolution and its aftermath
should mean. Key leaders, both during the revolution and after independence,
were committed to the idea that Haiti's economy could thrive only through
the continuation of some kind of plantation order. They sought a range of
strategies for maintaining aspects of the plantation economy without slavery.
In the process they faced constant, and at times successful, resistance from
what Haitian historian Jean Casimir calls the "counter-plantation" system.
The battle over what freedom, autonomy, and sovereignty truly meant began during the Haitian Revolution and, in a way, that battle has never truly
ended.

The excerpts in this section attempt to capture the dreams, struggles, and
contradictions of the colonial population as well as the first generation of
Haitians. They represent the beginning of a set of stories that would spiral
through the country's entire history.

An Account of the Antiquities of the Indians

Ramón Pané

A few years after Columbus's arrival in 1492 on the island that he dubbed "Hispaniola," a Spanish friar named Ramón Pané wrote a manuscript describing some of the practices and beliefs of the indigenous people who inhabited it.

Pané's text offers valuable descriptions of the way indigenous groups narrated their own history, as well as their religious beliefs and practices, including the use of carvings called zemis. The indigenous population was largely decimated through war, disease, and enslavement, dropping from perhaps 500,000 to 750,000 to just tens of thousands. By the time the French colony of Saint-Domingue was settled in the late seventeenth century, there were only scattered indigenous communities in the mountains. But the material culture of the indigenous societies was present throughout the island, and artifacts were sometimes found as fields were planted. Some of these remains, including zemis, were in fact preserved and used in the developing Vodou religion.

Though Pané calls the island Hispaniola, he notes that "before" colonization it was "called Haití, and the inhabitants call it by this name." Because the original indigenous name was preserved in the written record in this way, it was able to be recovered and redeployed in 1804 by the founders of the nation of Haiti.

I, Fray Ramón, a humble friar of the Order of Saint Jerome, am writing what I have been able to discover and understand of the beliefs and Idolatries of the Indians, and of how they worship their gods. . . .

In worshiping the idols they keep at home, which they call zemis, each one observes a particular manner and superstition. They believe that he is in heaven and is immortal, and that no one can see him, and that he has a mother. But He has no beginning, and they call him Yúcahu Bagua Marocoti, and they call his mother Atabey, Yermao, Guacar, Apito, and Zuimaco, which are five names. . . . They know likewise from whence they came, and where the sun and the moon had their beginning, and how the Sea was made, and where the dead go. And they believe the dead appear to them along the road when they travel alone because they do not appear when many of them travel together. Their ancestors have made them believe all this, for they do not know how to read, nor can they count except up to ten.

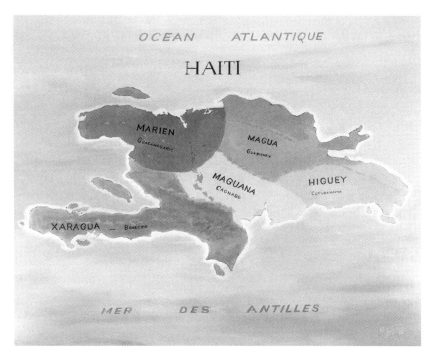

OCEAN ATLANTIQUE

HAITI

MARIEN
GUACANAGARIC

MAGUA
GUARIONEX

MAGUANA
CAONABO

HIGUEY
COTUBANAMA

XARAGUA — BOHECHIO

MER DES ANTILLES

Artist Ulrick Jean Pierre created this map of the indigenous kingdoms (headings) and their respective rulers (subheadings) as they are believed to have existed at the time Columbus arrived on the island the inhabitants called, according to early Spanish chroniclers, Ayïti. Courtesy of Ulrick Jean Pierre.

Chapter I

CONCERNING THE PLACE FROM WHICH THE INDIANS
HAVE COME AND IN WHAT MANNER

There is a province in Hispaniola called Caonao, in which there is a mountain called Cauta, which has two caves. The name of one of these is Cacibajagua, and Amayaúna the other. The majority of the people who populated the island came from Cacibajagua. . . .

Chapter IX

HOW THEY SAY THE SEA WAS MADE

There was a man called Yaya, whose name they do not know, and his son was called Yayael, which means son of Yaya. Because Yayael wanted to kill his father, the latter sent him into exile, and he was exiled for four months; and afterward his father killed him and put his bones in a gourd and hung it from the roof of his house, where it was hanging for some time. It happened one day that Yaya, desiring to see his son, said to his wife: "I want to see our son Yayael." And she was glad, and taking down the gourd, she turned it over to see the bones of their son. And many fish, large and small, emerged from it. Whereby, seeing that those bones had been changed into fish, they resolved to eat them.

. . . And they also say that the Sun and the Moon emerged from a cave located in the country of a cacique named Mautiatihuel, which cave is called Iguanaboina, and they hold it in great esteem, and they have it all painted in their fashion, without any figures, with a lot of foliage and other such things. And in the said cave there were two zemis made from stone, small ones, the size of half an arm, with their hands tied, and they seemed to be sweating. They valued those zemis very highly; and when it did not rain, they say that they would go in there to visit them, and it would rain at once. And one zemi they called Boinayel, and the other Márohu.

Chapter XII

CONCERNING WHAT THEY BELIEVE ABOUT THE DEAD WANDERING ABOUT, AND WHAT THEY ARE LIKE, AND WHAT THEY DO
They believe there is a place where the dead go, which is called Coaybay, and it is located on one side of the island, which is called Soraya. They say the first person in Coaybay was one who was called Maquetaurie Guayaba, who was the lord of said Coaybay, house and dwelling place of the dead.

Chapter XIII

CONCERNING THE SHAPE THEY SAY THE DEAD HAVE
They say that during the day they hide away, and at night they go out to walk about, and they eat a certain fruit that is called guayaba. . . . And at night they change into fruit, and they celebrate and accompany the living. And in order to recognize them, they observe this procedure: they touch one's belly with their hands, and if they do not find his navel they say he is *operito*, which means dead: that is why they say the dead have no navel. And thus they are sometimes fooled when they do not notice this, and they lie with one of the Coaybay women; when a man thinks he has her in his arms, he has nothing because the woman disappears in an instant. They still believe this even today. When the person is alive, they call his spirit *goeíza*, and when he is dead, they call it *opía*. They say this *goeíza* appears to them often, in a man's shape as well as a woman's, and they say they have been men who have wanted to do battle with it, and one such a man would let his hands on it, it would disappear, and the man would put his arms elsewhere into some trees, and he would end up hanging from those trees. And everyone generally believes this, the children as well as the adults, and that it appears to them in the shape of a father, mother, brothers, or relatives, and other forms. The fruit they say the dead eat is the size of the quince. And the aforesaid that do not

Images of zemi of Maquetaurie Guayaba (profile at left, front is below). Gift of the Austen-Stokes Ancient Americas Foundation, 2005, Walters Museum. Reprinted courtesy of the Walters Museum.

appear to them in the daytime, but always at night, and that is why one is very fearful to venture to walk alone at night.

Chapter XIV

CONCERNING WHENCE THEY DEDUCE THIS AND WHO LEADS THEM
TO HOLD SUCH A BELIEF

There are some men who are practitioners among them and are called *behiques*. . . . Just as the Moors, they have their laws gathered in ancient songs, by which they govern themselves, as do the Moors by their scriptures. And when they wish to sing their songs, they play a certain instrument that is called *moyahabao*, which is made of wood, hollow, strong, and very thin, the length of an arm and a half an arm in width. The part that is played is made in the shape of a blacksmith's tongs, and the other part resembles a mace so that it looks like a long-necked squash. And they play this instrument, which has a voice so loud that it can be heard from a distance of a league and a half. To its sound they sing their songs which they learn by heart and the principal men play it; they learn to play as children and to sing with it according to their custom. . . .

Chapter XV

CONCERNING THE OBSERVANCES OF THESE INDIAN *BEHIQUES*, AND
HOW THEY PRACTICE MEDICINE AND TEACH PEOPLE, AND IN THEIR
MEDICINAL CURES THEY ARE OFTEN DECEIVED

All of the majority of the people of the Island of Hispaniola have many zemis of various sorts. Some contain the bones of their father and mother and relatives and ancestors; they are made of stone or of wood. And they have many of both kinds, some that speak, and others that cause the things they eat to grow, and others that make it rain, and others that make the winds blow.

. . .

The zemi Opiyelguabirán has four feet, like a dog, they say, and is made of wood, and often at night he leaves the house and goes into the jungle. They went to look for him there, and when they brought him home, they would tie him up with a rope, but he would return to the jungle. And they tell that when the Christians arrived on the Island of Hispaniola, this zemi escaped and went into a lagoon; and they followed his tracks as far as the lagoon, but they never saw him again, nor did they hear anything about him.

Sou lanmè

Anonymous

This traditional Vodou song recounts the experience of the Middle Passage and presents it as a metaphor for the creation of a new culture in Haiti. Lasirèn and Agwe Tawoyo are lwa *(gods) in Haitian Vodou who live under the water and control the ocean, ocean crossings, and travel. When the song is sung in a ceremonial context, it places the assembled group back on the slave ship itself, from which entreaties are made to Agwe Tawoyo and Lasirèn and a future day of liberation is imagined. "In the bottom of the ship / We are all one," the song announces, capturing the ways in which many different African cultures came together in shaping Haitian culture. This process is made clear in the structures of Vodou itself, which organizes the* lwa *according to various African "nations" of origin, including Congo and Nago nations. But here is the most powerful and complex symbolism in the song: though the ship is sinking into the water, by singing the song the Vodou community makes clear that despite exile from Africa and the experiences of slavery they are still, as a community, recalling their history in order to continue struggling in the present.*

On the ocean we are sailing
Agwe Tawoyo
There's a time when they'll see us
On the ocean we are sailing

They took our feet
They chained our wrists
They dropped us in the bottom

They took our feet
They chained our wrists
They dropped us in the bottom of the ship

On the ocean we are sailing
Agwe Tawoyo
There's a time when they'll see us

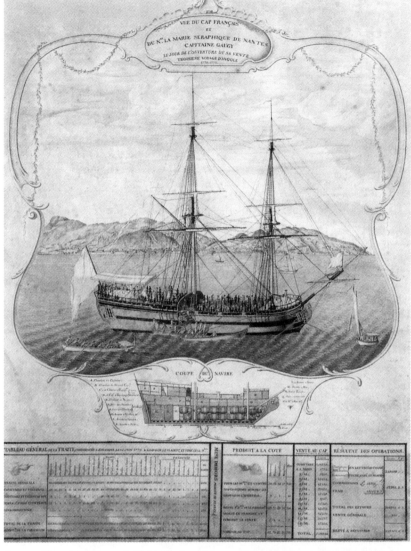

"View of Cap Français and the Marie Seraphique of Nantes, Captain Gaugy, third voyage from Angola, 1772–1773," watercolor, Musées du Château des Ducs de Bretagne. With the slave ship harbored in the port of Le Cap after crossing from Angola, residents are rowing out to purchase enslaved people. On the left side of the ship, a table is set offering refreshments to the buyers as they examine the slaves on display. Below, a diagram shows the organization of the hold of the ship, with merchant goods and enslaved people in different areas, and a chart summarizes the volume of the ship's trade.

Slave ship under the water
The ocean is bad
The ship is broken
It's ready to sink

Slave ship under the water
At the bottom of the ocean
It's covered in water
It's ready to sink

In the bottom of the ship
We are all one

In the bottom of the slave ship
If it sinks
No one will be saved
Agwe Tawoyo
We're all on board
Don't you see we're trapped

We're trapped, papa, we're trapped
We're trapped, Lasirèn, we're trapped

Translated by Erol Josué and Laurent Dubois

Account of a Conspiracy Organized by the Negroes, 1758

Anonymous

In 1758, an enslaved man named Makandal became the focus of planters and officials who believed that he was coordinating a campaign of poisoning across the colony. At the time of these events, the Jesuit order was active in Saint-Domingue, and they wrote the following account of Makandal's activities and his arrest, chronicling the subsequent executions and torture used by the planters in their attempts to suppress resistance among the enslaved. The document thus provides a striking portrait of the violence exercised by masters against slaves in Saint-Domingue. The Jesuit order did not take a position against slavery, and in fact there were Jesuit-run plantations with slaves in other parts of the Caribbean. Nevertheless, their missionizing among the enslaved worried planters in Saint-Domingue, who were always wary of any kind of intervention into their total control over their plantations and slaves. The planters came to perceive the Jesuits as too sympathetic to the slaves in the colony, and a few years later the Jesuits were expelled from Saint-Domingue.

We are here, Sir, in the midst of general consternation, perpetually caught between life and death. My description of our situation will horrify you. Last January, in the region of Limbé (which is five leagues from here), François Macandal, the negro slave of M. le Tellier, was arrested. He had been a maroon (fugitive) for eighteen years. By day he retreated to the mountains, and at night he came to the neighboring plantations, where he was in communication with the negroes. Together they created different poisons, which they sold to their comrades.

We put him on trial. He was condemned to be put to death in front of the main door of the church. . . . Under questioning, this villain revealed the names of a prodigious number of his accomplices, negro slaves belonging to different masters, who have been arrested. He killed an innumerable number of people during his eighteen years of marronage. He was finally executed on the 20th of January at five o'clock in the afternoon.

He was tied with iron chains to a post planted in the middle of the pyre. As soon as he felt the fire, he screamed horribly. But he made an effort that was so prodigious, so superior to the usual powers of man, that the necklace and the chain broke off the post, so that he escaped the flames, with part of his body burned. The police and residents prudently forced the negroes who were surrounding the plaza to leave. All these unfortunates, as they left, screamed loudly that François Macandal was a sorcerer, and incombustible; that he had been right when he told them that no one would be able to capture him, and that as soon as someone tried to grab him he would transform into a mosquito. Even the executioner couldn't believe what he was seeing. Nevertheless, he threw himself on the criminal, tied his feet and hands, and threw him back into the fire. The residents forced their negroes to come back, and as they watched him burn they understood that what they had been made to believe was false.

Since this execution, four or five are burned every month; already twenty-four enslaved negroes or negresses and three free blacks have suffered the same fate. But as each of them are questioned, the police arrest nine or ten others they named as accomplices. So the number of prisoners expands each time a criminal is executed. It is difficult to judge when this affair will end: there are 140 accused in prison.

Among the negroes who have been executed, some have declared that they poisoned 30 or 40 whites, even their own masters, and their wives and children; others claim they poisoned 200 or 300 negroes belonging to various masters.

There were some residents who had 50 to 60 negroes working on their plantation. In less than fifteen days all they had left were 4 or 5, and sometimes none at all. I know many who have suffered this misfortune. People didn't know what had caused this mortality, and it was impossible to help them, because no one suspected poison.

Several confessed they had poisoned negroes to whom they had at first offered poison, but who seemed too affectionate toward their masters and might expose them.

François Macandal discovered three types of poison, some of which are so dangerous and so violent that when doctors and surgeons gave some to dogs they died immediately. There are other poisons that work more slowly, make you languish for five or six months, but which inevitably kill you.

We are frightened to see that almost all of the guilty worked in the great houses, and are among the most trusted slaves: coachmen, cooks, and other domestics who serve us.

They specifically wait until their masters have 15 or 20 whites at the table and are throwing a party. They put the poison in the tea, in the soup, or in other dishes; they have no hesitation about killing inhabitants they have no reason to resent, as long as those they do resent die.

We tremble about going to one another's houses, and do not know who to trust, since it is impossible for us to go without the services of these wretches.

From a few of them we got the recipe for a remedy, which is an effective counter-poison, and that is a great help.

What alarms us even more is to see how little the fate of those we execute touches these wretches, and how little their torture leaves an impression on them. . . .

Here, Sir, is the state of our colony. For the time being the poisoners are mostly in the plain rather than in the town, because François Macandal only came here three times, whereas he was on the plantations of the plain every night. But one of the wretches he taught can teach a hundred more. . . .

Be aware that all those who are guilty are prize negroes, and even though they are worth 4,000 to 5,000 livres they are not spared for that reason. But their masters are all the more miserable because the King only gives them 600 livres for every negro who is executed.

Translated by Laurent Dubois

The Infamous Rosalie

Évelyne Trouillot

The Infamous Rosalie is Évelyne Trouillot's first novel. A member of one of Haiti's most important intellectual families (she is sister to internationally renowned anthropologist, historian, and political scientist Michel-Rolph Trouillot and novelist Lyonel Trouillot), Trouillot is herself a novelist, a poet, and a teacher. The novel's central narrative is inspired by the account of a Saint-Domingue colonist whose memoirs tell the story of an African midwife who kept a cord with seventy knots in it—one knot for each child she'd murdered at birth. Trouillot's novel fills in the gaps around that painful history via the memories of successive generations of enslaved women, taking the reader from the slave ship Rosalie *through to the first stirrings of revolution in Saint-Domingue. In her foregrounding of the particular role and struggles of women in Haitian colonial society, Trouillot suggests a complement to far more prevalent histories of the Haitian Revolution and its heroes, evoking less spectacular quotidian instances of rebellion and triumph. The excerpt that follows offers an example of the complex gendered realities that marked nineteenth-century Caribbean slave society. Told in the first person by a young slave woman—a so-called house Negress—the passage gives a sense of the broad historical phenomena of violence and intimacy underlying black-white relations during the period, and privileges in particular the delicate relationships between women. Far from focusing uniquely on the question of race, here and throughout the novel Trouillot is attentive to the public and private negotiations and hierarchies that were a matter of life and death for women and children in the brutally dehumanizing context of the plantation.*

"Lisette, where have you been? Madame will be sitting down to dinner any second now."

"I'm coming, I'm coming."

Hurriedly, I splash some water on my face, wash my hands and feet, shake out my skirt, flatten my bodice. Man Victor pours the sauces in the little earthenware bowls, complaining all the while. Man Augustine, my godmother, passes a clean apron around my neck and follows me into the dining room. A minute later, my mistress, Madame Clementine Fayot, enters the room in a swirl of silk and lace.

I've become an expert in the art of looking elsewhere. Past all the lace affixed to my mistress's wrists and neck, to the flounces of her skirt and underskirts, I shoot a glance at Gracieuse—half conspiratorial, half suspicious. Little whore, dear little whore, say my mocking eyes. Meanwhile my body play-acts docility so as to avoid any of the unwanted attention my excessively long absence might attract. My arms hang innocently down by my hips, my buttocks are tucked in. Gracieuse isn't fooled by my submissive posturing. A true Congo woman, she sways her hips as she follows her mistress; her smile lays bare my ruse.

"Little fool. Where are you coming from with that smell of hate on your breath? Will you never understand that when the sun sets in the sea, it doesn't get wet?"

Gracieuse holds the bamboo fan regally. Each movement of her hand sends a message infused with moist kisses, soft, languorous caresses, forbidden whispers, delicious pleasures. Madame lets herself lounge voluptuously in her seat. Monsieur seems unable to take his eyes off Gracieuse's arm. Her eyes are half-closed. Hypnotized by the lascivious suggestiveness of her movements, the slow, supple movement of the fan, the heavy, enticing pupils, my masters don't seem much interested in me for the moment.

"Don't you get mixed up in the affairs of your masters and their plaything. Things aren't as simple as you think," says Augustine oftentimes when I complain about the privileges Gracieuse has been enjoying, especially since the departure of Miss Sarah, the masters' daughter.

"Me, I'm Sarah's negress," I once said, a long time ago, back when Grann Charlotte was still alive. Later, in our little hut, grandmother had slapped me in the face. "Don't you ever believe what you just said, Lisette. Arada women belong to no one."

I have a long history of complicity and mistrust when it comes to beatings. Despite my privileged situation with Miss Sarah, I was never safe from them. Although she'd been forbidden to do so, Sarah wasn't always able to control herself and would strike me. Or sometimes she'd make up some story about a broken toy, a decapitated doll, or a soiled skirt just to show off her power as a little Creole girl, born to well-off planters—with her private tutors and music and dance teachers, her candied fruits and other sweets from France. From ten to twenty lashes, reaching up to around fifty in the worst cases, the whip and I have developed a long history of shocks and sidesteps, of clashes and near-misses. From tears to screams, whimperings to silences, my voice has mastered the dance of signs I deploy to spare my hide. The traces left behind on my skin aren't even visible. They've taken root in the hollow of my hand and sometimes I feel as if I'm dragging my insides under my feet and no one can see them. But back then, when Grann Charlotte was still alive, her slap left its mark on my cheek. She'd collected up the shells of my hidden sorrows, the pieces of shame thrown here and there, my urges to rage, my crusts of tears and my betrayals, and wrenched them sharply, with more force than any crack of the whip. I still feel that bitter, burning sound galloping inside me, without pity for my bowing and scraping, disdainful of my troubles and my fear. I sit down on its wing when my knees refuse to bend so that my pupils can warm themselves in the shadow of their truth.

I begin serving. First, the before-dinner drinks must be taken out of the locked cabinet. Next, I pour a spoonful of each dish into the bowl of Manon, Man Victor's grand-niece. Standing next to the tall mahogany dresser, just a few steps away from my mistress, Manon tastes all the dishes at every meal. Once she appears to have survived the food, I serve Madame, Monsieur, and their guests, if there are any. Then without saying a word, and with a bow befitting her eight years, the little girl leaves to join the other slaves in the kitchen.

We're right in the middle of the period of terror that is brutally shaking up the entire north of the great Island. Whites and Blacks, slaves and masters, all shake in fear and hardly dare to touch any of the food served to them. Husbands spy on their wives and mistresses. Mothers look suspiciously at their lovers, at their neighbors. The overwhelming fear of poison has invaded every home, giving rise to panic and paranoia. From the great houses to the smallest huts, from one carriage lane to the next, everyone is suspicious. Not a month goes by without the burning at the stake of four or five men or women accused of having poisoned Blacks or Whites. The Negro slave Paladin is only one of a long list.

For some time now, during dinner, that's all anyone talks about at the Fayot table. The guests seem to compete with each other to find examples of Negro poisoners, of a valet killing his longtime protector, of a mulatto woman getting rid of her master so as to more quickly acquire that promised freedom, of slaves killing one another to get out of slavery. The planters are fascinated by these incidents, recounting them to one another in hushed tones. They lower their voices noticeably each time Rose-Marie, broom or rag in hand, passes by in the corridor or in the entrance hall. They raise their heads in irritation whenever Florville comes to bother the master with some urgent matter or another, but speak freely before Gracieuse, Madame's favorite, and me. After all, aren't I just Lisette, Charlotte's granddaughter, Arada Negress who'd been head cook at the plantation until her death from smallpox? Man Augustine, she's always been responsible for all the housework, supervising Rose-Marie and the little Negro girls. And while it's true that Man Victor replaced Grann Charlotte, the masters don't trust her entirely. Fayot the planter was convinced, though, that she'd hesitate before imperiling her grand-niece's life if ever she thought to poison them. And so it is that Manon always eats before the masters. I wonder if she realizes that a single mouthful might someday cause her horrific suffering and kill her. And yet Manon is the daughter of Fanchette, who was the mistress's favorite for years, before Gracieuse. Madame Fayot used to say all the time that with Fanchette's hands to do their hair, she and her daughter were sure to be among the most elegant women of the town. Fanchette died giving birth to Manon and Man Victor had taken care of the little girl ever since. Man Augustine wasn't at all surprised by Madame's actions. "Believe me, Lisette, it isn't worth trying to understand these Creole women. They'll caress you in the morning, and whip you that same night."

The Declaration of Independence

Jean-Jacques Dessalines

On 1 January 1804, General Jean-Jacques Dessalines issued a proclamation declaring Haiti an independent country. Dessalines was a former slave who had risen through the ranks of the army during the Haitian Revolution and had become one of the leaders of the struggle against the French after the deportation of General Toussaint Louverture.

Written as a message from him to the nation, the Declaration lays out the Haitians' grievances against France and proclaims the determination of the Haitian people to resist the return of slavery and colonialism. Though linked in many ways to the principles and rhetoric of the broader currents of the Age of Revolution, it is also more radical than other documents of the period in its tone and implication, as it confronts the central institution of the Atlantic world at the time: slavery. In contrast to the United States' Declaration of Independence, this document was written at the end of several years of brutal conflict; consequently, it is infused with a sense of loss and mourning as well as anger. According to tradition, the document was drafted by Louis Boisrond-Tonnerre, one of Dessalines's secretaries, who had declared that the declaration "should be written with the skin of a white man for a parchment, his skull for a desk, his blood for ink, and a bayonet for a pen." But recent scholars have argued that Dessalines likely had a central role in shaping its language as well.

The Commander in Chief to the People of Haiti

Citizens:

It is not enough to have expelled the barbarians who have bloodied our land for two centuries; it is not enough to have restrained those ever-evolving factions that one after another mocked the specter of liberty that France dangled before you. We must, with one last act of national authority, forever assure the empire of liberty in the country of our birth; we must take any hope of re-enslaving us away from the inhuman government that for so long kept us in the most humiliating torpor. In the end we must live independent or die.

Independence or death . . . Let these sacred words unite us and be the signal of battle and of our reunion.

Citizens, my countrymen, on this solemn day I have brought together those courageous soldiers who, as liberty lay dying, spilled their blood to save it; these generals who have guided your efforts against tyranny have not yet done enough for your happiness; the French name still haunts our land.

Everything revives the memories of the cruelties of this barbarous people: our laws, our habits, our towns, everything still carries the stamp of the French. Indeed! There are still French in our island, and you believe yourself free and independent of that Republic which, it is true, has fought all the nations, but which has never defeated those who wanted to be free.

What! Victims of our [own] credulity and indulgence for 14 years; defeated not by French armies, but by the pathetic eloquence of their agents' proclamations; when will we tire of breathing the air that they breathe? What do we have in common with this nation of executioners? The difference between its cruelty and our patient moderation, its color and ours the great seas that separate us, our avenging climate, all tell us plainly that they are not our brothers, that they never will be, and that if they find refuge among us, they will plot again to trouble and divide us.

Native citizens, men, women, girls, and children, let your gaze extend on all parts of this island: look there for your spouses, your husbands, your brothers, your sisters. Indeed! Look there for your children, your suckling infants, what have they become? . . . I shudder to say it . . . the prey of these vultures.

Instead of these dear victims, your alarmed gaze will see only their assassins, these tigers still dripping with their blood, whose terrible presence indicts your lack of feeling and your guilty slowness in avenging them. What are you waiting for before appeasing their spirits? Remember that you had wanted your remains to rest next to those of your fathers, after you defeated tyranny; will you descend into their tombs without having avenged them? No! Their bones would reject yours.

And you, precious men, intrepid generals, who, without concern for your own pain, have revived liberty by shedding all your blood, know that you have done nothing if you do not give the nations a terrible, but just example of the vengeance that must be wrought by a people proud to have recovered its liberty and jealous to maintain it. Let us frighten all those who would dare try to take it from us again; let us begin with the French. Let them tremble when they approach our coast, if not from the memory of those cruelties they perpetrated here, then from the terrible resolution that we will have made to put to death anyone born French whose profane foot soils the land of liberty.

We have dared to be free, let us be thus by ourselves and for ourselves. Let us imitate the grown child: his own weight breaks the boundary that has become an obstacle to him. What people fought for us? What people wanted to gather the fruits of our labor? And what dishonorable absurdity to conquer in order to be enslaved. Enslaved? . . . Let us leave this description for the French; they have conquered but are no longer free.

Let us walk down another path; let us imitate those people who, extending their concern into the future, and dreading to leave an example of cowardice for posterity, preferred to be exterminated rather than lose their place as one of the world's free peoples.

Let us ensure, however, that a missionary spirit does not destroy our work; let us allow our neighbors to breathe in peace; may they live quietly under the laws that they have made for themselves, and let us not, as revolutionary firebrands, declare ourselves the lawgivers of the Caribbean, nor let our glory consist in troubling the peace of the neighboring islands. Unlike that which we inhabit, theirs has not been drenched in the innocent blood of its inhabitants; they have no vengeance to claim from the authority that protects them.

Fortunate to have never known the ideals that have destroyed us, they can only have good wishes for our prosperity.

Peace to our neighbors; but let this be our cry: "Anathema to the French name! Eternal hatred of France!"

Natives of Haiti! My happy fate was to be one day the sentinel who would watch over the idol to which you sacrifice; I have watched, sometimes fighting alone, and if I have been so fortunate as to return to your hands the sacred trust you confided to me, know that it is now your task to preserve it. In fighting for your liberty, I was working for my own happiness. Before consolidating it with laws that will guarantee your free individuality, your leaders, who I have assembled here, and I, owe you the final proof of our devotion.

Generals and you, leaders, collected here close to me for the good of our land, the day has come, the day which must make our glory, our independence, eternal.

If there could exist among us a lukewarm heart, let him distance himself and tremble to take the oath which must unite us. Let us vow to ourselves, to posterity, to the entire universe, to forever renounce France, and to die rather than live under its domination; to fight until our last breath for the independence of our country.

And you, a people so long without good fortune, witness to the oath we take, remember that I counted on your constancy and courage when I threw myself into the career of liberty to fight the despotism and tyranny you had struggled against for 14 years. Remember that I sacrificed everything to rally to your defense; family, children, fortune, and now I am rich only with your liberty; my name has become a horror to all those who want slavery. Despots and tyrants curse the day that I was born. If ever you refused or grumbled while receiving those laws that the spirit guarding your fate dictates to me for your own good, you would deserve the fate of an ungrateful people. But I reject that awful idea; you will sustain the liberty that you cherish and support the leader who commands you. Therefore vow before me to live free and independent, and to prefer death to anything that will try to place you back in chains. Swear, finally, to pursue forever the traitors and enemies of your independence.

Done at the headquarters at Gonaives,
the first day of January 1804,
the first year of independence.

The Deed of Independence

NATIVE ARMY

Today, January 1st 1804, the general in chief of the native army, accompanied by the generals of the army, assembled in order to take measures that will insure the good of the country;

After having told the assembled generals his true intentions, to assure forever a stable government for the natives of Haiti, the object of his greatest concern, which he has accomplished in a speech which declares to foreign powers the decision to make the country independent, and to enjoy a liberty consecrated by the blood of the people of this island; and after having gathered their responses has asked that each of the assembled generals take a vow to forever renounce France, to die rather than live under its domination, and to fight for independence until their last breath.

The generals, deeply moved by these sacred principles, after voting their unanimous attachment to the declared project of independence, have all sworn to posterity, to the universe, to forever renounce France, and to die rather than to live under its domination.

Haitian Hymn

This Haitian song was composed and sung for Jean-Jacques Dessalines, independent Haiti's new governor-general for life, in January 1804. It deploys the melody of the French revolutionary anthem "La marseillaise," which interestingly is described in the document itself as to the tune "Allons enfants de la patrie," perhaps because these opening lines would have been more familiar to Haitians than the official name of the song. But it uses the tune of this French nationalist anthem in order to celebrate the valor of Dessalines, who had just defeated the French. This version of the hymn appears at the end of a printed copy of Dessalines's Journal de campagne, *in which he narrates his attacks on Port-au-Prince and the North in late 1803 at the end of the war for independence.*
—Contributing Editor: Julia Gaffield

HAITIAN HYMN
(To the tune of "Allons enfants de la patrie")

What? You stay quiet, Native People!
When a Hero, through his exploits,
Avenging your name, breaking your chains,
Assures your rights forever?
Honor to his military valor!
Glory to his triumphant efforts!
Offer him our hearts, our praise;
Let us sing in a proud, masculine voice,
United under this good Father,
Forever reunited
Let us live and die his true children,
Free, independent.

Perfidious enemies of our rights,
The tyrants of the New World,
The homicidal French,
Once struck the children with the sun;
Oh! From the sky struck a miracle!
To raise up our battered foreheads,
Jacques appeared, they are no more,
Look and you won't find the ruins,

Under this good father, united,
Forever reunited.
Let us live and die his true children,
Free, independent.

On the ocean, on the plains, and on our mountaintops,
Listen to the sound, the explosions;
Friends, it is the cry of the victims
Denouncing the black attack.
The blood of a cruel horde,
Yes, when you water their bones,
They will hear these words
From the deepest dark of an eternal night,
United under this good Father,
Forever reunited,
Let us live and die his true children,
Free, independent.

Where is the unworthy islander,
Where is the cowardly heart, the vile soldier
Who, now under this banner,
Would not face death?
May he speak, for want of thunder
To expiate this attack,
Our arms raised against those unworthy,
Will know how to reduce him to dust.
United under this good Father
Forever reunited,
Let us live and die his true children,
Free, independent.

Friends, may your recognition
Consecrate these facts, their worth;
We will serve, under his power,
The sky, justice and honor:
So that our children, from the time of their birth,
Will love to murmur his name
From now on Jacques is the Patron
Of those who refuse slavery.
United under this good Father
Forever reunited,
Let us live and die his true children,
Free, independent.

Translated by Julia Gaffield

Writings

Jean-Jacques Dessalines

In the months after penning the Haitian Declaration of Independence, Jean-Jacques Dessalines issued a series of proclamations outlining and defending his political projects as the leader of independent Haiti.

In the first proclamation below, he defends his decision to massacre most of the French planters who remained on the island after independence, declaring that he had "avenged America." Dessalines presents the killings both as a necessary response to prior barbarism and as a source of unity among the different groups within Haiti. These included "blacks" (largely ex-slaves) and what were called "yellows," people of mixed European and African ancestry—many of whom who had been free and even wealthy landowners prior to the revolution. By massacring most of the remaining whites on the island, Dessalines insisted, they might develop the unity necessary for their collective survival as a nation.

—Contributing Editor: Julia Gaffield

Yes, we have replied to these real cannibals, war for war, crime for crime, outrage for outrage.

Yes, I have saved my country. I have avenged America. With all my pride and glory, I swear this in front of all mortals and the Gods. What does the judgment pronounced on me by contemporary and future races matter? I did my duty, and I have kept my own self-respect—that is enough for me. But what am I saying? The preservation of my unfortunate brothers, and the witness of my conscience are not my only recompense: I saw two classes of men who were born to love one another, to help and save one another, finally mixed and merged together, dashing toward vengeance, arguing who should have the honor of giving the first blow.

Black and yellow, which the refined duplicity of the Europeans have so long sought to divide: you who today comprise a whole, a single family: do not doubt it, your perfect reconciliation had to be sealed with the blood of your executioners. You shared the same calamities, weighing on your heads, the same ardor for attacking your enemies, and the same promised fate. Now your common interests must render you forever one, indivisible and inseparable. Maintain this precious concord, this happy harmony among you. It secures your happiness, your salvation, your success. It is the secret of the invincible.

In a private letter written soon afterward, part of an extended diplomatic dialogue between him and George Nugent, the governor of the nearby British colony of Jamaica, Dessalines explains that Haitian independence has transformed the relationship between Britain and the former French colony.

Your excellency will permit me to explain that the General Toussaint dealt with the British Government as the subject or employee of the French Government, while in the current circumstances I cannot and should not negotiate except as the leader of the people that I command. . . . The General Toussaint negotiated as a French General who was not certain about whether his government would approve the acts emanating from his authority, while I, the only leader of my country, I negotiate on behalf of my co-citizens, and don't have to explain my actions to any other power, nor do I depend on any other government to sign agreements or treaties.

Translated by Julia Gaffield

A Woman's Quest for Freedom in a Land of Re-enslavement

Marie Melie

*After the defeat of France's Napoleonic forces and the declaration of Haitian indepen-
dence in 1804, a French general named Jean-Louis Ferrand established a government
in Santo Domingo (present-day Dominican Republic), which lasted until Spanish and
British armies ejected the French from the colony in 1809. General Ferrand was an un-
repentant partisan of slavery, and his regime sought to place back into servitude thousands of men, women, and children in Santo Domingo who had won their freedom in
the French general emancipations of 1793–94. He also authorized slaving raids into
Haiti. Resistance to these measures took a variety of forms, ranging from violence to
the use of the legal and notarial systems to win and preserve freedom.*

*The following document, produced in a Santo Domingo city notary's office in early
1808, is an example of the latter. In this document, a woman claiming to be a refugee
from Haiti speaks on behalf of another woman called Marie Melie, declaring she had
been wrongfully sold into slavery despite being "free by birth." This case, like others
from the period, suggests how important social and familial networks were as people
struggled to guarantee and protect their freedom. It is just one part of a much larger
corpus of archival documents through which people of African descent who had been
become free during the Haitian Revolution sought to establish and protect their status
as free in various legal and political contexts outside the country.*

The label nommé, *translated here as "so-called," was generally used in official
documents in prerevolutionary Saint-Domingue and other French colonies to refer to
persons of color. And since slave status was transmitted through the mother, the claim
of having been born to a free mother would have been a particularly powerful claim
to freedom.*

—Contributing Editor: Graham Nessler

In the year 1808, on the eighteenth of March in the morning, in the fourth
[year] of the Reign of Napoléon.

Before me, Barthélemy Vallenet, imperial notary residing in the City
of Santo Domingo witness, and in the presence of the witnesses also
undersigned.

Appeared Marie Emilie, wife of Georges Hubé, property owner from the parish of Mirebalais [located in the] French part of Saint Domingue, a refugee and resident of this city [Santo Domingo]. She states to us, declaring and affirming under oath, that the so-called Marie Melie, black woman aged sixteen to seventeen years, who was sold on this past twenty-third of February . . . is in truth Free by birth being the daughter of the so-called Marianne also Free, residing in the district of Mirebalais, that [Emilie] held [Melie] at the Baptismal font and that the so-called Cadet Laumont resident of the said place of Mirebalais has been her godfather since he was named her tutor as well as [tutor] of the so-called Decossotier brother of the said Marie Melie who currently lives in Azua.

The said declarant has also stated to us that a great number of Mirebalais residents who currently live in this city [Santo Domingo] will be able to affirm the sincerity of her declaration.

The said declarant has requested the act [stating] all of the above to serve the said Marie Melie granted to her by law.

Done and received in Santo Domingo . . . undersigned in the presence of Mr. Frédéric Grand and Alexis Latour both merchants residing in this city [and serving as] required witnesses who after reading [the foregoing] have signed with us the notary . . .

(Signatures)

Translated by Graham Nessler and Lindsey Gish

An Exchange of Letters

Alexandre Pétion and Simón Bolívar

Alexandre Pétion served as president of the southern region of the Haitian Republic from 1808 until his death in 1818. During that time other nations, inspired in part by the Haitian Revolution, worked to throw off the yoke of their European masters. Simón Bolívar, whose armies eventually liberated Venezuela, Colombia, Ecuador, and Bolivia, needed financial and military assistance to complete his revolution. Driven away from New Granada by Spanish royalists in May 1815, Bolívar first sought assistance from the English in Jamaica, living under British sponsorship for eight months. During this time Bolívar came in contact with Robert Sutherland, an English commercial agent who worked closely in Haiti with President Pétion. It was due to this contact that Bolívar arrived in Port-au-Prince on 31 December 1815, met Sutherland, and was welcomed by General Marion of Haiti. On the following day he met with President Pétion, and the two men negotiated the terms and parameters of Haiti's support for the Venezuelan Revolution in return for the emancipation of slaves in all territories that Bolívar freed. In response to this agreement, Pétion wrote the following letter to General Marion, instructing him to provide weapons and a ship to Bolivar. The support provided from Haiti for the struggle for independence in Latin America is, to this day, commonly evoked in political circles, notably as a foundation for the contemporary assistance provided by Venezuela to Haiti.
—Contributing Editor: Andrew Manginn

In Port-Au-Prince, January 26, 1816, the 13th year of Independence

For reasons that I cannot commit to paper, my dear general, but to greatly strengthen the Republic, I command you to make available to General Bolívar, two thousand muskets and bayonets, that were deposited by Monsieur Brion at the arsenal of Les Cayes. You will also make available as many cartridges for these guns as you can. You cannot even keep the smallest amount. You will send these items as if they are going to the Grand-Anse. Load them on a vessel whose captain and crew are worthy of your trust. The destination will be given by General Bolívar once he is on board. This needs to happen quickly due to the number of precautions you need to take.

Hail of friendship,
Pétion

Once the preparations were started Bolívar wrote to thank Pétion for his contributions, asking him if he would like to be known as the "author of liberty" in the proclamation of emancipation that Bolívar was preparing to deliver.

Aux Cayes, February 8, 1816
To his Excellency the President of Haiti.

Mr. President:

I am overwhelmed with the magnitude of your benefactors. Monsieur Villares has returned through the exceeding promptness of Your Excellency: in everything you are magnanimous and indulgent.

Our affairs are nearly arranged and we shall surely be ready to depart in about fifteen days. I am only awaiting your final favors; and if it shall be possible for me I shall come in person to express to you the extent of my gratitude.

By Monsieur Inginac, your worthy secretary, I have the temerity to make some new requests of you.

In my proclamation to the inhabitants of Venezuela and in the decree that I shall issue, announcing liberty to the slaves, I do not know that it will be permitted to me to demonstrate the real sentiment of my heart towards your Excellency and to leave to posterity an undying monument to your philanthropy. I do not know, I repeat, if I ought to give publicity to your name as being in fact the author of our liberty. I pray Your Excellency to express to me your will in this regard.

Lieutenant-Colonel Valdes will present to you a petition which I beg to recommend to your generosity.

Receive, Mr. President, the respectful homage and the high consideration I have for the honored.

> *Your Humble and obedient servant,*
> *Bolívar*

President Pétion responded to this letter as follows:

Port-au-Prince, February 18, 1816
The 13th of Independence
To his Excellency, General Bolívar.

General:

I received yesterday, General, your estimable letter of the 8th of this month. I have written to General Marion on the subject you have inquired about and I refer you to him in that matter.

You know, General, my sentiments toward the cause that you have valor to defend and also toward yourself personally. You surely must feel how ardently I desire to see the oppressed delivered from the yoke of bondage; but because of certain diplomatic obligations which I am under toward a nation that has not yet taken an offensive attitude toward the Republic, I am obliged to ask you not to make public the aid I have given you, nor to mention my name in any of your official documents. In this matter I depend upon the sentiments that characterize you.

I have received the request of Colonel Juan Valdès and have attended to it. General Marion is charged to carry out the object of his request.

I extend my wishes of happiness to Your Excellency and pray you to believe me, with most perfect consideration,

Pétion

Translated by Andrew Maginn

The Code Henry

King Henry Christophe

The Code Henry was an extensive legal code promulgated by King Henry Christophe in 1812. Hundreds of pages of the 1812 Code Henry are devoted to detailed regulations concerning property law, marriage, inheritance, and the operation of the royal bureaucracy. The following excerpts, however, are from a section called "Loi concernant la culture" ("Law concerning Culture"), which laid out the regulations surrounding the agricultural labor on the plantations that were the economic engine of Christophe's kingdom. Although the Haitian Revolution was a movement against slavery and the plantation system, the country's early rulers—building on the policies of both French commissioners and Generals Toussaint Louverture and Jean-Jacques Dessalines during the Haitian Revolution—believed that it was necessary to maintain the preexisting plantation system to guarantee the nation's economic success and strength. They therefore reproduced a plantation order complete with overseers, absentee landowners, dawn-to-dusk labor, and restrictions on movement. While the systems of postemancipation forced labor were pioneered by Louverture and Dessalines, no early Haitian regime exported as much sugar and coffee or accumulated as large a treasury as the kingdom of Henry Christophe. The following articles are from chapter 2 of the "Loi concernant la culture," which is titled "The Obligations of Agricultural Laborers and the Regulation of the Workforce."
—Contributing Editor: Johnhenry Gonzales

16. The law having imposed upon landowners and lessees paternal duties toward the laborers, also demands certain reciprocal duties on the part of the laborers toward the landowners and leaseholders.

17. The law punishes the lazy vagabond; every individual must be useful to society.

Apart from the people comprised in the following article 19, the following will be considered vagabonds: laborers of both sexes who leave the plantations where they have chosen to make their residence in order to seek refuge without legitimate cause on another plantation, in the towns, cities, or any other place where their residence is prohibited by the law; consequently those among them who find themselves under such circumstances will be punished according to Article 115, Title VIII.

18. Marriage among the agricultural laborers will be essentially encouraged and protected, being the source of good conduct.

Diligent laborers who produce the most well-raised and well-mannered children from their legitimate union will be distinguished by the government and will receive encouragements.

19. Begging is severely prohibited; all laggards, beggars, and women of ill repute, rambling about in the towns, cities and roadways will be arrested by the police in order to be sent back to their plantations. Those that are not attached to any plantation will be sent to the plantation or worksite designated to them by the superior authorities.

The Governors, King's lieutenants, local commanders, and police officials will severely pursue the full and complete execution of the present article; and all good and faithful subjects of His Majesty are invited to denounce to the authorities the individuals mentioned above.

20. Every manager or overseer convicted of neglecting the operation of the plantation under his responsibility, or of diverting to his own profit the work of the laborers, whether employing them in fishing or hunting, or in having them perform work for themselves or others, or exercising bad treatment toward the laborers having committed an abuse of their authority will be punished according to Article 115, Title VIII.

21. Abuses arising directly from the actions of managers, when it is clearly proven that the owners and lessees have had no part, cannot in any case harm the interests of absentee owners and lessees. If these abuses are in fact the fault of the owners or lessees, the authorities will conform, according to the seriousness of the case, to the dispositions of the articles of the law concerning abuses on the part of landowners and leaseholders toward the laborers.

22. The hours of work of the agricultural laborers are irrevocably fixed as follows:

In the morning, starting at dawn work will begin, and last without interruption until eight o'clock; one hour's time is devoted to the laborers' breakfast, which will occur in the same place that they are working. At nine o'clock they recommence with work until noon at which point they are allowed two hours of rest. At exactly two o'clock they will begin work again and will not stop until nightfall.

23. Pregnant and nursing women are not subject to the rules established above.

24. Every night the owners, lessees, or managers are responsible for conducting prayers with the laborers and for inviting them to attend public prayer services in their parishes on Sundays and holidays.

25. Plantation owners, lessees, managers, and overseers are responsible for seeing that the provision gardens distributed to the laborers are always well taken care of. If not, they will oblige the laborers to work on the gardens on their own time.

26. Laborers cannot leave their plantations on work days without a permit from the local King's lieutenant which must be procured by the manager or overseer.

27. In case of any disorder or seditious movement on a plantation, the owners, lessees, managers, or overseers are charged with calling on the neighborhood to subdue the agitators. Once these are arrested they will call in the local King's lieutenant or police commander who will visit the location to receive the agitators of the public peace, incarcerate them, and determine culpability and the motives of their arrest.

28. Every time the King's lieutenant of a parish and the police commander are summoned, whether by the civil or administrative authorities or by plantation owners, lessees, or managers, to prevent disorder on a plantation, if they do not fulfill their duties exactly by employing the means at their disposal to repress any disorder, they will be personally responsible for the fatal consequences.

Translated by Johnhenry Gonzalez

Haitian Heraldry

Kingdom of Henry Christophe

As part of his project of creating a nobility to govern his kingdom in the North of Haiti, King Henry Christophe created a series of heraldic symbols gathered together in a remarkable manuscript today held in the College of Arms in London. Below is the arms of the capital of the kingdom, Le Cap Haïtien (then known as Cap-Henry). Christophe's crown decorates the top of the arms, which depict a ship on the seas off the coast of Haiti. It is flanked by two imposing-looking Africans figured as Hercules, wearing lion skins and bearing clubs, clearly ready to defend the country against foreign invaders. The ship itself might be seen as Haiti, making its way in rough seas, determined: the slogan below it reads, "Despite the waves and winds."

Another coat of arms (see color plates) was made for the Duc de Marmelade, Jean-Pierre Richard, an African-born man who was a high-ranking member of Christophe's regime. He was the governor of the city of Cap-Henry, a role depicted here in the key hanging from the sword in the center of the coat of arms. The slogan below insists on the duke's loyalty to his king—"I will only hand it over to my King"—though ultimately this loyalty was tested, as Richard led the uprising that overthrew Henry in 1820. The presence here of African animals, the hyenas flanking the coat of arms, is perhaps a way to highlight Richard's origins. Few among the new leadership in Haiti were African born, though the majority of the people in the colony were.

Alongside coats of arms created for himself and the members of his aristocracy, King Henry Christophe created this symbol for what had been the most important trading port and cultural capital in colonial Saint-Domingue, Cap Français, which he renamed Cap-Henry. College of Arms MS J. P. 177: Armorial General du Royaume d'Hayti. Reproduced by permission of the Kings, Heralds and Pursuivants of Arms.

Henry Christophe and the English Abolitionists

King Henry Christophe

*King Henry Christophe sought support for his regime outside Haiti, and found partic-
ularly eager allies among some English and North American abolitionists. They were
notably interested in helping him with one of his major projects: the development of
primary education within his kingdom. The following excerpt from his official newspaper, the* Gazette Royal d'Hayti, *lays out the project and announces the arrival
of teachers from outside the country. Ultimately, King Henry did construct a number
of schools and educate tens of thousands of young students. He drew on a model of
education developed in England by Joseph Lancaster, which was seen as an affordable
way of educating the working class.*

*Christophe's most prominent interlocutor and supporter was the British abolition-
ist Thomas Clarkson. He also worked with Prince Saunders (spelled "Sanders" in the
letter), a free black from New England who collaborated with the British abolitionists
and became one of Christophe's key supporters and allies. The following letter provides more details about the plans for education, which include the creation of a chair
of medicine in Le Cap Haïtien which was held by a Scottish doctor named Duncan
Stewart.*

*Christophe also sought Clarkson's help in gaining respect and recognition for Haiti
at a time when the country remained isolated diplomatically because of France's refusal to accept the country's independence. In the second letter, written just months before his overthrow, Christophe reaches out to the emperor of Russia and explains why
he should support the Haitian cause. The text—part history lesson, part treatise—
is one of Christophe's most impassioned and eloquent expressions of his vision for the
future of Haiti and the way he saw its broader mission in the world.*
—Contributing Editor: Julia Gaffield

His majesty, our very august and beloved sovereign, tirelessly works
towards the introduction of public education in our kingdom.

At this very moment, in Cap-Henry, excellent buildings are being
prepared to house new national schools, which will use the Lancaster
method. Similar establishments will be created in other towns in the
Kingdom.

His majesty offered a distinguished welcome to Professors, Artists, and Schoolteachers who have come to establish themselves in Haiti to educate the youth. They are treated very honorably and the government is offering them good salaries.

The King's plan is to introduce education in the English language in Haiti.

We must applaud the great intentions of our Majesty, who wishes to give the Haitian people the greatest gift one can give: that of education. It is urgent that we abandon French customs and habits in order to take on the customs and manners of the English, this brave and generous people who are friends of liberty. It is urgent that we receive a truly national education that will teach our children, from a young age, to love and idolize our kings, our liberty and our independence. And our progress in the Sciences and Arts will forever confound our detractors.

Translated by Julia Gaffield

King Henry to Thomas Clarkson
At the Palace of Sans-Souci, this 5th of February, 1816,
in the 13th year of our Independence
The King, to Mr. Thomas Clarkson, Member of the African Institute, etc.

Dear Sir,

I received with great satisfaction Mr. Prince Sanders. Your recommendation, and those of Messrs. Wilberforce and Stephen, insured him of being shown every possible consideration.

For a long while my intention, my dearest ambition, has been to secure for the nation which has confided to me its destiny the benefit of public instruction. . . . I am completely devoted to this project. The edifices necessary for the institutions of public instruction in the cities and in the country are under construction. I am awaiting the professors and craftsmen I requested, who will take upon themselves the training of our youth. . . . So if God blesses my handiwork, and grants me sufficient time, I hope that the inhabitants of Haiti, overcoming the shameful prejudice which has too long weighed upon them, will soon astonish the world by their knowledge. It is thus I should like to refute the calumny of our detractors, and justify the high opinion our friends, the philanthropists, have conceived of us. . . . I have before my eyes the record of history, and the approval of posterity, which I covet.

I rejoice, along with our kind friends, the philanthropists, at the action of the French Government in consenting finally to the abolition of the impious and abominable slave trade, and in abandoning the evil and impracticable idea of sending an expedition against Haiti. That Government should have taken such action long ago, instead of allowing itself to be led into disastrous measures by the claims and recriminations of those enemies of the human species, the ex-colonists, who declared in print that all our population above the age of six must be destroyed. We hope, if the French Cabinet is ever again led to attempt inhuman measures against us, that our virtuous defenders will enlighten European public opinion and strive to prevent the execution of such a project. If our friends do not succeed in the praiseworthy design of halting this abomination, we count on them at least to inform and warn us of any enterprises which may be undertaken for our destruction, so that we may be upon our guard.

The British Nation has long since earned a right to the gratitude of all Haitians. What it has just done, when it used its influence to obtain of France the abolition of the infamous slave trade, gives us new reasons for admiration and thankfulness. We are grateful also for the share Their Majesties, the Emperor of Russia, and the Sovereign of Germany, had in the abolition of the trade.

. . . Upon delivering to you my letter, Mr. Sanders has been asked to express to you, as well as to our friends, my warm and sincere thanks for all the efforts you have made, and the zeal you have shown for the triumph of the cause of the Africans and their descendants. The gratitude which I feel toward you, and toward our good and virtuous defenders, will never be effaced from my heart, and I shall ever seize all occasions to give proof of it.

Henry

King Henry to the Emperor Alexander
To his Imperial Majesty of all the Russias
March 20, 1819

Sire,

Fame has spread to the most distant countries the report of the noble and generous feelings with which your Imperial and Royal Majesty is inspired towards all nations. This universal benevolence has excited my admiration, which has been increased by the accounts I have received from my worthy friend, Mr. Clarkson, of the human and beneficent disposition of your Imperial and Royal Majesty towards the unfortunate Africans and their descendants, the Haytians; my gratitude and respect for your virtues have inspired me with the desire of addressing this letter to your Imperial and Royal Majesty as a tribute which I feel justly due.

. . .

Your Imperial and Royal Majesty must be undoubtedly aware of the events which have taken place in this country during the last thirty years;

it may, however, be well to revive in your memory the steps which have led the Haytians to liberty, and from liberty to independence.

. . .

After fighting many battles and at the expense of rivers of blood, we have driven these oppressors from our borders notwithstanding all their efforts; and to secure ourselves from the repetition of such unheard-of barbarities and crimes, such injustice and perfidy, the people of Hayti in a general assembly proclaimed their Independence the 1st of January, 1804! During the sixteen years that the nation has enjoyed independence, it has advanced rapidly towards civilization and its continually improving social situation.

As soon as the reins of government were consigned to me, it became my first care to give my fellow citizens a code of laws suited to their wants and to their morals. . . . Agriculture has received all possible encouragement by the multiplicity of farms; commerce and industry prosper, labour is honoured as the source of all blessings.

I trust that the motives which inspire me will influence your Imperial and Royal Majesty to excuse this apology for my labours. Too long has the African race been unjustly calumniated. Too long has it been represented as deprived of intellectual faculties, as scarcely susceptible of civilization or government by regular or established laws: these false assumptions spring from the avarice and injustice of men who have had the impiety to degrade the finest work of the Creator, as if mankind had not one common origin. These persons attribute to difference of colour that which is only the result of civilization and knowledge. . . .

I fear that I have already trespassed on the precious time of your Imperial and Royal Majesty. I believe I have sufficiently informed you of our situation to authorize the hope that you will grant your powerful and generous protection and benevolence to the cause of the unfortunate, oppressed Africans, and of the good and interesting people of Hayti. It is in their name that I have the honour of addressing myself to your Imperial and Royal Majesty and I beg you to accept the testimony of our great respect and gratitude and of the admiration which we feel of your virtues.

Henry

The Colonial System Unveiled

Baron de Vastey

The most influential man of letters to emerge in the decades following the independence of Haiti, Jean Louis Vastey was born in 1781 in the northern town of Ennery, the legitimate son of a French father, Jean Vastey, and a free "quadroon" mother, Élisabeth Dumas. Very little is known about Vastey's youth in Saint-Domingue or his exact whereabouts during the years of the Haitian Revolution, but as of 1804, Vastey served in the Ministry of Finance under Dessalines, and after the country split in two in 1807 he fulfilled similar administrative duties under Henry Christophe. In 1814 he was made a baron of the realm by King Christophe, and between 1814 and 1819 he served as the Christophean regime's chief intellectual spokesman, publishing over ten books and pamphlets, a number of which would be translated into English and gain the admiration of British abolitionist leaders such as William Wilberforce and Thomas Clarkson, with whom he corresponded, as well as of an emergent black intelligentsia in the United States. On 19 October 1820, Vastey was summarily executed by leaders of a military coup that had provoked Christophe's suicide earlier that month. His 1814 book The Colonial System Unveiled *is one of his most important works. It offers a pioneering critique of colonial racism and transatlantic slavery, ranging widely in its relentless unveiling of the physical violence of the slave trade and the epistemic violence of racial science, but at the heart of it, occupying the middle third of the book and constituting its most original contribution to the literature of antislavery, is an astonishing inventory of the names of well over a hundred French colonists and the horrifying crimes they perpetrated in Saint-Domingue against their human property before and during the Haitian Revolution. The following excerpt is taken from this central part of the book: it begins with the paragraphs immediately preceding Vastey's inventory, in which he offers a critique of "white" history and outlines the contours of the counter-history that his "Haytian pen" is going to undertake, then offers specific illustrations and a broad critique of the despotic rule of slavery and torture in colonial Saint-Domingue.*
—Contributing Editor: Chris Bongie

Most of the historians who have written about the colonies were *whites*, indeed *colonists*. They have entered into the greatest detail regarding crops, climate, the rural economy, but they have been careful not to rend the veil from the crimes of their accomplices. Precious few have had the courage to speak the truth, and even when speaking it they have sought to disguise it, to diminish the enormity of those crimes through their manner of expression. Thus, out of cowardice and self-interest, these writers have cast a veil over the outrageous crimes of the colonists. For centuries the voice of my unfortunate compatriots could not make itself heard beyond these shores, while here, in this theatre of oppression, they were being silenced by the ascendancy and unanimity of our tormentors.

"The erudition of the colonists," says the virtuous abbé Grégoire, *"abounds with passages cited in support of servitude; none are better acquainted than they with the tactics of despotism."* The time has finally arrived when the truth must come to light. I, who am neither a white man nor a colonist, may not possess the same erudition, but I will not be lacking when it comes to citing examples. My Haytian pen will be lacking in eloquence, no doubt, but it will be truthful. The scenes I describe will be without embellishments, but they will be striking. The words I use will not always be the proper ones, perhaps, but what does that matter? I will be heard and understood by the feeling and impartial European, and the brutal colonist will shake and tremble upon seeing his foul deeds brought to light.

This is not a novel I am writing. It is an exposé of the ordeals, the protracted suffering, and unparalleled acts of torture that an ill-fated people have experienced for centuries. My blood runs cold in my veins, my heart is overcome with sadness: the task I have set myself is one for which I have no aptitude. I lack the forms of expression to undertake it. What manner of pen would be required to describe crimes hitherto unknown to humankind? When depicting all these many horrors, what form of expression can I possibly employ? I know of none.

The flowers of rhetoric and embellishments of style are suitable for describing scenes that do not put a man to shame, but when it comes to such a lugubrious topic, when it comes to descending into a cesspool of crimes, they are useless. I will limit myself to reporting.

The facts I am going to recount bear the stamp of truth. They are a matter of common knowledge. I collected them from the survivors of families whose kinsfolk experienced the acts of torture I am going to try and sketch here, as well as from those unlucky enough to have lived through them. These witnesses are unimpeachable. As evidence in support of their acts of witnessing, they have shown me limbs mutilated by iron or roasted by fire. I have obtained these facts from a great many notable and credible people. Moreover, I am providing the names of the colonists who perpetrated these crimes, and I defy any of them to contradict me.

Poncet, settler, owner of a sugar plantation at Trou, had transformed his house into a veritable prison. No one could approach it without shuddering in horror. All one ever heard in that place was the clattering of chains;

every one of his house slaves and his natural children were loaded down with them. All one ever heard there was the cracking of the whip and the cry of the poor souls being subjected to those acts of torture. This monster had all his house slaves castrated, along with one of his quadroon offspring. After committing incest with his natural daughter, he had her put to a most excruciating death, along with her mother, by placing boiling wax in their ears and leaving it to melt. This inhuman barbarian was strangled by his son and the house slaves, provoked into taking their just revenge. They were broken alive on the wheel for that murder, which would never have taken place had Poncet not gone unpunished for committing such a shameful outrage against nature. The repressive laws were not made for the colonists, and especially not for the big planters; everything was permitted them.

Corbierre, settler, resident in the same parish, would have his blacks bled and use their blood to clarify the sugar. For a trivial offence, he would have them burned alive. Nothing gives better proof of the savagery of this monster than the following incident: an ox of his died one day from an epizootic disease; wishing to exact some revenge for this unavoidable loss on the unlucky person who was in charge of his animals, he had a large grave dug and buried both ox and cattle keeper in it.

Vosanges, settler, resident of La Mine, went one better than Corbierre: he had two of his luckless blacks chained together during their confinement; when one of them dies, the barbaric Vosanges has a grave dug and in one stroke buries the two victims in it.

. . .

We are going to report one last fact that will serve to characterize the colonists' soul in a single stroke.

Mistress Langlois was the owner of a sugar plantation in the plain of Les Cayes. One day, her overseer, as part of the report he was making on the day's activities at the plantation, said to her: "Madame, bad luck would have it tonight that a poor negress, who was feeding cane into the mill, was unlucky enough to get her arm caught in it. I had no choice but to chop the arm off right then and there, to save the rest of her body, which would have passed through it as well." Seated on her chair, Mistress Langlois listened coolly to the overseer, and then answered him: *"Gracious me, that wouldn't have been such a disaster when all's said and done, if it weren't that her body might have spoiled my cane-juice."*

No, it is impossible for me to keep on describing such atrocities. What courage and what strength of spirit it would require to write down the innumerable misdeeds of the colonists during the colonial regime. It would take me entire volumes. The slight account I have just given of the atrocities of which we have been the victims will suffice to give an idea of the colonists' character. The wives of these monsters proved equally proficient in the commission of such deeds: when it comes to debauched and indecent conduct, several of those furies—the shame and dishonour of their sex—equalled and even surpassed the men, committing the most abominable excesses, the most unimaginable crimes and unparalleled acts of cruelty.

To France's shame, not a single one of the monsters we have just cited has suffered the penalty that his foul deeds merit; not a single one has experienced even the slightest punishment for his crimes. Colonists, those of you who still draw breath, cite me a single one of your kind whose guilty head was struck down by the sword of the law. I defy you to prove me wrong.

History offers us no example of an aggregation of men resembling the colonists of Saint-Domingue in their criminality. Every nation has had its share of rank villains, to the great misfortune of humankind; but no other epoch or people has witnessed a rabble of this order, composed of *forty* to *fifty* thousand cut-throats, every single one of them a Nero, a Mezentius, a Phalaris, etc., and their women Messalinas and Fredegunds, etc. If, however, we think back to the impure origin of these colonists, one is readily persuaded that they could not have turned out any differently from what they were, and what they will always be: men descended from the dregs of the people, guilty of all manner of crimes; adventurers escaped from the gallows; vagrants; indentured servants; etc. From such men, only monstrous results could ensue. Fleeing a homeland that with horror drove them from its bosom, vomited forth onto these shores the better to hide their shame and, above all, to make their fortune at whatever cost, these villains employed the most illicit and criminal means imaginable to achieve their goal.

A long way from the metropole, whose laws were a dead letter (forever evaded and unenforced by administrators who were in their pay and under their influence), these arrogant colonists, accustomed to the despotism of the colonial regime, recognized no higher authority, nothing higher than the laws they held in contempt and the magistrates who were in their pocket. They committed every imaginable type of crime with the assurance of impunity, and oppressed the island's population in the most appalling manner.

Louis XIV attempted in vain, through his royal ordinances, to place restrictions on the cruel and dissolute conduct of the colonists by ameliorating the lot of the free people of colour and the slaves. His good intentions had no effect and the regulations were never enforced; in the beginning they were evaded, and soon thereafter they became a dead letter.

And so it was that on each plantation there existed *a white despot*, who had the barbaric right of life and death over the unfortunate blacks in his keep. Turning this atrocious privilege to account, death hovered over our heads as over those of the lowliest animals; and when they wanted to deal it out to us, the only thing that gave them any pause was the question of which form of punishment to choose. On all their plantations, the big planters had built dungeons of many different shapes and sizes, which were fitted out for the different types of torture they wished to inflict on their victims.

These dungeons contained cells that were exactly proportioned to the height and breadth of the victim who was to be confined in it, such that the victim would die standing, without being able to change posture. In other dungeons (those of Desdunes were built in this manner) the walls were lined with iron rings, such that the man fastened to them would have each of his limbs as well as his neck clamped to the wall; in this desperate situation, a sharp wooden stake was the only point of support on which the poor wretch could rest his buttocks and relieve himself of the weight of his body. In the furthest recess of that particular dungeon was a small hermetically sealed cell, where the victim could suffocate to death in a few short hours. Other dungeons were built in dank and miry locations (such were those of Gallifet, Montalibor, Milot, Latour Duroc, and almost all of the plantations belonging to the big planters), where the victims died a watery death, killed by the cold and the damp which cut off the circulation of the blood. In addition to these ghastly dungeons, the colonists in their savagery devised a thousand varied instruments of torture: iron bars; enormous iron collars with long prongs sticking out; thumbscrews; manacles; fetters; iron masks; chains; etc. Why! Why in heaven's name was all this apparatus of death and torture reserved for innocent victims, who would fall to their knees at the slightest sign!!! . . . And last of all, the terrifying punishment of the four posts, which was always at the ready on plantations, in cities and towns: the four limbs of the victim were fastened to the posts, and the middle of the body was held in place by an iron hoop, which prevented it from moving. Others would have the condemned slave stretched out on a ladder, and bound tight to it, while two drivers (who would be relieved by a fresh pair, when the first two tired) lashed the body, a hundred times over, tore it asunder, while the victim groaned in misery, called out for help, did whatever the pain prompted, whatever might incite the pity of a barbaric master. Alas! These unavailing cries would melt into air, they would merge with the sound of the whip that echoed through our mountains. The colonist in all his atrocity, unmoved, deaf to these cries, as unyielding as the powers of hell, gazed long and hard upon this horrifying spectacle! Far from being touched with pity, he would look on as new forms of torment were prepared, at his command, to stifle the cries of the victim: he would put a gag in the mouth, or a red-hot ember. To glut his frenzied rage the tormentor had his choice of caustic and burning matter—brine, salt, pepper, hot ash, boiling oil or lard, sealing wax, gunpowder—that he could spread over the bleeding body, and his ingredient of choice would mingle with the poor wretch's blood, causing him to suffer inexpressible pain; at other times, he would have irons brought to a red heat, which were then applied to the martyr's body.

Strokes of the whip and groans replaced the crowing of the cock, says Wimpffen, who wrote about Saint-Domingue during the revolution, and he spoke the truth. It passes belief that a white man with the name of Lataille [the Thrasher] openly advertised the fact that he was in the business of giving blacks a thrashing, at a modest salary of four bits for every hundred strokes of the whip, and ended up making a brilliant fortune. And yet this is a fact known throughout Cap-Henry, where he carried on that shameful profession.

The poor soul who had neither the courage nor the fortitude to endure the cruel punishments that, for the slightest offence, were going to be inflicted on him would escape into the forests to avoid such torments; his barbaric master, furious at seeing his prey escape, would pursue him there, in those places that offered the slave a refuge from tyranny. This is the origin of those notorious man-hunts, when maroons were pursued and destroyed as if they were ferocious beasts; if a dozen or so were destroyed then the hunt was considered a success. It often happened that, if there were no maroons to be found, those vile hunters would kill the unlucky slaves they had brought along with them to the forests, in order to collect the bounty the government awarded for each maroon's head.

And so it was that the unhappy slaves were put on a par with the lowliest animals. In the public records, entered on the very same line, one finds slaves, horses, cattle, mules, hogs, etc., all one and the same thing: a man was sold with pigs, it made no difference.

Hymn to Liberty

Antoine Dupré

Antoine Dupré is one of Haiti's earliest poets and playwrights. In fact, he began writing plays before the Haitian Revolution and continued writing through this period and in the early years of Haitian independence. Unfortunately, many of his works have been lost. Nonetheless, his best-known poem, "Hymne à la liberté" (also known as "Le dernier soupir de l'Haïtien"), especially the final stanza, continues to be learned and recited by Haitian schoolchildren today. It constitutes a warning to the French or any other would-be tyrants that the freedom so hard won by Haiti will not be conceded. Antoine Dupré died in a duel in January 1816.

O Sun, God of our ancestors,
Thou whose heat
Allows all beings to exist,
I, the creator's creation, am
Close to the end of my life,
May your majestic light
Illuminate my sight a while longer
That I may sing of Liberty!

Liberty, cherished maiden!
When my eye opened upon the day
To love you, I loved life
And you alone had my love,
The tomb destroys the flame,
Sentiment and desire
Ah! May my soul continue to burn
Beyond my final breath.

By the laws of nature,
Everything is born, lives, and dies.
The palm tree loses its green,
The lemon tree loses its fruit.
Man is born to cease to exist.

But, in posterity,
Would he not be reborn
If he loved Liberty?

Haiti, dear mother,
Receive my final farewell,
May love of country
Kindle our descendants' ardor.
And if ever on your banks
Our tyrants were to return
May their fleeing throngs
Fertilize our fields.

Translated by Nadève Ménard

The King's Hunting Party

Juste Chanlatte

Juste Chanlatte (1766–1828), the Comte de Roziers (also spelled Rosiers), was a histo-rian, poet, and playwright and an editor of the Gazette Royale d'Hayti, *the official newspaper of King Henry Christophe's kingdom. Born in Jacmel, Chanlatte became one of the principal leaders of the* hommes de couleur, *notably in the Arcahaie region during the August uprisings of 1791, and in the spring of 1792 he led several important strikes on French plantations in southwestern Saint-Domingue. A former secretary to Jean-Jacques Dessalines, Chanlatte played an important role in crafting the 28 April 1804 proclamation, which mandated death or expulsion to the major-ity of the French who remained in the colony after Haitian independence. After the assassination of Dessalines, whose 1805 constitution Chanlatte also helped to draft, Chanlatte would immediately join the ranks of Christophe's government.*

Chanlatte held many roles in Christophe's administration: he was a member of the Académie Royale de Musique and an actor in the Théâtre Royal, as well as the librarian of the king. After Christophe's suicide in October 1820, Chanlatte escaped execution, unlike many other members of Christophe's monarchy, and joined the gov-ernment of Christophe's rival, President Jean-Pierre Boyer.

A prolific writer, Chanlatte published many political pamphlets and historical articles in both colonial Saint-Domingue and independent Haiti. His most important historical writing is Le cri de la nature *(1810), one of the earliest histories of the revo-lution written by a Haitian historian. Chanlatte wrote over a dozen poems, many of which sing the glories of Haitian independence, and he also published the country's first operas and plays. His theatrical works—*L'entrée du roi dans sa capitale *(1818);* Néhri *(1819), an anagram of Henri; and the play excerpted here,* La partie de chasse du roi *(1820)—are especially noteworthy for their use of Haitian Creole in some of the dialogue. These works of theater, which are firmly grounded in Haitian rather than French history and mores, were part of a thriving national cultural life in the northern kingdom.*

The Hunting Party of the King *was first staged before the royal court on 1 Janu-ary 1820 in order to commemorate the seventeenth anniversary of Haitian indepen-dence. In it, the king goes missing but is happily found again and saved from a wild boar, ensuring his safe return to the throne. The piece is also a romance between the character Céliflore, and Zulimbo, the man who saves Christophe's life. But in retro-*

spect, the plotline in which the king goes missing and his absence produces "morbid imaginings" among members of the court—written and performed just ten months before Christophe committed suicide in the face of an uprising—seems strangely prophetic.

—*Contributing Editor: Marlene Daut*

Act 1

(The theater represents a convenient spot in the middle of the forest. In the background, a rustic pyramid consecrated to independence has been erected. On the right side is the altar of the Fatherland, on the left side is the altar of Liberty. Young Haitian women, interspersed with a battalion of troops from the Royal Dahomet army, dance around the trophies that they have raised, and gaily celebrate the eve of independence day.)

SCENE I

CHOIR: *(In Creole)* Oh! God! Oh God!
Oh! What sweet rejoicing!
God is good! God is good!
Here is something to dazzle God
We will call forth the *samba* [sorcerers],
We will sound the *bamboula* [drums],
We will dance the *bambocha* [traditional ritual dance]
Yes, we will dance the *calinda.* [traditional ritual dance]
     We will call forth the *samba*, etc.

YOUNG GIRL: His force gives him valor
Papa Henry
Founder of independence
In Haiti
     Oh! God! oh God! etc.

OLD BAYACOU: A cherished Phoenix
My tender heart! . . .
Decorated the crown
Of Papa Henry.
Our queen, the children,
From the heavens
Brought him down to the throne
A benevolent heart

     Oh! God! oh! God! etc.

COMMANDER OF *THE DAHOMETS*: You see, my brothers, on this joyous evening, we are celebrating the eve of the famous day when an entire people, righteously rebelling against tyranny, proclaimed its independence. Haiti is no longer in its political adolescence; in establishing a throne, a monument representative of its dignity and a sure guarantor of its rights, it has provided authentic proof of its physical and moral potency. Glory be to the All-Mighty who extended a helping hand to the innocently persecuted!

Name of a warrior nation from Africa given to the Royal military.

EVERYONE TOGETHER: Glory to the All-Mighty! (*Horn band.*)

COMMANDER: Long live, Henry, that beneficent hero, whose immortal arms, after having reclaimed our rights, constructed the edifice of our political existence upon an unshakeable foundation!

EVERYONE TOGETHER: Long live, Henry! (*Horn band.*)

COMMANDER: Eternal hatred to France!

EVERYONE TOGETHER: Eternal hatred to France! (*Horn band.*)

COMMANDER: Swear to die rather than to once again fall unto her unjust and cruel domination.

ALL TOGETHER: We swear it.

CAPTAIN OF *THE DAHOMETS*: After that homage rendered to the Eternal, after that very pleasing sermon, which has become the refrain of our appreciative hearts, let us deliver ourselves to the sweet transports that the preparations of this holy ceremony inspire in us. How sweet it is to leisurely soak our lips in the delicious cup of independence!

BRISE BATAILLE, *SOLDIER*: (*In Creole*) Yes, we will die for our King; yes, we will die for liberty and independence, and if the enemies come, make no mistake we will castle our king with our guns [*n'a pas piti rouqué fisi à nous va rouqué ça*].[1] We will surround them until the earth will tremble in this country. We asked them to make a choice to treat us justly, they did not listen with their own ears, well then, they are going to lose everything. We will control them, they are a controlling race, my goodness! If they are not happy about coming here, then how unreasonable of them to come. But let us directly quit all of this; tomorrow is independence day, the good Lord punished me, *ma candio* [my youthful desires], one time; if two are not rejoicing, Brise Bataille is going to make them rejoice.

OLD BAYACOU: When I see something as beautiful as this in our country, it makes me feel so young. You would say that it is a balm, that it is milk itself that is subsequently being slipped through my veins. Is it today that I desired the change of all this? Ask for the fish that is already in the hand of the fisherman if the water in the river is not sweet: there is not a bird in a cage that does not desire its own liberty. I shall not, no, be taken by them into the trap again! No way! A cat boiling in hot water is afraid of cool water. After all that, and to please the others, I will sing our song; the others see me there, but they did not see that the one who held my *ginga* [gamecock] is the one who held it last time too, it was not for nothing that the gods called me Bayacou, brilliant day ahead.

EVERYONE TOGETHER: Announcement, announcement, sing, old papa, we
   are listening to you.

OLD BAYACOU: Sing the glory
Of the Royal Dahomet;
Without any shame
He carries the musket
And into the black waves
Plunges every monster
In battle,
He is worse than a true goblin,
Cut and thrust
He shows his Latin,
Our high walls,
A steady fortification.

When we anger him
Better to encounter Lucifer,
He flies into rages
That one only sees in hell
When of slavery
He is shown the irons.

In ambush
He searches for his equal,
In shooting,
He has no rival,
And with the cannon
Fear his bacchanal.

The bayonet
Of the Royal Dahomet
Goes, without trumpet
Confounds, in its cackles,
The indiscreet band,
Perfidious, in its projects.

That a fire is being readied,
Is prelude to the laurels!
When in retreat
He leaves no trail;
And in defeat
He shows no mercy.

Throne and country,
Voilà his entire refrain;
Laws, industry,
Are his only obstacles:
And his battery
Is, my goodness! all his troops;

In time of war,
These sturdy warriors
In their careers
Offer the buccaneers
For use as a dwelling
The shadow of a banana tree

For food
From this tree, the fruit,
For a blanket
The leaves that it produces
And for shoes
The skin of the beef he cooks.

Voilà, despots!
Those who arm themselves;
Your proud boots
Have defeated soldiers;
With our *sans-culottes*,
You would not succeed.

(There, in the distance, the sound of the horns and several gunshots could be heard.)

Translated by Marlene Daut

Note

1. From the French verb *roquer*, to castle or protect the king in a game of chess.

Voyage to the North of Haiti

Hérard Dumesle

In 1821, the journalist and politician Hérard Dumesle traveled from his home in the city of Les Cayes, in the south of Haiti, to the northern areas of the country. His goal was to visit the sites where the history of Haiti's revolution had taken place, as well as to examine the ruins and traces left by the regime of King Henry Christophe. Like many political elites in the South, Dumesle was a strident critic of Christophe, whom he portrayed as a brutal despot, and a strident defender of Alexandre Pétion, whom he represented as the polar opposite, a man devoted to republican principles and the uplift of his people. The account Dumesle wrote of his journey to the North, published in his hometown in 1824, tells the history of Haiti's revolution and struggle for independence and of the subsequent regimes and civil wars that followed. It has long been a touchstone for historians of Haiti because it includes a speech purported to have been given by an insurgent leader at the Boïs-Caïman ceremony in August 1791. But Dumesle's work also offers us a fascinating entry point into the complexities and contradictions of political thought in early nineteenth-century Haiti, as the generation of leaders who followed those who had won independence tried to work through their relationship to their country's past and to what they saw as the unfinished business of the revolution that had created Haiti.

In the first excerpt, from chapter 1, Dumesle describes his departure and offers a set of philosophical reflections on nature and history based on his reading of the eighteenth-century naturalist Comte de Buffon and the English sentimental novelist Lawrence Stern.

Dumesle's text is organized around a series of dialogues with elders he encounters on his trip, with whom he discusses the history of the revolution and its aftermath. In the second excerpt, from chapter 6, he argues passionately against those abroad who denied the legitimacy of Haiti's independence.

Chapter 1: The Departure

A CONTEMPLATIVE GLANCE

We sailed farther and farther from the port, and as the objects paled in the distance, I was more and more disposed to meditation. Soon, that place that is the home of the ashes of the Rigauds, the Geffrards, of Benjamin Ogé, and of all the other illustrious men who made their country famous, disappeared from sight, just as they disappeared from the theater where they left behind so many glorious memories. . . .

As I looked at the coastline, sometimes crowned with green growth, sometimes savagely arid, a feeling of enthusiasm slowly electrified my senses. . . . What beauty there is in the relationships that form the chain of being! Who can pause to look at its innumerable links without feeling a profound admiration! Everywhere the world explodes with marvelous foresight, but it is only seen and appreciated by he who loves nature. He is the only one who sees that the universe is populated with feeling beings, while those who are indifferent see everything as inanimate. And the blind materialist, erring in the thick shadows of chance, abandons the light of reason and flees from nature. . . .

I would have passed the time in a tiring monotony . . . were it not for the company of Sterne and Buffon. Lying on the upper deck, I conversed in succession with these two friends, pulling them out of a small case where I had housed them. . . .

In laying out the system of the world, Buffon raised for me a small part of the veil behind which nature works. Putting aside its ingenious fictions, here, I saw a nursery of islands formed out of the debris of continents, advancing on the domains of the ocean, growing bigger, while farther away the ocean invaded entire countries, demanding on one side the rights it had lost on the other.

So it is, my friend, that empires succeed and replace one another; so we see a once fertile land struck with sterility, and flowers and fruits decorating a place once occupied by a pestilential swamp. Admirable equilibrium of the universe, which cannot be destroyed by our passions, always allied with error, in an attempt to overthrow the order of society and the harmony of nature!!

Sterne offered me less grandiose ideas; but, always sentimental, carried my imagination far from the lands where slavery burns incense at the foot of its idol, on the edge of a hill, next to pure water, or under a straw roof, where I dreamed next to a laborer with sweet illusions of happiness.

Traveling in this way, I resembled those Argonauts who traveled the world without leaving their room, and I had indeed traversed the immensity without even noticing the journey.

Chapter VI: The Founding of the Republic of Haiti

One would have to push skepticism to an extreme in order to doubt that this independence, acquired through the most glorious of sacrifices, does not exist in both right and fact. And if one called attention to the form, to that varnish which often services only to provide a legal appearance to outrages carried out against equality, one would find in place of that maxim of civil rights, *form is stronger than content*, that truth that defines the necessary alliance between politics and morality: *content governs form*. And no one can deny that this independence is not only the result of a struggle that liberty supported against tyranny in order to guarantee its own victory, but also the work of philosophy, and the conquest of reason over accumulated prejudice. To try and contest it would be to try and go back a century in time, and even the partisans of darkness have to accept that liberal principles can never be pushed back.

Translated by Laurent Dubois

On the Origins of the Counter-plantation System

Jean Casimir

Haitian sociologist Jean Casimir is one of the central theorists of the political and social structures in the country. Much of his work focuses on how the experience of slavery and revolution has shaped the long-term structures and practices of Haitian society. He coined the term "counter-plantation system" to describe the ways the en-slaved, having destroyed the plantation system and created an independent state, de-veloped an intricate and deeply rooted set of practices and structures meant to create an alternative, postslavery order that also was geared toward preventing the return of slavery or other forms of labor exploitation. This order was rooted in land ownership, the anchoring of family in this land over multiple generations, and structures of agri-cultural production and marketing in which women played central roles. It also was linked to the development of religious life, particularly the Vodou religion, and the Creole language as a form of communicating and articulating principles and visions. In the following excerpt, Casimir lays out the foundations for this broader process by exploring the experience of African slaves who were brought to Saint-Domingue, and theorizes the ways they were able to create a culture that allowed them both to survive within slavery and ultimately to create a new social order in independent Haiti.

To produce the plantation compound, the colonial state tried to appropriate the world of African village societies that the captives carried with them, to reduce it to silence and to annihilate it. It endeavored to institute a lack of history and tradition, and thus the absence of autonomous and sovereign production of knowledge by people originating from this underworld. To submit and to become functional slaves, the captives were commanded to resign their free will and live in a world structured to make them disappear by using their labor without any compensation.

For the colonial administration, the reality of Saint-Domingue was one and monolithic, made up of networks of slave plantations operating in com-pliance with the racialization of human relations. If the master of the slaves legally owned their body, their time, and their space, in order to make them useful, they still had to conquer, to invade, to occupy them, and to inculcate in their minds colonial ideas and values. Ultimately, they were not able to do that in Haiti. Instead, in the interstices of the social fabric that this administration strove to stitch up, the persons living in captivity patiently placed institutions challenging the external order and essential to the reproduction of their own awareness of the colonial order in which they were submerged.

The transition from freedom to mercantile slavery exceeded the imagination of African villagers captured by slave traders. In order to preserve or to recover their sanity, the kidnapped villagers embarked on a process of reeducation which enabled them to gradually recuperate their personality and shield it from abuse and harassment by the colonial plantation system. To avoid collapsing mentally and physically within the corset imposed by Europe, the prisoners had to find a balance. They had to sort out which of their jailer's demands they would comply with without complaining from those they could not accept. They had to find ways to separate what they were from what the plantation compound demanded from them.

To create standards to guide their conduct and improve their chances of survival, this collection of newly landed individuals needed to understand and deconstruct the logic of the plantation milieu, and to gradually elaborate a coherent set of reference points that could help them reverse it. Once they realized the critical role torture played in their socialization as slaves, they also understood the compelling interest they had in capturing and controlling the elements of the dominant culture that were essential for their survival. In this context, they welcomed the training sponsored by the master, understanding the need to be tutored. The planter chose aspects of his cultural frame of reference to try and inculcate in them. In response, they behaved as useful slaves, drawing on their background knowledge and experiences shared with their peers. They absorbed certain culture traits and norms of the dominant culture that were essential for their survival as they conceived of it.

The hostages began this journey in a deep solitude, since the arbitrariness of their abduction and exploitation had no logic they could spontaneously seize and share. Their fate was the result of a series of myths and justifications for racism that could only be perceived as utterly stupid. They therefore built a new pool of criteria out of daily practices, developed from the point of view of their particular cultural heritage. The introduction of new captives onto the plantation compound was a constant feature of daily life, such that various degrees of acculturation separated successive arrivals of prisoners. This gave rise to potential conflicts between the creolized people and those closer to their ancestral heritage.

Everyday life was the breeding ground in which prisoners cultivated and harmonized proposals relating to their way of conceptualizing the plantation compound and of interfacing with each other within it. Conviviality in the work gangs as well as conflicts between diverse ethnic groups became a laboratory where the captives discovered the principles and rules of solidarity in their opposition to the system and their pursuit of liberation. These interpersonal relations aimed at managing exchanges both with dominant institutions and with peer groups, and gave rise to what was later called family education, an education received from elders and necessarily distinct from instructions handed down by public authorities.

The person of the captives, their only asset, eluded the hold of both planters and the colonial state. They developed a form of self-reliance that enabled them to salvage their life, to protect and conserve this person which was a condensed version of a heritage in constant renewal. Drawing on scarce resources, these strangers restructured their individuality, while trying to invent a meaning and a rationale for the world surrounding them and a reason for the reception and training they were submitted to within the plantation compound. They had necessarily to combine the knowledge of the rules operating the plantation society, the development of a parallel set of knowledge to take care of them in lieu of the colonial state and of the institutions it created to extract their labor potential. This parallel system of knowledge became the backbone of the world that they built, and its primary function was to delay or possibly prevent their absorption by the plantation society.

By deepening their solidarity with their companions in misfortune, the enslaved developed a skillful comprehension of their new environment. Through this supportive surrounding they managed, by mutual agreement and for the benefit of their new community, to reorder their social world and begin to develop a counter-plantation order. Through their religious life, the Africans stated clearly that the foundations of their human dignity were not negotiable. They expressed without detour their refusal to accept the colonial state's version of God's truth and to bury themselves in the unexplainable dogmas conveyed by the dominant institutions. They lived according to values they gave themselves through processes defined in their traditions and endorsed by their peers.

The key issue to appreciate social exchanges during this period is not the content of the *wanga*—the fetish—and their virtues, but the simple fact that they were brandished as valid or at least plausible solutions. In other words, within the standards and principles of the plantation compound, there was a management and development of separate autonomies, the prelude to a collective and sovereign will imposing itself even in tiny and surreptitious spaces.

In reconditioning themselves in order to survive in the slave system, the captives enriched the knowledge they had inherited from their particular African ethnic group with an assessment of the order of the plantation compound. They expanded their cultural heritage to design survival strategies adapted to their new circumstances. In negotiating the implementation of these strategies they had to recognize, understand, and come to appreciate the perspectives of their fellow sufferers. At the same time, they codified the markers that separated them from their jailers. Networks of people sharing similar living conditions and behaviors developed. The borders keeping the French of the plantation compound from the African prisoners solidified even as the dividing lines separating different ethnic groups among the oppressed class were steadily blurred.

As they integrated into the plantation society, the captives explored not only the novelties of the dominant system but also those carried by their comrades in misfortune. They reorganized their universe by inventing an unprecedented one that both incorporated and outdistanced the African environment where they came from, as well as the mean-spirited landscape in which the master wished to enclose them. By so doing, without ever leaving the compound, they sidestepped the plantation society, dodging its negative effects.

Deprived of any future in their life as slaves, the captives had to refrain from accepting the contours of these predictable and hopeless figures. Instead, they created a milieu that was invisible to their masters. These worlds comprised ideas, meanings, beliefs, patterns of social relations, memories, even beings totally unknown to these masters. Using this unsuspected arsenal, the captives strove to people and reinvent their present by activating in a systematic manner these absences produced and reproduced deliberately by the plantation compound. They expanded their actual day-to-day living by exploiting all its avenues, and they learned how to move within this dimension beyond the dominant system.

Given the diagnostic of savagery they issued from their presumptuous and arrogant perspective, the masters remained unaware of the relevance of these new worlds. In their obsession with control and exploitation, they despised and ignored the multifaceted world of experiences and knowledge built by the incoming ethnic groups. The swarming experiments which led the newly arrived to join forces, as well as the logic of the answers they gave in response to the demands made by the plantation system, represented a form of education that evaded the field of vision of the authorities. The colonial system did not perceive its enemy, a fact which increased the range of movement of the latter.

The synchronization of the captives' defiant behavior relied on a form of self-management through which the oppressed community shared its experiences and its gradual mastery of the social environment. Their thinking depended on the daily, empirical testing of the appropriateness of any innovation. The oligarchs of the plantation compound could get by without an accurate appraisal of the abilities of the captives, compensating for their ignorance through the brutal imposition of the dominant culture and of the whims it enabled. But the prisoners could only defend themselves by managing a set of knowledge universally shared by their community. Beneath the surface of the dominant project of Western imperial mercantilism, the experience of the oppressed led to the invention of a reverse page to the plantation society: the new social fabric woven with an appreciation of the contributions by all actors of everyday life without exception.

When the opportunity arose through the outbreak of the French Revolution and the openings provided by imperial rivalry, the collective management of these unexpected forms of social life and solidarity developed into a revolutionary movement, encompassing practices of a larger scope that challenged the established order. The sedimentation of these practices through the course of the Haitian Revolution transformed the military victory of 1804 into a broader social transformation, one that converted the exploitation colony of Saint-Domingue into a settlement colony, with the formerly enslaved taking on the role of the settlers. This qualitatively new milieu could not have been foreseen or extrapolated from knowledge accessible to planters and colonial officials. For the planter and his or her entourage, the unexpected and unthinkable took hold of reality, renovated day-to-day living, and engendered a new social structure in which its architects could blossom.

In the new world that settled in Haiti after 1804, the original ethnic cultures —through their confrontations with the concrete experiences on the plantation society, and then during the ten years of the war for emancipation and independence—ultimately merged into a single oppressed culture. This culture was common to the insurgent agricultural workers and offered them the norms and principles necessary to carry out their life in independent Haiti. The women of the country could raise their children undisturbed, and the population no longer had to be recruited on the slave market. Deaths had always outnumbered births during the colonial period, but now children were born and raised in human conditions and the population grew steadily. The living conditions were modest indeed, but in time slavery and the slave trade became an unpleasant memory, buried in the deepest dungeon of collective memory.

Through this long process stretching from arrival in the plantation world through the successful overthrow of slavery through the Haitian Revolution, the weaving of relations of complicity and solidarity among companions in misfortune had revived a universe condemned by the imperial West. Gradually, the prisoners held hostage built their own world in the Americas, their own social order. In the very boat transporting them, in the slave gangs of the plantation, in the community of captives on same compound, in the *lakou* of Maroon villages, in the struggles of the revolution, the desire to live fully turned into the sovereignty of a community of peers. New identities evolved and created new reasons to appreciate oneself even as they offered instruments of defense against the abductors. People of the same condition, of the same social class, became in the long run people of similar birth—that is, of the same nation.

The birth of the Haitian nation cannot be distinguished from the Haitian Revolution; they produced each other reciprocally. The oppressed class and the emerging nation came into being through the same process. The nation evolved in opposition to the colonial state. It was the conversion of a set of isolated individuals into an organic totality, comprising networks of cohesive groups crucial to the existence and survival of the individuals. A culture, an elaboration of the experiences of the oppressed and the invention of new institutions ranging from groups of peers, to families, to the *lakou* and vil-lage communities, were structured daily in response to the misdeeds of the colonial state and its successors. This counter-plantation system represented a kind of internal sovereignty, embodying the aspirations for self-reliance and autonomy developed out of the historical experience of slavery and the Haitian Revolution.

Translated by Laurent Dubois

II

The Second Generation

By the mid-nineteenth century, Haiti's population included a new generation who had grown up in the wake of revolution and independence. They inherited the discourses, visions, and struggles of the revolutionary generation, but also sought to imagine new ways of configuring their society. They confronted many of the same challenges as their predecessors: until 1825, Haitian independence had not yet been formally recognized by any other nation. This hadn't stopped an active trade with other parts of the Caribbean, the Americas, and Europe, but it did maintain the Haitian government in a kind of strange limbo in relation to other countries. The struggle for recognition meant a confrontation with the often extremely negative attitudes and representations of Haiti that circulated outside the country, and intellectuals continued to be preoccupied with defending their country against ongoing attacks, as well as vindicating its culture and history.

Haiti's relationships with France, the United States, the Latin American republics, and the neighboring colony of Santo Domingo—involved in its own highly complex political conflicts over sovereignty—all shaped this period. So, too, did the ongoing struggles over land, labor, and power that erupted at different historical moments. These conflicts shaped state policy, such as Boyer's Code Rural, and drove political movements such as the uprisings of 1843. Haitian writers, meanwhile, produced works that sought to defend the country against its critics, as well as seeking out literary forms that could enable them to represent and express the experiences and aspirations of the country's people.

The Indemnity: French Royal Ordinance of 1825

King Charles X of France

For two decades following its military defeat in Saint-Domingue, France refused to recognize the independence of its former colony. The rest of the Atlantic powers followed suit, effectively isolating Haiti diplomatically. Finally, in 1825 Charles X issued a Royal Ordinance recognizing the independence of "the French side of Saint-Domingue" under the condition that the Haitian government agree to pay a substantial indemnity destined to compensate the former plantation owners for property lost during the revolution. When the ordinance was brought before Haitian president Jean-Pierre Boyer, it was accompanied by a French squadron prepared to start a blockade should the Haitian leader not accept the agreement. Although Boyer, under pressure, agreed to the terms, he also saw it as an opportunity to end Haiti's political and economic isolation.
—Contributing Editor: Claire Payton

No. 1798—ORDINANCE OF THE KING that concedes to the current inhabitants of the French part of Saint-Domingue the full and complete independence of their Government, under the conditions of the aforesaid Ordinance.

In Paris, 17 April 1825
CHARLES, by the grace of God, KING OF FRANCE AND NAVARRE, to all whom these presents may come, GREETINGS. . . .

Wanting to provide for those who claim the interests of French commerce, the misfortunes of the former colonists of Saint-Domingue, and the precarious state of the current inhabitants of that island,

WE HAVE COMMANDED and COMMAND the following:

Article 1. The ports of the French part of Saint-Domingue shall open to the commerce of all nations.

The duties levied in these ports, either on ships or on merchandise, upon entering as well as leaving, shall be equal and uniform for all flags, except the French flag, in favor of whom the duties shall be reduced by half.

2. The current inhabitants of the French part of Saint-Domingue will transfer to the French Deposits and Consignments Fund, in five equal terms, year after year, the first falling on 31 December 1825, the sum of 150 million francs, destined to compensate the former colonists who will claim an indemnity.

3. We concede, under these conditions, by the present ordinance, to the current inhabitants of the French part of the island of Saint-Domingue, the full and complete independence of their government.

And the present ordinance shall be sealed with the great seal.

Given in Paris, at Tuileries Palace,
on 17 April of the year of grace 1825,
and the first of our reign.
Signed, CHARLES

Translated by Claire Payton

Hymn to Independence

Jean-Baptiste Romane

Jean-Baptiste Romane (1807–58), one of Haiti's earliest poets and playwrights, composed the "Hymn to Independence" in 1825 to commemorate France's recognition of Haiti's independence. The poem attests to the ambiguous attitude many early Haitians, especially those in the upper classes, had toward France. On the one hand, the former colonizer was decried for the horrors of slavery and colonialism. On the other, the European country remained a model many sought to imitate in terms of its literature and societal mores.

The world has praised your sons,
Sun, today is your day!
See Haiti mingle lily
With the palms which cover her head.
Share in our joyous transports
On this day of rejoicing.
France has granted all wishes:
Long live Haiti! Long live France!

The day of glory has shone for you:
Majestic shadows of our Fathers,
Come celebrate with us
Our destiny, so beautiful, so prosperous.
France has sanctioned the efforts
Of our heroic bravery.
Sing, sing on the somber shores:
Long live Haiti! Long live France!

We salute you O great king of Frenchmen
You whom we saw crowned with glory,
Linking the ugliness of crimes
To the winged chariot of victory!

Your brow glows with immortality.
Our sons, admiring your mercy
Will say in posterity:
Long live Haiti, Long live France!

Translated by Nadève Ménard

Boyer's Rural Code

Jean-Pierre Boyer

A hero of the revolutionary fighting, President Jean-Pierre Boyer rose to power and held it for nearly two decades. He took power in the North of Haiti in 1818 and re-united the North and South in 1820. In 1826, in the wake of the indemnity agreement with France, he issued the Rural Code of 1826. It was designed to enforce standards of labor discipline and production in agriculture with the goal of boosting cash crop production in order to pay the debt of 150 million francs that his government incurred in exchange for French recognition of Haitian sovereignty.

While noticeably less draconian than Christophe's Code Henry, Boyer's regulations concerning agricultural labor constitute an important reflection of the persistence of elite fantasies of large-scale plantations, scrupulously taxed surpluses of cash crops, obedient laborers, and the swift repression of vagabondage. Much of what was laid out here, however, remained a dead letter. Poor Haitians could take advantage of the nationwide labor shortage and the sparsely populated rural hinterland to escape unfavorable contracts. And while the Rural Code attempted to prevent the establishment of unauthorized rural settlements, these measures met little success as independent farmsteads organically spread into the hinterlands with scant regard for formal property claims or conformity with state economic policy. As such, the details of the document are best read as an unsuccessful attempt to stop the progress of the "counter-plantation" system described by Jean Casimir (see part I).

Article 23 represents an interesting example of forward-thinking early nineteenth-century environmental policy. Fully aware that deforestation could undermine the nation's water supply and agriculture, Boyer hoped to continue with the profitable exportation of dyewoods and hardwoods while protecting indispensable rivers and mountain springs with forested buffers. But despite such enlightened planning, the growth of forest cover during the 1820s and 1830s primarily reflected the failure of Boyer's agrarian policy rather than the success of any environmental policy.
—Contributing Editor: Johnhenry Gonzalez

Article 4: Citizens of the agricultural profession cannot leave the countryside to live in the cities or towns without the authorization of the justice of the peace of the commune that they wish to leave and that of the commune where they will reside. The justice of the peace will not grant authorization until after being assured that the individual is of good customs, that they have maintained regular conduct in the district that they wish to leave, and that they possess the means of subsistence in the city that they wish to move to. All those who do not conform to the rules established above will be considered vagabonds and treated as such.

. . .

Article 23: It is especially forbidden to cut down trees along the mountaintops and for a distance of one hundred paces from their peak, nor at the head or alongside springs, or on the banks of rivers: owners of lands watered by springs or rivers must encircle the source of these springs and alongside the riverbanks they must plant bananas, bamboo, or other trees appropriate for maintaining coolness.

. . .

Article 30: No cooperative or association of agricultural laborers residing on the same plantation can become the leaseholder of the property that they inhabit to be administered by themselves collectively.

Article 31: The houses or quarters of the agricultural laborers must be constructed at the same place on the plantation to which they are attached.

. . .

Article 45: Everyone who is not working in the service of the state as soldiers, laborers or employees of any sort, and whose profession is to cultivate the land or to cut wood for export will be required, for the mutual guarantee of their interests, to sign a bilateral contract with the owner or principal leaseholder of the rural property or woodcutting operation on which they will be employed.

The contract can be signed collectively or individually according to the will of the parties involved.

Article 46: The duration of the contracts cannot be less than two years or more than nine years, for secondary cultivation and manufactures; for less than three years or more than nine, for woodcutting; less than six months or more than a year.

Article 47: The contract will be prepared on stamped paper before a notary who will take minutes and must clearly explain all of the conditions established among the contracting parties who can make any stipulations that they judge necessary, provided that they are not contrary to the positions of the present Code.

. . .

Article 50: The bosses of work gangs sharecropping by halves must share by the same proportion with the principal plantation owner half of all that they harvest on the land, in terms of fruits, ground provisions, vegetables, grains and cash crops of any kind.

. . .

Article 52: Sharecroppers receiving a quarter of the revenue of their produce will receive one fourth of the gross revenue of all that they produce: they will enjoy the entirety of the fruits harvested in their own gardens, which they will work during off hours and days of rest.

. . .

Article 69: Agricultural laborers will be submissive and respectful toward the plantation owners and leaseholders with whom they have contracted, as well as toward the managers.

Article 70: Agricultural laborers must execute with zeal and exactitude all of the agricultural work that is assigned to them by the owners, leaseholders, or managers with whom they have contracted.

Article 71: Agricultural laborers, whatever the conditions of their contracts, will be obliged to devote all their time to their work, and to not quit under any circumstances: they cannot leave their workplace except from Saturday morning until Monday morning before dawn without the permission of the plantation owners, principal leaseholders or managers; for all other working days they are required to have a permit from the landowner, principal leaseholder, or manager if they do not leave the district; if they do leave the district the permit will be issued by the local officer of the rural police and the local military commander.

Translated by Johnhenry Gonzalez

Le lambi

Ignace Nau

In this short story, Ignace Nau brings his readers back to the history of the Haitian Revolution through the words of an old veteran of that conflict named Jerome. He recounts the story of Halaou, an early leader of the revolt in the western part of Saint-Domingue. Halaou brought together many enslaved rebels under his leadership and collaborated with the white commissioner Leger Felicité Sonthonax, who decreed the abolition of slavery in the colony in 1793. The story also deals with the conflicts within the revolutionary movement, in this case between Halaou's band—composed largely of African-born men and women from the plantations—and other groups led by free people of color. The story emphasizes the sounds that accompanied revolt: of song, of clanging metal from sugar machinery taken from the plantations, and of the lambi, or conch shell. Looking back over the decades to the revolution, Nau suggests that the sound of the lambi—and therefore the spirit of revolt—still infuses and inspires Haitians of a new generation.

One night I was sitting by myself at the great house on the Dumé plantation. I could hear the sound of a few drums in the depths of the courtyard, where a few family members and friends were trying to pass the last hours of the night as happily as possible. But I, all alone, had nothing to distract me, except for the repetitive song of an owl sitting on the roof of the house. But this voice was not fit for serenading my imagination, and as sad and monotonous as it was I sensed it would end up irritating me. In that hour of vague reveries, if my spirit was going to rest in sad thoughts, I at least wanted them to be soft and persuasive. So I stood up and slowly walked toward the mill, which was plunged into rest and silence. The darkness was deepening all around me, and the moonless sky was nevertheless shining with an infinity of stars that projected a half-light on the objects around me. I'm not sure why I was drawn to the sound of the cascade falling from the top of the rock, but my intention was to go sit there in order to better dream alongside the falls, for its sound echoed soft and sonorous in my ears. As I was walking I looked up at the neighboring heights, so dark in that night of stars. All of a sudden, and on all parts of the mountain rising up around the town, there appeared fires beyond counting. I saw them disappear frequently only to appear anew elsewhere, and I presumed these intervals were the result of the ups and downs of the terrain. These fires without number moved here and there, but were all heading in the direction of the countryside, and under this fantastic illumination, the mountain seemed darker and more opaque: it looked like a giant tomb around which thousands of candles were burning. As I was preoccupied by this scene, I lightly felt someone alongside me. I turned around and to my great surprise saw an old man curved over a cane, walking next to me.

"Who are you?" I asked him, slightly surprised, for in that moment when my thoughts were mostly harvested from the field of the supernatural and the fantastical, I was tempted to take him too as a sudden apparition from a hollow, imagined world.

"I am," he replied, "the old Jérôme, former miller, Bourgeois. Old and crippled now, I can only see and walk with great difficulty in this darkness."

"I didn't see you either: I was busy watching the fires on the mountain go back and forth."

"And did that entertain you," he said with a slightly forced laugh. "That's for the best, my good Bourgeois."

"Yes, this scene seems very strange to me."

"Today is Saturday and the fires you see are nothing other than the pine torches used by those coming to the markets of Port-au-Prince. They come from so far away: from Bellevue, Grand-Fond, the new Touraine, and the other places at the base of the Selle mountain, over there, over there. That is how the mountains around us used to light up in times of upheaval and agitation, when each band of rebels and maroons, led by a bold and fearless chief, descended on the countryside and turned everything upside down. Night after night, there was a similar alert: an alarm here, an alarm there, and the miserable property-owners would constantly flee and then return, not knowing what to do, so harassed by these crises! These were all parallel shocks that preceded the great shock that came later, and overturned everything, as you can see.

But, stopping suddenly, he grabbed my arm. "What do I hear?" he cried. "Listen!" A lugubrious sound, the distant sound of the lambi! Despite the darkness I could see a little light in his half-hidden eyes. "But who would sound out the lambi in these plains?" I said to him. He cocked his ear: the sound repeated itself and then disappeared into the shadows. "That's what surprises me, it's true. Could it be children? But no, you can't play around like that with this instrument, right?" "In town," I replied, "it would be market women selling fish in the streets with their platters, calling out, sometimes even past eight o'clock. The mastiffs, lying in the dark hallways of the stores, lifted their big triangular heads, as usual, and howled at this sound, just as they howl when they hear some spirit lost in the night pass by outside their triple walls. But I don't think it could be children, Jérôme."

"Impossible, Bourgeois."

"And what is it that is so sinister in this sound of this instrument? After all, it is nothing more than a shell."

"Yes, a shell, a conch from the sea. But it is a memory. It is a charm, inseparable from that shell that makes our old hearts beat a little faster. Don't you see, in the interior, that bright red color?"

"Yes?"

"It is, for us, a bloodstain cemented by the revolution. For me, when I see a lambi, I want to pick it up and bring it to my lips. For me it is a dear relic that I would hang over my shrine. Whenever I look at it, an entire painting spreads out before me: a crowd of thoughts from my youth awaken when I hear this first trumpet of liberty. Wasn't it that instrument that first sounded out the accents of our victories? Isn't it this instrument that sowed the first seeds of terror in the hearts of our enemies? Its flesh fed our men, and more than once its shell made the horde of our executioners tremble with terror. But here is a mill. Let us sit down so that I can tell you a story. Let us hurry, it is late. I can't give you the precise dates, but not long after Sonthonax shelled Port-au-Prince and chased Borel out, when the entire country was in upheaval, when the slaves made their masters tremble, a man appeared, six feet tall and two feet wide. His name was Halaou. He first gathered a few partisans around him, but before the year was over his troupe had grown extraordinarily. Right now you see how the Grande-Rivière barely covers the rocks in its bed with its waves; but in April and May when the rains bring water to its spring, the water rises, and rises, and then overflows into the fields, carrying away trees, bits of mountain, and huge rocks. That was how this audacious chief carried everything in his wake. But one day, seeing that his army had grown considerably and that the men were coming to join him from everywhere in such great numbers that it seemed like they were bursting out of the earth, he wanted to divide them up into divisions and put a chief capable of leading them in charge of each one. It fell to me to lead one band. He ordered each chief to count their division, and we found that the men were more numerous than the leaves in a forest. Wherever we dug in the ground a wide, deep path carved itself under our footsteps. One night, a happy memory, he stopped and camped near the Meilleur and Lassère plantations. He summoned a *caplata* and asked him to start a ceremony he wanted to carry out in order to return to the work that the heavens had destined him to accomplish. This man, an expert in his profession, advanced with a calm look and presented to Halaou a large white rooster. 'This,' he told him, 'will be your magical rooster; you will never accomplish anything without picking it up and caressing it first; you and your men will protect it, for it is your banner, for it is your talisman. Each of your soldiers will carry the tails of horses and cattle that they will twirl in the air as they charge into battle: and then the cannon will melt away at your approach and the powder will turn to liquid under the wick of your enemies.' With these words there was an immense shout: the birds fled from where they were resting, and the colonists on the nearby plantations ran away, terrified. Then the *caplata* called up seventy to eighty men to whom he distributed *assotor* drums, lambi, and the debris from boilers from sugar plantations. They created a corps of musicians who surrounded Halaou. When the signal was given, they began a stunning serenade. The lambis sounded out high and piercing, the drums resonated, and the pieces from the boilers clapped against one another, created sounds so heart-rending and horrifying that they made your ears bleed. And the serenade was such, Bourgeois, that all the devils in hell would have run away, their talons over their heads! A choir gathered together and this famous song broke out:

Halaou! *Tym, pan, dam!*
The cannon is bamboo: *tymp, pan, dam!*
The powder is water: *tym, pan, dam!*

"In the midst of this army—all ears and all eyes—Halaou wandered about everywhere, delighted to the point of ecstasy at this music: and then in order to complete the scene and have the pleasure of seeing the flames spread wild with the wind, he ordered that the torches be put to the neighboring homes and buildings. The roar of the fire was joined by the cries of men dancing to the chords of the music. No: never, never in my life will I forget this scene! And when we saw that his army was complete and that everyone had armed themselves with weapons—war and hunting rifles, pistols, bayonets attached to poles, pikes hardened in fire, knives and daggers—he ordered the great march. Not one of us knew where he was going, not one of us knew where he would stop. Here is what happened at Croix-des-Bouquets tonight, we were told. The sentinel of the fort, overtaken for some reason by apprehension, called the officer on duty. 'Captain,' he said, 'put your ear to the ground and listen to this sound.' 'Yes,' he replied 'a strange noise, indeed. There's a muffled rumbling in the earth's entrails, as if a thousand chariots were rolling on the surface. Is it going to bury us under this landslide?'

"'By St. Denis, my Captain,' the sentinel said, 'stand up and take in the wind that is blowing from the mountains of the North.'

"The Captain stood up and smelled the wind.

"'What is it? I smell the smell of men, the warmth of breath. I hear a distant sound, like suffocated thunder that is being snuffed out and then reborn. Listen, soldier! The air is in motion. What do these strange things mean? Are volcanoes going to explode onto us and add their convulsions to the uprising of the slaves?' 'I don't know,' said the sentinel, 'but I'm seeing what look like giant shadows pass over the fields. Listen, again, an explosion over there! Look, over there a fire reddens the sky and the smoke coming towards us carries the smell of burning flesh!' The sentinel held his rifle close, the Captain convulsively grabbed his sword and both of them, pierced with fear, fixed their alarmed gaze on the redness of the sky.

"Over the course of the year we had a number of engagements through which our enemies learned to respect our considerable forces: we were the terror of the colonists, and the name Halaou made the white population tremble. A few months after Polverel proclaimed general liberty in the West and the South, our leader directed our columns toward Port-au-Prince. We marched all night, leaving Croix-des-Bouquets far behind us. The next morning, as soon as we saw the masts of the boats in the harbor, the order was given to start the music. With this extraordinary noise from all our instruments, the inhabitants of the town jumped, panicking, from their beds and gathered in the neighborhoods to watch our triumphal entrance.

"Our troops were lined up on all the great plazas of the town and were so numerous that they filled the streets of Belair. Commissioner Sonthonax came and asked to speak to our leader. We saw Halaou pick up his rooster and approach the commissioner with an audaciousness that inspired us all to firmness and even insolence. The white commissioner gave him a little slap on the shoulder, spoke quietly in his ear, and then brought him into his offices. There, a magnificent party awaited. There was a profusion of dishes set out on giant tables, luxurious drinks, and all kinds of fruit. The army could not contain its joy at seeing its magnanimous chief celebrated and honored by the commissioner. The *petits blancs*, who didn't know about Halaou's power, could not contain their surprise. And we, we could not stop complimenting the brilliant reception. 'Hola! Eh! My children,' cried the powerful chief, circulating among us; and all, the multitude we were, Aradas, Ibos, Congos, Poulards, Senegalese, Angolas, Dahomeans, jumped up in unison and created a circle around him. 'Let us retrace our steps, the Commissioner has given us a task in Croix-des-Bouquets, let us march there promptly, my children.' Ahead! And all the tails were twirling above our heads, and the instruments exploded with sound! The soldiers danced in the ranks and belted out amazing songs. I won't pause here and give you the irrelevant details of our return march; but before four in the afternoon that day, we flooded into the narrow space of Croix-des-Bouquets. We found General Beauvais with his troops. A large part of our army, finding no room in the town, camped outside of it, and our chief kept only a group of elite soldiers around him. That day, a deputation from General Beauvais came to invite Halaou to a great banquet that was to take place the next morning. He immediately took his white rooster, caressed it, and bending down from his great height, accepted the kind invitation of the general. So the next day our chief, accompanied by his officers, went to the designated location. But a rumor was spreading that the white commissioner had given Halaou an important and difficult task: was it an assassination, as was said at the time? To this day, I still don't know. But right after he left we saw two young officers from the legion of the West arriving at full gallop. One of them quickly assembled a detachment of the General's troops, and then came into the house where the feast was going on just as the food was being placed on the table. Surprised by this hostile and unexpected entrance, Beauvais got up, but the officer said: 'General, go into your room!' 'Who is giving me this order?' Beauvais demanded. 'Go to your room right away!' the officer repeated. The General was going to refuse again, but the officer insisted and Beauvais, furious, went into his room and grabbed his weapons. But before he left the room, Halaou and several of his officers fell dead under the fire of the detachment. Then everything became clear: Beauvais came out and shouted, 'To arms!' Our chiefs did the same thing and the signal was given for combat. A terrible melee ensued. Should I tell of the bloodshed? Should I count the hundreds of men who died? Pressed against each other, like cane in a field, our soldiers were indifferent to the cannonballs that dug wide and deep furrows in our ranks. They fell like leaves during a hurricane. For an instant our songs and the terrifying chords of our musicians made our enemies hesitate. But their numbers undermined our courage and soon we turned our backs and ran. Our bands dispersed into the countryside where, for a long time, they sowed terror and carnage accompanied by the sound of their magical lambi. Many times, when the white militias marched against the plantation workers, by then in open rebellion, you could see them stop—as if by enchantment—and clutch their rifles close to their chests when they heard the sound of the lambi. If lightning struck at the foot of a colonist, they would have been less surprised than when they heard the fanfare of this famous shell, the first chord of our liberty!"

With these words, the old man stood up, picked up his stick and went away, his heart full of sighs. Happy with my evening, I retraced my steps full of what the elderly Jerome had just told me. Since then, the fire on the mountains and the sound of the lambi at night in our streets, always awaken new and incredible feelings in me.

Translated by Laurent Dubois

An Experimental Farm

Victor Schoelcher

*Victor Schoelcher (1804–93) was a leading French abolitionist who played an impor-
tant role in the French abolition of slavery in 1848. In 1841 he traveled through the West
Indies, including Haiti, and wrote a vivid account of his voyage. Despite his commitment to ending slavery, he found Haiti a disappointment, in part because the system
of industrial agricultural production that had flourished under colonial rule had
been dismantled and had been almost entirely replaced by small farms. Schoelcher
was largely critical of this development, but here he describes his visit (he describes
himself in the third person as "the philanthropist") to an experimental farm run by
a man named James Blackhurst, who was likely an African American immigrant or
perhaps from the British West Indies. His politics of labor on the plantation are linked
to his opposition to the regime of President Boyer. This description gives us a glimpse
both of what attracted certain immigrants to Haiti, and of the alternative visions surrounding land and labor that were being developed in some quarters.
—Contributing Editor: Claire Payton*

In the middle of the Port-au-Prince plain, I met a Mulatto who was just
twenty-four years old. He had a vigorous spirit free from the general frivolity
and was striving to build up a plantation with few resources.

Mr. James Blackhurst has fields of sugarcane, and they are beginning to
expand. Each day he weeds new parcels of land with workers that he finds
without too much difficulty, because he lives fraternally with them, farms as
a collective, and does not take the lion's share of the produce.

However busy he may be with his work, Mr. Blackhurst never forgets that
he is a citizen. He sees it as his responsibility to think about policy, and dreams
of a noble regeneration for his country. He is already known as a member of
the extreme opposition. He knows that societies can become fields full of
weeds when they are not cared for, and soon he will found a school that he
will keep open no matter what. In the meantime, once a week he brings
together the most intelligent men of his workshop and leads a discussion
with them. His teachings are essentially moral; he attacks all superstition
and expresses himself with clear and precise language. That is the nature of
his mind. One day, he announced to his growers that they would be receiv-

ing a visit from a philanthropist. "What is a philanthropist?" asked one of these poor people. "It's a man," responded the young landowner, "who feels the pain and suffering of the unfortunate. We should love him as he loves us." These kinds of words entered into their hearts. So the next day when the philanthropist arrived, all the laborers gathered around him cordially and allowed him to enter into their huts, each of them as miserable as the next, because Mr. Blackhurst doesn't yet have the means to construct them properly.

As a result of this conduct, Mr. Blackhurst's property is already regarded by the men of the plantation almost as communal property. This protects it from the usual misuse. I spent two days there, and it was marvelous to see how Mr. Blackhurst, still so young, has already learned to shed all vanity. Under his thatched roof he did not try and hide his poverty. He served dinner with iron forks, telling me, "I could have gone to borrow some silver from a neighbor, but why bother with the shame of a lie? You are in the home of a peasant, sir." There was really a shimmer of antiquity in the character of this Haitian. Courage, generous child of the emancipated land, courage, you will succeed. Do not let yourself be weakened by deception or ingratitude, you will succeed. Yes, after a few years you will provide a great example to your brothers, you will become a noble subject of emulation.

Translated by Claire Payton

The 1842 Earthquake

Démesvar Delorme

Démesvar Delorme was born in 1831 in Cap Haïtien and became a prominent politician and writer. At the age of eleven, he lived through the 1842 earthquake that destroyed much of his city. In this account, written later in his life, he looks back at the experience. Delorme powerfully depicts the horror of the natural disaster by describing both his personal experience of it and the broader social trauma it caused. The earthquake contributed to the overthrow of President Boyer the following year and was the most devastating seismic event in Haitian history until the one that struck the country in 2010.

2. The Disaster

A muffled sound, a faraway rumbling, mournful, as if coming from a deep abyss, can be heard from the eastern side. Two soldiers from the regiment fall in a heap. Look, I say, to my brother, Darbelle, at those two soldiers who just collapsed. What is that? Other soldiers in the ranks fall. Spectators stumble and fall. The muffled sound becomes louder. We wobble, my brother and I, then fall, too. The northern wall of the barracks shakes and falls almost at the same time that we do. The sound becomes terrifying. I am lying on the ground, my head turned toward the street, shaking with fear. The cathedral's steeple in front of me begins to swing in the air, bells ringing and chiming with no rhythm, sinister; a horrible knell. The steeple falls, the top parts first. Then, the church falls, and all of the houses around it, and all the houses I see; and in the streets beyond, and at last the entire city.

All this, with a sound that could not be named, rumbling in the middle of a thick fog, coming from the cracked walls, and that, becoming thicker and thicker in mere instants, had become a black cloud, gloomy, like those of great storms at sea, and soon was surrounded like them by blazing red lights, moving around all over the place, filling the air. The city's flammable materials had already caught fire. Horrifying spectacle. True scene of a sudden and violent volcanic eruption. Arresting image of hell in its horrible, convulsive roar. That is how one must describe that day of final judgment of which they speak of to us in our childhood. The angel's trumpet was not missing, nor were the cries of distress, nor the wailing. Those cries were voiced from all around me and coming from afar along with the sounds of the disaster, they made one shudder. The angel of destruction passing by.

3. The Witness's Family

That was the idea that came to me right away. The end of the world, I cried to my brother, it's the end of the world. Following an instinct that I have never been able to understand afterward, I took off my shoes as if I'd heard that one had to appear barefoot before the Lord. At that moment, out of the gray cloud of slaked lime that covered everything around us, I saw a human form emerge, bent upon itself, hands outstretched, searching for a way. It was my mother. She was looking for us. After finding the last-born, Jules, who the nanny had been walking on the Place Montarcher, she was looking for us with the most profound anxiety. When she found us, she made us stay in the same spot, in the middle of the Place du Quartier; she made Louisine, the nanny, join us with the little one. And she returned to the ruins of the house to bring the other children. My sister, the only one I had then, had been half-buried beneath the rubble of the house. An artillery officer, a neighbor named Mr. Mesager, whose features I can still see, had helped my mother to free her. One of her legs was almost broken. Before going to get his mother, who lived next door to us, he had the goodness to carry Edelmone to the yard of the barracks where I was. She was covered in blood. My mother, with my two other brothers, Anderson and Bellomont, followed behind her. But the family was not complete. Where was my stepfather, my mother's husband? That question kept us in a state of anxiety. A few minutes later, he appeared, all bloody himself. At the time of the earthquake, he had been near the Marché Clugny. He had been able to throw himself onto the market square. After the disaster, trying to get to the house amid the rubble, he had to stop and help a poor woman called Augustine (Anet) who was trapped between the fallen walls and who was screaming loudly enough to alert the desert animals. Both her legs were broken. He had pulled her out of the rubble and carried her to the market, and was covered in her blood. Seeing him approach, we thought he was fatally wounded.

4. Father Torribio

At that moment, the parish priest, Abbot Torribio, a Spanish priest, who had been officiating in the city for many long years, came toward us, crucifix in hand and repeating in an emotion-filled voice that never left our ears, "My children, my children, go toward the mountain; as fast as you can, go to the mountain."

5. Fleeing to the Mountain

The sea was rising, coming into the city, drowning the poor people that the walls had spared. The poor priest, overcome by fear, thought it was a cataclysm, one of those geological revolutions that destroyed and remade the surface of the earth. He saw no salvation other than the top of the mountains that surround the Cap like a fence. Everyone got up and followed him; the inhabitants of the entire northern part of the city who had escaped from the murderous ruins of the crumbled houses had run to the big Place de la Caserne of the Thirtieth Regiment. The entire desolate crowd, haggard, distressed, aimless, got up and mechanically followed the priest. We went thus, stumbling, falling, getting up with great effort, falling again on the piled ruins where the fire had started, which the earthquake's aftershocks, continuing with hopeless frequency, shook from minute to minute.

The ground had hollowed in several places, and each person felt with horror the imminence of a supreme quake that would open the abyss of the earth and would swallow the city along with its remaining inhabitants.

We went on, we went on. Night was approaching. Even more horror! We passed among corpses, on top of corpses, passed by the wounded who screamed as they died, in agony mixed with torment. The long tongues of the immense fire twisted in the wind, threatened them from all sides. How to save them? When we wanted to go to their aid and tried to move the stones or pieces of wall that clutched them, flattened them, broke their limbs, an aftershock came that dropped onto our heads the disjointed stones of a shaky piece of wall, standing as if to continue the drama.

6. Refuge in Tifaine

It was the darkest of night, from eight to nine o'clock, when we arrived half-way up the mountain, at the Tifaine property where the priest made us stay to spend the night.

. . .

Nothing to give to the hungry children. Nothing to relieve the wounded who were able to follow us and continued to lose their blood. Not a roof under which to seek refuge. The Tifaine house had been toppled by the earthquake. I still see the debris of a beautiful fountain erected in the middle of the estate, which the quake had thrown beyond the entryway. Rain came. . . . A pretty strong rain. We had to stick the children under makeshift archways formed here and there by the house's debris. To do so was to risk them being crushed at the first tremor. But what could be done about the rain?

From the hole where they put me, I saw the fire over the ruins of the city. I closed my eyes to better form within myself the singular hope of seeing the city rise up the next morning.

7. Nightmare

After having believed in the end of the world, I had started to believe it was all a dream. I tried to convince myself that I was dreaming, that the nameless things I had just seen had not happened. It was a dream, a horrible nightmare. Also mixed in my mind was the idea of a miracle that would put the city on its feet at sunrise. I was eleven years old. I am recounting these things at forty-five years old. My imagination had been strongly nourished by marvelous legends. My father had been a believer, a pious man, who loved the beauties of worship and intoxicating himself with the grave harmonies of plain Gregorian chants mixed with the incense of church services. He never neglected to take me. I often heard him say that nothing is difficult for Him for whom everything has been easy, for Him who from nothing made all things. My grandmother, my mother's mother, had often talked to me about things similar to the story of the Seven Sleepers or the blessed Saint Denis, decapitated, carrying his head in his hand. It was above all another good woman, Madame Paul, whom we called Moumoute, almost a relative, a friend of my grandmother's and my sister's godmother, who had filled my head with the supernatural. She had told me everything with an unction that impressed me more than books: Joshua's adventure with the sun, the docility of the sea before Moses, Jonah's luck inside the whale, the lions kneeling before Daniel and all the best of those stories. I kept a faith in miracles that almost gave me the guarantee in the nervous weakened state in which the terrible catastrophe of the earthquake had put me that I would see the city intact the next morning.

Alas! That was not the case, and that next morning, when I opened my eyes and saw the immense mass of white rubble from which rose up in places black columns of smoke striped red by the flame's surge, an infinite sadness entered me and did not leave me but slowly for a year.

I do not recall having seen Father Torribio again. My family descended from the mountain. Around noon, having used up all our strength traversing the city lengthwise over the piles of ruins constantly moving beneath our feet, from the Ravine district to la Fossette, via Espagnol Street, we found ourselves at Loge Square, from which we headed off to the countryside.

. . .

11. Looting of the Cap

While tearful masses of helpless fugitives thus lingered everywhere, searching for refuge, unspeakably awful people were looting the ruins of the Cap. Those residents of the city who had land in the surrounding communes had headed out to their rural properties the next day to gather laborers to help them remove the rubble from their houses and to save what they could of their affairs, valuables, or money.

Seeing this, a few scoundrels who had nothing to save themselves arranged with the peasants to rob the victims. Thus began terrible scenes! Looters emboldened by the outright bandits. They killed anyone who tried to stop the looting, all those who merely criticized them for wanting to profit from such a disaster to seize the spoils. They even killed the poor people beneath the walls who were screaming for two days, asking for help, in order to plunder them without fear of later protests. They ended up killing each other over sharing their stolen goods. It was from then on, on the ruins of the Cap, a ferocious robbery. Nobodies, unknown the day before yesterday, have since become gentlemen, after the criminal and bloody looting of the Cap city. I don't want to name names. It was dangerous to venture into what was left of one's house to try to unbury something, in order to give the rest of the family something to live off of. You were killed with no mercy. The government had to send in troops. The chief looters were arrested and brought to Port-au-Prince. Several of those villains have since become important personalities. This is how human societies are often enough deplorable, disgusting.

12. The Plague

But soon these pirates of the rubble could no longer continue their exploits. A horrible plague, coming from the thousands of corpses rotting beneath the ruins, spread throughout the country for ten leagues around. A thousand people had remained crushed beneath the walls of the Cap.

Everyone was dying in Petite-Anse, in Haut-du-Cap, in Marchegal, in the heights of Lambert, all the way to the Plaine-du-Nord, all the way to Quartier Morin. Never was there a bigger calamity, more manifold, more murderous, more complete. The pestilent fever killed off those spared by the earthquake. All those whom hospitable peasants had welcomed under their roofs in the vicinity of the city fled in haste, heading for faraway villages. The number of refugees in Grande-Rivière grew considerably, two months after the event. All those unfortunate people required assistance. My uncle had had seized in all the habitations of the district the objects looted from the ruins of the Cap. He sent his report to the government, and President Boyer sent to him as well as to the commanders of the other neighboring districts of the Cap the order to auction off all of those objects and to distribute the proceeds to the refugees.

13. Commerce in Grande-Rivière

The sales took place. I remember it like it was yesterday. Those residents of the Cap who were able to save some money bought the merchandise and jewelry to establish themselves as merchants in Grande-Rivière. We bought objects of great value at low prices due to a lack of bidders. More than one fortune since made in commerce started in this way. That's how circumstances are in human affairs! Several commercial establishments were thus set up in the small towns; no one thought of going into the Cap. That city was a site of horror from which the contagion held everyone away. Foreign ships, no longer having cosignatories, went to Gonaives.

. . .

15. The Cap's Desolation

For an entire year, all commerce was dead in the Cap. How could one engage in commerce or anything else amid ruins set on an abyss, where with every step you could break a leg, break your neck, amid stinking ruins where in rummaging through the rubble you would find corpses that could immediately spread typhus or cholera again?

When one of those refugees of neighboring villages went several months later, called by the sweetest memories of his broken life, to visit the ruins of that opulent city where he had been happy, standing on the piles of stones of the Place de St. Victor neighborhood or of the Marché Clugny, he couldn't help being saddened to the point of tears before what was left of the Cap.

16. Description of the Colonial Cap

This city had been drawn and distributed by the French with the utmost care. They did their research. All the streets, lengthwise, from Carenage to Fossette, regularly cut at right angles by the crosswise roads, going from the mountain to the sea. Here and there, and in every neighborhood, beautiful public squares decorated with monumental fountains, in elegant style. The entire city in freestone or in brick, no wooden buildings. Very few one-story houses, a lot of two-story houses, all the rest made up of those gracious constructions of one story, with high ceilings, bringing to the angles those pretty wrought-iron balconies covered with laced marquise that made the houses look so much alike that strangers, the first days of their arrival, had some trouble distinguishing them from each other.

. . .

22. The Terror of the Earthquake

My family remained in Grande-Rivière for almost a year. We lived in fear of an earthquake all that time. For more than three months, the aftershocks repeated several times a day. When it was night, the terror was even stronger. We fled the houses in haste, any old way, in the most basic of outfits.

With each movement of the ground, at first, and afterward, two or three times a week, the parish priest would come out with the cross, the banner, the images of the saints, followed by the crowd, in a long procession, answering *ora pro nobis* to the somber litanies of the priest and his chants. If the tremor happened in the middle of these rogations, the crowd, in dismay, got on their knees, held their hands to the sky, smacked their foreheads to the ground, crying in a desolate voice, "Mercy! Mercy!" That cry has remained for me the final word in the lamentations of the afflicted, of ultimate recourse to divine mercy. The word still awakens in me an entire world of mournful impressions.

Never had more vivid terror been spread in a population. All of the towns near the Cap saw themselves on the verge of experiencing its situation, if not the falling of the walls, then the sudden opening of the entrails of the earth.

Translated by Nadève Ménard

Acaau and the Piquet Rebellion of 1843

Gustave d'Alaux

In 1843, Boyer was overthrown as the result of an uprising led by local elites from the southern peninsula of Haiti, who established themselves in Port-au-Prince and produced a new, more liberal, constitution. Soon afterward there was a second uprising in the South, this time among small farmers led by Jean-Jacques Acaau. Known as the Piquet Rebellion, this movement challenged the leadership that had replaced Boyer and demanded a set of far-reaching changes in governance and society. Acaau called for land redistribution, national education, and higher prices for their crops. Armed with sharp pikes (called piquet), they defeated government troops and gained control of much of the Southern Department, but their advance was halted. They eventually accepted the new presidency of Phillipe Guerrier, and Acaau and other leaders of the movement briefly took positions in the government.

A detailed account of these events was written by Maxime Reybaud, who was the French consul in Haiti at the time. First published in a French magazine and then as a book in 1856, both under the pseudonym Gustave d'Alaux, the account was translated and published in Richmond, Virginia, in 1861. Though Reybaud's account was clearly quite hostile to Acaau and his movement, it also provides us with some of the most detailed description of the philosophy and practice of this important political movement.

—Contributing Editor: Claire Payton

In the South there appeared a negro, the humanitarian negro, and eloquent speaker of the school of Jean-Francois. He was called Acaau, "General in chief of the demands of his fellow-citizens"; had gigantic spurs on his naked heals; and, followed by a troop of bandits, armed, for the most part, with *sharp stakes*, in place of guns, who overran the villages, which were depopulated by terror, at their approach, in the interest of "unfortunate innocence," and of "the *eventuality* of national education."

Acaau spoke especially "in the name of the country people, which were roused from the slumber, into which they had been plunged." "What says the cultivator?"—he would exclaim in one of his interminable harangues, in which the relentless obstinacy of the peasant was doubled in the negro, and refused to thank the Herard party for a single one of his promises—"What says the cultivator, to whom has been promised, by the revolution, a diminution of the price of his foreign provisions, and the augmentation of the value of his productions? He says, *he has been deceived!*" . . .

At the time of the black reaction of 1844, the bandit Acaau, barefooted, clothed in a sort of linen gown, and coiffed in a small straw hat, appeared at his parish church and there made a public vow not to change his costume until the orders of "divine Providence" should be executed. Then, turning himself toward the negro peasants, assembled at the sound of the *lambis* (a conch-shell), Acaau explained, that "divine Providence" commanded the poor people: in the first place, to hunt down the mulattoes; and second, to divide, among themselves, the property of the mulattoes. As indelicate as appeared this requirement to the higher class, the auditory could not call it in question, since it had the sanction of an *ex-garde champêtre*, strengthened by a lieutenant of the gendarmes; for such was Acaau's position when he announced himself, *"General-in-chief of the demands* of his fellow-citizens." A murmur of disapprobation, nevertheless, ran through the assembly, while its attention wandered from some well-clad blacks to a few ragged mulattoes, who were lost in the crowd. Acaau understood it:—"Oh! those are *negroes!*" he replied, pointing out the mulattoes, in question.

A black, thirty years of age, employed as a laborer at a *guildive* (rum factory) in the neighborhood, then issued from the ranks, and said to the crowd: "Acaau is right, for the Virgin has said: '*The rich negro, who knows how to read and write, is a mulatto; the poor mulatto, who neither knows how to read, nor write, is a negro!*'" He then earnestly added his appeals to those of Acaau. This black was called Joseph; and, from that day, he was called *Brother* Joseph. Having his head bound up, in a white handkerchief, and being clothed in a white gown that confined his pantaloons, which were also of white, he marched along, holding a wax taper in his hand, through the bands of Acaau. He edified these bands by his *neuvaines* to the Virgin, and subdued them by his well-known favor with the god Vaudoux; and whose rare opportunities of conscience, he decided in the hour of pillage, by the binding *distinction*: "*The rich negro, who knows how to read and write is a mulatto,—&c.*"

Negro communism was established, as we see, and nothing was wanting; neither that impartiality of proscription, which understood how to hold the balance even, between the aristocrats of blood, and those of fortune or of education; nor the mystical religiousness of grandsons of Babeuf; nor even their pacific and brotherly hypocrisy, as witness the bulletin of Acaau, in which, he relates his expedition against the shopkeeping reformists of Cayes. "It was far from our thoughts to give battle," said the paternal brigand; "but we only desired to present our demands, in an *attitude*, which would prove that we held to them." . . . What more natural!

As elsewhere, on the 16th of April, on the 15th of May, on the 23rd of June, it had been well understood, that, if there was a conflict, it was the reaction alone which would seek it. In fact, at Cayes, as at Paris, the incorrigible bourgeoisie, whom they only prayed to be pleased to leave the key under the door, received this request very badly. Let Acaau speak: "I have made known, by a letter, to the municipal council, the cause of our taking up arms. A verbal response, relying upon the Holy-Week, when no serious matter is allowed, was the *only honor* done us; and the same day, at eleven o'clock, in the morning, behold three columns marched upon us. . . .

"After an hour's combat, victory smiled upon us. We have had to *deplore in the enemy's ranks, the death of many of our brothers.* God willed, that we should have only, one killed, and three wounded. I could have pursued, with advantage, the vanquished army, and entered the city pell-mell with it; but the *sentiment of fraternity restrained our steps.*"

Before so much moderation, it would be certainly unjust to deny that: Acaau only desired the good of the mulattoes. But then, fraternity restrained his steps—just long enough to allow the frightened mulattoes to escape, from their stores and houses, and seek refuge on board the vessels in the roadstead. This done, he decided to direct two columns on Cayes. "They were in the city by ten o'clock, all having fled before us," added the bulletin, with modest simplicity. *"The justice of our demands are recognized, and property is respected."* What unction! what self-complacency! and above all, what scruples! The justice of his demands once recognized, Acaau had but one care: the respect of property. There was only a change of proprietors. If, by chance, I am accused of breaking these reconciliations, I will establish for them many others. Unfortunate innocence plays, for example, in the proclamation of Acaau, the same part that the working of man by man does in certain other proclamations. "The eventuality of national education," that other chord of Acaau's humanitarian lyre corresponded manifestly to gratuitous and obligatory instruction; and he demanded again, in the name of the cultivators, who are the laborers of the lower grades of society, the reduction of the price of exotic commodities, and the increase of the value of their products. The negro socialist had certainly found the clearest and most evident formula of this famous problem of the white Acaaus: reduction of labor and augmentation of wages. We have hit, ourselves, in going along, on some analogies much more conclusive; but, after these, we can no longer cry out against the counterfeit—if, indeed, the counterfeiters are not on this side of the Atlantic. Let us not forget that the publication, and the first working of Acaau's program, dates back to the spring of 1844.

Negro communism failed, like white communism, because of the extreme division of property. The first surprise having passed away, Acaau's army was reduced to a handful of vagabonds, which Guerrier easily brought to reason; which the feebleness, or complicity, of Pierrot recalled on the scene; and which Riché finished by dispersing. Hunted without cessation, and profoundly discouraged by the reception his fellow citizens gave the new science, Acaau resolved to abandon, to itself, that society which did not understand him; and, one fine day, he departed, by a pistol-shot in his mouth, for that Icaria, whence he will never return.

The Separation of Haiti and the Dominican Republic

Thomas Madiou

In 1822, as some Dominicans in Santo Domingo began organizing to gain indepen-dence from Spain, Haitian president Boyer joined the eastern part of the island, for-merly Spanish Santo Domingo, to the Haitian Republic. The Unification, which came to be known in later Dominican historiography as the Occupation, realized a goal enshrined in the constitution of the Haitian republic: unification of the whole island against outside aggression. But by the early 1840s, Dominicans joined in the wide-spread criticism of Boyer's regime. Soon after he was overthrown in 1843 and Gen-eral Charles Rivière-Hérard took power, a small group of activists in Santo Domingo overturned unified rule in the Dominican capital. Rivière-Hérard opposed separation and sent troops eastward, but his own rule was short. The document that announced Dominican separation was a manifesto penned by a large landowner, Tomas Boba-dilla. Bobadilla and its signatories were fiercely critical of Rivière-Hérard's betrayal of the 1842–43 reform efforts. On announcing the separation—avoiding the word "independence"—they expressed their disappointment with a litany of ills and the hope for a more democratic political future. The document rewrites history as well. Even as Bobadilla allowed that many Dominicans received the onset of unification in 1822 positively, he presents a narrative of economic and agricultural decline from that date, as well as major disruptions in land tenure. In the process he overlooks the near-total paralysis of nonsubsistence agriculture in the period of Spanish rule (1809–22) and the deep roots of party factionalism among Dominicans, which would resurface intensely in the months following the end of unified rule.
—Contributing Editor: Anne Eller

MANIFESTO OF THE INHABITANTS OF THE EASTERN PART OF THE ISLAND, FORMERLY SPANISH OR SANTO DOMINGO, ON THE CAUSES OF ITS SEPARATION FROM THE HAITIAN REPUBLIC, 16 JANUARY 1844

The due attention and respect for the opinion of all men and civilized na-tions, demands that when a people who have been joined with another de-sires to reassume its rights, reclaiming them and dissolving their political ties, they declare frankly and in good faith, the causes that motivate their separation, so that it is not believed that ambition or the spirit of novelty might motivate them. We believe to have demonstrated with heroic resolve that when the evils of a government are tolerable they should be endured, rather than doing justice by abolishing its means; but when a long series of injustices, violations, and injuries, continuing to the same end indicate the intention to reduce everything to despotism and the most absolute tyranny, it calls on the sacred right and duty of the people, to throw off the yoke of such a government and provide new guarantees, assuring its future stability and prosperity. . . .

This is why the inhabitants of the Eastern Part of the Island formerly known as Española or Santo Domingo, using their rights, spurred by twenty-two years of oppression and hearing from all parts clamors for the country, have made the firm resolution to separate permanently from the Haitian Republic, and to constitute a free and sovereign state.

Twenty-two years, for one of those accidents of fate, the Dominican People have suffered the most ignominious oppression. . . . Twenty-two years the inhabitants have been deprived of all of their rights, violently depriving them of what benefits they were due, considering them to be add-ons to the Republic. And before long they even lost the desire to free themselves from such humiliating slavery! . . .

No Dominican received Boyer then without showing signs of wanting to sympathize with his new co-citizens: the most common of the populations they were occupying, going out to greet him, thought they were getting from him, who had just received the title of Pacifier of the North [of Haiti], the protection he so hypocritically had promised. More slowly . . . they all became aware that they were in the hands of an oppressor, of a wild tyrant! . . .

Through a disruptive and Machiavellian system, Boyer forced the richest and most prominent families to emigrate, and with them the talent, wealth, commerce, and agriculture: he pushed away from his Cabinet and principal posts the men who could have represented the rights of their co-citizens, sought the remedy for ills and manifested the true needs of the country. Scorning all principles of public and human law, he reduced many families to indigence. . . . He destroyed agriculture, trade, shook the wealth from the churches, scornfully wore out and crushed religious ministers, taking from them their assets. . . .

Later, to give his injustices an appearance of legality, he dictated a law that the property of those who had migrated would devolve to the state. . . . Still not satisfied in his greed, with sacrilegious hand he attacked the property of the sons of the East; he authorized theft and fraud with the law of 8 July 1824; prohibiting the community of *terrenos comuneros* (commonly deeded lands), which through agreements and the utility and needs of families, had been conserved since the discovery of the island, to use them for the benefit of his state, ruining livestock raising and impoverishing a multitude of heads of family. He did not care! Destroy everything, ruin it! That was the goal of his insatiable greed!

Productive in coming up with ills to realize the work of our ruin and to reduce everything to nothing, [Boyer] put in place a monetary system that has senselessly reduced families, employees, merchants, and the general republic by degrees to the greatest misery. With such aims the Haitian government propagated its corruptive principles. . . .

This was the sad portrait of this part, when on 27 January of last year, from Les Cayes in the south of the island a cry for reform rose up: it inflamed the inhabitants; they adhered to the principles of the 1 September 1842 manifesto, and the Eastern Part entertained the idea of a happier future, but in vain! So much that good will got them! Commander Rivière proclaimed himself head of operations, interpreter of the will of the sovereign people: he dictated laws to his whims: he established a government with no legal basis, without taking into account any of the inhabitants of this part [of the island], who had proclaimed themselves in favor of his revolution; he traveled about the Island, and in the Santiago province, without legal base, a painful reminder of the sad epochs of *Toussaint* and *Dessalines*, bringing with him a monstrous administration that demoralized everyone; sold jobs, ripped off churches; destroyed the elections that the towns had set to give themselves representatives who would defend their rights; and this as ever to leave this part in misery with the same fate, and provide himself with candidates who would elevate him to the presidency even without special mandate of his principal supporters; so it was, by threatening the constituent assembly and giving strange messages to the army in his command, he became president of the Republic. . . .

On the pretext that this part contemplated a territorial separation, via Colombia, the prison cells of Port-au-Prince were filled with the most ardent Dominicans, in whose hearts love for the country ruled, with no other aspirations but those of bettering its fate . . .

Our condition has not improved at all: the same affronts, the same treatment as by the former administration, the same or higher taxes, the same baseless monetary system that works to the ruin of its inhabitants and a small-minded constitution that will never make the country happy, has sealed the ignominy, depriving us against natural right even the last thing that remained for us as Spaniards: of native tongue!, and cozying up on one hand to our august religion, so that it disappears among us. . . . [These violations] . . . decide the matter in favor of our country, as they did in favor of the Low Countries against Philip II in 1581. Under the authority of these principles, who would dare condemn the resolution of the people of Les Cayes, when it rose up against Boyer and declared him traitor to the country?

And who would dare critique ours, declaring the Eastern Part of the island separated from the Haitian Republic? . . .

If the Eastern Part was considered as voluntarily incorporated to the Haitian Republic, it ought to enjoy the same benefits as those whom it has joined. . . .

When the sons of the West revised the constitution in 1816, this part did not belong to Haiti, nor to France, the Spanish flag waved in its forts. . . . What is very clear is that, if this Eastern Part belongs to a dominion other than that of its own sons, it would be to France, or to Spain, not that of Haiti. . . . Considering . . . that a people has a right when it has voluntarily been dependent on another, for protection, to be free of its obligations in the moment that the other fails, even if for reasons of impossibility. . . . Considering, lastly, that for differences in customs and the rivalry that exists between one side and the other, there will never be perfect union nor harmony. . . . It is resolved to separate permanently . . . to protect and guarantee a democratic system; the liberty of citizens abolishing slavery forever; the equality of civil and political rights without regard to origin or place of birth; properties will be inviolable and sacred; the Apostolic and Roman Catholic religion will be protected in all its splendor as the state religion, but none will be persecuted nor punished for his religious opinions; freedom of the press will be protected; responsibility of public functionaries assured; there will be no seizure of goods for crimes or infractions; public education will be promoted and protected at the cost of the state; special privileges will be pared to the minimum possible; there will be a total forgetting of votes and political stands taken up to this date, as long as individuals subscribe in good faith to the new system. Military rank and office will be preserved under rules to be established. Agriculture, science, trade, sciences, and the arts will likewise be promoted and protected, for people who have come to live here just as those born in our soil. Lastly, as quickly as possible, a currency will be emitted that has a true and real backing, without the public losing what money it has with the Haitian seal. . . .

DOMINICANS! (This name includes all the sons of the Eastern Part and those who wish to follow our destiny). Our national interest calls us to unity! Through a firm resolution we show ourselves to be worthy defenders of liberty: we sacrifice hate and personalities on the altar of the country: that the sentiment of public interest be the motivation that brings us to the cause of liberty and of *Separation*; with it, we do not diminish the happiness of the Western Republic, we realize ours.

Our cause is holy; we will not lack resources . . . because if it were necessary to do so, we would in that case use those that we could obtain from abroad. . . .

Unite, Dominicans! Now is the opportune moment from Neiba to Samaná, from Azua to Monte Cristi, opinions are uniform and there is no Dominican who does not proclaim: SEPARATION, GOD, COUNTRY AND LIBERTY.

Santo Domingo,
16 January 1844 and Year 1 of the Country.

The second document details the withdrawal of Haitian families, officers, and functionaries from the eastern part of the island. As Thomas Madiou and others observed contemporaneously, the event was exceedingly calm. Rivière-Hérard had already taken most of the armory's weapons with him as he retreated. A Dominican regiment of formerly enslaved men and others known as the African Battalion initially opposed the handoff, and there were several small battles over the next months, but life largely continued as normal for the great bulk of the east's rural populace. In the larger work in which he included these documents, Madiou wrote favorably of the events of separation.

SURRENDER OF THE SANTO DOMINGO GARRISON

Today, 28 February 1844, year 41 of Independence and year 2 of Regeneration.

Under the mediation of the French Consul, and in the presence of members of the Commission designated by the governing Junta and those named by General Desgrottes, commander of the plaza of Santo Domingo and provisional commander of the arrondissement, undersigned, have arrived at the following capitulation:

Article I—Guarantee of property, particularly legally acquired.

Art. II—Respect to families and protection and support.

Art. III—Honorable departure of public functionaries.

Art. IV—Frankness and loyalty in both parties' conduct.

Art. V—Problem-free departure for all citizens.

Art. VI—Military officials or other citizens who want to leave can only do so ten days after the date of this surrender. Safe-conduct passes will be delivered by the Junta to those who prefer to travel by land rather than by sea; other citizens will have an entire month to leave the arrondissement, that month beginning 10 March.

Art. VII—The arms of the troops garrisoned in Santo Domingo will be turned over to the hands of the French Consul who will return them to soldiers belonging to Haitian regiments as soon as they return to their home; officers will keep their arms and will not be required to turn them over.

Art. VIII—The Fort and the Arsenal will be immediately evacuated by Haitian troops after the signature of this surrender.

Art. IX—The treasury and the archives likewise will be turned over to the hands of the governing Junta by the Administration, who will turn over accounts to the Commission designated by said Junta to review them, giving discharge and pay to the troops and functionaries from arrears to this date, this liquidating the debts contracted by the Haitian administration for services rendered.

Art. X—Given the advanced hour, it is agreed that the undersigned commissaries will not gather until tomorrow, 29 February, at precisely 8 A.M.

Two copies made on the below day,
month, and year.

Signed: DOUCET, PONTHIEUX,
DEO HERARD, PAUL JN-JACQUES, ROY,
BERNIER, CAMINERO, MD AYBAR,
CABRAL, FRANCISCON XAVIER,
DUCASTE aîné, PEDRO MENA.

Approved by the general, plaza commander
and chief of overseeing the Arrondissement.

Signed: DESGROTTES

Translated by Anne Eller

President Geffrard Protests the Spanish Annexation of the Dominican Republic

Fabre Geffrard

In 1859, Fabre Geffrard became president of Haiti, reestablishing republican rule on the island. During his time in office, he was able to overcome the final vestiges of the political isolation put in place at the time of Haitian independence by securing recognition from the two final holdouts: the Vatican and the United States. The U.S. Congress at last recognized Haitian independence after the outbreak of the civil war in 1861. Geffrard also had to negotiate a new relationship with the Dominican Republic. In 1861, strongman president Pedro Santana had ceded the territory—which had been independent since 1844—back to Spain. From Port-au-Prince, President Geffrard's response was immediate. He saw reoccupation by a slave power on the island as a threat not only to political autonomy on the island but also to the very autonomy of its citizens.

In the first document below, Geffrard addresses the Dominican people directly, urging a united front against outside incursion. In the second document, he calls on Haitian citizens to take up arms. Opposition to Spanish reoccupation brought new connections across the island. While no mobilization from Haiti ever materialized— Spanish warships quickly forced Geffrard into silence—Dominican rebels looked westward. Prominent exiles followed circuits that led them to Port-au-Prince, Cap Haïtien, and neighboring islands; a secret market of foodstuffs grew to feed rebels in the Cibao Valley. Though President Santana had invoked a fear of Haiti to justify his forfeiture of independence, the fighting demonstrated how cynical his claims had been. Rebels called for Haitian support, and one fighter in Baní was caught with a copy of one of Geffrard's proclamations in his pocket. Such support from Haiti played an important role in the ultimate victory of the struggle for independence, which culminated in the defeat of the Spanish by insurgents in 1865. And even as the fighting raged, a new potential foundation for unity between the two states grew, the possibility of two federated republics. In 1865, as the fighting ended, one newspaper in Puerto Plata, La Regeneración, even called for dual citizenship on the island. Political discord and disunity interrupted such idealistic visions in the east and west, but they embodied the creative responses of independent citizens grappling with a thoroughly colonial Caribbean.

—Contributing Editor: Anne Eller

General Santana, in realizing the coup that he has premeditated for a long time, has had the Spanish flag raised over the East of Haiti. Several acts emanating from that general have declared this fact, and a note, with the date of 6 April of this year, from the Consul of Her Catholic Majesty in Haiti, has notified the Haitian Government.

Certainly, the Government of Haiti could not have expected such an outcome. The friendly relations that the Madrid court had contracted with the government in recent years, accrediting it consuls, did not prepare it for this; yes, on the initiative of the mediating powers, *a treaty of five years* was rushed to be granted, it was not, no doubt, so that this development might be prepared in the shadow of that treaty and of the loyal mediation of France and England.

With what right does Spain today take possession of the East? Had this province not entirely ceased to be its colony, many years ago? Did it not in fact accept nearly a quarter of a century ago, voluntary incorporation of the Eastern Part to the Haitian Republic? Lastly, did Spain not recognize the independence of the Dominican Republic, and deal with her state to state?

Spain does not have today, then, any right over the Eastern Part of Haiti; it does not have any more right over this territory, than France or England could have; and the taking possession of the East by Spain is as enormous of an event as if it were done by France or by England. If it were necessary to admit that Spain still had rights over the Dominican Republic, then it would also be necessary to admit that she has them over Mexico, over Colombia, over Peru, over all of the independent Republics of América that are of Spanish origin.

Plus, with what right, on their end, do Santana and his faction turn over the Dominican territory to Spain? Such is the will of the people! they say. False claim! The population, trembling under the regime of terror Santana organized, cannot manifest any free vote. A good number of honorable, enlightened citizens, patriots loyal to the Dominican Republic, thrown out of their *patria* by General Santana, protest with all of their energy against the alienation of their country, which is cowardly treason!

No one can doubt that Haiti has a great interest that no foreign power establish itself in the East. From the moment that two peoples inhabit the same island, their destinies, relative to foreign initiatives, are necessarily shared. The political existence of one finds itself intimately tied with that of the other, and they are obliged to guarantee mutual security to each. Suppose it was possible that Scotland suddenly changed sovereigns suddenly, whether under Russian domination, or French: would it not be said that England's existence was not immediately threatened?

Such are the essential bonds that unite the two parts east and west of Haiti. Such are the powerful motives for which in all of our constitutions, since our political formation, we have constantly declared that *the entire island of Haiti will not comprise more than one State*; and it was not ambition for conquest that dictated that declaration; it was only a deep conviction for our own security; as the founders of our young society declared, at the same time, that Haiti forbade any enterprise that might disrupt the interior rule of neighboring islands.

The Haitian Government, better understanding the conditions of independence and security of nations, has wanted, then, to form with the Dominican people *a single and homogeneous State*. In the space of twenty-two years, the free and spontaneous will of the population of the East realized this grand vision. The two peoples have mixed, have lived the same political and social life, have formed but one and the same State; and the administration of this half of the shared country cost, in twenty-two years, great pecuniary sacrifices of the Haitian Government.

If the people of the East separated in 1844, they never had any other objective than to govern themselves. For purported motives of freedom, they wanted to substitute one unitary government with two separate governments, without nevertheless being ignorant of the intimate ties and community of interests of the two populations.

The separation of the East has never been, fundamentally, anything but a dispute over the form of government. Never would those populations, so jealous of their freedom, have gone so far as to turn themselves over to foreign domination; just as the Haitian Government will never consent but to their autonomy, the object of their most ardent will, to better ensure the common interests and the shared independence of the two peoples.

The Haitian Government protests, then, solemnly and in the face of Europe and América, against all occupation by Spain of the Dominican territory: it declares that Santana's faction does not have any right to alienate that territory, under any title whatsoever: *that it will never recognize such a cession: that it expresses all possible reservations, just as it reserves the use of all means which, per the circumstances, could be appropriate to assure and secure its most precious interest.*

Given in the Palais National of Port-au-Prince
on 6 April 1861, year 58 of independence.
GEFFRARD *[Fabre Geffrard,*
President of Haiti]

To the People and to the Army

Haitians

The Spanish Government, in favor of infamous intrigue and condemned plotting, tricking and seducing General Santana, who rules the fate of our brothers of the East of the island, has just raised its flag on the walls of Santo Domingo. You know that flag authorizes and protects the enslavement of the sons of Africa. In Cuba and Puerto Rico millions of our brothers and co-citizens groan, desperate, under the tyranny of a cruel master, who consider them to be more vile and miserable than the beasts of the fields and whom they mistreat without pity under the shade of that degraded flag, which in waving over Santo Domingo presages for us desperation and the end of our liberties.

Haitians! Will you consent to losing your freedom and to being reduced to slavery? Today, in the full nineteenth century, when Italy, Hungary, and Poland, peoples oppressed by an even less terrible regime than the one Spain imposes on our brothers in her colonies, fight to free themselves and win independence, can you consent that the authority of a strange Government put down roots in our soil, determined to conspire against our liberty and to destroy it by violence or guile? No, you would never suffer such a disgrace.

The country is in danger, our nationality threatened, our liberty compromised. To arms, Haitians! Let us run to arms using them to push back the invading hordes. May your motto be that immortal phrase that served to guide the founders of our Republic: *liberty or death*. Let us push back against force with force. We will not vacillate in the face of any sacrifice, nor retreat from any obstacle. All means are good ones when it comes to defending liberty. Even if we see our pueblos reduced to piles of rubble and the whole country converted into an immense sepulcher, we will fight without truce or quarter. God will make the Haitians win! After having drawn from us our last breath, Spain would not gain anything, because neither Europe nor América would ever consent to her planting her hated flag in the soil of our beloved country. To battle! Spain's domination in América must end. We will expel her from Santo Domingo and that defeat will be the precursor to her definitive expulsion from the Gulf of Mexico. Spain hopes to destroy our nationhood and does not realize that trying to do so will be her own tomb. The future will justify this prediction.

To arms, Haitians! We will march to combat and not drop them from our hands until the Spanish authority disappears from the territory of

Haiti. If luck is to be against us, which is implausible, we will make it so that the Spanish banner waves only over our ashes and our cadavers.

History and posterity will applaud our heroism. The educated nations will avenge our defeat and our ruin.

Given in the Palais National of Port-au-Prince
on 18 April 1861.
FABRE GEFFRARD

Translated by Anne Eller

Stella, the First Haitian Novel

Émeric Bergeaud

Émeric Bergeaud (1818–58) was a Haitian intellectual, politician, and author of the country's first novel, Stella, *which was published in Paris one year after his death. Along with Pierre Faubert's historical drama,* Ogé, ou Le préjugé de couleur *(1856),* Stella *is one of the first fictional portrayals of Haiti's revolution and independence written by a Haitian. The novel follows the fictional founders of Haiti, Romulus and Remus, sons of an enslaved woman named Marie the African, and their protector, Stella, who is the divine embodiment of Liberty. This excerpt narrates the moment of Haiti's birth, 1 January 1804.*

Bergeaud wrote Stella *in the late 1840s and 1850s, at a time when Haiti had many international detractors as well as serious internal fissures, and his work is allegorical and politically pointed: Stella's story unites both light- and dark-skinned Haitians in the founding and future of their nation. This excerpt describes the end of the revolution, at which time Stella reveals her identity to an audience of new Haitians gathered on the Place d'Armes.*

—Contributing Editors: Lesley S. Curtis and Christen Mucher

The moment had come for the virgin of the mountain to leave Marie's sons, the sons to whom she had given everything—glory, power, and freedom—and who had only to await that which they would produce themselves. We say "leave" because it is the most appropriate word to explain their simple parting of ways. Yet the generous daughter of heaven had promised never to abandon Romulus, Remus, or the island; she was merely returning to that eternal dwelling place on high from which invisible powers watch over the people below.

Stella took the approaching national solemnity as an occasion for revealing her true identity to the brothers, a mystery that they had desired to solve since her arrival on the mountain. Thanks to her great revelation, the ceremony took on new significance.

It was not yet night; the sun had just disappeared behind the high mountains lining the horizon. A sustained rumbling—the thunder of artillery fire—could be heard in the distance. The city was announcing the next day's celebration. Stella had only that night to spend on the mountain, to descend into her grotto, to walk along the banks of the river, and to visit for one last time all of the places that she had lived and blessed. She had the palm tree uprooted and the camp taken down to its ramparts: for there were no more enemies.

Awakening before daylight the next morning, Stella took the path to the city. The morning star was rising: it was the dawning of a new year. 1804 presented itself even before the sun. The month of January was born in the perfume of darkness. There are places where the year is first old so that it may next become young and finally mature into adulthood. Yet here the year started in youth so as to mature but never to age.

The path that Stella followed was lined with flowering logwoods; the brooks that she crossed flowed with crystal waters; the breeze that played in her hair was cool and sweet smelling; the sky overhead was a clear blue; the star that guided her was as bright as the sun. The first day of January began even more beautifully than the loveliest day of spring.

The daughter of heaven increased her pace toward the city and arrived just as the cannon saluted Apollo, ascending to the throne of infinity and lending the entirety of his splendor to the festivities. The two brothers waited for their protectress at the door. They bowed to her with new feelings of respect and love, and with great pageantry they accompanied her to the Place d'Armes. The army and the people were already there. The soldiers admirably and orderly lined the entire rectangular expanse of the square. The people gathered around the nation's altar, the wooden form of which—elevated in the center of the square—was decorated with flags, palm branches, and military articles. Shading the altar was the palm tree from the mountain, ornamental and symbolic at the same time. Stella had ordered that it be transported from her grotto and planted with care so that it would lose none of its beauty or vitality.

The procession stopped. Stella ascended slowly and majestically, like the Priestess of Victory. She positioned herself under the palm with Romulus and Remus at her side. A profound silence descended upon the square. The soldiers shouldered their weapons and the crowd waited attentively.

Remus read a Proclamation in which the violence and crimes of the former oppressors were described in lines of fire. The horrors of slavery and of masters burst forth from this document: in it, hate growled, anger twitched, and menace rumbled. At that moment, they all pledged never to disturb the peace of any neighboring island, but at the same time, they also made the solemn promise to live free or die. The people were moved to the last fiber of their being.

The Declaration of Independence, no less energetic despite its succinctness, was read by Romulus. This pact indissolubly tied together those generals who had taken part in the victories of the war so as to preserve their collaborative work indefinitely. The Declaration proclaimed to posterity and the universe that they would forever renounce France and would rather die than live again under French law. In the presence of Stella and in unison with the people, Romulus and Remus swore this oath. Fanfare, drumrolls, and artillery fire echoed the promise spoken by ten thousand mouths.

The procession, which had swelled in number, made its way from the Place d'Armes to the church. There, bells chimed, incense burned, and gratitude rose in hymns of praise. The priest blessed the laurels that were placed in the sanctuary, at the foot of God. During the Te Deum, the cannon did not cease its firing, the drum did not stop its sounding, and the trumpet did not end its blowing. Victory received the baptism of religion: it was now Christian, which is to say, everlasting.

They left the church strengthened by a new conviction drawn from the source of all strength. Prayer, that celestial vapor which rises and then falls upon the heart as beneficent dew, had replenished their souls.

Stella walked ahead, again leading the way toward the altar. This time, she climbed it alone. In a loud voice that could be heard on the far side of the square, she uttered these memorable words: "Citizens of a country henceforth independent and free: fourteen years ago, the common Father of Man and Sovereign Protector of Societies sent me to this colony to ensure the triumph of His justice. God forbids violence, condemns oppression, and denounces inequality. All tyranny is to Him an outrage. He did not create servitude; man imposed that yoke upon man. It is an attack upon His power. All of Creation is free. His laws, which are as gentle as they are wise, regulate a world that breathes nothing but happiness. Look at this land, so richly blessed, so poetically undulating, so wondrously decorated. It is always profuse in its greenery, always abundant in its fruits, and always covered in flowers! Here nothing suffers, nothing languishes, and nothing is endangered. The soil always produces without cultivation. If slavery is a monstrosity, it is seen nowhere more clearly than upon this island, where its hideousness is contrasted with the most ravishing beauties of Creation. Here, its barbarous rigors were in direct contradiction to God, who reveals Himself through such ineffable beauty.

"Make it your duty to hate oppression so as never to suffer under oppressors in the future, and never to become oppressors yourselves. You have suffered these long years under the soul-destroying weight of your chains; in your desperation, you have committed blasphemy more than once and denied that divine justice was waiting to shine. You did not understand that, while Heaven seemed deaf to your complaints, a century for man is only a minute for God. The Great Redeemer is more interested in compensating than in punishing. Merciful because He is strong, patient because He is eternal, the Supreme Arbiter often lets crime continue and He withholds punishment like a blade resting in its sheath. Due to this, we believe that Injustice has dethroned Justice, and that evil reigns over earth. The pious man is saddened and desolate; he hangs his head in silence while the wicked man becomes emboldened, increasing in pride as he looks defiantly toward the sky. Yet all of a sudden, the wicked man disappears, his good fortune gone with him. He whom the thunderbolt obeys does not strike only to punish: why would He listen to anger alone? He does not give in to the terrible demand for destruction; a more paternal reason guides His way. God avenges a portion of humanity. For this reason, His justice only bursts forth at a moment decided in advance, at an hour that is always propitious but sometimes far off. One must know how to wait with confidence. Woe beset the weak soul who doubts! . . .

"Nonetheless, your voice—the voice of your suffering—was heard. I was called to help you and that is what I did. I appeared to you in the midst of flames; you thought that you saw a fellow creature in peril, and you generously endangered yourselves for me. Then you had the idea to sacrifice me to your resentment; you mistook me for another. However, your hearts slowly brought you enlightenment: nothing is more intelligent than the heart. You loved me without knowing me and without fear of remorse. This love was a gift that was sincere and freely given, the kindest gift that you could offer.

"I returned this love to you: I supported, directed, and protected you. I watched over you from near and far; I guarded your arms and ammunition; I fought for you; I remained your friend, despite your errors and your faults. When Remus, at the time of your disagreement—of which I speak only to condemn and banish it from memory—took on the task of sacrificing himself, the supernatural being who advised him said that one day it would be reckoned. The Spirit of the Nation kept his word, and I can say that I have kept mine as well. Everything that exists at this moment is the work of my hands: I, Stella, am Liberty, Star of Nations! Each time that you raise your eyes to the heavens, you will see me. Like the unwavering celestial body guiding the sailor across vast expanses of the Ocean, I will guide you through the limitless fields of the future. Keep faith in me; you will be happy!"

The people, including the two brothers, knelt down, deeply moved by Stella's message. The revered virgin gave them her softest smile and, using her angel's wings, took flight toward the heavens. Everyone followed her path with tearful eyes until the moment she disappeared into space, leaving behind a long furrow of gold.

Haiti and Its Visitors and "Le vieux piquet"

Louis Joseph Janvier

Born in Port-au-Prince in 1855, Louis Joseph Janvier was part of a generation of elite young Haitians who spent a significant amount of time living abroad, where they studied, worked in diplomatic roles, and engaged broadly with contemporary intellectual debates. Having begun studies in medicine while in Haiti, Janvier traveled to France in 1877, where in 1881 he completed his doctorate in medicine in Paris. Janvier also received degrees in law and political science in Lille. In his book Haiti et ses visiteurs, Janvier described his time in France as the formative experience that led him to find his voice and to express it publicly, particularly on behalf of Haiti. A notable part of that process came from the intellectual exchanges he had in 1882 with fellow members of the Anthropology Society in Paris. Janvier's time abroad afforded him the opportunity to think critically about a broad range of topics. Perhaps most prominent among these was the condition of "the black race," both in Haiti specifically and more broadly.

Janvier was a prolific writer. He began publishing in 1881, using medical anthropology to challenge racist arguments about the conditions of blacks in the world. In 1883, he expounded on those ideas in Haiti and Its Visitors, which challenged Haiti's detractors. He countered Haiti's critics by discussing the revolutionary struggle as well as by emphasizing the challenges that Haitians faced in constructing an independent state in the face of international hostility. But Janvier did not reserve his critiques only for foreigners. He also denounced the acts of Haitian politicians, intellectuals, and members of the elite, as well as taking national authors to task for their representations of Haiti. Janvier criticized the authors of Haitian national literature and their representations of Haiti. He lamented the continuities between the racial ideology and practices of the colonial period and those of some of his contemporaries, and he criticized the centrality of the military in Haitian political life.

After his studies, Janvier worked in diplomatic posts and represented Haiti in London from 1889 to 1904. There he married a British woman in 1902. She died while birthing their daughter, the mother of the Haitian poet Ludovic Janvier. In 1905, after a twenty-eight-year absence, Janvier returned to Haiti. He sought political office but his bid failed, and he returned to Paris, where he died in 1911.

The first excerpts below are from The Republic of Haiti and Its Visitors. The book, totaling 636 pages, is a response to a series of columns by the black Martinican *journalist Victor Cochinat, who despite having spent just a few weeks in Haiti offered a withering criticism of the country's politics, culture, and society. They showcase Janvier's sharp and passionate wit, his critical perspective on foreign visions of Haiti, and his vindication of Haiti's political culture.*

For eighty years Haiti has been judged. Only rarely, and for short intervals, has the accused been able to respond. Its voice has almost never been heard.

It is asking for the right to speak.

This is a timely, opportune, and necessary book.

Only the demands of the polemic have prevented me from giving it a didactic, doctrinaire, and dogmatic form.

It nevertheless summarizes and examines the past, present, and future of the Haitian nation.

Between the 8th of September and the 31st of December 1881 there appeared, in a small daily newspaper in Paris, a series of columns that I found insulting and slanderous for my country.

I was shocked to see that they were signed by a man who, until then, had—rightly or wrongly—always been considered a friend to the Haitians.

I thought it was my urgent duty to protest the claims made in these columns.

That is how the following pages were born.

I know some will, later on, criticize me for the thoughts that have dictated them to me.

But my conscience, with which I have never compromised—and never will—is the only rule I obey.

Too bad for those who decide that I shouldn't have obeyed it in this circumstance.

No one can be judged except by their equals.

I worry only of the judgment of those who truly and fully love their country and all humanity, no matter what their nationality. They are the only ones with heart.

I dare flatter myself that they will always agree with me.

That will be enough for me.

Louis-Joseph Janvier
Paris, 4, rue de l'Ecole-de-Médecine
15 October 1882

. . .

A nation, like any moral person, does not have the right to allow themselves to be defamed. If it allows this and stays silent, it diminishes to that extent the sum of the good reputation and moral capital that it guards; it lessens the inheritance of glory that it received from the ancestors and which it is responsible for transmitting if not expanding, but at least not shrunken, to a renewed nation, that is to future generations.

Louis Joseph Janvier (1855–1911), Haitian nationalist, writer, and diplomat, Haitian Minister Resident in London ca. 1894–1903. Photo courtesy of CIDHICA.

. . .

A man who uses his intelligence in order to render a collection of men contemptible is himself essentially contemptible; he merits no respect, no compassion.

It is as dangerous for a people as for a man to be known through approximations, through rumors, through legends, through gossip and anecdotes. One is always somewhat disfigured; sometimes one is even killed in the spirit of generations and those of future races.

. . .

Haitians have already reached that level of intellectual culture that, following Bagehot, I call "the age of discussion."

And now I thank noble France, that breast of the world, which has fed my brain for almost six years now, and therefore enables me today to hold the pen in defense of my country, of my race—attacked, insulted, slandered by men from the Middle Ages lost in the middle of the nineteenth century, by a few individuals who refuse to understand this truth: that there will be no retreat by the Sun or the sublime French Revolution, or by Haiti, the daughter of one and godchild of the other, or by the awakening black race, finally escaping the material and intellectual prison in which slavery had kept it for so many years, forcing it to crouch in depressive abjection, moral pain, physical torture, and nameless villainy for such long and dark days.

. . .

It is a convention to claim that Haitians have always been, are, and will always be nothing but imitators. . . .

They always forget this marvelous, blinding, unparalleled invention, which surprised the world and surprises it still: the Republic of Haiti.

On 1 January 1804, when—surrounded by the triple azure ocean of the firmament, the ocean, and the mountains that surrounded Gonaïves—Dessalines and Boisrond-Tonnerre personified the Haitian nation and created it; while the cannons shouted with joy; while the flags waved and fluttered in the wind of the cheers of a people being born, smiling at the kisses of our mothers; as the eyes of our grandfathers shone, expansive, transported, ecstatic, and their transfigured and radiant foreheads burst, resplendent, under the rays of the newborn sun; on that day we were certainly not vulgar imitators. We were sublime inventors.

There are many other great and beautiful things that we did on our own, before anyone, but about which there is no point in dwelling and insisting on here, since my intention here is on the contrary to demonstrate that it is natural for men to imitate.

What, after all, is civilization? A pastiche, or a copy. Everywhere. All civilization consists in the exchange of imitations that are more or less appropriate, intelligent or opportune.

Railroads were invented in England (by Watt); it was an American, Fulton, who was the first to establish regular service by steamboat between New York and Albany. These two discoveries are the greatest of the century. Haven't other countries followed the model of the United States and England, once railroads were seen outside of the United Kingdom, and steamboats outside the Starred Federation? The telegraph was born in France (Chappe). Do we not see the telegraph now part of the economic tools of the great nations of Europe and the Americas, and telegraph lines creating great profits for countries other than France? . . . Electrical lighting through the Edison lamp is an invention that was realized barely two years ago in the New World, and already the Old World is using it to fulfill its needs. . . .

Some superficial people reproach blacks for having never invented anything, never discovered anything new in politics, industry, science, literature, or art. First, this is false. In the United States many blacks are inventors. They have invented in the realm of sentiment as well as industry.

. . .

If Haitians are said to have the genius of imitation because they have imitated England and France, then we must also conclude that France has the genius of imitation since it followed the example of the United States Republic whose Parliament is made up of a Chamber and a Senate, before France was born into true parliamentary life. It also copied England when it created a Chamber of Peers alongside the Lower Chamber.

In this sense, too, all countries that introduced a parliamentary system after Haiti, such as Belgium, Greece, Romania, and Italy, also imitated the Haitian Republic, along with all the states in South and Central America that gained their independence after us.

The 1816 Constitution, promulgated in Pétion's Republic, created a system with two Chambers. Before this period, there had only been one legislative assembly, the Senate, if we set aside the Constituent Assembly of 1807, and the Commission that produced Toussaint-Louverture's Constitution, and the Council of State under Christophe which, in the end, were not true assemblies that deliberated fully or with all the majesty of their rights as elected representatives of the nation.

When they promulgated the 1816 Constitution, Haitians were absolutely not modeling themselves on the French, who had just transformed their Senate into a Chamber of Peers and declared the positions hereditary or for life even as the Lower Chamber continued to be one of the cogs in their political organization.

Nor did the Haitians copy the English. They didn't borrow their rotten boroughs, where sometimes five electors were enough to constitute an electoral college and name a deputy, or their Chamber of Lords most of whom had hereditary seats.

The children of 1804 didn't imitate the United States, either, since their Senate is really an Assembly of ambassadors who are delegates of the States rather than a true higher Chamber with purely legislative attributes. The recruitment of Haitian Senators was not done in the same way as the recruitment of the members of the United States Senate, with two named from each State. Furthermore, there is a Supreme Court in the United States, established by the Constitution, which serves as the Highest Court of Appeals for the political actions of the House and Senate, something the 1816 Constitution did not establish in Haiti, instead creating a *Grand Juge*.

And even if Haitians had systematically borrowed their political institutions from France and England, what would be wrong with that? These European countries are much older than the Black Republic, and it would be irrational for us to reject the institutions they have judged to be good on the pretext that to do so would be a form of imitation.

Understand, Mr. Cochinat, that you are above all an animal of imitation and that you could do nothing without imitating someone else. So, when you criticize with so little competence the customs and habits of Haitians, you do so in the wake of Meignan, Lasselve, and others of the same ilk and you copy them in a servile manner, when you don't demonstrate even more ignorance than they do. When you sneeze, when you blow your nose, when you put on your boots, when you tie your tie, you again model yourself on someone. And if you eat with your hands you are imitating one of the ancestors of humanity, one of our common forefathers from the old land of Cham, or one of the anthropoids or troglodytes that we all descent from, white and black, according to Darwinian or Haeckelienne doctrine. . . .

. . .

The Haitian parliament rests on a very narrow electoral base! That is news to us! Charming! Mr. Cochinat doesn't even know how to lie well. Universal suffrage fully exists in our country and every Haitian citizen who reaches the age of twenty is an elector with full rights. . . .

A very narrow electoral base! My word, he is an idiot! As he was penning his wild imaginings he assumed there would be no Haitian audacious and knowledgeable enough about his country and other countries to stuff all his lies back in his throat.

The electoral base is much larger in Haiti than in Belgium, where there is a tax for Senatorial elections; it is larger than in France, where the electoral college for the Senate is made up of very few electors; it is larger than in Italy, where the elector has to pay a relatively high tax; larger than in England, where many citizens are not electors; larger than in Spain too.

And if, in Haiti, too many citizens neglect to put their ballot in the urn on Election Day, it is because not all understand how grand this act is, and not all understand that on that they truly constitute the *Sovereign* in the exercise and delegation of its functions. It took decades and repeated elections to make it so these ideas entered nine-tenths of the minds on this side of the Atlantic Ocean.

Janvier also expressed his interest in documenting and analyzing the political culture of Haiti through his literary work. "Le vieux piquet" is a short story published in 1884 in which Janvier describes how, from generation to generation, communities in the South of Haiti fought to gain access to land. The heroes of the tale are the "Piquets," peasants who at different times rose up against central authority demanding access to land and were repeatedly defeated by the military, seeing their leaders either killed or co-opted. The story begins in slavery and culminates in what Janvier presents as the ultimate victory of the peasants under the presidency of Salomon, who in 1883 issued a law ordering the distribution of government-owned land. The work clearly is meant to celebrate Salomon's regime. But it also powerfully presents a sense of how long-term political genealogies were constructed and foregrounded as part of ongoing political conflicts in Haiti.

We know the history of Haiti too little, or badly.

For too long people have imagined and repeated that the demands of the Piquets were unjust, illegitimate, unhealthy, or antisocial.

The opposite is true.

I will demonstrate it. I will prove it.

Until now those who have written the history of the Piquets were their enemies or their assassins.

Historical lies cannot last forever.

. . .

As far as the eye can see the land, it bathes in tides of red light.

The sun, like a ship burning and sinking, dives slowly and majestically into the tides of the Gulf of Mexico. The sky, already blue, seems to get bluer as the last of the daylight dies behind the nearly virgin forests of Grand-Doco.

In the depths of the valley, in the shadow of the trees—Campeche, Tamarind, Palm, Orange, Génipayer, Acoma—Jean-Louis Bon Dos's house sits on the banks of a limpid stream. It is silent at first, but then gradually fills with activity and noise.

One by one, the robust laborers who live in this big house and the small ones that surround it come back from the fields.

Ensconced in a rustic chair carried by his grandchildren, Jean-Louis Bon Dos has himself set down next to the cottage where he was born almost seventy-five years earlier.

Worn down by age and work and by much suffering, Jean-Louis Bon Dos seems very old. His wooly hair has turned almost silky because it is all white, his face is long, bony, dry, and wrinkled, but with a large and high forehead, prominent cheekbones, and a square chin.

His muscled neck, topping a large and roughly hewn chest, sticks out of his shirt of unbleached cloth and his open white cotton vest, while his gnarled and calloused hands play with the knob of an ironwood cane. His pupils dilate with delight as they receive the caresses of the blond rays of light from the Astral King, filtering like drops of water between the branches. The spectacle offered by nature at that moment is so beautiful, so grandiose, so striking that the pupils of the old man fill with tears. Seeing him cry, the wives of his sons, and his grandchildren, cry silently next to him.

"Children," says the Patriarch after having rubbed his eyes with the back of his hand, "I am going to die. But I die happy. In 1846, I was thirty-seven years old. My father was even older. One night, they brought him here bathed in blood. He had been wounded in combat saving the life of one of his companions."

"And why were they fighting, Grandfather?" interrupted Paul-François, his favorite grandchild, a little twelve-year-old boy, with his hands leaning on the chair.

"Listen, my little one, and remember this well, all of you.

" . . . My father had suffered a great deal in the old regime. In that time they treated us worse than animals. We were only men in name. They forced us to work under the whip each day, from four in the morning until six at night. We were the only ones who weren't allowed to profit from the riches we produced. Fathers had no right to their children; newborns were taken from mothers; males were chosen for girls, without consulting them, so that they could make *négrillons* for the plantations. . . . It was a terrible time, execrable, more barbarous than any other!

"When the creole blacks, exasperated by so many cruelties, tortures, and humiliations, had broken their chains and become masters of the country, they put their hope in Dessalines who, having led them to independence, had promised them land.

"But the Liberator was assassinated on the orders of Pétion, Gérin and their partisans who wanted to keep the best plantations of the former masters for themselves, and distributed only a few meager parcels of land to those naive enough to kneel before them.

"Goman, who lived with us in these mountains, was extremely sad when he learned about the death of Dessalines. Goman thought that all those who had fought for liberty should have their portion of material inheritance, and that the cultivator should be able to enjoy, by himself, the products he drew from his labor on the land and the sweat of his brow. He had fought like a lion in a hundred places, and his valor had earned him the rank of Chef de Batallion. He had prestige. My father and many others believed the same as he did.

"Armed with old flint rifles that they had put to good use during the War of Independence, along with Pikes whose points had been hardened with fire, the lads of Grand-Doco—those hardened companions!—rose up and held the countryside against Pétion and his troops as much to avenge the death of the Liberator as to conquer the ownership of the land."

Bon Dos then describes in detail how Goman's movement was able to hold on to its territory in the South, in part thanks to support from King Christophe. Ultimately, however, Pétion's successor, Boyer, succeeded in buying off many of Goman's followers with offers of land and defeating those who stood firm militarily.

They say that, desperate and wishing to die, Goman threw himself headfirst off a precipice. The truth is that he was killed, for they feared that as long as he lived the peasants of Marfranc and the heights would never be pacified, that the day they got more weapons from Christophe they would once again start demanding land for all.

My father was among the last to consent to surrender to Boyer's generals. To punish them for the tenacity with which they deployed in serving Goman, they gave them nothing and forced them to work on the plantations of the large landowners as they had before, or to rent their services to new small property-owners, or else to rent land from the state or from individual landowners which, if they had just conceded them full ownership, would have been ten times more productive.

My father rented ten *carreaux* from a city-dweller in Jérémie. Like many others like him, this man had gotten his land by stealing from the state. The people in the towns always arrange things between themselves so that they'll have power over us. My father worked long and hard. When, having toiled away all year, he went to town to sell his coffee, his cacao, his cotton, they disdainfully called him a *nègre* of the hills, or a *nègre* of Goman. He never whispered a word. He bought cloth, cuffs, hoes, and then quietly set off back to his house. His heart slowly filled with bile, bitterness, and rage.

Finally, Boyer was chased out of power. Here is how it happened. My father told the story to me just as I am telling it to you today, so that in fifty years you can in turn tell it to your grandchildren.

Philibert Lerraque had stirred up Jérémie against the old hypocrite who, for twenty-five years, had paraded around Port-au-Prince. He carried out this great action the day before New Year's. My father had gone into town to do his shopping. They grabbed him forcibly, put a rifle in his hands, and told him and the others—hill-dwellers and proletarians enlisted despite their strong protests—and shouted "To Port-au-Prince!" . . .

On 13 March 1843 Boyer went into exile. He never came back, the bad man!

When everything was finished and the country was freed of the one they called the tyrant, the new leaders created a Constitution on paper.

For them, the whole Revolution ended there. They didn't even think about the peasants, the popular masses. It was clumsy. Hérard Dumesle, Rivière Hérard, Segrettier, all of them pot-bellied gerontocrats, loud-mouthed lawyers, had done it just for themselves and not for everyone. They were chased out of power ignominiously in turn.

Then Guerrier was president. A good old man. He had white hair. And then, that was it.

He died quickly. They imposed Pierrot who passed for a friend of the poor rural folk. The wealthy people immediately found fault with him, though these faults were no worse than those of his predecessors.

He was overthrown and sent to live in the North. Riché was made president. All that happened in Port-au-Prince. The capital rarely consults us when it wants to take care of our business.

The overthrow of Pierrot angered us.

Riché, in fact, was nothing but a little Boyer, minus the ridiculous earrings. But he had a missing eye. He lacked prestige. He let himself be so perfectly led by those who thought of nothing but exploiting the peasants that, in the South, they rose up once again, demanding land.

That was in 1846.

This time, Acaau and the people of l'Anse-à-Veau and Nippes were with us. In Port-à-Piment, Petit-Jean and Paul-François had stirred up the masses of the peasants. Those robust lads fought madly at Côteaux, Port-Salut, Pestel, Platons, Corail, Fond-Bleu, Camp Périn, Plymouth—everywhere. All the peaks of the Hotte chain of mountains were on fire.

Sadly, Acaau was vanquished by Samedi Thélémaque, and the sublime though infamous man committed suicide. It is true that Samedi Thélémaque, having barely completed the work of exterminating our brothers, died suddenly and mysteriously in his camp in front of Corail.

We, on the heights of our good and loyal Macaya, from Marfranc to Cahouane, we ran and retreated, hid and trained, rested and fought, regrouped and fought still against Cayemitte, Fouchard, Marcel, Fleuriau, who, followed by a crowd of soldiers, had been sent from Jérémie against us.

It was then that we truly earned the proud name of "Piquets."

The old guns of the time of Independence, so rusted that they exploded in our hands on the second shot, were no help. With only our pikes, we were formidable and feared. My father was recognized as the chief of a band. He had fought in times past, under Goman. He became young again to lead us to the places where we could carry out the most audacious attacks. But one day, at Duranton, in the midst of battle, he was shot in his right leg. The wound bled a lot.

We bandaged him as well as we could. He couldn't walk. That night, he was brought here lying on a stretcher made of four pikes covered with green branches.

My mother, my sister, and my brother broke into tears when they saw him arrive, his skin already cold and ashen. He had the courage to sit on a large straw chair to say goodbye to us. He wanted to die outside, smelling the warm exhalations of the earth rising up out of the ground as the sun set. He ordered us to bury him in his soldier's tunic, insisting above all that we not put him in his good clothes and even that we not wash his corpse. He was obeyed immediately.

The day after his burial, I went back into battle with my older brothers and my younger brother.

He was only sixteen. He died at my side.

Before passing away, our father had left us with this supreme command: "Once I have been placed in the ground, you will return where duty calls: to combat. If necessary, in thirty years, in fifty years, you will return again at the first signal, for this land must belong to you."

After the battle at Duranton, things went from bad to worse. Our blood was spilled in floods. Once again we were vanquished, beaten, crushed.

It is especially since then that, in the books that they alone write or have others write, the sons of our executioners present us as miserable, vile, insolent pillagers! What a bunch of lying scoundrels! What bandits!

The year 1844 seemed like nothing more than a bad dream. We waited for a long time. But we never lost all hope. 1868 arrived. Jérémie rose up against President Salnave. A few elders from the mountain went from house to house, to the isolated huts, repeating everywhere: If the cities are rebelling against Salnave, it must be because he is a friend of the peasants, a true democrat, with a humble heart. It was true. When he came among us later, we could see that he was not a proud man, not only like the men of 1843, or his predecessor Geffrard who having overthrown Emperor Faustin ended up just continuing his policies as president.

I remembered my father's command. I was among the first to sharpen my pike, to put myself at the head of the men of the valley and the canton. I went with them to the camp of Délice Lésperance. Salnave had sent us good rifles. Many of those who accompanied the president had lived in the lands of the whites. At night, during our long evenings around the besieged town, they told us that there, in the midst of very old, civilized, well-governed societies, land had been returned to its legitimate masters, the peasants. Even a great emperor, the tsar of the Russians, an autocrat a hundred times more powerful than Haitian presidents, a hundred times more aristocratic than all of the self-styled aristocrats of Jérémie, had liberated the peasants of his empire, had placed the property of the soil in their hands, buying it from their lords. We had nothing to buy back, for we had conquered the land with Dessalines. We are the ones who have paid for everything since 1825, since our independence was recognized by France. The land of Haiti was meant for us. It is our right.

Bon Dos once again describes a series of battles that ultimately led to the defeat of the peasant movement in the countryside. He then returns to the consistent theme about the conflict between the interests of rural residents and city residents, particularly those in power in the capital of Port-au-Prince.

The city has never wanted to listen to us. If sometimes it hears us talk, it pays attention to what we are thinking and asking for only in order to massacre us. For itself, for its personal needs and interests, it has never accepted our grievances. It is the city that, now, like always, fattens itself on our labor and sweat.

Bon Dos then recounts the ultimate victory of President Salomon, whom he presents as a true friend of the peasants. Finally, he explains, the long struggle ended in victory.

"Abandoned to themselves in the little hold of Miragoâne, where they had locked themselves as if pushed on by an invisible hand, the sons of Boyer and Bazelais, our hereditary enemies, who had started a civil war purely to prevent us from becoming landowners, paid with their lives for all the iniquities committed earlier by Boyer and Bazelais.

"So here we are."

Having said this, the noble old man stopped talking. He was panting. His pupils were on fire, sequined with bright lightning. You would have sworn his eye was singing a fanfare of victory.

On the horizon, all the final light of evening was disappearing, paling. White and violet invaded the atmosphere. Soon the moon streaked the sky with silver rays and the diligent stars nailed diamonds into the great blue heavens.

The ancestor raised his resplendent face toward the ethereal depths and, three times, with his finger, made the sign of the cross.

His voice slower now, failing more and more, he continued:

"Now I am dying. I die happy. I worked for you. We worked for you. May each of you demand his portion of the national estate: five carreaux of land for each little family.

"Each head of household will plant on their concession coffee, cotton, cacao, manioc, plantains, green beans, rice, corn, malangas, eggplant, tobacco, potatoes, ignames, and also fruit trees. Mix your crops. Alternate them. Everything is good. You have to pull what you can from each parcel, mix and fertilize each bit of soil. Raise poultry in your farmyard and carry the milk from your cows, sheep and ewes to market. Eat the good bacon of the pigs you've fattened yourselves with the fruit of your avocado tree and the seeds from your palm trees.

"From now on, you must be full citizens. You all should know how to read and write, now that you are no longer pariahs, now that you must examine the electoral platforms of the deputies you'll have to elect. You therefore will help build or repair the local school and the teacher's house.

"Don't refuse to offer your services so that roads can be improved, so that bridges, canals, and dykes can be built.

"If you are asked to pay a land tax in the name of the state, pay it happily. If you are called to serve under the flag give yourself fully to military service, with joy in your heart. The nation has every right to it.

"Do not borrow anything from city-dwellers, and even less from those who come offering you money from abroad. There must be no justification for taking your land or pretexts to cheat and exploit you as has been done in the past.

"Be thrifty. Salomon is going to create savings banks and small community banks. . . . Give up the vain and useless expenses you previously spent on the souls of the dead. Dance as little as possible. Don't tire yourself out on Sunday, so that you'll be able to clear the land better on Monday.

"Whenever the occasion presents itself, rush to the village chapel, clean and rustic, garlanded with fresh, green foliage, to listen to the words of the priest, the Protestant pastor, the communal judge or the rural *chef de section*. As long as they cry: Long live the nation! Long live peace! Long live the black race! all will be well . . ."

His voice continued, tremulous but inexorable, mixed with little hiccups, like a voice that is about to go silent for good. The old man was tired. He blinked his eyes three times, opened them just a little and, through his already tight lips, these syllables—as if nailed together—passed in a whisper:

"Bury me in my good clothes. Today, and in the future, you will no longer lack clothes as we did in the past."

. . . He stood tall on his knotty legs, this very old man, and clearly he shouted under the clear sky: Long live Haiti!

The echo clearly repeated the cry.

The patriarch fell back in his chair, his arms open, his pupils dilated, his face totally serene, as if illuminated. He was dead. . . .

The next day, Jean-Louis Bon Dos was carried to the little cemetery in the valley. They had reopened the grave where, for years, the bones of his father, Goman's soldier, had been crumbling away. They lay him gently on a bed of sage, wild basil, and *vétiver*.

Both of them are now sleeping the long sleep, covered by the same simple tombstone.

Where the fathers rest, so will the children.

Once upon a time they were buried the way too many are still buried in too many latitudes, the way slaves, serfs, indentured laborers, proletarians, the disinherited are. From now on they will be placed in the true grandparent, the earth, respectfully, piously—the way free men are buried.

Where they were once slaves, valets, and vassals, there they will be masters and lords.

And it will be just!

Translated by Laurent Dubois

Atlas critique d'Haïti

Georges Anglade

Geographer and fiction writer Georges Anglade offers an analysis of the economic and political geography of Haiti in the nineteenth century. Taken from his richly illustrated Atlas critique d'Haïti, *these excerpts elaborate his broader argument that the nineteenth century represented a period of profound decentralization in the country, which was organized around eleven regions focused on eleven ports. He emphasizes the ways in which the regionalized system created spaces for the development and anchoring of the rural system based on agricultural production of food for local markets as well as coffee and dyewood for export. While celebrating the forms of autonomy and self-reliance made possible through this system, Anglade also acknowledges the often-overlooked long-term environmental effects, particularly of the export of dyewood.*

Dyewood was the most important tinting wood until the invention of the chemical colorants that replaced it. The cycle of exportation of this wood is fundamental for understanding the ecological disaster of the Haitian space. . . . Over the long term, during the national period, it is to the irresponsibility of clear-cutting the dyewood, yellow wood, guayacan, *brésillet* trees . . . at the rhythm of hundreds of millions of pounds each year, to the profit of lumber exporters in each of the ports, that we owe the degradation of our natural habitat.

. . .

From 1791 to 1804, the conflicts of the slaves' war of liberation ravaged the infrastructure of the plantations. At the time of independence, there were three main problems that had to be confronted: first, the distribution of the plantations, or more precisely the process through which they were grabbed up by the new oligarchies in formation; second, the construction of a new relationship between agricultural work and a labor force that was now free and the artisans of the victory; and finally, the reconstruction of the means of production which it had been necessary to destroy in order to win independence or, barring that, the adoption of other means of production. Within the broader context of the plantation Americas at the beginning of the nineteenth century, the conjuncture in Haiti was unique because this society in formation was cut off from direct external influences.

The endogenous process that took place produced a set of adaptations in which different, more or less pronounced regional variations coexisted. Groups were formed on a local basis, centered on port towns from which products were exported. The run on the large plantations was accompanied by access to smaller properties on the part of workers. The juridical order did not allow either for the reconstruction of the colonial plantations or the constitution of a proletariat composed of agricultural laborers. An authentic peasantry with parcels of land emerged even as the dominant groups were formed, along with commerce and profits, rent and land, armies and administrations.

Within a broader context of federation, the general tendencies were the same in all of the provinces. But large property was maintained more easily in the regions where oligarchies were stronger, such as Le Cap and Port-au-Prince, than in those where they were weaker, such as the regions of Aquin and Miragoâne. There were additional variations: Gonaïves, Jacmel, and Cayes, closer to Le Cap and Port-au-Prince in terms of the strength of the oligarchy, developed similar solutions. Petit-Goâve, Jérémie, and Saint-Marc, with weaker oligarchies, also lived through very similar adaptations. The structure of regionalized space allowed for the constitution of eleven peasantries, who resisted the levies organized in each province.

The nation didn't spring up fully constituted and uniform, and neither did the peasantry. Upon a common foundation composed of Vodou, music, communal practices, family structure, there were regional variations which had the time to grow strong before the centralization of the twentieth century. This context provided time and plentiful space that enabled the genesis of a civilization. It is also the origin of the local variations that remain significant.

. . .

The nation and the Haitian state were not born at all once on 1 January 1804. One and the other were forged slowly, and with difficulty, over the course of the nineteenth century.

Regional oligarchies opposed one another to the point that there were splits into several Republics and wars placing regional armies in conflict with one another. Popular uprisings contested the power of the capital port towns of the provinces, and territorial war temporarily unified the provinces through the conquest of the East of the island, the future Dominican Republic.

. . .

During the period of the regionalized space of the nineteenth century, links of consanguinity tied together generations cultivating the same land. The *lakou* brought together the habitat and gardens of peasants sharing a

Bread market in St. Michel, ca. 1928. Courtesy of Smithsonian Institution Archives. Image #SIA2008-2521.

family farm, which had often been received as a concession to an ancestor who served in the armies of the war of independence. The extended kinship networks of the *lakou* constituted a core of resistance to plantation work and to the powers of taxation of the eleven port towns. The *lakou* was a mode of organization born of regionalization. My main hypothesis is that each of the federated provinces lacked the coercive force of a strong state that would have enabled the maintenance of workers in a plantation system. The access of peasant farmers to parcels of land enabled by the regionalized space made it possible for them to impose their will against oligarchies who wished to privilege the plantation.

. . .

The market is not simply a mechanism for commercial exchange, but a fundamental element of rural life. Each market and its zone of influence functions as a community, a center through which the orders and rules of political and administrative power are transmitted, through the section chief, who is aptly nicknamed *Leta*, or "the state." It is also the location and the time for the organization of local celebration, the public site of the diffusion of information, and the seat of secret organizations. In sum, the market is the node of rural distribution for town garden plots, the "town center" whose periodic animation unites thousands of people, some days, in a space that is otherwise deserted.

Open-air market in Gros Morne, Haiti. Estus H. Magoon Collection, Cuban Heritage Collection, University of Miami Libraries, Coral Gables, Florida.

The site of the market is layered with forms of centralization. It is the *potomitan* loaded with signs, the crossroads of all commercial and symbolic circulation. The market is the knot for circuits of levies: there rent is collected, profits realized, available labor hired, advances paid back through the delivery of products. It is also a bottleneck, an unavoidable passageway on the margins of which camp the professionals of chicanery and usury, alongside speculators charged with the task of collecting taxes for the Haitian state which will ultimately be deposited into the customs house of Port-au-Prince, the end point of all these circuits.

The market is also a center of resistance on the part of the rural world. While the town garden plots are the main site for phenomena linked to production, the market is the locus of the phenomena of commercialization. The rural collectivity creates there an infinite number of small intermediaries who share the crumbs left to the countryside: market women, resellers, brokers, porters, artisans all toil to collect a few pennies. These activities are scattered precisely in order to give resources to the greatest number of people possible, notably the landless peasants who also work at numerous tasks in the town garden plots.

This center of resistance is an object within the localized space, which is itself defined as a collective organization for survival of the masses confronted with the rigors of levies of all kinds on the part of the networks that enervate the Haitian space.

Translated by Claire Payton and Laurent Dubois

III

The Birth of Modern-Day Haiti

The late nineteenth and early twentieth centuries were a time of profound transformation in Haiti. The political conflicts of earlier decades intensified, as did fiscal and economic problems, notably those surrounding external debt. There was an increase in migration in all directions—into and out of the country, and from the rural areas to the cities. In many ways, it is during this time that modern-day Haiti was born.

These were decades of tremendous political turmoil. A series of presidents installed themselves in the National Palace, often through force, only to be overthrown soon afterward. Intellectual Anténor Firmin and military officer Nord Alexis, for instance, engaged in a struggle for power that spanned several years and cost many lives. Alexis, the grandson of King Henry Christophe, ultimately won this conflict and seized the presidency in 1902. During his six years in power, he carried out political arrests, controversial executions, and a trial against high-ranking officials. He was overthrown in 1908, and over the following years the political conflicts accelerated. In 1912, President Cincinnatus Leconte along with hundreds of others was killed in a violent explosion at the Haitian National Palace. This explosion can be read as a symbol of the disintegration of the Haitian state. Three years later, U.S. Marines would disembark to occupy the country.

Part of what drove this political turmoil was the pressure placed on the Haitian state by powerful foreign nations attempting to exert control over its financial and political affairs. There was a long series of diplomatic incidents between Germany and Haiti: Germany frequently sent warships into Haiti's harbors to back up its claims against the state. The United States regularly intervened in Haitian political conflicts, and tried and failed to gain control over the territory of Mole Saint-Nicolas, which the U.S. wished to use as a coaling station for its navy. Even as representatives of the Haitian state confronted suspicion and discrimination from other countries, they also discriminated against some groups within the country, particularly those known as Syrians—immigrants from different parts of the Middle East, many of whom also had ties with the United States.

Somewhat paradoxically, this period of political fragmentation and conflict was also when many of the country's national symbols were established and consolidated, including the national anthem. But the claims of unity made through such symbols remained superficial. Projects for the expansion of education into rural areas were largely neglected by the state. The dramatic drop in coffee prices around the world at the end of the nineteenth century undermined the economy of many rural areas and helped to spur the beginnings of rural migration to the cities and of Haitian migration to Cuba, both of which would intensify during the U.S. occupation.

The turn of the century was also a time of urban renewal. There were many technological advances: railroads were built and cars imported. Street electrification became a reality and telephones were introduced. New, more modern marketplaces were built. This renewal took place not only in Port-au-Prince but also in Cap-Haïtien. These developments impacted social life, as a Haitian nightlife began to develop that went beyond people's homes and *lakous* (communal yard space within a family compound).

Although the urban and the rural commingled constantly through movement and markets, there was tremendous tension between them. Color dynamics and gender relations were constantly being questioned and renegotiated. These tensions shaped the literary and cultural life of the period, as some artists sought to incorporate Haiti's vernacular and rural cultures into their writing. Some began to use Haitian Creole as a literary language and developed a new literary form, the *lodyans*, from oral storytelling traditions. The transition from the nineteenth century to the twentieth also marked the decline of French cultural influence in Haiti and the concurrent rise of North American influence, which would only deepen with the U.S. occupation. At the same time, some Haitian thinkers sought to establish connections and alliances with Latin America, as a way of countering and at other times, relating to U.S. influence and power, from a hemispheric or linguistic origins perspective.

Nineteenth-Century Haiti by the Numbers

Louis Gentil Tippenhauer

Louis Gentil Tippenhauer was a German who spent many years in Haiti. In 1892 he published a detailed analysis of Haiti's population and economy. Tippenhauer emphasized the expansion of the coffee industry, which soon after independence had replaced sugar as the main source of foreign exchange. Coffee production was ideally suited to the small-scale peasantry that had replaced the large estates under French colonial rule. Haiti came to be the world's fourth largest exporter of coffee in the nineteenth century. Coffee exports paid for imports and were also critical to government revenue, which was almost entirely based on taxation of both coffee exports and imports. The work points out the success of the Haitian coffee industry in the nineteenth century: in 1890, Haitian exports per head were nearly US$10, a figure similar to that in the Dominican Republic and Puerto Rico and higher than that in several other Caribbean countries. By the time Tippenhauer's book was published, the industry was starting to decline as a result of overproduction in Brazil and the collapse of world prices. Tippenhauer also addressed the thorny question of Haiti's demographics. Because no census had been taken since the 1820s, there was great uncertainty about the size of the population. Tippenhauer sifts through the various estimates with great care and eventually settles on what he thinks is the most reliable figure.
—Contributing Editor: Victor Bulmer-Thomas

On Foreign Trade

It is clear from this list of coffee exports that it is quite wrong to assert that the republic has made no progress. Since the declaration of independence coffee production has tripled. In 1820, 25 million pounds were exported; today 75 million pounds are exported, apart from the low values in 1879 and 1883, both of which were filled with revolutions. In the colony's most flourishing years no more coffee was produced than it is today.

On Population

The Haitian A. Paul, in a pamphlet published in 1875, calculated the population at 943,000. From a brief consideration of the details, it is obvious that this is a significant overestimate. For of these 943,000 people—in his own quite private opinion—495,000 were black, 420,000 mulatto, and 28,000 white or foreign! Since when have there been 28,000 white people or foreigners living in Haiti, or indeed 420,000 mulattos? If we accept the figure of 393,000 Haitian inhabitants in 1815, and of 650,000 by 1860—which means believing that the population almost doubled in forty-five years—we base our opinion on the fact that these included the peaceful years of Boyer's presidency and Soulouque's long regime: a period in which the political upheavals were not too stormy; in which the revolutions were not accompanied by as much bloodshed as they were later on; in which the population was able to develop almost normally. However, Paul's calculation is untenable; according to him the population would have to have increased by 300,000 after 1860—that is, within fifteen years. But in that case, where is the evidence of the dreadful influence on the land and its inhabitants of Salnave's wars? The eighteen-month-long civil war was certainly atrocious enough.

We would do better to follow A. Thoby's estimate. Thoby was for a short while a minister of the country and is recognized as an authority on his people (A. Thoby, *Questions Politiques d'Haïti*, Paris 1883). In his opinion, the population of the Republic of Haiti was 800,000 in 1879; for, he adds, although only 40,000 votes were cast in the last parliamentary election, 160,000 inhabitants of the country were entitled to vote. In the following year (1878), the Catholic clergy, in the *Bulletin religieux*, was already putting the population at 960,000. However, it is well known that, as far as the outside world is concerned, it is in the strong interest of the Catholic clergy to find the highest possible number of believers.

The view that 800,000 is not too low a figure for 1879 is strengthened by Guridi's opinion. In his geographical account he gives a figure of only 725,000 inhabitants for the Haitian republic in 1880. As a zealous Dominican, however, he will have claimed for Saint-Domingue the 10,100 square kilometres of Haitian-occupied border territory and its 70,000 inhabitants, so that according to him there were 795,000 people living in Haiti in 1880. Edgar la Selve (*Le Pays des Nègres*, p. 2), who traveled through most of the Haitian republic, agrees with Thoby and Guridi: he puts the number of inhabitants during the years 1870–80 at 800,000.

The younger Thébaud claims that in 1886 there were already 990,000 people in Haiti, divided as follows: Département de l'Ouest 350,000; Département du Sud 200,000; Département de l'Artibonite 120,000; Département du Nord-Ouest 70,000; Département du Nord 250,000. Total 990,000.

Translated by Victor Bulmer-Thomas

Family Portraits

This portrait, probably from the early twentieth century, offers a glimpse of how certain urban Haitian families saw and represented themselves. Since the arrival of photography in Haiti, there has been a rich tradition of portraiture, providing images of family life and dress that counter many of the assumptions outsiders have about the country. But these photographs were most of all ways of documenting and preserving kinship and domestic life. "I always search for my dead relatives in archival photographs," writes Edwidge Danticat, "as if I might actually find them there." Such photographs "connect us to parts of people and places that have already ceased to exist."[1]

Untitled (Family of Ten), n.d., gelatin silver plate, 8" × 10". Photo courtesy of CIDHICA.

Note

1. Edwidge Danticat, "'My Misery Is Mine!,'" in *From Within and Without: The History of Haitian Photography*, edited by Barbara Buhler Lynes (Fort Lauderdale: NSU Art Museum, 2015), 60–73.

My Panama Hat Fell Off

Anonymous

It is said that this traditional Haitian folksong, "Panama m tonbe," was inspired by an event in which President Louis Mondestin Florvil Hyppolite (1889–96) journeyed to Jacmel to try to quash an uprising headed by Merisier Jeannis, a Caco leader. Before he left, the president's hat fell from his head, which was considered a bad omen. However, Hyppolite did not cancel his trip or turn back. Some accounts state that the falling-hat incident actually occurred several years before the trip to Jacmel. In any case, on his way to Jacmel, Hyppolite suffered a heart attack, fell from his horse, and died. At the time, panama hats were popular and often worn by dignitaries. They were made in Ecuador, yet distributed globally from Panama. President Florvil Hyppolite died on 24 March 1896. There are other, lesser, known songs that also commemorate this event, but "Panama m tonbe" remains a staple of Haitian music even today, with recent interpretations by Réginald Policard (2004) and Strings (2013). The date of the first recording as well as the song's original composer(s) remain unknown.

I left the city of Jakmèl,
Headed to Lavale.
As I approached the Benè crossroads,
Off fell my panama hat!
My panama hat fell.

My panama hat fell.
My panama hat fell.
Whoever's behind me, pick it up for me.

Translated by Nadève Ménard

God, Work, and Liberty!

Oswald Durand

Known for his patriotism and his avant-garde writing in Haitian Creole, Oswald Durand (1840–1906) is one of Haiti's most renowned poets. His poem "Chant national" was used as an unofficial national anthem throughout the late nineteenth century. In 1888, Haitian composer Occide Jeanty wrote music to accompany it. And in 1893, when the German legation needed a Haitian anthem to be played at an event held on a ship, an orchestral arrangement was composed in the space of a few hours. A new national anthem was created in 1904, but Durand's "Chant national" has continued to be performed at official events. Today the song is commonly referred to as the presidential hymn.

The poem calls on the spirit of the country's forefathers (Dessalines, Toussaint, Capoix-la-mort, Chavannes, Ogé) to guide the current citizenry in their management of the new nation, warning that independence will be fleeting if Haitian citizens do not work to maintain it and to constantly live up to their place in history.

I

When our forefathers broke their chains,
It was not to sit back and cross their arms.
In order to work as masters, the slaves
Had to embrace death.
Their blood fed our hills in torrents.
It is now up to us, yellow and black, let's go!
Let us work the land Dessalines left us:
In our valleys, therein lies our fortune.

Independence is fleeting
Without the right to equality!
To happily tread this land,
We need the strict motto:
"God! Work! Liberty!"

II

What could be more beautiful than these sons of Africa
Who, plunged into all manner of ills for three hundred years,
Turn their shackles, their bonds, their cudgel
Against might and old prejudice!

Down there, look! It is the noble banner
Surrounding the blacks who will die there . . .
—No! Their stream, with Lamartinière,
Steadily pours down from la Crête-à-Pierrot!

All that would be fleeting
Without the right to equality.
To happily tread this land,
We need the strict motto:
"God! Work! Liberty!"

III

Rochambeau's proud troops
For several moments held their fire,
To salute the hero of Vertières,
Capoix la mort, great and god-like!
Toward progress, let us cry like that worthy man:
"Onward, Blacks, onward!" And let us toil
The soil soaked through with the sweat of slaves!
We have here what we search for elsewhere!

Otherwise, all becomes fleeting:
No order, and no equality.
To happily tread our land,
We need the strict motto:
"God! Work! Liberty!"

IV

Martyrs' blood whose frothing purple
Shook our chains and yokes!
Chavanne, Ogé, on the infamous wheel of torture,
You, old Toussaint, in your dungeon at Joux:

O ancestors, whose last fibers
Must have trembled—you the torch-bearers—
Seeing us now proud and free,
Advise us from the depths of your tombs!

—"Your happiness is fleeting;
Claim the right to equality!
To happily tread your land,
You need the strict motto:
God! Work! Liberty!"

To work, then, children of Africa
Yellow and black, sons of the same cradle!
Ancient Europe and young America
Watch us attempting the difficult feat from afar.
Working the land that in the year eighteen oh four
Our ancestors conquered for us with their might.
It is our turn now to fight
With this cry: "Progress or death!"

To work, or all is fleeting!
Let us claim the right to equality!
We will tread the land more proudly
With this strict motto:
"God! Work! Liberty!"

Translated by Nadève Ménard

The National Anthem, "La Dessalinienne"

Justin Lhérisson and Nicolas Geffrard

To celebrate the centennial of Haiti's independence, a contest was held in 1903 to establish a national anthem. Author and journalist Justin Lhérisson (1873–1907) was declared the winner. Nicolas Fénélon Geffrard (1871–1930) composed the music to accompany Lhérisson's lyrics. The song's title, "La Dessalinienne," refers to Jean-Jacques Dessalines, father of Haitian independence. In the 1980s Raymond Moïse created a Haitian Creole adaptation of the song, and it was popularized by singer Ansy Dérose. Today children typically begin the school day by singing one verse each from the French and Creole versions.

March on! For ancestors and country,
United march, united march;
Loyal subjects all remain,
And lords of our domain.
United march, march on!
United march for ancestors and country,
March on, united march, march on!
Unite for ancestors and country!

For sacred soil,
For sires of old
We gladly toil.
When team field and wold
The soul is strong and bold.
We gladly toil, we gladly toil
For sacred soil,
For sires of old.

For land we love
And sires of old
We give our sons.
Free, happy, and bold,
Our brotherhood we'll hold.
We give our sons, we give our sons

For land we love
And sires of old.

For those who gave
For country all,
God of the brave,
To thee, O God, we call;
Without thee we must fall,
God of the brave, God of the brave.
For those who gave
For country all.

For flag on high
For Native land
'Tis fine to die.
Our traditions demand
Be ready, heart and hand,
'Tis fine to die, 'tis fine to die
For flag on high,
For Native land.

Trial about the Consolidation of Debt

Various Authors

Throughout the nineteenth and early twentieth centuries, the Haitian government was burdened by the weight of its foreign debt, which it consistently paid, to the detriment of other national expenditures. During his presidency (1896–1902), Tirésias Simon Sam decided to consolidate the nation's debts in an attempt to facilitate repayment. However, his successor to the presidency, Nord Alexis, charged that Sam and his family, along with other high government officials, had committed fraud in this debt consolidation process in order to enrich themselves. A trial was held from 28 November to 25 December 1904, and several people were condemned to prison and forced labor. Interestingly, three of those condemned during the trial went on to become president of the Haitian Republic (Cincinnatus Leconte in 1911, Tancrède Auguste in 1912, and Vilbrun Guillaume Sam in 1915). This remains the biggest financial trial in Haiti's history to date.

The first letter, from the president to the secretary of state, started the process that eventually led to the trial.

Key details were provided by Thimoclès Lafontant, government commissioner to the bank, in the following interrogation.

Port-au-Prince, March 20th 1903, year 100 of independence
Nord Alexis, President of Haiti
To the Secretary of State of Justice

Mister Secretary of State,

I send to you, as a matter pertaining to your department, documents which, presented to be consolidated, were submitted to me by the Government Commissioner to the bank. These receipts having already been paid, they are obviously duplicates. I invite you to command the appropriate parties so that government action can be set in motion against the authors and accomplices in this matter.

Receive, Mister Secretary of State, the assurance of my utmost consideration.

(Signed) Nord Alexis
CC: Ch. Bouchereau, Division Head
at the Department of Justice

Pierre Nord Alexis (1820–1910). This photograph from 1908 depicts Alexis (seated in carriage) returning to Port-au-Prince from a military review. Reprinted by permission of Photo 12/Alamy Stock Photo.

Year one thousand nine hundred three, March 25, at ten o'clock and fifteen minutes in the morning.

Question put forth: What are your last and first names, your age, status, profession, place of birth and residence?

Responded: My name is Thimoclès Lafontant, thirty-six years of age, Government Commissioner to the National Bank of Haiti, residing in Port-au-Prince.

Ques.: Tell us under what circumstances you came to refuse to sign certain effects presented for consolidation.

Resp.: After my nomination, once I arrived at the Commissariat, I only found incomplete archives. I noticed that certain registers had blank pages and others stopped in the year 1895 and in the year 1896 according to the report I made to my immediate superiors.

When I resumed the consolidation service that had been stopped before my nomination, I received a letter dated the current 16th of March from the Ministry of Finances, making me responsible for any errors that might slip into the documents that would be sent to me. This letter will be communicated to your chamber of instruction. One afternoon, before having received the letter from the Ministry of Finances, bearing the date of current 16th March, Mister Edmond Lallemand, employee of the Ahrendts house, presented himself to me as a friend, requesting the prompt dispatch of certain documents that would be sent to me for consolidation, which I promised him.—Upon receipt of the letter from the Ministry of Finance dated 16 March, accompanied by a statement of six payment authorizations with the numbers 87, 80, 90, 107, 77, 76, presenting a total of 2,640 gourdes of Haiti and 10,500 gold coins of the United States, which statement named as bearer the payer of the Department of Foreign Relations. After having verified all the documents, several things held my attention: first, I asked myself whether the State had the right to consolidate documents belonging to the State, for these payment authorizations, although they were established for the personnel account of the stated Department in the year 1889 were not accompanied by any certificate, either from the bearers or their rights holders, nor from the Administrative Commission of 89/90.

On the other hand, since a balance of 2,640 gourdes is declared in the statement accompanied by the Minister's letter and in the report by the Commission 89/90, it seems to me that the balance of these payment authorizations should be accompanied by certificates from the bearers or by some title delivered by the Verification Commission in favor of the interested parties. Such was not the case; it was for me to verify the accuracy of this balance by addressing either the Finance Department, or by doing research.—The evening of the same day, upon leaving the office, I met Mister Edmond Lallemand in front of the Bar de la Bourse who asked me if I had dispatched those documents to the Bank for him. I answered him that these documents, to my mind, did not meet the necessary conditions to be consolidated; therefore I was reserving the right to verify their accuracy. Then, he, to answer me that the documents did not belong to him, that if he was getting involved, it was only to receive a brokerage fee for the prompt dispatch of the aforementioned documents.

On the morning of the 18th, the payer of Foreign Relations, having presented himself at my offices, Mister Régnier acting as head of office in the absence of the bearer asked the payer if he had come to receive the documents of the current service. The latter responded in the affirmative and received the documents of the current service.

At that time, Mister Viaud, Jr., employee of the Commissariat, asked the same payer if he had also come for the consolidated items mentioned in the Finance Minister's letter dated 16th March current. Upon his affirmative response, I introduced myself and told him that in my opinion, those papers did not present the desired level of authenticity;

I would speak to the Minister about it and undertake research. The payer then showed to Mister Régnier and myself a certificate signed by him of which he was the carrier, attesting to the validity of the aforementioned documents in question. I again made the same observations to him as above, that first I needed to do research before coming to any type of decision on the subject of those documents.

Upon which, he answered that, since that's how it was, the Department of Foreign Relations would write to the Finance Minister so the latter could do what was necessary. The same day, at eleven o'clock, having needed some information from the Department of Finances and not finding it necessary to ask for it in writing, I asked Mister Léonce Régnier to go get it. Upon Mister Régnier's return, he informed me that Mister Desravines, division head at the Department of Finances had told him that the payer of the Foreign Relations had returned to the Ministry quite indignant and that he reserved the right to see his Minister so that the latter could write to his colleague in Finances in order to do the necessary; that Desravines added that he was surprised to see the Government Commissioner to the Bank make observations about the documents signed by the Minister, when he was only there to register and stamp the documents that were sent to him.

The evening of that same day, around five o'clock, having learned from Mister Viaud, Jr., that Mister Roland Michel was an honest man, I hurried to charge Mister Régnier to tell him that my intention was not to wound his susceptibility, but rather to do my duty. And on Friday, March 20th, rumors of my dismissal having circulated in town, I thought it necessary, not having the books necessary to enlighten me at hand, to go to the bank to undertake the necessary research concerning the documents that had been presented to me by the payer of Foreign Relations to be consolidated as pink titles. I thus addressed myself to Mister Thibault, the Treasury's head of service, to have precise information about the consolidation or the non consolidation of the documents in question. He replied to me that he had to have the name of the bearers without which it was impossible for him to do any research. Faced with this response, I proceeded to do research myself which allowed me to find a bundle of receipts in a cabinet that had been addressed to whom it may concern. Said receipts were in reference to the payment authorizations of Nos. 87, 80, 90, and 107. The Bank's Director having come to declare to me in my office that the balance of 2,640 gourdes was correct, considering that his books stated that the balance had never been paid, I maintain that these payment authorizations should be accompanied by payable sheets, because I found receipts that were already paid related to these payment authorizations. And with respect to the payment authorizations in gold, the Bank declared not to have paid them, I thus also maintain that those payment authorizations should be accompanied by certificates or papers from the bearers or their right holders. Nothing more was heard. The declaration having been read to the witness, he declares it to be true and to persevere. Required to sign, he did so before us.

Signed: A. Poujol, Thimoclès Lafontant,
Ls. Jh. Lebrun.

Below is an excerpt of the sentences rendered by the Court.

On these grounds, the Court, after deliberation, sentences the named:

1. Marie Jean Joseph de la Myre Mory, forty-two years of age, former director of the National Bank of Haiti, born in Villeneuve-sur-Lot (France), residing in Port-au-Prince, to four years of hard labor;
2. Georges Théodore Ohlrich, forty-four years of age, former assistant director of the National Bank of Haiti, born in Achim (Hanovre), residing in Port-au-Prince, to four years of hard labor;
3. Henri Rodolphe Tippenhauer, thirty-five years of age, former chief of the National Bank of Haiti's portfolio, born in Cap-Haïtien, residing in Port-au-Prince, to the same sentence;
4. Jean-Baptiste Poute de Puydaubet, forty-three years of age, employee of the National Bank of Haiti, born in Nouix (France), residing in Port-au-Prince, to the same sentence;
5. Brutus Saint-Victor, sixty-four years of age, proprietor and former secretary of state, born and residing in Port-au-Prince, to three years of imprisonment;
6. Vilbrun Sam, forty-five years of age, planter and merchant, born in Grande-Rivière-du-Nord, residing in Cap Haïtien, to hard labor in perpetuity;
7. Gédéus Gédéon, forty-eight years of age, lawyer, born and residing in Port-au-Prince;
8. Désmosthènes Simon Sam, thirty-seven years of age, speculator in commodities, born in Cap-Haïtien, residing in Port-au-Prince;
9. Lycurgue Simon Sam, thirty-three years of age, speculator in commodities, born in Trou, residing in Port-au-Prince, to three years of hard labor;

. . .

11. Fénélon Laraque, forty-one years of age, born and residing in Port-au-Prince, to three years of imprisonment.

Consequently, sentences them jointly and severally to the restitution of the diverted values and properties and to a fine equal to the quarter of the aforementioned values;

Declares null the consolidated 12 percent bonds, the obligations of the converted interior debt and the pink 5 percent titles issued fraudulently with regard to the State's rights;

Declares the sentenced Haitians barred from their civil and political rights and unable henceforth to exercise a state function.

Translated by Nadève Ménard

The Execution of the Coicou Brothers

Nord Alexis and Anténor Firmin

During the first decade of the twentieth century an intense political battle developed between Anténor Firmin, a prominent intellectual, and Nord Alexis, a powerful member of the military. Alexis assumed the presidency in 1902, but Firmin organized opposition to his rule, with a strong base of supporters. Among them was writer and diplomat Massillon Coicou, who accused Nord Alexis of being a tool of European and North American imperialism and of serving U.S. interests in Haiti.

In January 1908, several Firmin supporters launched an uprising in the city of Gonaïves. The uprising was crushed, and several participants were executed. Firmin himself took refuge at the French consulate in the city. During the night of 14–15 March 1908, three Coicou brothers, including forty-year-old poet Massillon, were pulled from their beds. The brothers had been accused by a relative, Jules Coicou, of being behind the uprising. Along with about two dozen others, they were brought near the cemetery and executed for plotting against the state. This repression effectively ended the opposition, and Firmin soon went into exile.

Nord Alexis's Version of Events

Haitians,

For several days, the rumor has been circulating that Firmin, having now taken refuge in the French consulate in Gonaïves, had delegated several of his supporters to again stage in the capital and other cities of the Republic the criminal enterprise of last January 15th.

The government, having wind of this, hurried to take all necessary measures to safeguard public order, and to this end, had the goings-on of individuals denounced by the police and notorious for their Firminist and antipatriotic opinions closely monitored.

Worthy and honest citizens who received propositions from the leaders of the conspiracy came to express their outrage to the government as well as their devotion to public order, and submitted letters from Firmin, who from the consulate in Gonaïves, thus kept the revolt going within the population and cultivated treachery among army officers.

The government thus doubled its vigilance, and last night, a patrol managed to arrest the main leaders of the conspiracy with weapons and munitions intended for the insurrection that was to take place this morning at ten o'clock.

Mr. Massillon Coicou, in the presence of proof establishing his guilt, did not hesitate to confess his crime and to denounce his accomplices.

The documents found in his possession allowed the police to realize that officers, and even some of the government guard, won over to the cause of the conspirators, were to have assured the success of the movement by making an attempt on the lives of the head of state, and of the government's principal lieutenants.

The individuals caught with weapons in hand received the only punishment befitting their archaic enterprise, and the officers identified as traitors to their duty were deferred to the military council.

The government congratulates the population of Port-au-Prince for its calm attitude which condemns this latest attempt by the troublemakers, and hurries to reassure families by promising to maintain, with the help of its assistants and its friends, public peace, order, and security, in spite of the nonsensical plans of those who premeditate the toppling of the established government to satisfy their guilty ambition.

Given at the National Palace,
in Port-au-Prince, 15 March 1908,
year 108 of independence.
Nord Alexis.

Anténor Firmin's Reaction to the Events

Saint-Thomas, May 29th, 1908
To Sirs Camille Coicou, Emmanuel Coicou, Christian Coicou
and Clément Coicou—Kingston

Dear compatriots and friends:
It is only in the latter half of this month that I learned of your presence in Kingston. Without this delay in my information, I would have already written you a few lines to express my deep chagrin and the vivid regrets that the assassination of my three friends, of whom I was very fond: Massillon, Horace and Pierre-Louis caused me; your beloved relatives. . . . They fell victim to their devotion to our worthy cause and their personal affection for me. There were no limits to their zeal nor to their noble efforts toward the goal of trying to extract me from the hands of those so thirsty for my blood. Alas! How I would have preferred to spill that blood as a burnt offering for our country, instead of theirs, so full of sap and generous ardor! For I am already descending the ladder of life and they

Execution of Massillon Coicou and others on the front page of the French newspaper *Le Petit Journal*. Reprinted by permission of Bibliotheque Nationale de France.

were young and strong, harboring all the noble aspirations that inspire me in the battle for the development of our race. What a bitter and sad thing this suffering and the grief triply and brutally inflicted upon our unfortunate family.

But God in allowing the executioners to accomplish their impious and cruel act no doubt leaves us with a pious task to accomplish even in the midst of our anguish and tears. We must internalize the virile intentions of which our dearly departed—patriots and martyrs—gave unsurpassable evidence and we should live only to satisfy what their heroic sacrifice claims of our dignity and our courage. It is in joining my heart with yours that I affectionately press your hands and that I assure you that the name Coicou (except for the traitor) will be eternally sacred to me; to mine and to all the friends of our noble cause.

Believe that I am, dear compatriots and
friends, your cordially devoted
Anténor Firmin

Translated by Nadève Ménard

The Luders Affair

Solon Ménos

Solon Ménos was a prominent politician in late nineteenth-century Haiti, serving in a range of government positions including minister of justice, minister of foreign affairs, and foreign minister to Washington, DC. In this excerpt he offers an account of the Luders Affair, which crystallized conflicts between German merchants, the German government, and Haiti, and meditates on the need for a strong national consciousness in the country to resist the incursions of foreign governments.

Emile Luders was of German and Haitian ancestry. In 1897, police came to arrest his coachman Dorléus Présumé, and Luders tried to stop them. He was arrested and put in prison, and requested help from the German embassy. The conflict escalated over several months, and Germany ultimately dispatched warships into the Port-au-Prince harbor to force his release. This kind of "gunboat diplomacy" was strikingly common during the nineteenth century. Many foreign businessmen in Haiti used the threat of their respective nations' naval force to their financial advantage. In 1872, for instance, during the presidency of Nissage Saget, the German Captain Basch captured two Haitian ships and held two Haitian citizens hostage, demanding reparations for German businessmen who had suffered financial losses in Haiti. The Haitian president paid the sum demanded, and the Germans returned the Haitian ships, but not before defecating on the Haitian flag. And in 1902, Germans intervened in the conflict between Firmin and Nord Alexis, providing ammunition to Alexis. The Luders Affair, then, was but one chapter that bolstered the financial and political prominence of German descendants in Haitian society. It also illustrates the ways that foreign extraction of wealth from the island nation contributed to the demise of Haiti's finances.

Ménos's analysis of the event represents a broader attempt to grapple with the history and impact of foreign intervention in Haiti over the course of the nineteenth century.

Upon returning home, I became lost in thought pondering the reasons that had dictated to the diplomatic agent his sudden and quite irregular determination. Amid my reflections, the memory of the Batsch affair suddenly reared its head. The facts are known and it is not necessary to relate nor to recall the unanimous indignation that swept across the country when we learned how, following an ultimatum addressed to the Haitian government in the name of the German Empire by the ship captain Batsch, "expedition chief," for the payment of an indemnity of three thousand sterling pounds in favor of German subjects Dickmann and Stapenhorst, the frigates *Vineta* and *Gazelle* had surprised us at nightfall, and seized two Haitian dispatch boats. The indemnity was but a pretext. The real accusation was that we had loudly demonstrated sympathy for France during the 1870 war. We were anxious, sad and revolted on hearing the news of the disasters that fell upon that tired and suffering, but noble country, felt boundless hopelessness when faced with its definitive defeat and its inevitable dismemberment. We sang a "mourning hymn"—echoing the general emotion—in which the poet Oswald Durand reproached Napoleon I for not having broken

That haughty Prussia and struck from the map

Its name and its past

It was natural, for the government at the time protested against the act of violence committed on 11 June 1872 and "denounced these facts to all nations of the globe." It was natural for it to proclaim that it was time to "tighten our ranks, chase from our hearts all resentment, in order to foster an invincible resistance to attacks that might be made against our nationality." Naturally the people leapt at the insult, blustered, grumbled, and naturally everyone— the rulers and the ruled—then promptly forgot. Paul and Victor Margueritte recently said that in France, people only remember at set times. In Haiti, we do not remember the foreigner's affronts at all. But oh! Wouldn't even a periodic reminder of the humiliations that have befallen our Republic so many times be useful? Shouldn't we use the painful anniversaries of these crises, which are so lethal to our pride, as a kind of virile education? Wouldn't this at least have the virtue of uniting those of us who, pulsing with tireless hope, persist in believing in civic duty, the efficacy of sacrifice, and the possibility of reparation, at the foot of the national flag, dressed in mourning?

Alas! Our indignations have no tomorrows, our patriotic anger evaporates in a blink, the next day there is no trace of the terrible tearing of our bruised and lacerated souls. Somehow a kind of complacency and a series of compromises soon restore the subjects of the very nations who insulted us yesterday, and will do so again tomorrow, to positions of power. They gorge once again with all the lifeblood of a country whose governments will probably end up commissioning them as pawnbrokers.

In truth, since the Batsch affair, the agents accredited to Port-au-Prince by the German empire had generally been correct in their relations with us, maintaining a strict neutrality between the internal parties whose silly blindness had too often bloodied the Haitian territory to the benefit of exotic agitators. . . . Following the deplorable bad habits of the preceding regime, the people became used to seeing the foreigner sojourning in Haiti as a beneficiary or, at the very least, an aspiring beneficiary. But we must acknowledge that many of those who receive the most straightforward hospitality here all too often end up being the instigators of our discords; with the objective of extreme exploitation, they become stakeholders and usurers in insurrections, and since they always have a claim at the end of the riot or revolution, the Republic's weakness or its rulers' weakness seems to inevitably make them the nurslings of our civil wars.

In light of such actions, which have the tendency to become a habit, we can honestly fear that a general concession of the right to property to foreigners might ultimately become a new source of revenue, drawn from state funds, for these beneficiaries—who are waiting for just such a development.

Translated by Nadève Ménard

Anti-Syrian Legislation

Haitian Legislature

Over the course of the nineteenth century, immigrants came to Haiti from the Middle East, mostly from the region that is today Lebanon. In Haiti they came to be known as "Syrians." Many worked first as street vendors, but in time they established themselves as owners of shops and other businesses. But their integration into Haitian society was not an easy one. Established businesspeople in Haiti, including French and German merchants, saw their arrival as a threat to their established commercial activity. Through family networks, many Syrian merchants developed connections with the United States (including securing U.S. passports), which facilitated the Syrian community's ability to begin importing goods from the United States that competed with European products in Haiti. These commercial tensions led to attacks on the Syrian community. A small newspaper, L'Anti-Syrien, was even published in the late nineteenth century with financial backing from foreign groups. As the following law shows, at times the Haitian government also saw the presence of these immigrants and their descendants as a threat.

LAW OF AUGUST 10TH 1903 RELATING TO SYRIANS

The Legislature

Using the initiative accorded to it by Article 69 of the Constitution;

Considering that the arrival en masse of individuals said to be Syrians or so-called in the popular language, far from remaining a moderate immigration, is taking on the proportions of a true invasion;

That their very high number demands the attention of the public authorities and can be the source of grave dangers;

That conflicts have already arisen between them and nationals; and each day more threaten to develop;

Considering that the Syrians, in only undertaking commercial operations, do not provide any service to the nation deserving of the State's solicitude; that an experience of almost fifteen years has not shown the benefits that the Haitian nation receives from their presence on its land; that no fusion seems to be possible between their respective customs, and that they form within the Republic something akin to a foreign state;

Considering that one of the main duties of a government is to protect its nationals, and to facilitate their livelihoods and to improve their living conditions;

That all the laws on direct taxes from 1804 to 1904 guaranteed preferential treatment to national trade, justified by the inferior state in which the social condition of the Haitian people placed it at the time, its lack of capital and the sacred obligation to ensure that it receive the benefits of Independence;

With regard to articles 4 of the Constitution and 14 of the civil code;

With regard to the laws of October 27th 1876 and August 3rd 1900 on direct taxation;

Following the Senate's proposal,

Voted the following law:

Art. 1. From the promulgation of the present law, no individual said to be Syrian or so-called in the popular language will be admitted to the territory of the Republic. Any Syrian, who, with the objective of circumventing the law, should leave the country to return with an act of naturalization, will not be admitted to the territory of the Republic either. On penalty of dismissal, ministers, chargé d'affaires, Haitian consuls abroad are forbidden from delivering passports to any of them, except those carrying a passport from the Haitian government.

Any head of movement at the port who has gone against the dispositions of the present article, by allowing Syrians to land without passports, or even with irregular passports, will be placed in police court and punished by a fine of two hundred gourdes.

Art. 2. From now on, no license will be accorded to a Syrian by the President of Haiti to establish a commercial establishment other than that of co-signatory trader.

Art. 3. Licenses accorded until now to Syrians to practice trade in a capacity other than that of cosignatory traders will not be renewed.

A deadline of six months, expiring at the end of the year is accorded to them to liquidate and close their wholesale and retail commercial establishments.

Art. 4. It is forbidden for any Syrian in possession of the license to have more than one commercial establishment.

Art. 5. Any Syrian who should undertake a business without having a patent and license or who should be caught practicing the profession of junk seller, hawker, foodstuff speculator, or any other retail business will be hit with a fine of five hundred dollars and punished by an imprisonment of three to six months. Repeat offenders will be expelled from the territory of the Republic.

Art. 6. Any Communal magistrate who would have delivered to a Syrian a patent to which the latter has no right or without requiring him to show his license:

Any commune commander who would have let establish or circulate in his commune Syrians to practice a trade that is forbidden to them by law will be subject to removal from office and a fine of two hundred gourdes.

A patent thusly delivered will be legally void.

Art. 7. Pending the promulgation of a law on naturalization, henceforth, no naturalization shall be accorded to Syrians until after a period of ten years in the Republic's territory.

Art. 8. Any customs director who would have verified merchandise for a Syrian without first verifying that he has the patent and license required by law will be removed from office and punished by a fine of five hundred dollars.

Art. 9. Upon promulgation of the present law, the State Secretary of the Interior will publish in the *Moniteur Officiel*:

(1) The list of naturalized Syrians, their date of naturalization, their place of residence;

(2) The list of those who asked for and received the license from the President of Haiti to practice trade in Haiti.

Art. 10. Any Syrian who would have tried to break the law, by presenting to Haitian authorities a naturalization act, a patent or a license delivered to another than himself will be hit with a fine of five hundred dollars and punished by an imprisonment of six months to a year.

Repeat offenders will be expelled from the territory of the Republic.

Art. 11. The present law abrogates all laws or law provisions contrary to it. It will be executed with the diligence of the State Secretaries of the Interior, of Finances and of Commerce, of Foreign Relations and of Justice, each for that which concerns him.

Given at the national house,
in Port-au-Prince, July 24th 1903,
100th year of Independence.
Senate President, STEWART

. . .

In the name of the Republic

The President of Haiti orders that the above law of the Legislature be stamped with the Republic's seal, published, printed and applied.

Given at the National Palace,
in Port-au-Prince, August 13th,
100th year of independence.
NORD ALEXIS

Translated by Nadève Ménard

Choucoune

Oswald Durand

Oswald Durand, author of "Chant national" (see above), also wrote one of the earliest and most famous poems in Haitian Creole. Durand's poem tells the story of a young Haitian woman who rejects her Haitian suitor in favor of a white foreigner. As such, it speaks to the ways in which tensions around class and race impacted relationships in the country. "Choucoune" was put to music by Michel Mauléart Monton in 1893. The poem is better known internationally through its English-language adaptation as the song "Yellow Bird," interpreted by various musicians, including Harry Belafonte.

Behind a big shrub,
The other day I met Choucoune;
She smiled when she saw me,
I said: "Heavens, what beauty!"
She said: "You think so, dear?"
Little birds were listening to us above
When I remember it, I am in pain,
For ever since that day, my two feet are in chains!

Choucoune was a marabout:
Her eyes were bright as candles
She had perky breasts
Oh, if only Choucoune were faithful!
We talked for a long time . . .
Even the birds in the woods seemed happy.
Better forget that, it's too much pain,
For ever since that day, my two feet are in chains!

Choucoune's little teeth are white as milk,
Her mouth the color of star apples.
She's not a fat woman, she's plump
Women like that please me right away
Yesterday is not today

Charles Alexis Oswald
Durand (1840–1906).
Photo courtesy of
CIDHICA.

Birds heard every word she said
If they remember it, they are most likely in pain
For ever since that day, my two feet are in chains.

We went to her mother's house
An honest old woman,
As soon as she saw me, she said:
He pleases me very much
We drank hot cocoa with cashews
Is it all over, little birds in the woods?
Better forget it, it's much too painful
For ever since that day my two feet are in chains

Furniture was ready, nice sleigh bed
Wicker chairs, round table, rocking chair
Two mattresses, a hat stand,
Tablecloths, towels, chiffon curtains
Only fifteen days remained . . .
Little birds in the woods, hear this, listen!

You will understand if I am in pain
If ever since that day my two feet are in chains

A white man showed up
Red beard, nice pink face
Watch at his side, pretty hair
He is the cause of my troubles
He found Choucoune beautiful
He spoke French, Choucoune loved him
Better forget it, it's much too painful
Choucoune left me, my two feet are in chains!

What is even sadder in all this
What will surprise everyone
Is to see that in spite of the time that's passed
I still love Choucoune!
She will have a little quadroon . . .
Little birds, look, her little tummy is nice and round!
Hush! Close your beak. It's much too painful:
Ti Pierre's two feet, his two feet are in chains!

Translated by Nadève Ménard

Bouqui's Bath

Suzanne Comhaire-Sylvain

Bouqui and Malice ("Bouki ak Malis" in Creole) are two recurring figures in Haitian folktales. In 1940, pioneer anthropologist Suzanne Comhaire-Sylvain gathered fifty of these tales into a book entitled Le roman de Bouqui. *They were all collected from Haitian peasants. In the book's introduction, Comhaire-Sylvain seeks to establish the similarities between the Haitian folktales and those from Africa, Europe, and across the Americas.*

In "Bouqui's Bath," the storyteller introduces Bouqui and Malice, explaining the relationship between them and describing their principal characteristics. This tale sets the tone for the rest of the book, introducing readers to a Bouqui who is physically strong, but not too bright, and speaks with a lisp. Malice is younger and smaller than Bouqui, but also much smarter. "Bouqui's Bath" contains many elements of traditional rural Haitian culture, with allusions to farming, market days, traditional medicine, and a heightened sense of community.

Cric? Crac!

In those times, Bouqui was very young. Along with his nephew Malice, he lived with his old grandmother who had raised both of them. There are people who say, when they tell this story, that the old lady was his mother. They're wrong. I knew them all at the time: there was Mrs. Bouqui, whom the kids lived with, and then in another village, there was her daughter Mrs. Gaïnedé, who was Bouqui's mother. Mrs. Gaïnedé had married her eldest daughter to Mr. Guianacou, father of the young Malice kids who lived in a third village. Bouqui carried his grandfather's name, whom he strongly favored. That's why people today when they hear about Mrs. Bouqui think she's Bouqui's mother and not his grandmother. They also don't know that Malice never belonged to the Bouqui family: he was raised by them, but was the son of Guianacou with another woman.

So, Mrs. Bouqui had become very old, she was weak and semiparalyzed. The two children helped her and kept her company: Bouqui, who was bigger, stayed with her to serve the clients at the corner store, and little Malice went to the market to sell produce from the garden or the farmyard and stock up on provisions. Bouqui was very dumb. He always needed someone to guide him and tell him what to do. That's why Mrs. Bouqui had taken the habit of keeping him near her. Malice, on the other hand, was the smartest kid in the area. She would thus send him far, sure that he would never let others take advantage of him.

One day, Mrs. Bouqui fell ill. She had such a high fever that she did not recognize the children and kept talking about things that made no sense. An old neighbor came to see her in the morning and in the evening and Malice was careful to follow the prescribed treatment faithfully. Tuesday came and she was not doing any better. But Tuesday was market day. Malice said to Bouqui:

"I have to go buy provisions for the week. I also have to sell the little goat. You will take care of Grandmother. Look, I've prepared the leaves for her bath. When the sun gets to be above the palm tree, you will put water on the fire. When the water is hot, you will pour it onto the leaves, you will add cold water until it's warm. Then you will give Grandmother a bath. Remember, the neighbor said: 'a warm bath.'"

Malice left. Bouqui set up in the little store after having put the water on the fire. There were no clients that morning and the child was bored. He decided to move up bath time.

He poured several buckets of cold water in the tub, then he ran to call his grandmother. Since she didn't seem to understand, he picked her up (he was very strong) and placed her in the tub. Then he went to get the water that he had put on to heat and poured a pot of boiling water over the poor woman. Mrs. Bouqui made a horrible grimace and without a word, without a cry, passed from life to death.

Her grandson did not understand the meaning of this teeth-baring grimace and asked her:

"Do you want your pipe? Aren't you pleased with your little Bouqui's bath?"

She did not respond at all. He brought her her pipe and kindly placed it between her teeth himself.

"I am leaving you, Grandmother. I'm going to watch the store. You'll call me when you want to get out, right?"

When Malice returned, he immediately asked:

"What about Grandmother, Bouqui? Does she need anything?"

"Grandmother is so happy with her bath that she doesn't want to get out. I told her to call me, she never called. If you see her with her pipe, she is smiling nonstop!"

Worried, Malice ran to the room. The old lady was already stiff. He cried out.

"Bouqui! You killed Grandmother!"

"I didn't touch her. She died by herself! Woy, woy!"

They both started to shout. The neighbors ran over, took care of the deceased and alerted the family. That was a very long time ago! It was never forgotten, however. The accident made a big impression on everyone. Ever since then, we prefer to heat water for baths in the sun and if it happens that the doctor says to heat it over fire, we always put a hand in the water to check the temperature. It is also since then that we say about a bath that's too hot: it's a Bouqui bath.

Translated by Nadève Ménard

Zoune at Her Godmother's

Justin Lhérisson

Justin Lhérisson's "Zoune at Her Godmother's" ("Zoune chez sa ninnaine"), first published in 1906, is an example of the Haitian literary genre called audience *in French, or* lodyans *in Creole, and popularized by Lhérisson in its written form. This literary form uses humor and inflections of oral storytelling to make incisive social commentary.*

"Zoune at Her Godmother's" is a short tale that narrates how a young girl from the countryside transitions to life in the city. The comparisons between rural and urban life are particularly astute, but the main focus is on the particular problems faced by girls and women. The work is subtitled "Fanm gen sèt so pou li pase," which roughly translates to "Women Have Seven Trials to Overcome." During the course of the work, Zoune is harassed and eventually violated by a character named Cadet Jacques. This name has become synonymous with rape, the word for which is kade-jak in Haitian Creole. Indeed, a distinctive aspect of Lhérisson's fiction writing is his use of Haitian Creole interspersed with French. We have left many of these original terms, notably for food and plants, in the original italics in order to communicate the flavor and style of the work.

Zoune's father was a short peasant, with broad shoulders, solidly built. He had the look of a "bocor," with thick, tangled hair. He was known for his endurance when it came to work. No one could manage the hoe or the *couteaudigo* like him, with his hard and calloused hands.

The soles of his feet were an oddity; more solid, more resistant than the best cowhide leather. They crushed the spokes of *acacia* and *bayahonde*, whose dangerous points never dared sting him. So he went barefoot in the crabinages and the thickets.

Very talkative with his people, he was excessively shy in the presence of strangers, especially people from the city. He could barely talk to them: he invariably answered the questions they asked him with a bunch of "yeses." He only added an *apisollement* or a *ce parole* to break the monotony of his speech. In truth, with his side-eyed looks, he was a *madré compère*. Beneath the rough exterior of a Bouqui, he hid the soul of a Ti Malice.

He owned three *carreaux* of land. He inherited one and earned the other two through his sweat and hard work. Since he had as many *menagères* as there were days in the week, he had divided his property, and had given a parcel to each one, of which they were in charge and cultivated for themselves. He had only reserved for himself a garden planted with fruit trees, with coffee plants, with cassava and yams—and a *barré* of guinea grass. The only payment he asked for from his *maman-pitites* was drink, food, and bed. When they were in service, they all applied themselves with much devotion, since they were all fighting to keep him at home. They had even consulted witches to bring about such a happy ending. In spite of the *précipité*, of which they made great use, their man did not sway to one side or the other. In fact, he showed more love and more devotion to his parcel of land than to any of them. He loved it above all else. In the morning, at the time of day when the chickens came down from the trees, that was where he headed with his steps, his hoe on his shoulder, his machete in hand. It was there that he hid, enclosed in a calabash, his titles, his *d'Haiti*, *gourdins*, and *calins*. Rain or shine, it was the land that he worked or planted. Often, at high noon, bare-chested, with only a straw hat on his head, he weeded, *balisait, brulait le bois-neuf*, or dried coffee on the *glacis*.

This hard worker was the thirteenth son of Tichéry Bodio. Although the name on his birth certificate was Ismael Tichéry, he was called Maréchal Ticoq. He never complained about that nickname. On the contrary, he was very attached to it.

That was because he probably did not want it forgotten that, for some time, he had held rank in our rural constabulary, and therefore no one in his section could more justifiably claim the title of "cock."

"As for that!" his beak was solid and prompt; also, in any little skirmish, he used his preferred strike, the strike of his *lière*. . . .

You would be surprised at the extent to which I am interested in these small naming issues. They are sometimes very amusing riddles. I admit that I find it very entertaining. If our Ticoq, TiCrabe, Tizo put me in a good mood, I positively chuckle in the presence of our Napoleons, who, annoyed at not resembling, even in profile, the Corsican with flat hair, come to you one fine morning and say: "From now on, our name is Lindor," that is when they don't send you the announcement columns from the newspaper in which they ask the public to consider them as Jacques the elder, Jules Cadet, Charles fils, or Mentor jeune . . . with the same last name.

In our countryside, these name changes are common to the point of making it difficult to establish a person's identity or to write their genealogical tree: one error, an infirmity, some infidelity can promptly debaptize a man. Add to that the fact that we can easily be induced into error by the words "uncle," "brother," and "cousin" to which our peasants give an extensive meaning. Any old man for them is a grandparent; they call him indistinctly, with the respect due to white hair, tonton or uncle; they embrace with the same love their brothers of baptism and those of the same womb or blood; finally, they call each other cousins among themselves.

Generally, in these rural centers, names are nicknames, "play names" or shortened names, "revenge names" or war names. Without such explanations, could you have understood that Zoune, in reality, should be called Zétrenne Bodio and Maréchal Ticoq, Ismael Tichéry Bodio?

Would you believe me on the other hand, if I tell you that the malicious residents of Pays pourri found a way to turn Zoune's mother from Chérise Boisblanc into Sor Poum?

Yes, my friend, it is by that strange noise that they called that peasant woman, and, what is even more shocking, she bravely accepted the nickname and wore it "with no noise, no trouble."

There's one that would fit in in the court of King Pétaud!

To see Sor Poum's vacant eyes, her calm face where was flattened a nose with large nostrils: to consider her savage and embarrassed air, to hear her weak and whiny voice, you'd think she was incapable of killing a flea. However, never had appearance been more misleading. Of Ticoq's wives, she was the most cunning, the most enterprising, the most intelligent. She knew very well how to count on her fingers, or with the help of grains of corn or beans; she sold rotten eggs for fresh ones; in her calabash of palma-christi oil, she always poured some syrup; her bag of coffee contained at least five pounds of small stones that imitated the color of that bean; finally, in her way, she responded, an eye for an eye, tooth for tooth to the disloyal practices of the cityfolk who, speculating on the ignorance of our peasants, saving for them all they have that is inferior, falsified or *zabrigay,* that is when they do not apply to them, in buying their foodstuff, a special arithmetic whose beauty shines in this extremely fantastical math: 9 times 9 = 42, we give 4 but we carry nothing.

Sor Poum only allowed her man to lead her around willy-nilly; Ticoq alone was her lord and master; before this robust male she was nothing but a passive and respectful female; pregnant or nursing (these two states forever alternating) she harnessed to work like a donkey. Every day, bright and early, followed by a line of her little troop of brats, some completely naked, the others in *tanga,* she went to draw water at the nearby source or to get dry wood in the forest, then she went to the field.

Once or twice a month, you could find her by the river washing smocks, pants, camisoles, and jackets with powerful strikes from a racket.

At harvest time, she was the one who went into town. With her tireless feet, she would walk miles and miles. Preceded by her beast of burden, holding its long halter, carrying on her head a basket filled with fruit and provisions, she walked over rutted and rocky roads. People were surprised to see her walking so easily, for she also had a child sitting astride on her hips and held on to her back by a piece of cloth whose ends formed a solid knot beneath her sagging breasts.

She never spent more than a day in Port-au-Prince. Her foodstuff sold, she put her money in a big *saquitte* stuffed in her blouse, its cord passed around her neck. She would touch it, open it, close it from time to time. If by some misfortune, a "gourdin" happened to be missing, she would frighten an entire crowd with her noisy lamentations.

Calmly, she took care of errands; without rushing she would also take care of the shopping. And what shopping?

Her provisions consisted almost entirely of the following articles: salt, one or two "marques" of codfish, or of *petit-salé*; cow or lamb *suif*; packets of *afibas*; occasionally a kerchief from India or a few lengths of *gros bleu* or *ginga*. But she would invariably bring for her brood some *bonbon-sirop* or *doucounou* and to her Ticoq one or two vials of rum or a measure of *mannoc* tobacco (it's the city of New York that suffered this transformation).

She reserved the *cacaboeufs* and the candy canes for her little Zoune, so frail and so scrubby.

Indeed, the poor child had a deplorable complexion. She was always sick. Instead of getting her the care required by her condition, her parents, superstitious to the nth degree, preferred to put around her neck a *rangé* necklace, made of knotted string, and to plunge her twice a day in a repulsive-smelling bath. As far as they were concerned, Zoune was under the influence of bad air. They insisted to the hearing of people in the neighborhood, of whom they suspected a few, that it was indeed zombies, hairless pigs, who, with the help of an invisible calumet, sucked their daughter's blood from a distance.

You could not get that out of their heads. Thus, each night, to ward off those demons, they would burn bull horns and *assa-foetida* and they would throw onto the roof of their shack salt and some grains of *hoholi*. . . .

Since this foolishness brought no change, Sor Poum, following her grandmother's advice, decided to have the child baptized. It was more than about time: Zoune must have been more than ten years old.

Translated by Nadève Ménard and Laurent Dubois

The Haytian Question

Hannibal Price

*Haitian intellectuals have long been preoccupied with the question of how to guaran-
tee and protect Haitian sovereignty and independence in the context of foreign pres-
sures and intervention. In his classic text* The Haytian Question, *Hannibal Price,
then Haitian ambassador to the United States, examines the controversy surrounding
Washington's attempt to establish a naval base and coaling station at Mole Saint-
Nicolas in 1891. The U.S. ambassador to Haiti at the time was the ex-slave Frederick
Douglass, who was deeply respected by the Haitian population. Nevertheless, President Florvil Hyppolite's administration, particularly the minister of foreign relations,
Anténor Firmin, remained steadfast in their refusal to cede land to the United States,
considering such a gesture an unacceptable surrendering of sovereignty. Price's work
places these events in Haiti within the broader context of an emerging U.S. technical,
military, and commercial dominance in the Caribbean and Central America in the
late nineteenth century. It also positions them as part of a longer history of foreign
aggression against the Haitian state.*

Hayti, it is scarcely necessary to remark, is a nation numbering not over a
million inhabitants, as against the sixty-four millions of the United States: in
view of which fact it would seem clear enough that whatever the Washington Government might see fit to ask, the "black republic" could not oppose a
refusal without laying itself open to the charge of insolence.

Nevertheless, it is to be observed that the little nation of the Antilles is not
the only one in the New World whose strength is in pitiful disproportion to
that of the United States; she is not the only one which may have to look up
to the colossus of the North, and to ask herself what she may expect from that
quarter, good or ill.

The *Haytian Question,* then should be regarded as of a nature to create a
precedent, the importance of which the other American nations, particularly
the more feeble ones, will not fail to recognize, inasmuch as it affords a guarantee of what they may hope from the *sincerity* and *integrity* of the people of
the United States.

Mr. Blaine, or Mr. Harrison, and the Government, may shape their exterior policy as they see fit—that is not the most important point in the rela-

163

tions of the United States with foreign peoples. For these latter, the capital question is entirely in the *American public opinion*; and of this opinion, the press is, or ought to be, the organ. It is known, abroad, that the American people are sincerely republican, profoundly imbued with the democratic spirit; and that, consequently, no international action ought to be taken by the Government without the popular consent.

. . .

It is also known,—or, at least, it has been always believed—that American public opinion is generally on the side of justice and truth; and for this reason the other nations of the New World have been accustomed to regard the growing power of the United States as a protection, rather than a menace. For this reason the Monroe Doctrine has been ever regarded, throughout Latin America, not only as an assurance against European intervention in cis-Atlantic affairs, but above all as an efficacious guarantee of independence to the old-time colonies. In a word, this is the reason why the Monroe Doctrine of the United States has had the enthusiastic adhesion of all the other American nations.

Is it now to be revealed to these Latin colonies, to these younger American nations—who also have shed their blood in external and internal strife to win a place in the sunlight of freedom, and to assure to themselves the benefits of a democratic regime—is it now to be revealed to them that the Monroe Doctrine is a fallacy, a mirage, serving but to withdraw them from all political relations, from any friendship with the great European powers, so that they may be the more completely isolated and left defenseless against foreign covetousness, and under the domination of the United States? Are they to behold the republic of Washington, of Franklin, of Hamilton, passing insensibly into the condition of a *conquering nation*, and abdicating the proud part it has hitherto played in the world's history in conforming to the spirit of its founders, who meant to make it "the hearthstone of liberty"? No! It is not to be believed that such a deviation from the old principles of the Union is possible in the minds of the American people.

Loud has been the clamor about the "breach of faith" on the part of President Hyppolite, who, it is alleged, first promised and then refused to cede the Mole Saint-Nicolas to the United States. There is complaint, moreover, of this "ingratitude," and of the "insolence" or "ill will" of his government toward that of the United States.

We will examine, presently, these divers points, and get at the truth of the matter, supported by the official documents; but let this principle be recognized, to begin with, that throughout this affair two *sovereign nations*, independent of one another, are engaged, the one of which is in possession of an object that the other wishes to acquire. The United States, the nation making the demand, is beside the other, Hayti, like a giant beside a child. But is it not at this time, more than ever, that sincerity and loyalty of conduct should be a question of the national dignity? Whatever the disproportion of the two nations, they are nonetheless, in their relations towards one another, two absolutely sovereign States.

Now, if there is one undisputed principle of modern international law, it is that the sovereignty of a State, consisting *essentially* in the independence of all foreign influence in the exercise of the rights of sovereignty, *ought*, by its very nature, to be exercised not only without regard to the age of the State, to the form of its constitution or government, to the established order of succession to the throne or the seat of executive power, to the rank and title of the State or its sovereign, but also "without taking into account the extent of its territory, its population, its political importance, its customs and religion, the condition of its general culture, the commerce of its people, etc., etc."

In virtue of this principle, the Haytian people, unable to support any comparison whatever with the United States, should be permitted, by right of their very feebleness, to count more particularly upon the equity and the chivalry of Americans.

However insignificant in the extent of its territory, the number of its population, and in its political importance, the Republic of Hayti, like all the other American republics, is in possession of a dearly bought independence. She is jealous of this independence, and of the integrity of her territory. Her just desire is to remain a sovereign republic, and not to become a dependent one.

Surely the American people would not, in the honesty of their conscience and the depth of their democratic convictions, make a crime of the Haytians' patriotism, their attachment to their national independence and the integrity of their territory.

It is to be remarked here, that, in order to mislead American opinion upon this story of the Mole Saint-Nicolas, there has been, and still is, in the utterances of political circles, a lack of frankness as to the exact nature of the demands made upon the Haytian Government.

How is it that the press of the United States, whose mission it should be to enlighten the people upon the veritable sense and import of the acts of the national Government, has in this instance failed in its duty? Certainly not for want of the official documents, communicated to Congress, and published by the Federal Government itself. Why has this same press supplemented the unfair reproaches and false insinuations upon the affair of the Mole Saint-Nicolas, with violent attacks upon the past history of the Republic of Hayti, and against the negro race, with gross and ridiculous insults to President Hyppolite? It is a curious problem, not to be solved at the present moment. But if this be not the time for investigating such a question, it may be proper to take a calm and dispassionate survey of essential points, as follows:

. . .

1st. To re-establish the historic verity regarding the alleged promise of cession of the Mole Saint-Nicolas, said to have been made by President Hyppolite to Mr. Bayard, Secretary of State under the Cleveland administration. (So-called Elie mission. Mission of Dr. Auguste Nemours.)

2nd. To say a few words as to what has been characterized as the intervention of the United States in Haytian affairs.

3rd. To present the real story of the Môle, and to make known the exact nature of the demand addressed to the Government of Hayti by the Washington Government under the Harrison-Blaine administration (Douglass-Gherardi mission).

4th. To state why this demand had to be refused by the Haitian Government.

5th. To furnish some indications as to the parties or factions in the Republic of Hayti; and, in replying to certain accusations, to endeavor to ascertain what, from our point of view, would be the policy most desirable for the United States to pursue towards the Government of General Hyppolite.

Appended to this pamphlet will be found, moreover, the text of the principal official documents, in support of the explanation and statements herein submitted.

African Americans Defend Haiti

Ebenezer Don Carlos Bassett

At the beginning of the Civil War in the United States, in 1862, Massachusetts sena-
tor Charles Sumner pushed through a bill offering diplomatic recognition to the na-
tions of Haiti and Liberia. African Americans celebrated the reversal of a policy of
nonrecognition toward Haiti, which had been put in place by Thomas Jefferson in
1804. Many among them had long seen Haiti as a beacon of racial equality and black
progress. Ebenezer Don Carlos Bassett (1833–1908), who was of mixed black, white,
and Indian heritage, took particular interest in the newly recognized Black Republic.
In 1869, Bassett became the consul general and minister resident to Haiti and the
United States' first black diplomat. He later served as Frederick Douglass's secretary
and interpreter in Haiti. His sympathy for Haitians and skilled diplomacy also led to
his appointment as Haiti's consul general in New York.

Throughout his diplomatic career, Bassett wrote about Haitian history, contempo-
rary Haitian politics, and the unique bond between African Americans and Haitians.
In 1904, when a U.S. senator introduced a resolution advocating the annexation of
Haiti, he responded with this passionate defense of Haitian sovereignty, published in
an African American newspaper.
—Contributing Editor: Brandon Byrd

To sum up the whole question as I have presented it, repeating myself here
somewhat, it appears,

1st. That the fixed policy of the United States from their beginning has
been against the extension of their dominion over territory lying beyond in-
tervening seas; the annexation of Hawaii in 1894 (brought about by means
which will, in all probability, never again be employed or even tolerated toward any other country), being the only exception to the rule, and there is
very high authority for the general statement, that in a broad sense, conditions which have long existed, are likely to continue.

2nd. That the altogether unfavorable reception accorded to the resolutions
presented in the Senate of the United States as lately as November and December last on the annexation of Cuba and San Domingo and Haiti, as well
as the authoritative, public declaration of the Assistant Secretary of State in
the New York Independent of March 3rd, 1904, that "there is no thought and

no possibility of the annexation of San Domingo," tends to show, at least, that annexation is not within the scope of the policy of this government for the near future.

3rd. That, nevertheless, it is well to keep an eye open for the first dawning or the dim approach in the distance of possible future contingencies in lines leading out toward annexation.

4th. That the government and the people of Haiti are, and for one hundred years have been, an inflexible, indivisible unit against every possible scheme insidious and otherwise, for the alienation of any part of their territory and independence. It can be safely set down as a positive fact that Haiti does not now and in all probability, never will desire or consent to share her sovereignty with any other power whatsoever.

Furthermore, Haiti is by far the most advanced, the most important and the best established of the only three Republics in the world, where alone the Negro race has full and untrammeled liberty to develop its faculties and its possibilities.

As a general rule, American publications speak only evil of Haiti. This is wholly unfair. If we look back at the real condition of things existing in Haiti at the time when she achieved her independence, her cities and villages, her roads, her industries, her aqueducts, her mills, her plantations, her commerce, her families and fortunes, all in ruins from the desolations of several years of war, so that she had to begin her life from nothing—if we look back at all this and then turning to her as she is today, consider the gigantic difficulties which she has had to meet and overcome in order to maintain her independence, I think that there can be no question that her growth and development intellectually, morally, and materially have been in every way remarkable and merit at least the considerate and generous judgment of mankind.

Should Haiti then be annexed to the United States? Should either one be called upon to do that which is repugnant to both? Why, no, no! Let Haiti alone; let her alone to work out her mission for the children of Africa in the New World and to fulfill her destiny among the Nations of the Earth.

On the Caribbean Confederation

Anténor Firmin

Anténor Firmin was a prolific intellectual and political figure who profoundly shaped Haiti's nineteenth-century culture and the then-emerging field of modern anthropology. Firmin's most famous work, The Equality of the Human Races *(1885), is largely known as his response to Count de Arthur Gobineau's two-volume work* The Inequality of the Human Races *(1853–55). He also wrote widely about Caribbean development and foreign relations and was an ardent supporter of Pan-American ideals. This excerpt from* Lettres de St. *Thomas (1910), written after he went into exile following his political struggle with Nord Alexis, explores the possibilities for Pan-Caribbean unity. Firmin seeks to imagine a way to address and overcome the many divisions in the region, so that Caribbean societies can collectively address their stark economic difficulties in the wake of emancipation. Firmin is clearly in dialogue with and inspired by his hispanophone intellectual contemporaries, such as José Martí of Cuba and Ramón Emeterio Betances of Puerto Rico. In this essay, titled "Haiti and the Caribbean Confederation," Firmin introduces his thoughts on Pan-American solidarity and includes correspondence to and from Latin American thinkers on the subject, including the Cuban writer F. Carvajal.*

Around the year 1880, there were a remarkable group of Latin Americans in Paris, almost all Spanish speakers. Educated men, enthusiastic about ideas of solidarity among Latin peoples, they were mainly influenced by the political freedom in America, the powerful leaven of all fine qualities and all the superior skills that render man fit to proudly wear the grand title of king of creation. Their dream was the intellectual and moral emancipation of all those whose growth is compressed by some external force, national despotism or colonial exploitation. They aspired to establish an international link between each Latin American nation in effort and in development.

How will we proceed? Could it be a constitutional and positive confederation that while respecting the national autonomy of constituent states, would create a center for leadership, a capital whose unifying actions would support a patriotic beam, their various moral and material interests, by projecting the spirit of order and rational progress, maintained by administrative discipline and legal uniformity? Would it simply be via an amphictyonic organization

Joseph Auguste Anténor Firmin (1850–1911). Photo courtesy of CIDHICA.

whose weakest link would nevertheless provide a means of normal and regular contact between the young American nations that belong to a different ethnicity than Anglo-Americans? Would it and could it have the same cohesive force as the ancient Greek amphictyony, which gained its religious and sacred character during the historical periods of ancient Hellas? . . .

Among these elite men, we must mention two names, the most famous, who were like stars in the meetings where the broad aspirations of a world of thinkers, writers, and scholars dominated. They are too little known, with a reputation below their true personal value. I refer to Torres-Caicedo, a diplomat, and Dr. Betances, a physician.

[Torres-Caicedo] . . . was the personification, so to speak, of the Spanish America that he embraced with equal and constant worship. On occasion, he took up the pen and lifted his voice in favor of Venezuela, Mexico, Chile, Peru, Argentina, and other South American republics, with a zeal similar to his efforts to defend his homeland, the former New Granada, currently the United States of Colombia. This character of a Spanish American patriot was sealed by the fact that Torres-Caicedo represented, either in Paris or London or Brussels, in turn, Venezuela, Colombia, and El Salvador, changing republics, without ever losing his national loyalty.

. . .

After the death of Torres-Caicedo, Doctor Betances—who had become the principal star by which were guided all the generous aspirations of the Latin race in America—became convinced that the confederation of all the states of South and Central America was a phenomenal and majestic conception, but one whose realization seemed impossible. Indeed, the chief sociological cause of political cohesion, which consists in the frequent, easy, and continuous contact of the federated peoples, would necessarily be lacking in this case, because of the immense extent of the countries, whose interior populations are not to be reached, except with great difficulty, even for the affairs of national existence. He thought, besides, that Puerto Rico and Cuba, freed from the sovereignty of Spain, would not be sufficient to constitute, separately, a power capable of making itself felt abroad. Thence sprang the idea of the confederation of the Antilles.

. . .

What distinguished individuals of Puerto Rico, Cuba, and the republics of Central and South America have I not met in the salon of the illustrious Antillean! Doctor Betances, after having read my book, *De l'égalité des races humaines,* manifested an esteem for me that at times surprised me very much, but which strengthened me in my ideas of progress and of the rehabilitation of the negro race. The truth is that there was between us an affinity of points of view and aspirations, which constituted a powerful and consistent bond, although I had less enthusiasm and fewer illusions than he as to the immediate realization of our patriotic ideals, which would have to pass through a long incubation the better to germinate in the countries in which they would have to sprout and grow. He never failed to introduce me with overwhelming eulogies to those that chanced to be present in his well-frequented salon. Even in my absence, whenever the problem of the Antilles came up for discussion, he cited me among those he believed to be destined to play an important part in this respect. This appreciation is certainly above my merits; but Doctor Betances's word has perhaps been enough for many to take it as an article of faith.

In 1893, I had occasion to confer with the incomparable José Martí in Cap Haïtien. The great patriot, upon whom a grateful Cuba later bestowed the title of apostle, presented himself in the name of Doctor Betances, who had recommended that he see me. Our meetings revolved around the great question of Cuban independence, and the possibility of an Antillean confederation. With the exception of certain practical reservations, we were in absolute accord as to principles. We were drawn to each other by an irresistible sympathy. Informed of the audacious enterprise that this man—eloquent, well-informed, inspired and of an unusually broad spirit, determined and

tenacious—was fostering, preparing and heralding, with the zeal of an il-
luminato and an apostolic devotion, I did what I ought to do everywhere on
behalf of a sacred cause.

. . .

During the same period the Cuban revolution had broken out, the stirring
events of which already form a part of contemporary history. Impressed by
the inhumane proceedings of General Weyler, who shut up women, children, and the elderly in places of confinement, where they died of hunger and
of every kind of deprivation—a measure decorated with the hateful name
of *reconcentración*—and, using the catastrophe of the *Maine*, blown up in the
bay of Havana, as pretext, the North Americans, "in the name of humanity,"
came to the aid of the revolutionaries of February 24, 1895, in a spontaneous
and popular movement, that swept up President McKinley after the congress
in Washington.

Puerto Rican patriots were stirred to an effervescent exaltation. When the
United States invaded the former Borinquén [Puerto Rico], they welcomed
the American troops as liberators. They too entertained hopes of national
independence and they conceived that it ought to be the logical result of the
termination of Spain's colonial domination. In Paris, Doctor Betances experienced a triumphant joy. He thought to behold at last the realization of a
dream, tenderly, ardently cherished for the almost thirty years that he had
lived far from his native soil, having sworn never to set foot upon it save as
free and independent.

Spain—after the destruction of Admiral Cervera's fleet, after the military
defeats sustained in the battles of El Caney, Guantánamo, Las Guéasimas,
Santiago de Cuba, and on the heights of San Juan de Puerto Rico—was forced
to withdraw from the Antilles; but, while Cuba, which had possessed the
energy and virility to raise the standard of revolt, was recognized as independent, Puerto Rico was released from Spanish domination only to fall into the
grasp of the United States.

When I read in the Charleston harbor (South Carolina), in the prelimi-
nary peace protocol between Spain and the United States, the clause of the
cession of Puerto Rico to the North Americans, I experienced the sensation
of something like a fatal blow, aimed at the heart of Doctor Betances, with
the irremediable failure of his long-cherished and patriotic hopes. I was not
deceived. Indeed, I found him, soon afterward in Paris, broken and prostrate,
more undermined by the overthrow of his generous aspirations than by the
disease from which he apparently suffered. Moved by a delicacy with which
hearts that have already suffered great disillusionments and that have loved
deeply are acquainted, I did not utter a word regarding the dénouement of
the bloody struggle between the successors of the Cid Campeador and the
descendants of the pilgrims, over the land lighted by the sun of the old Caribs. However, this very silence regarding the stirring events of the day was

one more sorrow. The martyrdom of thought is usually mute. There is a concentrated bitterness that the soul suffers with impassiveness when it is strong and brave, but the corrosive virtue of which eats it away and undermines it, just as the beak of the Jovian eagle tore out the entrails of Prometheus. He spoke no more, but he suffered frightfully, lamentably. Fortunately, his mortal agony did not last long. The first apostle of the Antillean evangel was extinguished silently in the throes of a supreme anguish.

. . .

Since then the dream of a confederation of the Antilles has always remained alive in a corner of my brain, but the idea causes me, whenever it presents itself, a sorrowful shiver. It inevitably reminds me of the two great deceased that were its distinguished champions—José Martí, who was killed by Spanish bullets at Dos Ríos, and Betances, wounded to death by a lack of generosity on the part of the United States.

. . .

The proselytic ardor that shines from the lines of Monsieur F. Carvajal proves that that idea of the Antillean confederation still burns in more than one Latin American brain. It holds a real ascendancy over those that in their enlightened conception experience a discerning desire to constitute in our Caribbean region an important state that shall have as a basis the ever closer union of the material and moral interests of these superb, verdant and fruitful islands, forever washed by the warm, blue, limpid, swaying waters of the sea of the Antilles. . . .

It was very agreeable to me to discover in Havana a swell of sympathy and admiration that seemed to belie the legend of a disdainful repulsion on the part of the white Cuban toward all persons that had in their veins even a small infusion of African blood. I am absolutely black, and, nevertheless, I received in the capital of Cuba an enthusiastic welcome unequaled by any offered to any other diplomat that has gone to that country. What, however, explains the great enthusiasm aroused by my presence, as the minister of Haiti, was—in addition to a literary and scientific reputation, disputable, perhaps—the sympathetic and moral ties that had existed between Doctor Betances, José Martí, and myself, and that I am acquainted with the former workers for Cuban independence, the "irredentists" of the idea of an Antillean confederation.

One of the paladins of El Yara wrote: "We who have a good memory and who recall the revolutionary past have felt as if the spirit of Antillean solidarity had revived when we saw Firmin, the eminent statesman admired by Martí, received today by the president of the republic of Cuba."

In evoking this recollection and the recent proposal made by the popular chamber of Puerto Rico, we reaffirm this declaration of the old program: "The Cuban revolutionary party is constituted to achieve the independence of Cuba and to aid in fostering that of Puerto Rico."

Indeed, on 27 February 1909, at San Juan, Puerto Rico, nine members of the chamber of delegates met to present the resolution on the confederation of Puerto Rico, Cuba, Santo Domingo, and Haiti, with the name of the "República Antilliana."

The plan provided for a president and a supreme court of justice for the four states, and the election for each of them of a governor and administrative and judicial functionaries. It was also "enunciated" in that "resolution" that the United States could have naval stations in the República Antilliana and the right to interfere in case of revolution, in exchange for her protection and for freedom of commerce with American ports. This proposal was discussed in a secret session, but, without its being formally rejected, no decided action was taken. . . .

A trial balloon was thus officially launched in the full assembly of the representatives of Puerto Rico. It still remains in the air, and no one can predict its political fate. The government of the Puerto Ricans is already becoming more and more difficult for the Americans. It would be in no way extraordinary that, sooner or later, the United States should change her colonial rule over Puerto Rico into a sort of intangible protectorate, from a political point of view, but very real and positive from the economic and financial standpoint. Uncle Sam knows how to content himself with these practical compromises, according to the opportunities presented. The national independence of the fourth of the Greater Antilles is within the category of things possible or very probable; but even in this case it may be asked what would be the probability of realizing the great dream of Hostos, Betances, Luperón, Martí, and so many other illustrious Antilleans, dead or still living! When will the day come for this federation of the Antilles: the ideal and sacred aim of such continuous and generous efforts? How can it be attained and what chance of immediate and peaceful success would so noble and delicate an enterprise have? For my reply to these questions, I give to the reader my letter addressed to Monsieur Carvajal. I have nothing to add to it, save the profound and sincere joy that the happy termination of the second American intervention, which has left the republic of Cuba independent and mistress of her own national destiny has caused me.

LETTER TO F. CARVAJAL: 15 MARCH 1907

. . .

Your idea to trigger a moral and intellectual movement in favor of a future Caribbean Confederation is most generous. In 1893, I remember being in Cap Haïtien and I heard your remarkable and late compatriot, José Martí, present it with that passionate conviction and enthusiastic eloquence with which he was so beautifully gifted. But the aspirations manifested in this idea are also difficult to realize because they are high and noble.

Besides, for it to triumph and translate itself into tangible fact, it takes a long, constant, and saintly propaganda from those who are driven by the sacred fire of a broad, intelligent, and far-sighted patriotism, inspired mainly by the truth that three small nations that currently make up the two largest Caribbean islands—as long as they are left to an isolated existence—will never constitute, separately, a power capable of imposing respect. On the contrary, by combining their national destinies and attracting all the other Antillean islands, now living under colonial rule, they would finally form a substantial state, adept at maintaining itself and establishing such a name for itself that it would garner the esteem and respect of other nations.

It is to this end that you work.

All kind-hearted men can only applaud your magnificent idea. You were thus right to believe that I cannot refuse to lend my moral support. However, as I wrote last year, to a publicist from Guadeloupe who had shared with me ideas extremely similar to yours, "I believe that this enterprise can only achieve complete success with difficulty, given the little sociological substance that can be found in political groups, even in those lands in the Caribbean long established as independent states such as Haiti and the Dominican Republic, to say nothing of Cuba, which is still in a period of national trial and error." Since then, the political occurrences brought about in your country by the antagonism between the group of the conservatives, at the head of which was President Palma, and that of the liberals, with General José Miguel Gómez at its head, have brought on a fresh intervention on the part of the North Americans. It is with an interest that approaches anguish that the friends of Cuban liberty and independence await the outcome of this painful situation.

And what are we to think of the French West Indies, the British, Dutch, or American? Not only is it not clear that they all want to change from colonial existence to formal national autonomy or independence, but we do not even know to what extent they would be able to retain a constitutional organization without any administrative supervision from a foreign power.

Your ideal is infinitely appealing and noble, it bears repeating, but its practical realization requires a ripening of the idea that inspires it, facilitated by a happy evolution of human elements called to be infused with it, for the greater honor and glory of the Caribbean archipelago, that we can consider, today, *as our largest homeland*, helping in the genesis of a real and powerful sympathy between Antilleans outside of and above all distinctions of race, origin, and nationality.

It is in this spirit that I join your fine aspirations with all my heart and all my soul.

Translated by Millery Polyné and Nadève Ménard

IV

Occupied Haiti (1915–1934)

On 28 July 1915, U.S. Marines landed on Haitian soil, initiating what would be a nineteen-year military occupation. Pierre Sully, the soldier guarding the Haitian military arsenal, refused to allow the Marines access, famously declaring that the Marines would only enter "over his dead body." He was shot. Sully is generally regarded as the only member of the Haitian military to have resisted the Americans' arrival. But other patriots would soon emerge. Among them were Jean Price-Mars, Raymond Cabèche, Georges Sylvain, and Charlemagne Péralte, symbol of the Cacos' armed resistance against the occupation.

Ten years into the occupation, in 1925, Jacques Roumain, then barely eighteen years old, wrote to Joseph Jolibois, director of the Haitian newspaper *Le Courrier Haïtien*, from Switzerland, where he was studying to become an engineer. In his letter, Roumain expressed his admiration for Jolibois's outspoken stance against the occupation and stated that he looked forward to "returning to Haiti, in order to help revive the courage of the masses and relieve the people." He also stated that "patriotism, as well as valor" do not depend on one's age. After his return to Haiti, he penned the country's most celebrated novel, *Masters of the Dew*.

The texts in this section—essays, letters, speeches, fiction, and poetry—reveal the myriad Haitian reactions to the occupation of their country by the United States. Furthermore, the stakes involved in the U.S. occupation of Haiti reached well beyond those two countries. In the context of World War I, the United States demanded that Haiti declare war on Germany. It used the opportunity provided by the occupation to seize German property in the country, and over twenty Germans in Haiti were detained in a U.S. internment camp. They were released when the war ended in 1919, but the United States maintained pressure on Haitian president Sudre Dartiguenave to deport nearly one-fourth of Haiti's German population in 1920. The idea was to reduce German influence and interests in Haiti in order to facilitate those of the United States. Nevertheless, the Germans remained important in Haiti, and certain families of German origin are established members of the contemporary Haitian bourgeoisie.

Haitian thinkers and artists were well aware of the global implications of U.S. action in Haiti. Georges Sylvain, for example, was acutely conscious of Haiti's importance in the world and was convinced that the fight against the occupation could be successful only if it was an international effort. He forged alliances both with associations in the Dominican Republic and, through the help of James Weldon Johnson, with African Americans.

The occupation years were a period of intense encounters throughout Haiti, including armed skirmishes between U.S. Marines and Haitian Cacos, and political maneuvering between the two governments and their representatives. Among other things, Americans strong-armed the Haitian parliament and pushed aside Rosalvo Bobo in favor of more cooperative presidents like Sudre Dartiguenave and Louis Borno. In their attempts to preside over Haitian national interests by working with occupation officials, these two Haitian heads of state authorized the creation of U.S.-led public institutions charged with training Haitian men and women in fields governed by the 1915 treaty that established the official terms of the occupation.

In addition to being a time of urban renewal, financial uncertainty, and social conflicts, the occupation was also a period of profound artistic activity. The short-lived but highly influential *Revue Indigène* was published between 1927 and 1928. Many of Haiti's most important writers published within its pages: Carl Brouard, Philippe Thoby-Marcelin, Jacques Roumain, Fernand Hibbert, and Emile Roumer. Those who participated in the journal wanted to present a "vibrant portrait of contemporary Haitian life and thought." They were also interested in maintaining ties with France, especially with its avant-garde literary production, and forging a stronger connection with Latin American writers and the region in general. Though the occupation itself was not a central theme of the journal, many of those who contributed to it were also involved in resistance efforts.

In spite of censorship, Haitian journalists and writers were very active during the occupation, publishing articles against the intervention, organizing and leading marches, as well as offering support to the armed resistance. President Louis Borno was especially zealous in having vocal opponents of the occupation imprisoned. In his first three years in office, over twenty journalists were arrested. Journalists and newspaper owners like Georges Petit, Daniel Heurtelou, Georges Sylvain, Carl Brouard, Joseph Jolibois, Jacques Roumain, and Elie Guerin were arrested several times. In addition to being arrested himself for his journalistic writings, Georges Sylvain sometimes served as lawyer to imprisoned writers. Jacques Roumain, among others, experienced solitary confinement and even undertook a hunger strike.

Writers were not the only artists using their voices to protest the occupation of their country. Several musicians did as well, including the classical composer Ludovic Lamothe. His 1934 Carnival meringue "Nibo" (which won the competition that year) came to symbolize Haitian resistance and triumph over the occupation. French-born Auguste de Pradines, known as Candio or Kandjo, was also very active in the resistance against the occupation. Even before 1915, he was known for the biting social commentary of his songs. He continued this tradition during the occupation, leading anti-Borno marches and singing songs critical of the occupation forces and the Haitian government. Other songs written during this period became classics of the Haitian repertoire due more to nostalgic sentiments than to patriotic ones. Songs like Marcel Sylvain's "Ayiti cheri" and Othello Bayard's "Souvenir d'Haïti," both written in the 1920s, offer the perspective of Haitian migrants forced by circumstances to live abroad and express their longing for the homeland.

1915 Treaty between the United States and Haiti

Robert Beale Davis Jr. and Louis Borno

U.S. Marines landed in Haiti on 28 July 1915, beginning a nineteen-year occupation of the country. There was almost no armed resistance to the invasion—only one Haitian soldier was killed that night, and the only U.S. casualty was killed by accident by other Marines. In fact, many among the political elite seemed to welcome the occupation. During the next months, U.S. officials negotiated with Haitian leaders to produce the following treaty, which was signed on 16 September 1915 by Louis Borno, Haiti's secretary of state for foreign affairs, and Beale Davis Jr., the United States' chargé d'affaires in Port-au-Prince.

The treaty codified the goals of the U.S. occupation, presented here as a project to improve the country's institutions, focusing on Haiti's finances, safety from internal and external aggression, and agricultural economic development. The treaty also outlines the general structure through which the United States was to supervise and carry out this mission.

The language of the treaty was one of collaboration, illustrating the relationship publicly agreed upon between Haitian and U.S. actors. But it clearly compromised Haitian political sovereignty in many ways. While the Haitian president retained the right to fill government posts, for instance, it was the U.S. president who would nominate candidates for those positions, thus controlling the process. Similarly, U.S. officials used the treaty to circumvent Haitian resistance: for example, U.S. officials created a Central School of Agriculture that emphasized an applied curriculum rather than the classical curriculum traditionally preferred in Haiti, ignoring the critiques of Haitian officials, such as Dantès Bellegarde, regarding their approach to reforming Haiti's education system. This domineering approach by U.S. officials was foremost among the factors that undermined the possibilities of any joint effort that emerged from the treaty. Despite any initial welcome, within a few years residents across Haiti were challenging the occupation regime, and many political elites also rescinded their support for the occupation.

Preamble

The United States and the Republic of Haiti desiring to confirm and strengthen the amity existing between them by the most cordial cooperation in measures for their common advantage;

And the Republic of Haiti desiring to remedy the present condition of its revenues and finances, to maintain the tranquility of the Republic, to carry out plans for the economic development and prosperity of the Republic and its people;

And the United States being in full sympathy with all of these aims and objects and desiring to contribute in all proper ways to their accomplishment;

The United States and the Republic of Haiti have resolved to conclude a Convention with these objects in view, and have appointed for that purpose, Plenipotentiaries,

The President of the United States, Robert Beale Davis, Junior, Charge d'Affaires of the United States;

And the President of the Republic of Haiti, Louis Borno, Secretary of State for Foreign Affairs and Public Instruction, who, having exhibited to each other their respective powers, which are seen to be full in good and true form, have agreed as follows:

Article I

The Government of the United States will, by its good offices, aid the Haitian Government in the proper and efficient development of its agricultural, mineral and commercial resources and in the establishment of the finances of Haiti on a firm and solid basis.

Article II

The President of Haiti shall appoint, upon nomination by the President of the United States, a General Receiver and such aids and employees as may be necessary, who shall collect, receive and apply all customs duties on imports and exports accruing at the several custom houses and ports of entry of the Republic of Haiti.

The President of Haiti shall appoint, upon nomination by the President of the United States, a Financial Adviser, who shall be an officer attached to the Ministry of Finance, to give effect to whose proposals and labors the Minister will lend efficient aid. The Financial Adviser shall devise an adequate system of public accounting, aid in increasing the revenues and adjusting them to the expenses, inquire into the validity of the debts of the Republic, enlighten both Governments with reference to all eventual debts, recommend improved methods of collecting and applying the revenues, and make such other recommendations to the Minister of Finance as may be deemed necessary for the welfare and prosperity of Haiti.

Article III

The Government of the Republic of Haiti will provide by law or appropriate decrees for the payment of all customs duties to the General Receiver, and will extend to the Receivership, and to the Financial Adviser, all needful aid and full protection in the execution of the powers conferred and duties imposed herein; and the United States on its part will extend like aid and protection.

Article IV

Upon the appointment of the Financial Adviser, the Government of the Republic of Haiti, in cooperation with the Financial Adviser, shall collate, classify, arrange and make full statement of all the debts of the Republic, the amounts, character, maturity and condition thereof, and the interest accruing and the sinking fund requisite to their final discharge.

Article V

All sums collected and received by the General Receiver shall be applied, first, to the payment of the salaries and allowances of the General Receiver, his assistants and employees and expenses of the Receivership, including the salary and expenses of the Financial Adviser, which salaries will be determined by previous agreement; second, to the interest and sinking fund of the public debt of the Republic of Haiti; and, third, to the maintenance of the constabulary referred to in Article X, and then the remainder to the Haitian Government for purposes of current expenses.

In making these applications the General Receiver will proceed to pay salaries and allowances monthly and expenses as they arise, and on the first of each calendar month, will set aside in a separate fund the quantum of the collection and receipts of the previous month.

Article VI

The expenses of the Receivership, including salaries and allowances of the General Receiver, his assistants and employees, and the salary and expenses of the Financial Adviser, shall not exceed five per centum of the collections and receipts from customs duties, unless by agreement by the two Governments.

Article VII

The General Receiver shall make monthly reports of all collections, receipts and disbursements to the appropriate officer of the Republic of Haiti and to the Department of State of the United States, which reports shall be open to inspection and verification at all times by the appropriate authorities of each of the said Governments.

Article VIII

The Republic of Haiti shall not increase its public debt except by previous agreement with the President of the United States, and shall not contract any debt or assume any financial obligation unless the ordinary revenues of the Republic available for that purpose, after defraying the expenses of the Government, shall be adequate to pay the interest and provide a sinking fund for the final discharge of such debt.

Article IX

The Republic of Haiti will not, without a previous agreement with the President of the United States, modify the customs duties in a manner to reduce the revenues therefrom; and in order that the revenues of the Republic may be adequate to meet the public debt and the expenses of the Government, to preserve tranquility and to promote material prosperity, the Republic of Haiti will cooperate with the Financial Adviser in his recommendations for improvement in the methods of collecting and disbursing the revenues and for new sources of needed income.

Article X

The Haitian Government obligates itself, for the preservation of domestic peace, the security of individual rights and full observance of the provisions of this treaty, to create without delay an efficient constabulary, urban and rural, composed of native Haitians. This constabulary shall be organized and officered by Americans, appointed by the President of Haiti, upon nomination by the President of the United States. The Haitian Government shall clothe these officers with the proper and necessary authority and uphold them in the performance of their functions. These officers will be replaced by Haitians as they, by examination, conducted under direction of a board to be selected by the senior American officer of this constabulary and in the presence of a representative of the Haitian Government, are found to be qualified to assume such duties. The constabulary herein provided for, shall, under the direction of the Haitian Government, have supervision and control of arms and ammunition, military supplies, and traffic therein, throughout the country. The high contracting parties agree that the stipulations in this Article are necessary to prevent factional strife and disturbances.

Article XI

The Government of Haiti agrees not to surrender any of the territory of the Republic of Haiti by sale, lease, or otherwise, or jurisdiction over such territory, to any foreign government or power, nor to enter into any treaty or contract with any foreign power or powers that will impair or tend to impair the independence of Haiti.

Article XII

The Haitian Government agrees to execute with the United States a protocol for the settlement, by arbitration or otherwise, of all pending pecuniary claims of foreign corporations, companies, citizens or subjects against Haiti.

Article XIII

The Republic of Haiti, being desirous to further the development of its natural resources, agrees to undertake and execute such measures as in the opinion of the high contracting parties may be necessary for the sanitation and public improvement of the Republic under the supervision and direction of an engineer or engineers, to be appointed by the President of Haiti upon nomination by the President of the United States, and authorized for that purpose by the Government of Haiti.

Article XIV

The high contracting parties shall have authority to take such steps as may be necessary to insure the complete attainment of any of the objects comprehended in this treaty; and, should the necessity occur, the United States will lend an efficient aid for the preservation of Haitian Independence and the maintenance of a government adequate for the protection of life, property and individual liberty.

Article XV

The present treaty shall be approved and ratified by the high contracting parties in conformity with their respective laws, and the ratifications thereof shall be exchanged in the City of Washington as soon as may be possible.

Article XVI

The present treaty shall remain in full force and virtue for the term of ten years, to be counted from the day of exchange of ratifications, and further for another term of ten years if, for specific reasons presented by either of the high contracting parties, the purpose of this treaty has not been fully accomplished.

In faith whereof, the respective Plenipotentiaries have signed the present convention in duplicate, in the English and French languages, and have thereunto affixed their seals.

Done at Port-au-Prince, Haiti,
the 16th day of September in the year of our Lord
one thousand nine hundred and fifteen.
Robert Beale Davis, Jr.,
Charge d'Affaires
of the United States.
Louis Borno, Secretary of State for Foreign
Affairs and Public Instruction

The Patriotic Union of Haiti Protests the U.S. Occupation

Union Patriotique d'Haiti

Haitian resistance to the military and financial intervention of the United States developed quickly, drawing on the intellectual and political traditions of Haitian nationalism. The Union Patriotique d'Haiti (Patriotic Union of Haiti), which was initially conceived of in Port-au-Prince in 1915 and founded anew in November 1920, was a self-defined international nonpartisan organization dedicated to the reimplementation of Haitian sovereignty. With members in Haiti and the United States, an array of writers, intellectuals, and former statesmen raised awareness of and funds to abolish Washington's control of Haitian affairs. Key activists and statesmen, particularly Sténio Vincent (future president 1930–41); Perceval Thoby, former chargé d'affaires of the Haitian legation at Washington; and Pauléus Sannon, former secretary of foreign affairs, sought to document the political and economic transgressions of U.S. military personnel in charge of the occupation. The Union lobbied U.S. officials, notably during U.S. congressional investigations in 1920 and 1921 to relay their concerns about the occupations of Haiti and the Dominican Republic.

In the memoir excerpted here, produced in 1921, they provided an account of the occupation from their perspective, in which they asserted their political contentions and their aspirations for the future of Haiti-U.S. relations in the context of a U.S. congressional hearing. The narration of this history, which included a discussion of the long-term impact of the 1825 indemnity levied by the French, was itself a political act, communicating the expectations and frustrations of the political elite during this period of the abrogation of Haitian independence. Their sentiment of protest also reveals the hope that these elites had for reaching terms of agreement with the United States that would offer Haiti "friendly aid," as their northern neighbor had pledged to do. The stance presented by the Union Patriotique's leaders ultimately led U.S. president Harding to restructure the occupation from a military to a civilian-led mission and to the creation of several public institutions, directed by U.S. officials, who trained Haitians across social classes in fields outlined in the 1915 treaty. These shifts tempered but did not fully resolve the Union's claims against U.S. involvement in Haitian affairs, as evidenced by the continued push for the end of the occupation and the ongoing challenge of these leaders to identify a structure under which Haiti could secure "impartial and altruistic aid" from the United States that did not compromise its sovereignty.

Landing of American Troops in Haiti—Treaty of September 16, 1915

On July 27, 1915, an attack was directed during the night against the President's palace by a revolutionary group—a group which militantly represented amid other antagonisms the overwhelming sentiment against any policies which tended or seemed to tend to the compromising of Haitian independence. On the next day President Vilbrun Guillaume Sam, wounded in the struggle, abandoned the palace and took refuge in the Legation of the French Republic.

On the morning of the same day, the rumor spread through the town that some political prisoners had been summarily executed in the prisons of Port-au-Prince during the attack on the national palace. This terrible and deplorable news was only too true. A great cry of grief arose from all classes of the people and soon changed into indignation and anger. Agitation was increasing. On July 28, the relatives of the victims, mostly young people, carried away by grief, invaded the French Legation, seized the ex-President, who was thrown into the street and killed. At the time when these confused scenes occurred, there was for the moment no government, nor any kind of an organization capable of preventing them. Yet there was no burning or robbing, and no one except the ex-President and the ex-Governor of Port-au-Prince, who were held responsible for the execution of the political prisoners, met death through this tragic incident.

After this act of reprisal, quiet was promptly restored, and a Committee of Public Safety assumed responsibility for order.

Meanwhile, on July 28, the American cruiser *George Washington*, bearing the flag of Rear-Admiral W. B. Caperton, anchored in the harbor of Port-au-Prince. No notice was taken of it, because it was generally believed that the presence of this vessel had no other object than that of protecting foreign interests if necessary, since Europe was at that time plunged in war.

On July 29, the population awoke to learn that the territory of Haiti was invaded by American forces that had landed at the extreme south of the city the night before. Hundreds and soon thousands of American marines occupied the town and disarmed the surprised Haitians, who were completely bowled over by the terrible events of the last two days—and so the American forces did not meet with any resistance from the population. Two weeks passed, during which the landed forces succeeded in getting control of Port-au-Prince and its immediate vicinity. Meanwhile other American troops had occupied the city of Cap Haïtien, in the northern part of the country. On August 12, 1915, after numerous conferences between leading members of the Haitian Chamber and Senate with the American naval authorities, at the United States Legation and elsewhere, a Presidential election was held by permission of the Occupation, and M. Dartiguenave, president of the Senate, was elected, the majority of the members of the two houses agreeing to support him. It was made clear that the choice of M. Dartiguenave was essentially agreeable to the American Occupation. He was therefore elected for a term of seven years in accordance with the Haitian Constitution then in force.

Two days after the establishment of the new government, Mr. Robert Beale Davis, Jr., American Chargé d'Affaires, in the name of his Government, presented to President Dartiguenave a project for a treaty. This project was accompanied by a memorandum, in which the President was informed "that the State Department at Washington expected that the Haitian National Assembly, warranting the sincerity and the interest of the Haitians, would immediately pass a resolution authorizing the President of Haiti to accept the proposed treaty without modification." Since this request indicated a certain ignorance of Haitian constitutional practice, as regards the negotiation of treaties, the Government hastened to call Mr. Davis's attention to the article of the Constitution relating to this subject, and showed him that the President of Haiti did not need special authority of the Chambers to negotiate and sign treaties with a foreign Power.

The American Chargé d'Affaires, after examining the constitutional text, readily acknowledged it and withdrew. Imagine the surprise of the Government on receiving the next day a threatening note signed by the Chargé d'Affaires, insisting that the resolution indicated in the memorandum should be passed by the Haitian Chambers, and setting in the form of an ultimatum a time limit within which that resolution must be passed.

To this demand the Haitian Government replied, through the State Secretary of Foreign Affairs, M. Pauléus Sannon, that it was guided by the most friendly disposition and was ready to negotiate a treaty with the United States, but that rather than accept without *modification* the project presented it would prefer to resign as a body.

By the occupation of its territory the Government which had been deprived of even its police power and which had none of the essential attributes of authority, was in reality without independence, without liberty of action. Its existence and its working depended upon the invading American forces, equipped with all modern armaments and now occupying the country.

While the negotiations were being continued laboriously as a result of the determination of the American representative not to accept any modifications in the project of the treaty, Rear-Admiral W. B. Caperton, commander-in-chief of the expeditionary force of the United States, seized the custom houses of Port-de-Paix, Cap, and St. Marc on August 24, driving out the Haitian officials. And in spite of the repeated official protestations of the Government to the American Legation, all the custom houses of the Republic were successively occupied and thus came under the control of the officers of the

United States Navy. On September 1, 1915, President Dartiguenave solemnly protested in a proclamation against this long series of violations of law, which had just resulted in the occupation of the custom house of Port-au-Prince. On the 3rd, Rear-Admiral W. B. Caperton issued a proclamation in which he declared that he had assumed control of the Government, and the town of Port-au-Prince (the seat of the Government) and its vicinity were under martial law.

In the face of the impossibility of getting certain modifications of the project accepted, two members of President Dartiguenave's Cabinet, the State Secretary of Foreign Affairs and the State Secretary of Public Works, handed in their resignations on September 8, 1915.

The treaty was signed on the 16th of the same month by M. Louis Borno, the new State Secretary of Foreign Affairs, and Mr. Robert Beale Davis, Jr., American Chargé d'Affaires at Port-au-Prince.

In reality the Government had been, from the beginning to end, oppressed by a series of violent acts. Apart from the occupation of its territory, the custom houses, which were the chief object of the treaty, had been seized *manumilitari*, and the funds belonging to the Haitian Treasury and deposited in the National Bank of the Haitian Republic had been transferred to the account of Rear-Admiral W. B. Caperton, by his orders.

Haitian Finances

THE FINANCIAL AID PROMISED BY THE UNITED STATES

Haiti has always lived up loyally to her financial agreements. One of the reasons given for American intervention is the breaking of these agreements. As those of many other countries, Haitian finances have passed through critical periods, but the leaders of the country have always been able to find the necessary solution to the problems that confronted them.

For a long time Haiti has borne the weight of a heavy debt which has hindered her economic development.

By a royal decree, King Charles X of France, in return for 150 million francs as indemnity for the losses incurred by the former colonists and payable in five equal instalments, granted to Haiti on April 17, 1825, an independence which the Haitians had conquered at the price of hard and bloody sacrifices. In the continual expectation of the offensive return of the French, and weary of maintaining the country for more than twenty years in a state of war, the Government of President Boyer accepted the arrangement of the King of France which stipulated these painful conditions.

By means of a loan of 24 million francs, issued at Paris at the rate of 80 per cent and bearing 6 per cent interest, to which was added 6 million francs paid in specie by the Haitian Treasury, the first instalment of the indemnity was paid.

But owing to the energetic protests of the Haitian people and the refusal of the French Government to reduce this heavy indemnity, the Haitian Government suspended the payment of the four other instalments of the indemnity with the clear intention, however, of paying the annuities (interest and principal) of the loan. After long and delicate negotiations, the Government of Louis Philippe consented, on February 12, 1838, to recognize the independence of Haiti by treaty. At the same time a financial convention was signed, reducing the balance of the indemnity from 120 million francs to 60 million.

The loan of 24 million francs and the indemnity were known as "the Double French Debt." It was entirely paid off in 1893, after 58 years.

Soon after the first payments of the 30 million francs, the Haitian Government found itself handicapped in meeting its most urgent budget expenses. In 1826 it had to resort to paper money. The burdens imposed upon the country were too heavy; this was the beginning of all its troubles. The nation was barely able to recover from the losses incurred by the wars of Santo Domingo, the war with the English, the struggle of the French against Toussaint-Louverture, and the war of Independence, which started in 1802 and ended with the surrender of Rochambeau at Cap Haïtien in November, 1803. The plantations had disappeared, the towns and villages had been nearly all destroyed—nearly a hundred thousand Haitians had lost their lives in the pitiless struggle for liberty. Sugar and indigo, the chief exports of the island, had no more markets in France, and there was not enough capital to revive the sugar mills. Courageously the Haitian people undertook and intensified other forms of cultivation, and in this way coffee, cotton, and cocoa became the principal products of the land. In spite of so many misfortunes the country continually made sacrifices to live loyally up to its agreements.

. . .

From the time of the landing of American troops on July 28, 1915, the Military Occupation suspended payment of the foreign debt of the Republic which the Haitian Government had been able to carry on until then to the satisfaction of its creditors. But not even the signing and execution of the treaty of September 16, 1915, was to put an end to this state of affairs, which was so injurious to the credit of the country. This decision was even more incomprehensible when the special funds for the payment of the interest and amortization of this debt had accumulated and were remaining unproductive in the vaults of the National Bank of the Republic of Haiti. It was not until last year (1920) that the interest due was finally paid, upon the repeated demands of the bondholders, almost all foreigners, and upheld by their respective Governments. As for the internal debt, except for a partial payment made in April, 1916, no payment of interest has been made up to now, in spite of the demands of the bondholders. Their voices were not heard for the simple reason that they were nearly all Haitians.

In a report of March 20, 1917, the Consul-General of the United States at Port-au-Prince said on this subject: "It is unfortunate for commerce that the internal debt has not been adjusted nor the interest paid, this default having resulted in reducing sales very materially for 1917. Most of the bonds are held by the people, who have been expecting the interest to be paid *as formerly*, thereby to meet their living expenses. The failure to do this has embarrassed them financially and will tend to diminish the sale of imported goods."

Thus, the principal object of the treaty, which was to place Haitian finances on a solid basis, has not been fulfilled, nor has the financial aid which was promised by the United States been effectively given. In fact, up to the present time, the monetary circulation of Haiti is still paper money, and instead of substituting metal money for it, the Financial Adviser has fixed the Haitian gourde at 1/5 of the American dollar, to the detriment of all those who receive it in payment for their work. A further resulting injustice is involved in the fact that, in conformity with the budget of the Haitian Republic, certain officials are paid in American gold and others are paid in Haitian money, no calculation being made in favor of these latter, in consideration of the depreciation of this money in relation to the American dollar. Naturally, all the officials from the United States are in the first category.

. . .

Conclusion

The Haitian Republic was the second nation of the New World—second only to the United States—to conquer its national independence. We have our own history, our own traditions, customs, and national spirit, our own institutions, laws, and social and political organization, our own culture, our own literature (French language), and our own religion. For 111 years the little Haitian nation has managed its own affairs; for 111 years it has made the necessary effort for its material, intellectual, and moral development as well as any other nation—better than any other nation, because it has been from the start absolutely alone in its difficult task, without any aid from the outside, bearing with it along the harsh road of civilization the glorious misery of its beginning. And then, one fine day, under the merest pretext, without any possible explanation or justification on the grounds of *violation of any American right or interest*, American forces landed on our national territory and actually abolished the sovereignty and independence of the Haitian Republic.

We have just given an account of the chief aspects of the American Military Occupation in our country since July 28, 1915.

It is the most terrible regime of military autocracy which has ever been carried on in the name of the great American democracy.

The Haitian people, during these past five years, has passed through such sacrifices, tortures, destructions, humiliations, and misery as have never before been known in the course of its unhappy history.

The American Government, in spite of the attitude of wisdom, moderation, and even submission which it has always found in dealing with the Haitian Government, has never lived up to any of the agreements which it had solemnly entered into with regard to the Haitian people.

The Haitian people is entitled to reparations for the wrongs and injuries committed against it.

The great American people can only honor themselves and rise in universal esteem by hastening the restoration of justice—of all the justice due a weak and friendly nation which the agents of its Government have systematically abused.

Reparations are due for the human lives that have been taken and for the property that has been destroyed or abstracted. An impartial investigation will provide the necessary statements and supply the basis for the estimates to be determined.

The present political aspirations of the Haitian nation have been formulated by the Union Patriotique, a comprehensive national association which, through its numerous branches throughout the country and in all levels of society, includes virtually all the Haitian people. The undersigned have been sent to the United States by this association to make the will of the country clearly known.

The Haitian people are filled with peaceful sentiments, but there is no doubt that they intend to recover definitely the administration of their own affairs and to resume under their own responsibility the entire life of the country, with full sovereignty and independence. They will never rest until they have obtained them.

The salient aspirations of the Haitian people are summarized as follows:

1. Immediate abolition of martial law and courts martial.
2. Immediate reorganization of the Haitian police and military forces, and withdrawal within a short period of the United States Military Occupation.
3. Abrogation of the convention of 1915.
4. Convocation within a short period of a Constituent Assembly, with all the guarantees of electoral liberty.

But the Haitian people desire too strongly the friendship of the great American people, and are too anxious for their own material, intellectual, and moral development not to wish and bespeak for themselves the impartial and altruistic aid of the United States Government. They have urgent needs, vital to the development of the natural resources of the country and essential to the full expansion of its agricultural, industrial, and commercial activity.

The satisfying of these needs is absolutely necessary for the continued progress of the Haitian community.

Nothing would serve better to bring about the speedy reestablishment of normal relations between the two countries than the friendly aid of the United States Government in the economic prosperity and social progress of the Haitian Republic.

H. Pauléus Sannon
Sténio Vincent
Perceval Thoby

Memories of Corvée Labor
and the Caco Revolt

Roger Gaillard

In the late 1970s and early 1980s, historian Roger Gaillard produced a multivolume study of the U.S. occupation of Haiti. It drew on a range of sources from Haitian and U.S. archives, but also on extensive oral histories gathered by Gaillard among Haitians who remembered the occupation. In the first excerpt, two of his interviewees remember the corvée practiced by the U.S. Marines in the country. The use of this form of forced labor was the major spur to uprisings, which started in 1918 and were led by Charlemagne Péralte, a former Haitian army officer. Gaillard narrated these events in rich detail. The first account comes from Narcisse Malary, a local official in the commune of Hinche who worked with the local gendarmes as they captured rural Haitians to put them to work on road construction under the orders of the U.S. Marines.

Once there were three of them (three gendarmes and a Sergeant of Dominican origin, whose name was Francisco) and they had searched the countryside in vain: men, particularly wary at that time, had left their houses and taken refuge in the woods.

At three in the morning we heard singing in the distance, indicating that a wake was taking place in the distance. We walked in that direction. After an hour, we found ourselves in front of a house, in front of which were three carpenters sawing, nailing, making a coffin. While one of the guards pointed his gun at them to prevent them from fleeing, the others burst into the house, blocking the entrance.

The singing stopped. The parents and friends of the deceased looked at us, frightened. In the room next door the corpse was laid out, ready to be placed in the coffin. It had already been "imbibed," covered in leaves and moistened with rum.

The gendarmes quickly grabbed the petrified men and, with the ten ropes they had brought, tied them tightly together by their forearms. Then, in the midst of the moaning and shouting of the women, they walked out in order to capture the carpenters too.

I interceded in their favor, explaining that the dead had to be buried, and therefore the artisans had to finish the coffin and help the women with the burial. Francisco responded that if he didn't come back with at least thirty men, [U.S. Marine] Lang would demote him. We need, he said, the three inhabitants; and the three carpenters were, in turn, tied up.

As we walked away, cries of pain from the women replaced the singing. I learned later that they had themselves lifted up and carried the corpse and, without a coffin, placed it in the grave that had been dug.

Another of those Gaillard interviewed had escaped doing corvée labor himself because his father was a chef de section. But he described it as a form of slavery, and when Gaillard asked him why he used that term, the man answered with a list, delivered in Creole:

First, the work isn't paid.
Second, you work under the sun, with nothing but a scrap of pants on.
Third, they don't send you home if you are sick.
Fourth, you don't eat enough, just corn and congo peas.
Fifth, you sleep in a prison or at the construction site.
Sixth, when you try and escape they kill you.
So that, isn't that slavery?

The use of corvée labor helped to trigger an armed uprising against the U.S. occupation, led by Péralte. Gaillard offers a detailed account of his background and leadership of the struggle. In 1980, Gaillard interviewed a resident of Zeb-Guinée, Stephen Gautier, who had been one of Péralte's officers, and remembered how he had begun organizing the resistance after he escaped from prison in Le Cap in September 1918.

I was among the officers who later surrounded Péralte. He told me that after he secretly escaped Le Cap, he had disguised himself as a woman and headed on foot toward Grande-Rivière. As he walked he sang religious songs. When people asked him where he was going, he replied that he was heading to a *renvoyénamn* ceremony, to offer a "last prayer" for a deceased relative. Everyone let him pass without hassling him. He arrived without difficulty in Saint-Raphaël, where he revealed himself to one of his friends, who dropped everything to follow him. He returned to the region of Hinche, living in the bush, inviting trustworthy friends to join him, gathering guns, bullets, and powder in calabashes.

This photograph of a female Caco soldier seems to have been mailed from within the country in 1924. Neither the sender nor the recipient is clearly indicated. Courtesy of CIDHICA.

a Caco's wife Caco herself

In 1971, Gaillard interviewed another man, Lagneau Augustin Sylvain, who was a child in Hinche at the time Péralte began organizing his insurrection.

I remember seeing Charlemagne in 1918 after his escape. He came to my father's house at Los Palis, near Hinche. My father, who raised, kept and sold cattle, knew him. Charlemagne came with two other horsemen. It must have been ten in the morning. My father greeted them, asked them to come inside, and ordered that food be prepared for them. They stayed together for two to three hours. Then the three horsemen left, happy, after having shaken the hand of my father and saluted my mother.

I was nine years old. When they had left, my father, in my presence, told my mother that a very hard civil war was about to start, a revolutionary war, and that Charlemagne was recruiting men and gathering his friends. That was why he had come to ask my father to join his troop. My father went on to explain that because he was *chef de section* he couldn't actively participate in the movement, but that he would support it in all kinds of ways, particularly by offering cattle to them: Charlemagne and his envoys could serve themselves.

Translated by Laurent Dubois

The Crucifixion of Charlemagne Péralte

Philomé Obin

Charlemagne Péralte led the Caco revolt against the U.S. occupation of Haiti, which begin in 1915. Beginning in May 1919, the U.S. Marines designed a covert operation to eliminate Charlemagne Péralte. On 31 October, working with a Haitian collaborator, soldiers were able to sneak into his camp at night and assassinate him. They brought his body back to the city of Le Cap and displayed it so that local residents could see that the rebel leader had been killed. A Marine photographer took this image of the body, and copies of it were distributed in the countryside in the hopes that it would quell resistance. Instead the photograph became an iconic depiction of Péralte as a martyr for liberty. He looks Christ-like, with his head against his battle flag (the Haitian flag), with a crucifix attached to the pole above him. This has become one of the most recognizable and famous photographs in Haitian history, a kind of monument to the cruelties of the U.S. occupation of Haiti—and one produced, ironically, by the occupying power itself.

Haitian painter Philomé Obin drew on this image to produce a series of paintings, one of which is titled The Crucifixion of Charlemagne Péralte. *Obin reinterpreted the U.S. troops' portrayal of Péralte as a hunted and dispossessed guerrilla fighter, turning the black and white of the photograph into an image bursting with the colors of the Haitian flag. Here Péralte's symbols—the flag and the crucifix—are clearly seen. And the horror of his death is emphasized by the presence of his mother, looking at the corpse and weeping at his side. Obin's painting captured and helped to crystallize the popular historical memory of Péralte as a martyr.*

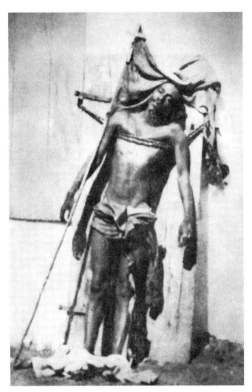

Charlemagne Péralte's corpse was displayed to the public in Le Cap after his assassination. This photograph, taken by a U.S. Marine photographer, was then distributed in Haiti in the hopes of helping to crush the Caco revolt. Photo originally from U.S. National Archives, reprinted in *From Within and Without: The History of Haitian Photography* (NSU Art Museum Fort Lauderdale, 2015).

Philomé Obin (Haitian, 1891–1986), *Crucifixion de Charlemagne Péralte pour la liberté*, 1970, Milwaukee Art Museum. Reprinted with permission of the Milwaukee Art Museum.

"My Dear Charlemagne"

Widow Massena Péralte

The following letter was written to Charlemagne Péralte by his mother, Marie-Claire Emmanuel, who signed her letters Widow Massena Péralte. Though undated, it seems to have been written during the period when Péralte was preparing to launch a Caco uprising. The letter is now in the U.S. Marine Archives in the United States. U.S. Marines often intercepted Caco correspondence in order to mine it for intelligence information. The letter was typed and translated into English by the marines, and we have used this version of the letter here, preserving the precise punctuation and grammar. The letter reads as both an intimate and public exchange between mother and son. Mrs. Péralte offered both words of caution and encouragement for his anticipated or existing opposition to the occupation. As such, it provides critical and coded information about Haitian resistance against U.S. troops during the early twentieth century.
—Contributing Editor: Yveline Alexis

My dear Charlemagne.

You who are more than I and are nearer the town, you can see how things are advancing, you have the information to know what you should do, yourself well to see how the things are going advancing. I have heard that all these big men of Port-au-Prince have left inform yourself well to see if this is true. We have no communication with the North, every one here has doubts. Saul and St. Remy have already left. Keep yourself hidden, do not hurry to enter into anything because we do not know the mind of the North and everyone is bursting out against the whites, no one accepts this condition. They are saying they would rather rebel than be under the white orders. You see the intentions of the people of Leogane how it is if you cannot remain out of it yourself because I believe that that is not good for the people of Haiti. And also do not let anyone put their hands on you, better you are in the woods than under arrest. Make sure to see if it is true that the gentlemen have left, to see how things are. You who are there can see how they go here—you will guard yourself well if you decide to remain at peace—you are intelligent—

you will wait—you will be careful of yourself while waiting—people are keeping things to themselves—you will not put yourself into it too quickly—listen well before you will do anything—you will also see the overseer of your command and the actions of the people towards you. You have more intelligence than I. I did not know about the situation of our country.

Nothing more to tell you—
Your mother
Widow Masséna Peralte.

If you have bought the mule for me, send it to me and if you have animals send them also to me. And also I am down to the last penny see if you cannot send me a little help because I am a little more embarrassed for some time past on account of the money that I spend in the works which I have done. You weigh things to see what you should do. You are a politician. It is not for me to tell you facts upon facts you see the situation only it is for you to know what you should do in order not to be arrested like President Oreste—take care of yourself—keep always ready—Be on the lookout for whatever may turnup to know the road you should follow for that particular situation. I do not know if it is true if there gentlemen have left—I do not know if it is propaganda, it is not official news—if you hear all the North is in movement you know what to do, and if you hear nothing you will remain peaceably in your place. God alone who knows. but lay low and get information from all the country.

Nothing more to tell you
Widow MassénaPeralte

If you have any bit of money exchange it and arrange your affairs well or you can not go to Domingo, try and see if you can remain quiet and peaceful. I am more than pleased to hear that the people of Leogane are charmed with you. And try to conduct yourself always to do good rather than harm to the rich as well as the poor. I pray the Immaculate One night and day for you. If you can remain quiet and peaceable, God and the people of Leogane will save you in all circumstances because you have acted well towards the people. If you see that things are quiet remain quiet also. Mind well the situation of the country. Pray the Immaculate One your father to protect you in every case—do good works and do no evil to anyone—you have not done harm to anyone—you cannot do harm to anyone, also if we have quiet I will go there to thank St Rose and the people of Leogane who are so charmed with you.

Your mother
Widow Péralte

La vocation de l'élite

Jean Price-Mars

The political oppression and violence of the U.S. occupation of Haiti helped to incite a profound shift in intellectual thought within the country. The best-known and most influential voice to emerge during this period was that of Jean Price-Mars, who came to be known as l'Oncle (the Uncle) in Haiti and the Father of Négritude by intellectuals, artists, and activists involved in discussions about Pan-Africanism around the world. Price-Mars's most widely celebrated work is Ainsi parla l'oncle, *a collection of his ethnographic findings about Haitian folk culture, published in 1928. The volume called for politically and economically privileged Haitians who traditionally celebrated France as the source of Haitian culture and national identity to look instead to Haiti's rural traditions as a source of inspiration.*

A decade earlier, in 1919, Price-Mars had published La vocation de l'élite, *a compilation of his early writings including a series of speeches. In these writings, dating from 1906 to 1917, Price-Mars argued that people in the capital city of Port-au-Prince, as well as in other major Haitian cities, ought to respect and learn from the cultural traditions of Haiti's laboring and rural citizens. It was only by doing so, and by dedicating their own knowledge and resources to improving the well-being of all classes of people, that Haiti's elite could effectively defend the integrity and sovereignty of their nation.*

—Contributing Editor: Claire Payton

One of the things that struck me the most, upon my return from a mission to France two years ago, was the disarray in which I found this country's elite since the American intervention in Haiti's affairs.

We would be justified in thinking that after the vote of the Haitian-American convention—the bitter discussion of which had exacerbated the division between learned men—"the new era" would have brought calm and quiet to the conscience of those who had been sincere and disinterested supporters. From many of them, as from their adversaries of yesterday, I was astonished to hear the same tone of lamentation and skepticism. From the ones and the others, I heard so many times, alas!, the same bitter expression that returned to their lips like a refrain: "There is nothing left to do."

Furthermore, I thought I noticed in the attitude of most people, at the

Jean Price-Mars (1876–1969). Photo courtesy of CIDHICA.

same time as this renouncing of effort, a weakening of the will to live, a sort of aspiration toward death in order to relieve oneself from fears of the future. Even among the rare beneficiaries of the present situation, I thought I sometimes discerned worries, uneasiness barely hidden beneath a superficial self-confidence. It seemed to me that this state of mind had many consequences for the existence of the Haitian people and I resolved to fight it with a campaign of moral uplift in the press and at the tribune of conference rooms.

. . .

Without doubt, some of the ideas on which we've lived up until now have been violently shaken by the events. In this sense, I will call particular attention to the idea that we had of the state. We thought of it as a very high abstraction, according Divine attributes to it: omnipotence and omniscience. Instinctively knowing, however, that the state, in the end, is only worth the men who hold the power, and in spite of repeated deceptions, all the same, we put our last hope in the wait for He who would come one day to fulfill our most fanciful desires and most extravagant aspirations. It is all that that we express with the catchphrases—the new era, adaptation to progress, to modern civilization, etc.—which saturate our specious political phraseology and which can periodically be found with disconcerting persistence in programs, speeches, proclamations, decrees, and laws since 1804.

Yet the dramatic adventure of 1915 has had the immediate result of putting us face to face with another understanding of the state: that which, pushed to its extreme and ideal consequences, restrains and limits the actions of power to established conditions and areas and lets the individual's activity thrive. It has particular pride of place in certain Anglo-Saxon societies.

. . .

The campaign that I've undertaken has no other goal than to ask the elite to pull itself together and to only count on itself if it wants to keep its role of representation and leadership.

To attain this result, it particularly has to give up the bogus antagonisms between classes and political parties and unite according to the manners of human activity. Of course, we can differ in opinion on such or such doctrine, on the advisability or nonadvisability of its application. Should these diverging views necessarily lead to hatred, taking sides, humiliating campaigns of disparagement and character assassination? Is it not possible to not share the sentiments of such or such personality without calling into question the honesty of his intentions, without condemning him to public execration?

If Haitian life offers to the observer the sad evidence of ruffian customs, it does so precisely when it shows the spectacle of the dirty tricks in which the elite partake in order to board the gravy train. All of my ambition would be to remind this elite of the simple dignity of its vocation by advising it to make better use of its moral, social, and intellectual value.

I would thus wish that the studies published in this volume contribute to achieve such a noble objective. If I could convert just one man to my ideas, I would consider that my efforts have not been in vain.

. . .

First, what does this elite represent and from which elements is it composed?

We partially responded to this two-sided question when we analyzed the role of men and the influence of events in the formation of Haitian society. We tried to demonstrate—you will remember—that the transformation of the colonial society into a politically and economically independent society had as its starting point the removal of the previous leadership and the nearly automatic replacement of the landowners by the leaders of the rebel masses. This well-established historical fact had a very clear social and political significance for the later development of the nation. This is a point we have insisted on, and one on which we believe we find the unanimous agreement of our thinkers.

Thus, it follows that the national elite was—in the past—the slow and laborious creation of the race's genius that carried from distant homelands, into the land of exile, the hidden possibilities of an ethnic rehabilitation. In the past, the national elite was the end point of a long process of accumulated suffering. It was also the product of unconscious choices made since time immemorial, drawing on the reserves of the sensibilities and latent intelligence of African tribes. Which brings us to more recent times that, because of crossings under our skies, marked a decisive era of evolution during which leaders of men sprang up from the subjugated masses and liberated the race from the forces of oppression and debasement.

So, if our definition is accurate, the elite of yesterday was not only a product of its milieu and in perfect concordance with this milieu, but also, despite all of our efforts at imagining something different, we have not been able to conceive of being in our society without these organs of discipline and direction. But then, by what strange and disconcerting phenomenon has what in the past was the norm become today nothing more than a memory that each day is coated with more melancholy regret.

How can one explain the distance that separates our current elite from the masses, so much so that even the least sophisticated eyes can see that our nation is divided into distinct factions, separate and watertight compartments? How can we explain the fact that we have arrived at such a level of social division that our elite seems to be a foreign organism, superimposed on the rest of the nation, living a relationship to the people that is essentially a state of parasitism?

Two categories of facts—facts of an economic order and facts of a psychological order—dominate the discussion. By analyzing them we can clarify the singularity of the phenomenon and help dispel some misunderstandings.

As to the first, I have explained enough—or so I flatter myself at least— when I tried in my earlier lectures to highlight the fact that the abolition of servile work, obtained at the price of so much sacrificial blood, changed the condition of the masses only in appearance. In reality, legal slavery was replaced by a hybrid form of servitude, through the simple shifting around of people and responsibilities. Despite the exclusion and the subsequent dispossession of the large landowners, despite the emphasis of legal texts and the goodwill of ideologues, the new indigenous society tacitly conserved the framework of class. The most obvious consequence of this state of things was the perpetuation among the lower classes of the same roles as before, with some very minor modifications, among which a somewhat crude mode of wage labor was the only obvious novelty. We know that in this regime, which endures today, almost sacrosanct, the work contract does not introduce the principle of daily wages, instead allowing the farm laborer the share, in kind, of a fourth first, and then half of all the produce that he harvests.

But it would take a lot for this regime to become a principle of progress. For it to become such, it would have had to be considered less an end than a means, one means to take a step between servile work and work directly remunerated according to the value of the work and the technical abilities of the worker, which is one of the means by which men everywhere gradually elevate themselves to a higher dignity through wealth and knowledge. It is unfortunate to note that tenant farming, known by the name "de moitié," has, up to this point, been the only form of wage system offered by landowners to the masses of farmers. For, the result has been that the landowning regime and the labor regime not only exercised on one another a spirit of routine that was harmful to progress and the renewal of agricultural methods, but also engendered other evils from which we are still suffering. The state, as you know, took possession of most of the land by invoking the law of conquest. It then distributed it by large blocks or in smaller parcels to its favorites, either in the form of a land donation or by renting it out or as farms (though it received payments only sporadically). The state therefore created a new privileged class, which reinforced the remnants of the former upper classes that survived the revolutionary upheaval. If they had had a clear sense of their responsibilities, those granted these privileges would have been the agents of progress by virtue of example, by intelligently cultivating their lands themselves, lands where not long before the overseer's whip had been the only discipline and the only method of cultivation. But alas! They had neither the energy nor the good sense, and probably lacked the capital, to raise up the domains they had inherited thanks to the generosity of the prince from their ruins, preferring instead—all while keeping a nominal right of control over the acquired properties—to live elsewhere, in the cities, off the easier and more immediate profits of politics, while leaving the administration of these properties to the haphazard ignorance and the routine of "de moitié." This was the first great fault of the elite: the desertion of the land.

We also should not lose sight of the fact that this distribution of land took place in conformity with the topography of the country and, to a certain measure, according to the aptitude of different areas for different crops. I mean that if collectively the rural properties were divided since colonial times into mountainous areas and the low plains—the former more appropriate for crops like coffee, for instance, and the others devoted to extensive crops like sugarcane—the distribution that was carried out afterward largely respected this older concept of property, so that today the large and medium-sized domains are 80 percent in our various plains, while the infinitely fragmented parcels are found particularly in the mountain districts. The result of this state of things was that the mountainous zones fragmented into a large number of "habitations" offered a considerable attraction to the recently freed poor devils, who found there the possibility of living more or less at their ease, having for several generations known no alternative except for working for someone else.

And as the problem of existence was not complicated for them by any clothing luxury, finery nor even minimum comfort, they contented themselves with sowing the land that generously provided beyond that which was absolutely necessary for a primitive life, without horizons, without doubt, without troubles. That is how this class of peasants living scattered in the solitude of high summits or dispersed along the slopes and in the valleys—in conditions of isolation that the often tormented nature of the soil often makes quite impressive—was formed, and have remained until our time. Many among them, the majority, were then and now tenant farmers like those in the plains. But the latter enjoy a more or less developed network of communication, are involved in lucrative industrial farming and remain in contact with the urban bourgeoisie, drawing from all these conditions an incontestable benefit of cultural refinement. As a result they have become resourceful. But the others, who form two-thirds of the country's total population, are left to themselves, resigned in advance to their fate—whose tragic misery they do not suspect. They live to the alternating rhythm of the clash of hoes in the earth and the clinking of pruning knives. The same ancestral gesture that attaches them to the fields gives birth to an agglomeration of men different and distinct from the rest of the nation by language, custom, morals, unsophisticated and primitive mental development. They are nothing more than a simple sketch, a crude image, a distant caricature of the other element of Haitian society, the elite.

. . .

. . . In order to complete our explanation, we now need to underline the role of psychological facts on the same phenomenon.

One of the least unpredictable consequences of the horrors of slavery was to inspire a characteristic repulsion toward manual work among those who liberated themselves through the atrocities of war. That was in the nature of things.

Indeed, if we remember that the colony of Saint-Domingue was nothing more than a vast agricultural operation, that the different kinds of professions that were represented were only practiced by the poor whites and the free people—a class of free men, no doubt, but mistrusted and ridiculed by the big planters, and that artisans who became successful hurried to flaunt the same sentiment of shame toward their recent past, it is not difficult to understand that for the freed slave, there needed to be a certain ideal, a standard of value that was outside of wealth and that competed with it, the unavoidable sign of social superiority. That ideal was, and could only be, that of intellectual cultivation. To think—with courage, audacity, and good fortune one could reach the highest levels of leadership, acquire wealth and honors. But beyond that there was above all something mysterious, fascinating, and irritating all at the same time—knowledge—toward which one was often pressured to give a discreet homage, unavowed perhaps, because of its effectiveness, its distinction and rarity. Such was the likely prestige of intellectual culture that it must have seemed in the eyes of the new masters a mark of the greatest nobility, certainly more inaccessible than leadership or wealth itself. This assertion is backed up by the consideration and general esteem with which the nascent society covered not only the very small number of those reputed to be educated, but even some of the men against whom it had just waged war and against whom it still frothed with formidable anger despite its recent victory.

. . .

We can affirm that at the dawn of our national life, at the moment when the power of weapons was only of mediocre assistance in the process of re-organizing government services, the prestige of knowledge exercised a profound influence on the new society. But it is also easy to understand that, if on the one hand manual labor was stripped of its attraction and tacitly discredited because of the way it evoked abolished servitude, if on the other hand, intellectual culture seemed to confer a certain ennobling dignity, then we can easily understand that the small number of men who brought together the power of money with that of knowledge came to constitute a kind of aristocracy very distinct from the rest of the flock. Nevertheless, it is important to add that this took place not long after the period when suffering affected all equally and disdain was the general law, and at a time when the threat of external danger directed the collective worry toward a common defense of the rights so dearly acquired. Not enough time had passed for this transmutation of values to incite a sharp and sudden change in the relationship between people. On the contrary, a certain social solidarity, more intuitive than voluntary, blunted the antagonisms between groups, even as the economic and psychological causes that made the divisions even deeper were crystallizing.

And that, in my opinion, is where we must go to search for the origin of this devastating separation of the elite and the masses, which has gotten to a point that they currently form two nations within the nation, each having its own interests, tendencies, and objectives.

And that is also how a definition of our elite can only be understood in relation to the workings of the mental development of a minority of men whose life unfolds on the sidelines of collective life, like a kind of artificial mandarinate. Because at the end of the day, my dear sirs, if there is an established truth it is that in all the countries of the world where the law of castes does not stereotype social groups into fixed attitudes, the elite is recruited from all domains of social activity.

The elite must be simultaneously, and pragmatically, industrial, commercial, and agricultural, without being exclusively intellectual.

. . .

You well understand that if education is an attempt to model man according to a determined ideal, it seems to me that all systems of pedagogy must first begin with a familiarity with the temperament of the people to whom it will be applied. This is the first consideration, and I am tempted to affirm that it is the essential consideration that must determine any collective educational enterprise. Yet, we know that such concerns have never crossed the minds of our men of state and our past public figures, and I regret to note that even today when people talk so much of reforming public education, neither the majority of our writers nor the official authorities have the slightest inkling of this elementary truth.

In any case, it is most likely due to having ignored this fundamental law of pedagogy that we have established schools from 1804 to today, all based on the same teaching principle, that is to say: force-feeding a given child or adolescent with the greatest amount of knowledge, without bothering to know whether this knowledge is digestible and assimilated by the minds of those to whom it is destined. Or whether this knowledge relates to the needs or conditions of evolution, historical or otherwise, of the society these beneficiaries belong to, or finally whether, in its ultimate form, this knowledge can develop or contribute to developing—beyond the intrinsic qualities of intelligence—that equally great and precious element of character which imprints the dignity of life and the sense of responsibility in the hearts of men.

. . .

A few of my friends, very much alarmed by the unease suffered by our democracy, have rightly understood that it was urgent to undertake the study of the issues of interest to the country's life force, in order to create a movement of ideas, of sentiments, and of aspirations of which the ultimate goal is the organization of the nation's moral forces by giving them a clearer conscience of their capacity for action and resistance and by bringing national thought to a more methodical and deeper meditation about the new problems that demand our attention.

. . .

I mean, . . . by social education the discipline we must enforce upon ourselves, the obligation we should take upon ourselves to participate either directly or indirectly in the creation and the maintenance of works that clearly have as their goal an attenuation of the material or moral misery: postschool works, night schools, founding nurseries and workrooms, sponsoring dispensaries, and leagues against the illnesses that attack the biological vitality of the race: tuberculosis, rot, alcoholism, etc.

You see that such disciplines do not necessarily imply that the individuals that benefit from them know how to read and write. On the contrary, we owe them more sympathy and more goodness directly because of the heavy tribute they pay to ignorance. For tell yourselves that the only measure of an elite's value is its social utility. If ever in your soul and conscience you have never been inclined toward a serious meditation on these problems of social education such as I have tried to define the postulates before you, well, to-night I am directing a fervent appeal to your good sense and your reason so that from now on your pity leans toward the humble less like charity from your weary elegance, but as a manifestation of your greatly understood and firmly accepted duty.

Translated by Claire Payton

Guillaume Guillon-Lethière, *Le Serment des ancêtres* (*The Oath of the Ancestors*), 1822, oil on canvas. This image, painted by a French painter of Guadeloupean descent and offered to the nation of Haiti as a gift, depicts the founding of the country through the collaboration of Alexandre Pétion and Jean-Jacques Dessalines. At their feet lie the broken chains of slavery. Image courtesy of CIDHICA.

Coat of Arms of the Duc de la Marmelade, 1812. College of Arms MS J. P. 177: Armorial General du Royaume d'Hayti. Reproduced by permission of the Kings, Heralds and Pursuivants of Arms.

Haiti was among the first stops in early tourist packages. Promotional materials (including this one from around 1937) often featured romanticized representations of Haitian history and culture. Image reprinted courtesy of Frank R. Crumbie Papers, Special and Area Studies Collections, George A. Smathers Libraries, University of Florida, Gainesville.

Children playing in front of the Sans-Souci Palace in Milot, Haiti. Sans-Souci, once the residence of King Henry Christophe, is now a World Heritage Site. Photo courtesy of Myrmara Prophète/FotoKonbit.

Painting of President Florvil Hyppolite by renowned early twentieth-century Haitian artist Hector Hyppolite (1894–1948). *Le President Florvil Hyppolite*, ca. 1945–47, oil and pencil on paper board, 30" × 24", Figge Art Museum, Davenport, Iowa, City of Davenport Art Collection, museum purchase with funds from the Beaux Arts Committee, Inc., 1992.13. Reprinted with permission of the Figge Art Museum.

Vote on Demand, Port-au-Prince, Haiti 2006: Voters form lines in all directions as they stand surrounding election workers demanding the right to vote. Thousands of Cité Soleil residents gathered at 5 A.M. to vote at the former state employee housing building known as Building 2004 in Port-au-Prince, Haiti. The large building was the residence of high Lavalas officials and was built under Aristide's guidance. Photo: Carl Juste.

This photograph shows the intricate land use on the hills above Pétionville, with terracing on many farms. Photo by Viran De Silva. Reprinted courtesy of www.ExperienceHaiti.org.

Pauleus Vital, *Bees Attack Loner while Combit Workers Prepare the Fields*, 23 January 1964, oil on Masonite, 24" × 48", private collection. This image shows the many different types of agriculture practiced in the hills outside Jacmel and the rich vegetation on the hillsides. While workers have gathered for a collective work gathering, or *konbit*, accompanied by music, one man who has refused to join in finds himself punished by a swarm of bees.

Frankétienne, *Les Dénerflés*, 1983, oil on canvas. This work, one of many canvases by the novelist, exemplifies a swirling, vivid style and depiction of movement and intensity. Image courtesy of Frankétienne. Image credit: Max Nucci.

Phyllis Galembo, "Portrait of ounsi Paule of Souvenance." Photo from *Vodou: Visions and Voices of Haiti* (Berkeley: Ten Speed Press, 1998), 97.

A sugarcane cutter in Cadouche, a sugar-producing suburb of Cap-Haïtien, Haiti. Photo courtesy of Myrmara Prophète/ FotoKonbit.

Phyllis Galembo, "Oungan Castra Philippe poses by a mural of Azaka Mede, displaying the symbols of bag, pipe, and denim clothing." Photo from *Vodou: Visions and Voices of Haiti* (Berkeley: Ten Speed Press, 1998), 23.

Milocan; Le Monde Actuel—Erzulie Interceptée, 1996, oil on canvas in artist frame, detail of one of four panels, each panel 241 cm × 165 cm. Courtesy of the Bass Museum, Miami Beach. Artist Edouard Duval-Carrié offers a powerful critique of Ronald Reagan's 1981 Haitian Interdiction Program, which ordered the Coast Guard to intercept boats carrying Haitian migrants seeking refuge in the United States. Duval-Carrié depicts the Vodou *lwa* of love, Ezili Dantò, as a migrant, carrying a child, seeking refuge. Stopped by the Coast Guard, she remains resplendent, powerful, a signal of the determination and will that enabled migrants to make and survive the journey against the odds.

Edouard Duval-Carrié, *Cargo Bounty*, 2016, mixed media on aluminum in artist frame, 60" × 96". Courtesy of the artist.

Dix années de lutte pour la liberté

Georges Sylvain

Georges Sylvain was born in 1866 in Puerto Plata in the Dominican Republic to Haitian parents who had taken refuge there after the city of Cap Haïtien was bombed by English ships in 1865. However, he grew up in Haiti and after obtaining a law degree in Paris, he returned to Haiti in 1888. He founded the country's first law school in 1900. Sylvain represented Haiti in France and at the Vatican. He was also an accomplished writer, publishing a volume of poetry and a Haitian Creole adaptation of La Fontaine's Fables, both in 1901. Several of Sylvain's children went on to become influential and pioneering members of society in their own rights, such as anthropologist Suzanne Comhaire-Sylvain; feminist activist Madeleine Bouchereau-Sylvain; Normil Sylvain, poet and cofounder of La Revue Indigène; and Yvonne Sylvain, Haiti's first female medical doctor.

Georges Sylvain is perhaps best known for his role in the resistance against the U.S. occupation. He was a founding member of the Patriotic Union in 1915, whose principal objective was to fight the occupation. At its height, members of the Patriotic Union numbered in the tens of thousands, and were spread in branches throughout the country and even abroad. Thirty years after Sylvain's death in 1925, his friends and colleagues went through his papers to select speeches, articles and correspondence and gathered them under the title Dix années de lutte pour la liberté, *which they published in two volumes. In addition to chronicling Sylvain's fight against the occupation, the volumes also describe some of Haiti's ongoing environmental and political problems, including deforestation, the practice of preventive detention, and fraudulent elections.*

First Founding

Charles Bouchereau, Dr. Carré, V. Cauvin, F. Féquière, Dr. S. Holly, Occide Jeanty, Edmond Laforest, Lys Lafortune, L. C. Lhérisson, F. Porsenna, Joseph Sylvain, and Georges Sylvain met on 10 August 1915 at 11 A.M. to found the Patriotic Union. What follows is the speech given by Georges Sylvain to start the session.

Georges Sylvain's funeral in August 1925 was a national event. Photographer and date of photo unknown.

Sirs,

I could have convened a much greater number of friends whose support I can vouch for without even having to check with them to this first meeting. But wanting to move quickly, I stopped at the twentieth. . . .

Of the twenty called, eleven were able to come. We are thus twelve at the start of the session. Twelve bodes well, when we have to take on the duties of apostles. Sirs T. Guilbaud, A. Villejoint, E. Morel, D. Bellegarde, J. Lizaire, Georges and Charles Régnier, C. Benoit, Léo Alexis, kept far from us through circumstances independent of their will, enthusiastically applaud the idea that brings us together and approve our resolutions in advance. Others still, closely related to us, await the word to take their places at our side.

I thank you all for the large amount of trust that you have placed in me. My explanations, for most of you, have necessarily been short. It is time to complete them.

Our country, you know, is going through one of the most painful periods of its existence. For the first time since it constituted itself as a sovereign state, foreigners occupy its territory militarily. Taking advantage of our civil unrest, the United States, a friendly nation, without having been called by us, without making any formal grievances against us, is helping us—weapons in hand—demonstrating their intention of putting an end to, even through coercive means, the anarchy that, for some time, seems to have become for the Republic of Haiti, somewhat of a chronic state. Temporary or permanent assistance? It all depends on our behavior. Yet we seem not to understand the necessity of changing behavior.

Since there is no longer a president nor ministers, and no one is exercising authority, one could say that national life is paused. On the political stage, where the most active artisans of our ruin continue to parade, each one thinks only of fighting over the little we have left. Not knowing where to alight, [public] opinion is adrift, bewildered. Outside of the capital, people are not well informed. Only one side of the story is heard abroad, that given by U.S. newspapers.

I thought, you thought as I did, that in these troubled times, when the legacy of our forebears and the future of our children is at stake, something has to be done, for our collective honor: hold the national flag high above the factions!

Scattered across the country, kept out of public affairs by concern for their dignity and by our detestable government customs, some Haitians, respectable in every way, who represent honest work, family virtues, patriotism in action, live without almost any bonds between them. Because they are not noisily protesting and because they abhor violent acts, they are readily considered to be negligible quantities. In truth, their regrouping would constitute one of our major social forces. It seemed to me that the time had come to organize for them a rallying point, an association they could join. By remaining in constant communion of ideas and feelings with them, we will give them the means to make their voices heard and to dominate this clamor of personal appetites, the impact of which has never been more jarring.

Thus, the foreigner will note that, outside of politics and its leaders, there are thoughtful minds in our society, sound consciences and firm wills, capable of a common effort, when the fate of the homeland is at stake.

On the solid ground where we have stationed ourselves, completely disinterested from any ambition other than that of helping our people to regain a clear sense of its duties, agreement is easy between citizens of goodwill. A common worry brings us together: that Haiti remain ours and progress on the right path! The events taking place give this goal a precise meaning. Our action plan will be to make the best use of the present situation.

Onward, then, for the nation's salvation, and may God bless our endeavor!

The first incarnation of the Patriotic Union ended soon after the convention between Haiti and the United States was signed in September 1915. Georges Sylvain continued to protest the occupation of his country in newspapers and other venues. In November 1920, encouraged by James Weldon Johnson, Sylvain and others relaunched the association. The inaugural session of the union's second incarnation took place at the Parisiana Theater. What follows is the resolution signed by the founders.

Considering that experience has shown the necessity of restoring the political relations between Haiti and the United States of America to normalcy,

Considering that the coexistence of two powers, one foreign, the other native, simultaneously exercising their authority over a same territory, leads to anarchy; that such a regime, applied to the Republic of Haiti, cannot be prolonged without serious harm for the country that is affected by it without its consent;

Considering that it is important to Haitians to take advantage of the sympathy and to support the goodwill which has been set in motion in favor of their national cause abroad, especially in the United States.

The Haitians who have signed below, wanting to affirm their faith in their homeland's future, their devotion to its interests, and their unshakable commitment to the integrity of its territory

Solemnly swear to work in close union, by all peaceful means, to hasten the moment when the Haitian people will unequivocally regain the management of their destiny and will once again take under their responsibility full power to manage their own affairs in full sovereignty, in full independence:

Agree of a common accord that to effectively assist in the realization of their national aspirations:

1. An Association is constituted, known as the *Patriotic Union*, between all those who across the breadth of the Republic adhere to or will adhere to the views and purposes listed hereunder. It will last until its objective is attained.

2. The Association is represented by a Central Committee of Action and Propaganda, consisting of fifty-five members, located in Port-au-Prince. The committee is itself represented by a board of fifteen of its own members.

3. The Patriotic Union will meet, whenever opportune, at the call of the Central Committee. The Committee will meet each month, and will hold special meetings when the board deems it necessary. The board is continuously in session.

4. The Association delegates full powers to the Committee to develop and implement the statutes that will govern its workings. The board is especially tasked with linking the Patriotic Union's action to that of the various local committees, as well as to that of groups abroad which have captured [public] opinion with the Haitian issue and are involved in ensuring a solution consistent with national interest. It makes all practical decisions and takes every measure apt to bring about this solution.

Long live Haiti!

Written and signed at Port-au-Prince,
the twenty-second of November, 1920.
(signed) Baussan, F. L. Cauvin, Lespinasse,

M. Morpeau, D. Jeannot, Pauléus Sannon,
D. Bourand, Georges Sylvain, Ls. Ed. Pouget,
Léon Nau, Sténio Vincent, C. Rosemond,
P. Thoby, Price Mars, Léon Liautaud, Abel N.
Léger, Victor Cauvin, C. Vieux, V. Delbeau,
Rigal, Clément Lespinasse, Boco, Is. Vieux,
Dr. Salomon, F. Viard, Dr. F. Coicou.

In June 1922, Georges Sylvain wrote to the director of the Courrier Haïtien *newspaper with an account of his tour in the north of the country on behalf of the Patriotic Union. The account which summarizes the results obtained by the Union to date was printed in the 16–17 June edition of the newspaper.*

A Tour in the North

Mr. J. Jolibois, Jr.
Director of "Courrier Haïtien"
In Town.

My dear director,
Here I am returned from my short tour in Cap [Haïtien], Port-de-Paix, Gonaïves and St. Marc.

Although too rare and too short for our liking, these trips, where we have the chance to confer with the heads of our regional committees, and have direct contact with the people, to inform them of the results of our action, and to sustain a unity of vision, are precious.

Everywhere I went, I found the people thirsty for comforting news, if only to strike a balance against the endless chatter of those begging for posts and the outrageous character of the government projects regarding the loan law and internal taxes which overwhelm and bewilder them. I had no trouble showing that in the opinion campaign we are waging in the United States with the help of the defenders of our national cause, our ambition has always leaned toward a complete recovery of our confiscated rights and not toward an adjustment of the protectorate, in McCormick's turn of phrase. Any partial improvement obtained through the condescension of those in power, whether Republicans or Democrats, can only be uncertain, liable to disappear with the Administration that agreed to it. We are attacking imperial policy itself as an instrument of oppression, of violence and of ruin. And imperialism, strengthened by the United States' current financial dominance, is not a fortress we can strike down on the first try. "The battle will be long," our friends told us as soon as we entered into action. "There will be inevitable ups and downs. Stay strong and you will gain the advantage in the end!"

Two years had not gone by before we saw the effectiveness of a plan based on these projections justified. By asking for more, we have obtained less, without abandoning any of our claims. No one can deny that the treatment to which the country is currently subjected is not that to which it was subjected six years ago. To what do our people owe this softening of the regime, if not to the energy of its defenders? Hog-tied and handed over by its own government to the mercy of the United States, where would it be now without the intervention of the Patriotic Union along with the National Association for Advancement of Colored People and the writers of *The Nation*? When our delegates left for New York, the Dartiguenave government, deprived of its salary by the plenipotentiary Minister of the United States with the approval of the State Department, was so discredited in the eyes of its foreign guardians that a report from the President of Haiti, sent in accordance with all forms of protocol to President Harding, spent several months without an acknowledgment of receipt!

So all those who purport that our fight has been in vain or that no results can be seen, obviously have their eyes closed, due to their own bias and disparagement.

The truth is that having the firm intention of effecting a profound change in the relationship between the United States and the small countries of this hemisphere through the pressure of public opinion, enlightened with regard to the processes of the imperialist system, we have, thanks to the intelligent zeal of friends of our cause, provoked in all the states of the federal union a strong current of opinion that is favorable to the restitution of our independence and of our national sovereignty. An association is working, which has given itself the task of defending our interests and extending our propaganda. Important leagues, in terms of members and objectives, such as the General Federation of Labor, the League of Voting Women, the Society of Foreign Policy, the Popular Government League, the main Catholic and Protestant associations, have taken this movement under their wing. Newspapers and magazines with large circulations and with great influence, aside from or outside of *The Nation* unhesitatingly participate.

In the Senate itself, the formidable and feared group of the die-hards, that most solid core of the Liberal Party that seems destined in the near future to supplant the two big historical parties worn out by the routine of power, is acting in our favor. Those are all positive results that anyone can verify.

A recent event has just thrust them into the light. Its importance and reach cannot be exaggerated. Twenty-four men of law, of those whose word carries authority in the United States, former judges of the Supreme Court, law professors, presidents of the Bar and former presidents of the Bar, lawyers and attorneys, diplomats, members of judicial congresses, authors of universally appreciated law books, have signed a legal opinion, in which they denounce the illegality and the injustice of the United States' intervention in Haiti and in the Dominican Republic, and conclude with the necessity of putting an end to the military occupation of these two territories, for the honor and the good reputation of the starred union.

. . . We are thus founded in affirming that in the match at hand, victory remains ours, resounding, undeniable. The most authoritative voices in the country of our occupiers have proclaimed that we are well within our rights.

We have thus won our battle of the Marne.

There is no example of a great people that cares about its honor, content with living indefinitely in illegality and injustice.

Politicians can agitate, financiers can multiply their plundering and extortion of businesses. The seed of truth scattered to the . . . winds . . . by the twenty-four jurists will sooner or later be sanctioned in the annals of history.

Very cordially yours,
Georges Sylvain

On 19 August 1923, Georges Sylvain gave a speech in the northern city of Jean-Rabel. He begins by stressing his ties to the area, as well as the importance of family and community. He then provides an update on the struggle to end the U.S. occupation of Haiti, exhorting his audience to join the fight. He evokes the international support the Haitian cause has garnered, citing populations in the United States and in Latin American countries. Sylvain also evokes migration, deforestation, elections, and taxes, citing them as issues that need to be addressed for the fight against the occupation to be effective. The speech begins and ends with historical references.

My friends,

Have no doubt that it is a joy for me to be among you today. Child of the North-West, I belong no less to Jean-Rabel, to the Mole, to Bombarde, to Baie-de-Henne, to Port-de-Paix, to St. Louis or to Anse à Foleur, by virtue of multiple familial and affective ties that throughout time have made of all the great families of our region a single family within which we willingly unite and support each other when needed.

. . .

Seeing you so numerous and so refreshed, I thought this was a good occasion to talk to you about a subject that is dear to all of our hearts: our country's future. I will present the situation to you as it is, what a group of patriots has tried to do to improve it and what still remains to be done so that the Haitian nation can recover its normal living conditions.

May you glean from my words a new reason for comfort! May the spirit of our ancestors inspire me with the words most likely to touch your consciences!

Where are we? A foreign government, the United States of North America occupies our territory and is ruling as master. Some Haitians are associated with them in this labor of subservience and exploitation. The vast majority of the nation is opposed to the foreign domination and protests against the indigenous power's actions: the invaders' puppet, the support it lends them is self-serving. But powerless to demand its sovereignty with weapons, it is a spectator to its ruin, seemingly with no strength to achieve moral unity, the prerequisite for any effective reaction. However, the work is there, urging us to act. Although the solution to the problem of our liberation may be painful, it is not practically unsolvable. We have to solve it, and it can only be solved by us. Whatever way we approach it, we can only begin by an act of faith and of will. As long as you tell yourselves that there is nothing left to do, you will not engage in the battle, or if you engage in it with the idea that victory is impossible, you are already beaten. Only fighters win: certain of ultimate success and determined to make all sacrifices to obtain it, no matter what!

Have we really been reduced to the state of those who are doomed, waiting for nothing more than the final punishment! Far from it!

Sylvain evokes how the tide of public opinion is turning in the United States, with more and more people in favor of ending the occupation in Haiti and the Dominican Republic. He also evokes support for the Haitian cause in Latin America.

Against the external danger we have two weapons—all powerful, if we know how to use them: our rights and our unshakable persistence in claiming them. All over the world, where opinion no longer accepts that we purport to subjugate a people against their will, Haiti is considered to be a victim of a misuse of force.

Let us stay on this solid ground: let us use our money, our information, our encouragement to help those generous hearts abroad, especially in the United States and in other countries of the Americas, work to rally even more support.

At home, let us control our outrage and our impatience, however sharp certain forms of provocation might be! Faced with a revolutionary and anarchic power, let us protest vigorously; let us protest together against all attacks on our rights, against everything that tends to worsen our fate!

Let us not be afraid to descend en masse to the public arena from time to time to better assert the steadfastness of our claims, and our unshakable solidarity! But, let us show ourselves to be worthy of freedom, by showing impeccable discipline. Let us know what we want and where we should stop. Let justice remain our shield! Let us not do anything that our enemies can use as an excuse to justify upholding an indefinite occupation of our territory to the new President of the United States!

. . .

Without abandoning our opinion campaign, that we want, on the contrary, to intensify, it seems to me opportune for us to develop our internal activities more vigorously from now on. Resisting oppression, illegality, anarchy, is not enough: we must fight for a reform of the communal institution, which has at its core the autonomy of the communes; fight for the adoption of measures conducive to ensuring the freedom and fairness of the electoral vote, and to exclude any measures that would be contrary [to that]; fight for the return to legal order with legislative elections! We must, in addition, organize ourselves in light of these elections in a way to only send to the chambers, through rigorous discipline, only those citizens sincerely devoted to the superior interests of the country in all ways.

Is such a result, desirable as it may be, still possible, given the electoral practices you all know? I would not dare affirm it. But whatever the outcome, the time has come to undertake the cleansing of those practices, in preparation for the great work that will fall to the liberating chambers. It is one of the tasks included in our duty to educate the lower classes, [a duty that is now] more pressing and more urgent than at any other time of our history. . . .

But who am I to thus pretend to light your way, at the troubled hour when consciences seem to float aimlessly; when the need for a guiding principle of conduct, for firm direction, flusters our bewildered population everywhere? A Haitian of goodwill, who has never despaired of his country, a mere servant of the homeland in mortal danger, who asks nothing of it, who wants nothing but its salvation.

If one day someone were to come say to you that I aspire to anything that resembles an award, boldly denounce the lie. My only ambition is to be useful! Anywhere I can fight to ensure a better future for your children, for mine, I will be in my place!

What more is there to do to make that happen? Let's go to the people, my friends, to raise them from their miserable conditions: *drought*, the consequence of an imprudent deforestation . . . (Do we have a forestry office, forestry legislation, no one to warn the man of the countryside of the wrong he does to himself in thoughtlessly cutting down trees?); *emigration*, the most certain effect of which, in absence of any preventative measure is the disintegration of the peasant family; the state's retaking of domain concessions endowed with long-term leases and exploitation monopolies for the benefit of foreign countries; *internal taxes* in the hands of gendarmes; the rural police in the hands of the section chiefs—all of these ills at once have brought our people in the plains and the mountains way down and will continue to bring them down! Let us unhesitatingly go to the people to instruct and preach to them! Let us set our honor to it, let us set our pride to it! Have you counted up what delaying this necessary vocation for too long might have cost us? Quite simply our country's independence! My dream, you see, would be that each of our Patriotic Union committees have its . . . school, that it would maintain and endow! And may each city, each town, each village, have its committee, a rich scholarly crop, in communication with the Head Office, receiving the seed of life from it and spreading it little by little! Yes, that would really be a touching sight! Why should your city not give the signal for this new crusade? Noblesse oblige! Remember! Was it not a few hours from Jean-Rabel on the Fouré Plantation that Joseph Pourcely determined the liberation of this part of the territory by inciting the slave workshops to rise up? Here, behind the hillock that dominates the church square, did the residents of this town not sustain a Homeric battle for two months against one of Christophe's divisions, led by the terrible Riché?

Men, women, old people, children, everyone was involved! Men of Jean-Rabel, where is your soul of yesteryear? Women of Jean-Rabel, of the land from which the cornelian soul of Jeanne Maurepas sprung like a flame, what have you done with your heart?

Rise up! It is not too late! Let us recover our faith, the male energy of the forefathers! Rise up around the flag, symbol of national unity!

The following excerpts are from the statement prepared by members of the Patriotic Union and presented to the committee established by the U.S. Senate to look into allegations of abuse under the occupation regime in Haiti and the Dominican Republic. They explicitly reference international law as well as the national myths on which the United States was founded to demonstrate why the occupation was unacceptable.

Protest by the "Society for the Independence of Haiti and Santo Domingo" and of the "National Association for the Advancement of Colored People" before the Senate Inquiry Committee.

In the name of the Society for the Independence of Haiti and of Santo Domingo, of the Patriotic Union of Haiti and of the National Association for the Advancement of Colored People;

We respectfully protest against the conditions in Haiti and in Santo Domingo, against the current occupation of the Republics of Haiti and of Santo Domingo by the armed forces of the United States before the Senate Inquiry Committee and we ask for their withdrawal and the restoration of the two republics to their complete and absolute independence in accordance with their former constitution, and this as soon as effective national civil governments can be established.

We make this request in the name of justice, of liberty and of the sacred right, fortified by the results of the world war, for a separate existence and complete freedom for all small nations in keeping with our historical American traditions.

We declare that the violent overthrow of these Republics happened without sufficient reason, that it was not justified by American nor international law nor did the political conditions that existed at the time warrant it, and it is in direct violation of the fourteenth point of the principles of peace, such as they were evoked by President Woodrow Wilson, guaranteeing "political independence and territorial integrity of big and small states alike."

We declare that the American occupation of these countries has since been destructive and without fundamental constructive value; that no foundation has been established for the permanent reconstruction of these governments; that the physical improvements made, such as the construction of roads and the sanitation of cities, were accomplished by inexcusable means—in Haiti at the cost of a forced slavery, such as the corvée, that the American conscience would never have permitted to exist had it not been hidden by an impenetrable naval censure.

We declare that the American domination in Haiti and Santo Domingo has been accompanied by individual wrongs and military excesses exacerbated by the difference in language, race and traditions, and that it has offered the most complete proof of the truth of Abraham Lincoln's immortal words that "no man is good enough to govern another man without the other's consent."

We declare that the Constitution and the treaty imposed on the Haitian people and the military regime imposed on the Dominican people without even the sanction of a constitution or a treaty, are unworthy of the genius and the generosity of the American people and tend toward the establishment of perpetual protectorates implying that the development of these Republics will be dominated by a foreign government.

We declare that the efforts of the State Department to force the Dominicans to sign a treaty ratifying and approving all official acts of this government are absolutely unworthy of any country with a decent and wholesome public spirit; we affirm the rights of these people to a complete recovery of all the injustices committed by the military government.

We declare that the acts of this government in Haiti and in Santo Domingo since July 29, 1915, have troubled our relationships with the Republics of Central and South America, have seriously threatened our commerce with these countries and gravely intensified the defiance toward the United States on the part of these small American nations.

The Republic of Haiti

The report presented to the senate committee of Foreign Affairs by the delegation of the Patriotic Union of Haiti contains serious and documented accusations against the American administration in this republic, accusations that demand the most pressing investigation.

These accusations attack the motivation of the intervention, the mode of the intervention, the imposition of a treaty on Haiti, the subsequent repeated violations of the Modus Vivendi imposed by the American forces onto Haiti, the failure to pay the interests of the Haitian debt under the American regime, which had never happened before, the suppression of the Haitian legislature by armed American officers, the regime of martial law and of censure, the refusal of the Mayo court to call Haitian witnesses or to hear Haitian complaints. The report also records twenty-five cases of atrocities with names and dates attributed to the American forces.

. . .

Respectfully submitted,
Haiti, Santo Domingo, Independence Society,
by Oswald Garrison Villard
National Association for the Advancement
of Colored People
by James Weldon Johnson, Secretary
Patriotic Union of Haiti by Sténio Vincent
Ernest Angell, Advisor

Disappointed with the investigation conducted by the 1920 court of inquiry established jointly by the U.S. Marine Corps and the U.S. Navy, the Patriotic Union used the press to render public various crimes committed in Haiti by the Marines. Below is an excerpt from their list.

List of Crimes Committed by U.S. Marines

1. Hanging of Mr. Cicéron Lacroix, execution of Léon Moricet Téca and other individuals, in October and November 1918, by Lieutenant Lang, facts denounced to the Navy Court of Inquiry by Mister Philoclès Lacroix in his letter dated 20 October 1920.

2. Execution in Mirebalais of the Péralte brothers by Lieutenant Wallace. Here are the names of those shot: Philoxène Péralte, Emmanuel Péralte, Péralte Jr., and Léosthènes Péralte in December 1918.

3. Execution by Marines of the man called Joseph Marseille and of his two sons, Michel and Estima Marseille, of Princil Mesadieux, Baye section, district of Mirebalais; murder in his house of Guerrier Josaphat, with one of his

children, aged fourteen years—facts denounced by Mr. Louis Charles Aîné on December 8th 1920.

4. Arrest by an American officer and mysterious disappearance of Mister Charrite Fleuristone, former school inspector, in la Chapelle, district of Saint-Marc. He was arrested in early 1919, at the same time as Mr. S. Jean-Baptiste and Mr. Clément Clerjeune.

5. In Marin, district of Mirebalais, in December 1919, the murder and mutilation by Marines, accompanied by gendarmes, of Joseph Duclerc, respectable old man, aged sixty years. After the crime, they burned down his house.

6. During the same period of time and in the same section, the same group shot at a schoolteacher, Mrs. Frédéric, and wounded her in the mouth. She managed to escape. The Marines and gendarmes burned down her house, as well as all the outbuildings. They were accompanied by an American officer, a lieutenant, whose name can be established with an investigation.

7. Near Marin, in Collier, in the district of Mirebalais, the same gang cut off a blind man's head. His name was Néis, he was twenty-five years old, and they cut off the head of a child who was with him, named Jules Louisville.

8. In Marin, during the same period of time, another group of gendarmes and Marines attacked Mathieu Cadet, aged fifty-five years, in his house with gunfire. Despite being wounded in the shoulder, he managed to escape his attackers through a side door. His house was pillaged and burned. The gendarme Josias took a mule belonging to Mathieu.

9. In January 1919, in Nouailles, Marines and gendarmes, having come from Beaurepos, killed Jean Luc, an invalid. Torn from his house, he was shot point blank. His house was pillaged and burned.

10. The same day, the same gang of Marines and gendarmes caught Esca Estinfil with her young sons in her house at Caye-Beau. They shot all three of them. Then they pillaged the house and burned it. Esca, an important planter, had a large quantity of coffee and a large sum of money for commercial transactions in storage.

. . .

25. In a petition addressed to Mr. Barnave Dartiguenave, Haitian Secretary of the Interior, on December 16th 1920, by the members of the League of Public Good, located in Cap Haïtien and presided by Pastor Auguste Albert of the Baptist Church, petition published in the *Courrier Haïtien* on February 26th, 1921, we highlight the following facts:

1. In the prison at Cap Haïtien, over four thousand prisoners died during the years 1918, 1919, and 1920.
2. At Chambert, American camp, during those three years, 5,475 prisoners died, for an average of five deaths a day.
3. In Cap Haïtien, in 1919, up to eight corpses of prisoners were thrown into pits each day.

4. The mortality rate is just as intense in the prisons of Port-au-Prince and Gonaïves.

5. In Cap Haïtien, for a population of five hundred prisoners, the death average is four a day, meaning 24 percent a month, or a quarter of this population, give or take 1 percent.

6. Before the American occupation and the takeover of prisons by American officers, the number of detainees did not surpass forty per year on average in the prison at Cap Haïtien.

7. At that time, the mortality rate rarely got as high as four prisoners in a year.

Translated by Nadève Ménard

Les simulacres

Fernand Hibbert

Fernand Hibbert was one of Haiti's most important early twentieth-century writers. A teacher at the Lycée Petion in Port-au-Prince, he first published articles in the journal La Ronde, *and went on to write a series of novels. His 1923 novella,* Les simulacres, *holds the distinction of being the first book-length work of fiction published during the U.S. occupation to take the occupation as its subject. The main character is a member of the Haitian elite who is hoodwinked by both the occupation forces and a Cuban schemer who seduces his wife and cons him out of thousands of dollars. This work is typical of Hibbert's fiction, which often pokes fun at the bourgeois class to which he himself belonged. At the same time, the tale also contains a serious commentary on the country's political plight. The character Mr. Brion, often read as the author's stand-in, demands: "May all those to whom a talent for writing has been given take up their pens and discuss their country's interests." * Les simulacres *ends with the author addressing a passionate plea directly to his readers, exhorting them to change their own behavior and that of their children in order to preserve and protect the nation in the future.*

Mr. Héllenus Caton was about fifty-eight years old, but looked young. He had contributed to the establishment of one of those governments of long ago that did not last long, but were very profitable for the "entitled," as they were called at the time. He was appointed minister, persecuted his compatriots, committed a few crimes and after a year spent in the ministry which he had entered poor, he left with a small fortune that he was able to conserve—which is pretty rare for politicians of that category. The American intervention bothered him in his ascension, "crushed his future," as he sometimes complained. Regret filled his soul; he became an ardent patriot and a bitter progressive.

. . .

Mr. Héllenus Caton had not always been as hardened as he wanted to appear. Mr. Brion even recalled that not too long ago—it was soon after the visit to Port-au-Prince of the fine, elegant, and sophisticated MacCormick, who advised the occupation to have more contact with Haitian society—one day, Mrs. Russell, accompanied by Mrs. Henry Roberts, had come to visit Céphise Caton. Héllenus was so proud that he stayed puffed up like a balloon for days. And Céphise, too. Think of it! The sole visit of Mrs. Roberts would have been sufficient to flatter her—and here the wife of the head of the Occupation joined her to call on her, taking the initiative—she was all aflutter! Mrs. Roberts, who had never known the Héllenus Caton couple, made the introductions with remarkable ease. Mrs. Russell found Céphise to be pretty, feisty, which was true, and despite Héllenus's earnestness which made her want to laugh, she was able to contain herself, congratulate him on being the husband of a charming woman, then she left with her friend.

That was all, but it was enough. We can guess what this simple courtesy visit opened as far as a future outlook in Héllenus Caton's soul! The next week, Céphise returned the visit, accompanied by her husband. They also went to see the Robertses. For a few weeks, Mr. Héllenus Caton transformed into an Americanizing-Americanist and stopped, during that period, paying visits to Mr. Brion. But when he realized that the Americans were not thinking of him for president of the Republic, he began to slowly deflate, became a patriot again and began to see Mr. Brion again who welcomed him with a smile born of kindness and gentle irony.

Translated by Nadève Ménard

La Revue Indigène: The Project

Normil Sylvain

La Revue Indigène *was a short-lived but influential literary magazine founded in 1927 as part of a broader cultural movement. It is often celebrated as a pivotal moment in Haitian literature, symbolizing the turn toward more authentically Haitian writing. But as this introductory text shows, its founders did not see it as a radical break with prior literary traditions and figures. Rather, they presented themselves as following in the footsteps of literary predecessors from previous generations, such as Georges Sylvain and Massillon Coicou. In this text from the first issue, Normil Sylvain (son of Georges Sylvain) lays out the project's objectives, including the need for a literary celebration of "haitienneté," of "Haitianity." At the same time, Sylvain emphasizes the importance of establishing connections with Spanish-speaking counterparts on the American continent and refers repeatedly to literary production in France. Sylvain acknowledges that in the context of the occupation the creation of a literary journal may seem frivolous, but insists that in fact poetry—and beauty—are necessary to the rebirth of the nation.*

Georges Sylvain's Dream

During a conference tour he once undertook in the South of the island, Georges Sylvain wrote to his collaborators at *La Ronde* with his impressions of the various cities he passed through, and he finished thus, sharing his ideal of a Haitian journal, hyphen and meeting place for all brotherly souls haunted by a same dream of art and beauty.

"To find outside of politics, for all Haitians of goodwill, a common ground of unity, to have all of the nation's intellectual forces contribute toward the civilization of their shared homeland, to render them conscious of themselves by teaching them to know themselves better; to show the new generations who have come into the world at a time of transition that their special mission is to *prepare the future*, to help the people become more moral through the revelation of the artistic ideal[,] to instruct them via a gradual initiation to knowledge of French language and civilization, acquired with the help of our Creole dialect, to lastly save us from ourselves, by diverting toward

Good all the restless activities that require nourishment, all the latent energy that withers and is depleted due to idleness.

One fact that any of us, provided he gives it some thought, cannot help but be struck by, is our society's lack of cohesion. We are lacking the overall picture, a continuity of effort, because we do not know each other. Today does not know what yesterday was, even stranger, we do not know each other from one city to the next. Revive interrupted traditions, unite the past with the present and prepare the future by spreading throughout the country a taste for a national understanding.

A love of letters will thus be a link that will unite hearts, a sort of religion that will speed up the arrival of that Brotherhood that up until now has only found its place on our official acts and in our newspaper columns. Popularize the works of our good authors, help the youth who deserve attention become known to the public. Who does not see the hope it is reasonable to expect from such an undertaking! . . ."

That much would be sufficient as a program and would spare me from having to keep you longer, but we must specify our leanings and add some new thoughts to the old ideal.

Why We Accord Such Importance to Poetry

And I was told, "Think of it! An art and literature journal at this time. Don't you realize that those are games and entertainment for happy times, work for fortunate days, no one cares about joy, your call will fall on deaf ears, who reads verse in our rushed times; romantic young women and lovelorn adolescents, c'mon, be serious. I don't advise you to try this adventure."

It's true that this is not a time for laughter. In the whirlwind of our existence, however, don't you think that it would be enjoyable to allow for a pause, a break in the shade listening to poets sing before again picking up the collar of daily troubles. Don't you think that the burden would be lighter, that the road would seem shorter, the sun less hot. Song is not only a pretty tune that speaks your joy, orchestrates your sufferings, it helps us to discover the landscape contemplated with a distracted gaze, sliding over the surface of things, without trying for one minute to possess them, it allows us to see within ourselves more easily, to partake of the interior landscape, to penetrate the mysterious domain of the soul. . . . Is that not the problem in its entirety? Poetry is an instrument of knowledge.

We are not only hungry for bread!

. . .

We want other voices to respond from all over the country. The singers are from the North and they are from the South; they sing the Haitian land. They help make it known, love it through knowing it, revealing us to ourselves, giving us motive for national pride.

The ideas we have of a country, whether true or false, are those given by poets, novelists, painters, sculptors, faithful image or false painting. . . . During the war, the propaganda service was headed by worthy writers and the best talents of the warring countries presided over the moral offensive constituted by the communiqués. . . . Literature provides the unerring expression of a people's soul.

What We Want

Testimonials of our time, of our generation, [or,] as we say in medicine or chemistry, our reaction, the reflexes of our sensitivity when in contact with things.

The message we are bringing—no matter that it is heard, another age will come that will welcome it, we are sure. Before entering into the night of forgetfulness, we want to release our sincere cry. A stormy night, tousled waves, blowing gusts of wind, the dismasted boat is adrift. In its cabin, the telegraph operator is making conventional calls at his post, calm in the midst of chaos and confusion. The captain at his command post takes the logbook, inscribes his latest observations and flings to the coast a bottle into the sea. Our stubborn hopes send out a station's cry . . . it is our bottle in the sea . . .

Together, we want to try to find reasons to love one another within reasons to believe. Unite in unanimous accord souls of goodwill searching for their way and aimlessly wandering in the dark; unite them in art, in Beauty.

Go back to the times when Haitians loved each other, when living here was sweet, a sweetness enclosed in our tranquil landscapes between our blue mountains and the singing sea.

Our Public . . .

The reader we choose, the one dearest to us, is the young man of twenty years carried away by a noble and generous enthusiasm, who still has a heroic and excessive soul, who is obsessed with heights, tortured by the desire for excellence, and who dreams of the absolute. . . . O, you the great yeast of future crops, young man who embodies our hopes, I trust you. And you, the anxious mothers, you the worried fathers troubled by his pensive gaze, frightened by his fever and exaltation, rest assured that he is born to accomplish great things.

Young girls not yet troubled by the painful problems of our oppressed existence, mothers of tomorrow who will have to knead the loose clay, the fragile clay of the souls of children yet to be born, we want them to listen to us, we will try to keep their attention, to move them, to make them think with us about collective duties.

Our Ideas: A Doctrine

Our country is sick not only in the heart, but also in the head. The problem is first one of intelligence, then one of sensitivity. We have to attempt a therapy of national renaissance at home, guided by the fine parallel effort conducted with uncommon good fortune in France. There are too many misconceptions currently on the market.

We must reestablish the notion of order, of basic required hierarchy, a healthy logic, more just criteria. First establish the library of an honest man, chase off those who are selling junk, the fortune tellers, the acrobats and the jugglers, make known the upstanding writers, the serious thinkers who are preparing a healthy and vigorous youth for France.

The work of an Auguste Comte, commented by Maurras, Valois, Galéot, Daudet, the intellectual and moral reform of Renan, Taine, Eustel, Barrès, Le Play . . . and so on.

From these thinkers we will take methods of reasoning and modes of action, they will serve as models for us and will allow us to build an original doctrine.

Latin America and Us

In this Spanish and English America, we have the glorious destiny of maintaining along with Canada and the French Antilles the traditions of the French language, dire and dangerous honor, for it earned us a century of isolation. . . . The Dominican Republic which shares our territory does not share this misfortune; she belongs to a Latin America of eighteen republics. Writers speak to a public of 90 million men, her joys and pains are acknowledged.

We have to know the literature and the soul of Latin America.

The peoples have lived a life as difficult as ours, they have known the same fumblings, similar vicissitudes, the era of *caudillos* and *pronunciamientos*, the period when forces of anarchy and forces of cohesion and order confronted each other, the painful times of puberty for young nationalities.

Historians of the causes of their misfortune try, like us, to explain race, that simple phenomenon of social physics, that game of antagonistic forces that clash before finding their balance in a perfect static. They say "we acted that way because Indians." For our part, we readily say "because Black."

That has nothing to do with it. If we have suffered, if we have known the same anxieties placed beneath similar skies, in almost identical circumstances, it is neither because Indians nor because Black, but because men. All men, whoever they may be, placed in the same climate, faced with the same difficulties, would probably have acted or reacted the same . . . as men. Paul Morand, returning from a long journey wrote "nothing but the Earth." And another great traveler of whom they asked his opinion on what he had seen answered, "I met men and women."

We are guilty for not knowing Latin America because the origins are similar and a great common danger threatens us.

. . .

"Brothers of the other race," the writers of Latin America sometimes say when speaking of us and hereditary prejudices raise their fence.

The language difference isolates us more than an ocean.

. . .

More Human

Finally, we must work to create the man who is to be, citizen of the future, citizen of humanity, of a renewed humanity—I hear the cries and the chaos of Pharisees—for whom the barriers, the borders, racial differences, geographical positions have only their necessary accidental value that limit the fields we cultivate, but in no way hinder the painful identity of consciences. Here is the one we are looking for: the man on his way, the one called by and waited upon by Massillon Coicou, the friend, the brother for whom we have a tenderness at the ready. We will try to create him within ourselves, around us. However, let there be no mistake about our intentions or our thoughts and let us not be betrayed in the ways we are interpreted: diversity between countries is necessary. "Happy are they who die for their cities of earth; they are the outward forms of the City above," said Péguy. They are lands of choice, predetermined settings for the wonderful blooming of dissimilar yet closely related plants.

What We Will Try to Do with Our Journal

A faithful and living portrait of the different expressions of contemporary Haitian life and thought. Intellectual and artistic life, economic and commercial life. The Haitian point of view on issues, the way in which we see things and since the word "native" is used as a type of insult, we claim it as a title, the native's point of view. A return to simplicity and to what is natural, to the living model, to direct description, a more pronounced flavor of Haitian-ness, that is what seems to characterize our young poetry.

. . .

As soon as our next delivery, one of us will provide an overview of contemporary French poetry in order to initiate the public here and to introduce it to this select audience.

We have chosen tales, and especially wanted them from those of our storytellers who have been able to see and understand Haiti. We start with an episode of peasant life deliciously sketched by the tender philosopher, that man of charming spirit who is called Price-Mars. It is an excerpt of our friend's lovely, substantial, and profound work on Haitian folklore, wakes, legends, old customs inherited from the African past or the colonial period. Tales from Marcelin, Hibbert and others . . . let's not get ahead of ourselves . . . will help to set the face of Haiti, its true face.

. . .

We want to continue, to take our place in the ranks, behind those who struggled so that one day there could be a prosperous, happy, and free Haiti.

Translated by Nadève Ménard

La Revue Indigène: The Poetry

Various Authors

The following selection of seven poems reflects the range of themes and styles to be found in La Revue Indigène. *Among the poets who published in* La Revue Indigène *are many of Haiti's best-known writers, including Jacques Roumain, Emile Roumer, Philippe Thoby-Marcelin, and Carl Brouard. Like early Haitian poetry, the works in the magazine often described and celebrated particular geographical locations—Sacré-Coeur, Croix des Missions, Savanne Désolée, Grand-Rue, Kenscoff, Bois-Verna—and made references to Vodou, folk culture, and tributes to "women of the people" that can be found in the writing of previous decades. But the inclusion of technological innovations—the poets evoke subways, cars, steamers, typewriters, and phonographs—is new and a reflection of the time. They also reference new dances like the Charleston, tango, and fox-trot, musical instruments, and movies of the period. The poets who participated in* La Revue Indigène *had a lasting impact on Haitian poetry. They were especially innovative with regard to form, penning extremely short or long poems with unconventional line breaks. They also often included English words and phrases in their poems or lines written in Haitian Creole within predominantly French poems.*

SUBWAY
Bells!
The sound of scrap metal,
grating!
A tunnel's
black maw.
Men, girls and children[1]
abruptly thrown:
stop.[2]

—André Liautaud

MAIN STREET
>   Car horns
>   buses
>   crowd
>   donkeys
>   peasants

Under big-straw-hats
The market and its colored sounds
Hustle and bustle
>   pell-mell
The new houses are white
And square
You shouldn't daydream in the street
Drivers politely teach you that lesson in their own way
Konpè ou fou? (You crazy, Brother?)
>   Locomotive
>   bell
>   HASCO-5
The convoy roars
30 wagons of sugarcane
Pass by.
—Philippe Thoby-Marcelin

TAKE ELEGANCE AND WRING ITS NECK
Lolotte with shorn hair
no butt
 no breasts either
O palm-tree-like typist
With tortoiseshell glasses
who goes by bicycle
plays tennis
dances the Charleston
chews gum
You thumb your nose at callipygian beef stews
Yes, my dear[3]
And your handshake is very masculine
You play scales
On a Remington universal keyboard
It's as poetic as a xylophone
And my friend Jacques Roumain
Compares you to the rain

English correspondence holds no secrets for you
Sir—You would greatly oblige us forwarding the amount
of your bill enclosed by bearer[4]
I never sent you love letters
No, my dear[5]
And when Roumer began
ELEGIE:
We'll to the woods no more
O palm-tree-like typist
With tortoiseshell glasses
 you laughed
Not too practical
is he?
that young man
—Philippe Thoby-Marcelin

POEM
The road,
insatiable belly,
drinks
the car, that goes by gasping
in jolts.
My soul
has the hiccups.
I am thirsty for a woman's kiss.
The paddle cactus,
flea-ridden vagrants,
seem to laugh,
laugh at my pain.
I dream of being a cow
along the main road.
—Daniel Heurtelou

WE
We, the extravagant, the bohemian, the insane
We
Who love girls
strong liquor
the moving nudity of tables
Where the dice-box stands,
phallus-like.

We
the ones who are skinned alive, the poets.
We
who love everything.
everything;
church,
the tavern
the ancient
the modern
theosophy
cubism.
We
with hearts
powerful as motors
who love
cockfights
elegiac nights
the buzz of bees
in golden mornings.
the savage melody of tam-tams,
the husky harmony of car horns,
the poignant nostalgia of banjos.
We
the insane, the poets,
we
who write our most tender lines in hovels
and who read *Imitation* in dancing halls.
We
who do not bring peace at all
but the sad dagger
of our pen
and the red ink of our heart!

O LOULOUSE
Sweet Loulouse,
you drank crème de menthe,
gin,
"Black and White,"[6]
and you died.
O Loulouse,
you smelled of beef marrow pomade,
Pompeia,

you smoked tobacco from Virginia,
and you died.
Loulouse,
you took off all of your clothes
when making love,
but you are dead
and will forever gaze upon
the tips of your toes.

YOU
You
the beggars,
the filthy
who stink:
peasants coming down from the mountains with a
kid in your belly,
calloused peasants, with feet streaked with vermin,
whores,
invalids who drag your stench heavy with flies.
You
all the common folk,
Rise up!
for the great sweep of the broom.
You are the pillars of the building;
Take off
and it all collapses, house of cards.
Then, then
you will understand that you are a great wave
who does not know its power.
Oh! Wave,
gather yourself,
bubble up,
howl,
and may nothing subsist
beneath your shroud of foam,
nothing
but that which is nice and clean,
freshly washed,
bleached to the bone.
—Carl Brouard

Translated by Nadève Ménard

Notes

1. This line in English in the original text.
2. The title of the original poem is in English.
3. Original in English.
4. Original in English.
5. Original in English.
6. Original in English.

La blanche négresse

Cléante Valcin

Born Cléante Desgraves, Valcin holds the distinction of being the first woman to publish a novel in Haiti. She was also a founding member of the Ligue Féminine d'Action Sociale. Published in 1934, the final year of the U.S. occupation, La blanche négresse *is Valcin's second novel. It tells the story of Laurence Desvallons, a young Frenchwoman who moves to Haiti with her father and stepmother. She falls in love with a Haitian man but is pressured by her parents to marry a white American instead. The latter abandons her on discovering that one of her ancestors is black.*

Set against the backdrop of the occupation, the novel references several events that actually occurred at the time, including the student strike at the agriculture school, an event that helped bring about the end of the occupation. One American character is named Yen Leabrook, a clear reference to William Seabrook, author of The Magic Island. *Indeed, in Valcin's novel, Leabrook writes a book about Haiti that focuses on Vodou rituals and admits that most of it is made up. Major themes in the novel include racism (the first mention of the United States is within the context of a lynching), international relations, capitalism, and women's rights. The text draws continuous parallels between the institutions of marriage and slavery.*

Myrtana Durand is a staunch feminist and the novel's most patriotic voice. In the following excerpt, she responds to the overt racism expressed by the American Robert Watson, who objects that Laurence cannot possibly consider marrying the Haitian Guy Vanel because the latter is black.

"Selfless love is rare, Miss Laurence. It is sometimes found in marriage, when there is either wealth or poverty on both sides. There are exceptions, of course. Take me, I am rich and want to marry you, because you resist me. I'll have the ultimate pride of making you my wife in spite of yourself. Don't go thinking that because of that, I don't love you. Oh, no! I haven't been able to sleep since I found out that the poor president of our circle hopes to marry you. It makes me laugh sometimes . . . but.

"Could you forget that Mr. Vanel's fathers were the slaves of yours? . . . Would you dare to place this beautiful white hand in that of that black man and tell him, on your knees before the altar of God: 'I am yours forever?' You would not do that, Miss Laurence, the colonizers' spirits would tremble in their graves. Have you forgotten or better yet do you not know how cruel the rebellious Haitians were to the poor distraught colonizers? Haiti, ingrate Haiti, was the first black land to give the signal to revolt and massacre the Whites. If not for its temerity, your father would be rich and Guy Vanel, who has risen to the level of your generous love, Guy Vanel, who today is a renowned lawyer, the president of our club, would just be a vulgar nigger in some white person's service—in yours, who knows?"

"Shut up," said Myrtana, brusquely. "Our ancestors were not the only black slaves in the world, but only they hold the glory of having conquered their freedom."

"Yellow fever was their most powerful ally," said Leabrook.

"You're lying," continued the black woman, "the men of 1804, who, a short time later, helped Bolivar achieve his country's independence, but only under the condition of freeing the slaves of his land, did not need such a measly alliance. Yellow fever. Come on!"

Turning to Miss Desvallons, she said: "Laurence, whatever discomfort I may feel talking about colonizers, the ancestors, I cannot not defend the memory of the black heroes of Haitian independence."

Robert Watson is ultimately successful in his bid to marry Laurence. After their marriage, he complains of how he suffers from her indifference. Her reply:

"I know. Is it reasonable to waste two lives this way, each of which could, apart, have created an Eden? Ah! If I am causing you trouble, you can only blame my parents and your own stubbornness, I've already told you, sir. You bought me like one buys a trinket. Satisfy yourself with that, but don't ask me for anything. A trinket gives nothing . . .

[Robert:] "Ah, because I don't scatter the secrets of my life in the wind, even Mr. and Mrs. Desvallons have not guessed the depths of my torment.

"I can no longer suffer this compromise that forces us to [show] a radiant face, while on the inside, a sharp weapon pierces each of our hearts. Let's be loyal to ourselves. I have suffered this existence for a month. That's enough . . . I have lost hope of moving you even to pity . . . Mr. Guy Vanel will always remain the gulf that separates us, but as long as I live, you cannot be his mistress."

"Be quiet, sir, be quiet."

"You still love him . . . And I will not divorce, no, never . . . "

"You have no right to use that name as a weapon to insult me. When you asked me to marry you, I was informally engaged to Mr. Vanel, you knew that. What are you complaining about?

I had declined the honor of marrying you because I was against the horrible transaction this marriage was to be, but I was sold . . . "

She fell into a chair and added:

"Yes, I am your slave. But I call upon your generosity. Give me my freedom."

With this last word, she had a sudden jolt of revolt.

"No, a subjugated people, like an oppressed person does not ask for freedom, they take it: even if they have to spill their blood or die in its conquest: I will have my revenge upon you. Upon your dollars. I want to be free, I want to escape this golden prison, I want to retake my name, I want to live. Your wealth is for me the deepest of tombs. Haven't you already made thoroughly rich those who wanted to be wealthy at the expense of my happiness? Do they not plan to return to France to set up a department store with the proceeds of the big check you wrote them? Are they not driving around in a car? Aren't they happy at last?

Well! I am indifferent to all that. Me, I want only freedom. If you are not a tyrant, you will not place any obstacles to the battles I will wage to obtain it."

"Laurence, it's true I had always told you that I would marry you in spite of your refusal, thanks to my wealth, without letting you see that I adore you, that behind the proud American's dollars hid a poor lover's soul. I didn't know how to let you penetrate that soul so that you could read all the silent pain, all the selflessness it held captive. I was wrong, maybe. . . . Well, I release you from all the commitments we solemnly swore at City Hall, at your church, and before our God, that cruel God that you forced me to adopt."

The young woman lifted startled eyes to her husband. Robert, without waiting for her answer, brusquely left the room, slamming the door.

"Free!" repeated Laurence, "free with so little struggle." It seemed like a dream. Free! The word she had been waiting for for so long, that happy word fell upon her heart like a weight. Free. Is it divorce?

When her parents learn that her husband has left, they rush to Laurence's side. Her father tells her,

"Laurence, I married you to the most generous, the most loyal man there is. I made you a . . . " "A martyr," she added, "less than a slave, it's true . . . "

"No, a woman who could have been happy if she did not cling to unhappy memories. . . . Many a time we have seen people join in union who were not in love and who during the course of their life as a couple, discovered unsuspected qualities, unforeseen delicacies of the soul. Laurence, the law obliges you to follow Mr. Watson . . ."

"The marriage law? But, it's barbaric. It was clearly written by men to terrorize women, to make them eternal minors. Don't speak to me of that, oh no!"

"You owe your husband obedience, dear little one, remember that . . ."

"Woman will soon bury that word in her briefcase, as a lawyer, jurist, deputy, senator, minister . . .

Obedience! Oh! If you could only know how much that word hurt me when the mayor pronounced it.

It's time that marriage no longer turns a free woman into an oppressed one. See, thanks to this marriage I am a slave that only divorce can free."

After that speech, Laurence's stepmother admonishes her for having made "too great a stride into feminism."

Laurence and Robert Watson eventually resume life as husband and wife. They have a daughter together, Eveline. One day, while the couple is hosting a small party to celebrate Robert's birthday, Laurence receives a letter and photograph from her mother's great-uncle which reveal that she has black ancestors. One of the guests asks the others to take pity on Laurence and to promise her their silence on the matter. Laurence declares:

"No, sir, keep your pity and your silence, I have no use for them. . . . Is there misfortune or shame in having in one's veins a few drops of the blood of those men whose genius and courage surprised the whole world? I mean Toussaint Louverture, Dessalines, Pétion, François Capois, Boisrond Tonnerre and so many other illustrious blacks . . .

Their story is beautiful; I know it and I love it. I do not feel at all diminished to learn that in addition to the noble French blood that simmers within me, another one, just as noble is mixed. . . . No, keep your pity, sir, for I glory in being the granddaughter of the unfortunate Africa."

Robert declares that the letter and photograph make of Laurence "the woman he should not have married and of Eveline the child he should not have fathered." He proposes that they divorce and offers to set up Laurence in a house in the country as his mistress. She refuses.

Translated by Nadève Ménard

Souvenir d'Haïti

Othello Bayard

Written during the early twentieth century, most likely when Louis Achille Othello Bayard was a student in Germany in the 1920s, "Souvenir d'Haiti," often called "Haïti chérie," is one of the best-known and most often performed traditional Haitian songs. (Composer Robert Durand put Bayard's poem to music.) The speaker in the poem expresses his nostalgia for Haiti's faces, customs, and tropical environment when living abroad, "nan peyi blan" (in the white man's land). Although likely written at the time of the U.S. occupation of Haiti, there is no explicit reference to the imperial event, leaving unanswered the question of whether such a context informed or enhanced Bayard's longing. For many Haitians who have emigrated since the mid-twentieth century, the song has remained relevant. Although its title is in French, the song was written in Haitian Creole.

Sweet Haiti, there is no country better than you
I had to leave you to understand your worth
I had to miss you in order to appreciate you,
So I could really feel all that you are to me.
There's good sun, good rivers and good shade,
There's a nice breeze to keep us nice and cool
Haiti Thomas, you are a country dear to me.

In the white man's land, there's a nasty cold that's never good
And all day long, charcoal is kept burning
You can never see clearly, the sky is always in mourning
And for six months, not one of the trees has leaves
In my country, there is a sun to give heat
During the year, all the trees provide good shade
A nice sea breeze blows on our beaches
Haiti Thomas, is a country dear to me

In the white man's land, all the faces are one color
There are no mulatto women, no nice *marabou* or nice creole *griffonne*
Who like pretty dresses, nice powder, and nice smells,
Nor pretty young black women who like to say sweet words

In my country, when all those pretty people
Step out of church or the movies
You can't help but look, your mouth waters
What a great country is Haiti Thomas!

In the white man's land, you don't see mangoes or roosters at all,
No sapodilla, nor pretty green or violet star apples
No pineapples, nor pretty cashew apples
That give us good nuts to make nice hard candy.
You find oranges that come from Italy
But that are withered, and always half rotten.
In Haiti, they are finger-licking good
And in that sense, we beat all other countries

In my country, wherever you go, all down the road,
It's good morning, brother, and my sister how are the kids?
How come we don't see each other, come on in for a while
To drink a little something, to play some dominoes
After the handshake, it's great conversation
Politics, bad situations
What should we do, we have to deal with it now
But God is so good, he will bless us

In the white man's land, if you walk around, night or day
Everyone is in a hurry like mad dogs
Where are they going? Why are they running?
They're scared of wasting time, they never say, "How goes things?"
In my country, people are not slave to time
There is freedom, you have time to catch a breeze
Wherever you go, it's hello, handshake
People are never in a hurry, they chitchat all day long.

In Haiti, you never lack for downtime
What you don't do today, you can do tomorrow if you want
When tomorrow comes, whether it's good or not
Doesn't matter, everyone says God is good
In Haiti, people never despair
We have faith in a God who never lies
We will do today for sure, when tomorrow is not certain
My God, What a great country Haiti is!

Translated by Nadève Ménard

Veneer of Modernization

Suzy Castor

Many have criticized the U.S. government for infringing on Haiti's political and eco-nomic sovereignty, as well as for the racism of U.S. occupation officials between 1915 and 1934. But some Haitians who lived through the period, as well as other observers since, have also celebrated the occupation for its "modernization" of Haitian society through the construction of roads, buildings, and telecommunications technologies. The occupation era was also the period when institutions such as the Garde d'Haiti and the Central School of Agriculture were created, and served as training grounds for the professionalization and reform of Haitian bureaucracies. In her history of the occupation, Haitian historian and political activist Suzy Castor argues that in fact the occupation brought a "veneer of modernization, not development" to Haiti. She focuses on the U.S. political and commercial figures who sought economic gain in Haiti, as well as members of Haiti's political and economic classes who initially saw in the occupation an opportunity to consolidate their own wealth and political power. Castor's stance takes on even broader significance when we consider that even celebrated nationalists, such as the leaders of l'Union Patriotique and Jean Price-Mars, respectively advocated for the aid of Americans and spoke favorably about the agro-industrial training that U.S. officials emphasized as a means of attending to the needs of Haitian society. In the following passage, Castor questions the ultimate advantage of the occupation's investments, reforms, and training, if socioeconomic structures in Haiti continued to favor a select few. In this Marxist analysis of Haiti's economy, Castor challenges those who saw themselves as advocates for the larger society's greatest good—be they foreign or Haitian—by pointing to the limits of the occupation's contributions to Haitian society.

The occupation initiated a process of modernization that gave the country a veneer of apparent civilization. The traditional mulatto elite and certain groups among the nascent middle class, both mulatto and black, integrated themselves to a certain extent with the managers of this modernization. The inauguration of urbanization projects, especially in the capital, gave the impression of a change that was favorable for development. This was the period of the construction of the Palais National (National Palace), the Casernes Dessalines (Dessalines Garrison), the Palais de Justice (Palace of Justice) and the Palais Législatif (Legislative Palace), the Faculté de Médicine (Medical School), etc. These urbanization projects transformed Port-au-Prince, which ceased to be a "large village."

There was also a reform of public administration through the creation of new institutions, the renovation of certain others, and the formation of an effective cadre of administrators.

It was during the occupation that the Direction Générale des Travaux Publics (General Direction of Public Works) was inaugurated, with the goal of constructing bridges, roads, and rural byroads and providing potable water supplies to the towns. The Service d'Hygiène et d'Assistance Publique (Hygiene and Public Assistance Service) was also created, with the goal of training nurses, treating endemic illnesses, and constructing hospitals and rural clinics. The Service Technique d'Agriculture (STA; Technical Agriculture Service) opened, and launched experimental farm schools. In addition, the Ministère des Finances (Ministry of Finance; an organization of a technical-administrative character) began to regularize the financial life of the country. The Service des Douanes (Customs Service) and the Service des Contributions (Tax Service) were reformed, which made the functioning of public finance more effective and resolved the administrative and financial imbroglio that had characterized life in Haiti during the period before the occupation.

We cannot insist enough on the superficial and utilitarian characteristic of this modernization, since the changes that were produced through the occupation left the fundamental structure of the country intact. The impetus given to the development of the cities and the creation of administrative institutions could not in any way resolve the serious economic and social problems Haiti suffered from.

The archaic agriculture structures remained intact. Changes were only adopted to the extent that they showed themselves to be indispensable to assure the success of American investors. But in fact there were very few changes introduced into the agrarian structure.

Land ownership, as was the case before 1915, was characterized by a large concentration of property in the hands of the State and large property-owners. At the same time, the fragmentation of the "habitation" (small land-holdings) had increased, along with the lack of land among the peasantry. In 1941, the agronomist Schiller Nicolas (a specialist in Agricultural Economy) estimated that the State owned thirty percent of the total land in the country.[1]

The massive dispossessions carried out to benefit American capitalists increased the number of peasants without land, leading to the pauperization of the middle levels of the peasantry.

There was some element of modernization in agriculture that came along with the installation of the large companies who were putting plantation agriculture in place. The sisal industry (the largest in the world at the time) known by the name of Plantation Dauphin, and the Haytian American Sugar Co. (HASCO), focused on the cultivation of tropical products on large tracts of land, creating an agricultural industry oriented towards the treatment of sisal and sugar production. So was born an innovative capitalist sector that introduced salaries into the countryside and contributed to the formation of a class of agricultural workers. Nonetheless, this change in agricultural relationships did not provide the impetus for a significant capitalist development. Its influence was reduced to the employment of 10,000 workers, most of them seasonal, hired according to the rhythm of the harvest of sugarcane or sisal. The Dauphin Company functioned as a classic "colonial enclave"; only the sugar industry stimulated commercial relationships because—in addition to the cane from its plantations—it purchased cane from individual property-owners. But in reality, it tied itself to the dominant feudal structure, which itself didn't change.

We also have to mention the vicissitudes of this cultivation, the result of the global economic crises in capitalism. Those of 1920–21 and 1929–33 in the United States had catastrophic repercussions on the Haitian sugar industry.

Nor did production relationships evolve in a significant way during or after the occupation. They were dominated by the use of agricultural income in the form of products, by relationships of dependency between tenant farmers or agricultural workers and landowners, by an almost inexistent use of money in work relationships and its limited use as a form of exchange. In a considerable sector of agriculture, the State along with absentee landowners continued to receive revenue from their land and used it to pay for their consumption and the maintenance of their social status.

Even the rent paid in money by small renters, especially to the State, remained definitively a disguised form of natural rent. As Gérald Brisson notes, "through this form of rent, the parasitic and wasteful State received, all the surplus production and even a part of the necessary production created by the small renter in primitive conditions, and supported none of the expenses for production."[2]

In 1938, the number of people renting land from the State was estimated to be 11,086; in 1943, it had increased to 35,506.[3] At the time, the State and landowners received the equivalent of six million dollars per year in rent.[4]

The weight of feudal-style rents within the broader economy approached the total amount of Haitian exports, which continued to be insignificant, impacted by the weak volume of production of commercial goods and by the restrictions on demand (both in terms of volume and price) resulting from the global crisis in capitalism. During the period from 1932 to 1940, the total of Haitian exports amounted to barely nine million dollars per year. Only forty to fifty percent of this total reached peasant producers, most of it being instead grabbed by the State, speculators, and the export sector.

As a result the amounts paid by the peasants to the landowners were more than that received from the sale of their most commercialized products. Based on this relationship we can conclude, taking into account the weight of self-subsistence within the agrarian economy, that feudal rents continued to dominate the Haitian economy, not only at the level of production but also as a category of exchange.

Not a single infrastructure project, such as irrigation or a network of roads, was carried out to support the entirety of the agricultural system. Agricultural techniques remained as primitive as before, based on rudimentary manual tools like the hoe, the machete, pikes, etc.; tools with animal traction like the plow, along with chemical fertilizers, remained unknown.

Mechanization and other modern agricultural techniques were only adopted in the plantation sector. The introduction of these technological changes only deepened the gap between this sector and that of traditional cultivation, where archaic techniques continued to dominate.

Given the continuation of the same anti-economic models of land appropriation, the same methods of cultivation, and the old relations of production, it is not a surprise that there was no progress in agricultural production, except in the sugar and sisal sectors, which within the national economy had all the characteristics of colonial enclaves fundamentally linked to the metropolitan economy.

In these conditions, one can conclude that the U.S. occupation was not able to develop capitalist agriculture, or to create the infrastructural foundations for the establishment of industry. It also did not spur the creation of a consumer market that could have driven industrial manufacturing. And it also was not able to propel an expansion, in quantitative terms, in the commercial relations with global capitalism. Despite the absorption of a large quantity of commercial profits, the commercial sector was unable to push the larger economy of Haiti towards a market economy. Haiti remained a pre-capitalist country, where the small capitalist sector was subordinated to an American economy and the commercial relations with global capitalism; it had a specific, and reduced, influence within the broader society that continued to be dominated by a subsistence economy and feudal relations of production.

Translated by Laurent Dubois

Notes

1. Schiller Nicolas, *Bases essentielles d'un redressement économique* (Port-au Prince: Imprimerie de l'État, 1940), 23.

2. Gérald Brisson, *Les relations agraires dans l'Haïti contemporaine* (Port-au-Prince: 1968), 37.

3. Jean Dartigue, "La situation agraire dans Haiti," in *Caribbean Land Tenure Symposium*, Washington, D.C.: Caribbean Research Council, 1946, 317.

4. Nicolas, *Bases essentielles d'un redressement économique*, 11.

V

Second Independence

As men and women across Haitian cities and provinces did their part to re-claim their national sovereignty and establish more equitable relations with Americans by demanding that U.S. officials respect their humanity, many of them saw their efforts as a path to a second national independence. The tran-sition from the occupation to the postoccupation period began in 1930, with the reinstitution of legislative and presidential elections in Haiti, and ended in 1934, with the departure of the U.S. occupying forces on 14 August. These turning point events ushered in a fresh opportunity for self-rule in Haiti.

Negotiations to end the occupation, a process known as *désoccupation*, came about after a culmination of events on and off the island in late 1929. Most notable were protests across Haiti, particularly those that took place in the capital, Port-au-Prince, in November, and in the southern province of Les Cayes in December. In the capital, students who had been enrolled in courses at public institutions supervised by occupation officials, such as the School of Agriculture, went on strike to challenge policy changes that reduced their scholarship funding. With each new day, politicians, businessmen, custom-house workers, French Catholic clergy, and other residents across the country capitalized on the protests to advance their own dissatisfaction with occupa-tion officials, as well as with standing president Louis Borno. Locals critiqued Borno for being overly complicit with U.S. officials in ways that negatively impacted Haitian workers, such as supporting policies and proposals that dis-proportionately hurt Haitian sugar and coffee workers, and for taking actions to extend his own authority, such as delaying elections. The spirit of dissent spread as students and residents elsewhere on the island joined in to support their counterparts in Port-au-Prince. Tensions mounted even further when rural workers gathered to contest hikes in taxes on their products and were met with armed assault by U.S. military officers in a southern town called Marchaterre. These financial circumstances were linked to economic dis-tress taking place abroad, as reduced agricultural prices caused an economic depression to set in worldwide. Dissent in Haiti reinforced the sentiments of anti-imperialists in the United States and around the world who argued against the rule of foreigners in other territories. In an effort to manage the cost of foreign engagements and the reputation of the United States in global affairs, newly elected U.S. president Herbert Hoover appointed commissions that ultimately recommended an election and arrangements for the termination of U.S. military rule in Haiti. Those elections began with a popular vote for the Haitian legislature, which then selected the nationalist senator Sténio Vincent to serve as Haiti's new president.

After Vincent's election, a wide range of negotiations continued to take place, making the transition to Haiti's Second Independence a diplomatic process, compared to the military campaigns that led to Haitian independence from France in 1804. Still, the "new era" sustained the diplomatic challenge of securing Haiti's political and economic sovereignty, as well as respect for the humanity of its citizens, in ways quite similar to what took place during the nineteenth century. As with the indemnity payable to France, Haiti's second independence came with a financial burden, payable to the United States. U.S. president Franklin D. Roosevelt, who followed Hoover, agreed with Haitian president Sténio Vincent to have the U.S. Marine forces occupying Haiti depart on 14 August 1934, but to retain the financial receivership that oversaw the Haitian state's revenues and expenses. This was set to continue until the New York City–based loans acquired during the long nineteenth century were paid. Such a condition belied the fact that throughout the nineteenth century and through the occupation, Haiti was the sole nation in the region that did not default on its loans. The influence of U.S. financiers in Haiti only deepened as Vincent's successor, Élie Lescot (elected in 1941), enthusiastically pursued ties with the United States based on the assumption that agricultural pursuits such as SHADA (Haitian-American Society for Agricultural Development) would generate financial and political gains for Haiti. In reality, the greatest impacts of these circumstances were constraints on the Haitian budget and land use that privileged the priorities of foreigners above the well-being of Haitians and the Haitian economy.

What marked the "new era" quite notably, however, was an internationalist climate from the 1930s through the early 1950s in which the ideals of regional and global cooperation circulated widely. This brought new connections between Haitian history and world history, as major developments in the two arenas mirrored one another. The end of the occupation foreshadowed what was to come after the Second World War ended in 1945, an era of decolonization. Haitian intellectuals and officials, like their counterparts around the world, drew on folk identity to develop a distinct national identity. This practice nourished Haiti's already prolific literary traditions, while also contributing to increased promotion of Haiti as an ideal destination in the world's emerging tourist economy.

But the repression in postoccupation Haiti also reveals a profound disconnect between popular, state, and foreign ideas about who and what could have a legitimate place in the society. These internal tensions shaped every-

Photograph of monument to the Battle of Vertières (18 November 1803), on the road to Haut du Cap near Cap Haïtien; President Paul Magloire (r. 1950–56) commissioned a series of monuments to commemorate the 150th anniversary of Vertières, the decisive battle of the Haitian Revolution. Cuban sculptor Juan José Sicre was selected to create this monument in Cap Haïtien. Photo courtesy of Paul Clammer.

day life in Haiti, affected political and economic opportunities, and established rich ground on which some Haitians used international platforms to mobilize. For example, a new wave of assaults on practitioners of Vodou, or *les actes superstitieux* (superstitious acts), made clear the terms on which Haitian folk culture would be considered acceptable and discussed with the world. More broadly, debate about the state of Haitian society played itself out in the color and class politics of the era, which led a cross-section of Haitians—most visibly, laborers, students, and middle- and upper-class women—to organize. These developments led to Lescot's ousting through the so-called Noirist Revolution in 1946 (described in this section's final excerpt by historian Matthew J. Smith), named for ending the succession of mulatto rule and for promising to end a period of mulatto privilege. This gave rise to the election of dark-skinned men to the Haitian presidency: Dumarsais Estimé (elected 1946), Paul Eugène Magloire (elected 1950), and later François Duvalier (elected 1957).

Genocide and internationalism during Haiti's Second Independence also underscore the links between Haitian history and foreign, or world histories. While the selections in this section highlight some familiar narratives, they also accentuate lesser-known voices and experiences. Alongside accounting for the numbers and the horror of massacre in the Dominican Republic in October 1937, there are the testimonies of those who fled and those who witnessed the unsettling nature of this moment from Haiti. And, while prominent Haitian statesmen and male intellectuals represented Haiti in political and cultural arenas, their female counterparts gained increasing visibility doing the same domestically and on inter-American and global platforms. In the midst of trying moments, Haitians across social classes and gender lines advocated in an array of arenas for what they regarded as valuable ways to uphold a sovereign, prosperous, and internationally respected Haiti.

Vincent and Trujillo

Diplomatic exchanges between Haitian executive officials have been commonplace since the nineteenth century. This photo captures one of several meetings between Dominican president Rafael Trujillo (in military attire) and Haitian president Sténio Vincent who met on both sides of the border to negotiate and display amicable ties between the two nations. Strikingly, these negotiations took place during the years and months that preceded the massacre of Haitians ordered by Rafael Trujillo in 1937, highlighting the limits of the diplomatic negotiations. After the massacre, the Haitian government did little to condemn Trujillo's actions, to the dismay of intellectuals including Jacques Roumain, who wrote about and denounced the massacre at the time.

Rafael Trujillo and Sténio Vincent, presidents of the Dominican Republic and Haiti, meet at the border between the two countries as part of diplomatic negotiations. Courtesy of Frank R. Crumbie Papers, Special and Area Studies Collections, George A. Smathers Libraries, University of Florida, Gainesville.

Proud Haiti

Edouard A. Tardieu

The period after the U.S. occupation saw a flourishing of patriotic song and symbolism in the country. In 1937, the Department of Public Instruction held a song contest, inviting people to submit compositions that could be sung by schoolchildren to celebrate Haiti. Edouard A. Tardieu submitted this song and won the contest. The accompanying music was composed by Desaix Baptiste. Since 1938, it has been widely adopted, and it is sung at parades on Haitian Flag Day (18 May), one of Haiti's most animated national holidays, and during related festivities. Through such songs, and public celebrations of the nation, new ideas about the Haitian nation and Haitian nationalism gained traction across the society.

The song invites the youth of the country to see themselves as part of a long lineage of struggle going back to the period of the Haitian Revolution, to identify as the "sons of titans" who were the "proud conquerers of Haiti." In these gendered sections it becomes clear that the ideal citizen is conceived of as a "strong man" and a potential soldier. The song claims that if Haitians do need to go to war, they will do so "fearlessly and bravely," as their ancestors did at Vertières, the decisive final battle that expelled the French from the island in 1803. Written in the years soon after the U.S. occupation, during which Caco armies fought an unsuccessful campaign against Marine forces, the song has an undercurrent of needing to reestablish a sense of national dignity and pride. In this sense, the evocation of the Haitian revolution perhaps served as a way to overcome the wounds of the recent occupation. The fierceness of the song, directed against any who might "insult" the "reputation" of the country, may also have been a call to never allow what happened during the previous decades to happen again. To future attackers or invaders, the schoolchildren are asked to call out: "We shall say no!"

CHORUS
It is us: we, the youth, we the students,
The big ones and the small ones,
Who tomorrow will be Haiti's glory.
We shall always go forth
With joyful hearts and fervent souls,
And always with our heads held high.

I

Dear homeland, we want you to be
Powerful and strong in everyone's eyes
Blessed land, we want you to always be
Worthy of our ancestors.
Free and prosperous, they bequeathed you
To their children, we who love you
Will fight zealously
For your salvation in any battle.

II

Onward all, and of firm foot,
For we want to make it felt
That beneath our skin
Flows the purest blood, ready to gush forth
To wash you, to defend you
Against any insult to your reputation
To all who attempt to
Tarnish you, we shall say no!

III

Let us stand proud, youth.
To protect our flag
We will have to fight relentlessly.
Our ideal is fine and good
Let us not be afraid, but full of hope
Let us always march toward the future
Let us always steadily march
If we do not want to falter

IV

Yes, for the honor of our race
We need strong men
Everyone, the elite and the masses,
Let us unite in this effort
To renew our country.
May your children be hardy
Beautiful Haiti, dear mother,
And forever brave, like our heroes

V

Let us unfurl our banner here
That it may brightly shine for all time
In the light
Of a peaceful Haiti.
And if we must go to war
Fearlessly and bravely
We will all go just like at Vertières
To fight for freedom

FINAL CHORUS

We are the valiant race
We are the sons of titans
The proud conquerors of Haiti
Nourished by their resounding glory
We shall always go forth
With our heads held high

Translated by Nadève Ménard

Color Prejudice

Jacques Roumain

Jacques Roumain, one of Haiti's best-known writers, earned a favorable reputation as a gifted poet in the 1920s and 1930s and was a leading light among a highly talented generation of Haitian intellectuals who came of age in the years of the U.S. occupation (1915–34). His major novel, Gouverneurs de la rosée *(Masters of the Dew) published after his death in 1944, was translated into several languages, extending admiration for Roumain's work far beyond Haiti.*

Roumain was also a political activist. In 1932 he was a principal organizer of the Parti Communiste Haïtien (PCH). After two years of clandestine activity, the PCH surfaced with the release of its powerful manifesto, Analyse schématique, *which appeared just as U.S. Marines were making their final withdrawal from Haiti. The document was a perceptive critique of the Haitian nationalist movement—which gained considerable force in the late 1920s and throughout the 1930s—and an attempt to analyze the country's political problems through a Marxist framework. In this excerpt Roumain engages with the question of color and addresses the divisions between light-skinned and dark-skinned Haitians. This had been a preoccupation of many intellectuals since the nineteenth century and was often considered one of the causes of the country's political and social disunity. But Roumain argues that color in Haiti is a dangerous smokescreen that conceals the more exploitative class divisions in the society. This point was captured in the PCH slogan: "Color is nothing, class is everything."*

Following the appearance of Analyse schématique, *Roumain was arrested, imprisoned, and briefly exiled by Sténio Vincent. And though Haitian Marxism would remain marginal during Roumain's lifetime, his example would lead subsequent generations of radical youth to Marxist activism.*
—Contributing Editor: Matthew J. Smith

Color prejudice is a reality and it is pointless trying to hide it. And pretending that it is a moral issue is equivalent to taking a Jesuit approach to the problem. Color prejudice is the sentimental expression of class confrontation, class struggle: the psychological manifestation of a historic or economic fact: the unrelenting exploitation of the Haitian masses by the upper and upper-middle classes. It is revealing to note the resurgence of this more-than-secular question, just when the poverty of the workers and peasants is at its worst,

Jacques Roumain (1907–44). Photo courtesy of CIDHICA.

that the proletarianization of the lower-middle class is being pursued with greater fervor. The Haitian Communist Party (Parti Communiste Haïtien—PCH) wields exceptional importance, because it is the mask behind which black and mulatto politicians want to disguise the class warfare. Nowadays, various manifestos in which the issue is raised are being circulated covertly. It should be noted that these manifestos expose: (1) in a sentimental way, truths that are in fact economic and therefore social and political, as well; (2) the pauperization of the middle class, the reasons for which are explained in the manifesto's critique of the "Democratic Reaction" [Réaction Démocratique, another group of Haitian political leftists]. But the issue here is (about) explaining that the social, economic, and political debasement of Blacks is in no way due to a simple confrontation of color. The hard fact is this: a black proletariat and a predominantly black lower-middle class are mercilessly oppressed by a very small minority: the upper and upper-middle class (mulattoes, for the most part) and proletarianized by large-scale international industry.

As we can see, what is at work here is an economic oppression that has a social and political ripple effect. The objective basis for the problem, then, is undoubtedly rooted in class warfare.

The PCH states the problem scientifically without negating in the least the well-founded psychological reactions of Blacks who have had their dignity crushed, by the stupid disdain of Mulattoes, an attitude which is but the social expression of economic oppression by the upper class.

But the duty of the PCH—a party which, by the way, is 98 percent black, since it is a workers' party and within which the issue of color is systematically stripped of its sensitive and epidermal content and is firmly set in the arena of class warfare—is to caution the proletariat, the lower-middle class and black working-class intellectuals against black upper-class politicians who would want to use to their own benefit the justified anger of their poorer compatriots. They must be sensitized to the reality of class warfare that tends to be overshadowed by color prejudice. One black person from the upper classes is no better than his mulatto or white counterpart. One black, upper-class politician is just as despicable as a mulatto or white politician. The motto of the Haitian Communist Party (PCH) is:

FIGHTING AGAINST UPPER-CLASS SOLIDARITY—BLACK, MULATTO OR WHITE CAPITALISTS: A UNITED PROLETARIAN FRONT IRRESPEC-TIVE OF COLOR!

The lower-middle class must form ranks beside the lower classes, because the upper classes and imperialists are increasingly and rapidly proletarianizing them.

The Haitian Communist Party (PCH), acting on its slogan—"Color is nothing, class is everything"—issues a call to the masses to join the class warfare under its banner. It is only by fighting against the nation's capitalist upper class (with a yellow-skinned majority and a black-skinned minority) and against the international capitalist upper classes, that a relentless battle, a battle devoid of epidermal content and rooted in class warfare is possible. It is only by destroying privileges gained through oppression and exploitation that we can wipe out color prejudice and at the same time eliminate the social, economic, and political debasement that come with it.

Translated by Matthew J. Smith

Migration to Cuba

Maurice Casséus and Jacques Roumain

During the first decades of the twentieth century, particularly at the time of the U.S. occupation of Haiti and in the years that immediately followed, U.S. capitalists and government officials encouraged regional labor migration—most notably to Cuba and the Dominican Republic—in order to benefit their sugar industry. In this period, as many as 200,000 Haitians traveled to work in eastern Cuba. As the industry flourished, thousands of Haitian women and men traveled back and forth, bringing with them both the dollars they earned and stories of opportunity and abuses, soon represented in Haitian fiction. Authors Maurice Casséus and Jacques Roumain both constructed novels around Haitian heroes who worked in Cuba before returning to their homeland. While Casséus stresses the ways worker exploitation remains a constant throughout the region, Roumain presents a more romanticized view of Cuba, presenting it as a model for Haitians to follow. This distinction may be explained by the differences in time periods—Casséus's novel was published shortly after thousands of Haitians were expelled from Cuba—and by Roumain's leading role in promoting communism in Haiti (he founded the Haitian Communist Party in 1934). In both texts, however, Cuba is represented as a place to acquire knowledge that can then be applied to transform Haitian society. Maurice Casséus's novel offers perspectives on the different types of foreigners inhabiting Haitian space. Among the characters are Americans, Syrians, and a Martinican. In the literary landscape, Viejo serves as a transition from the occupation novel to the peasant and proletariat novels of later decades. Roumain's Masters of the Dew, *a classic of Haitian literature, recounts one community's plight as it faces drought and famine. Manuel, the protagonist, has recently returned from Cuba and brings a heightened sense of worker solidarity back to his hometown of Fonds-Rouge. He evokes the power of the peasantry.*

Maurice Casséus, Viejo (1935)

Mario was having sliced sweet potatoes served to him when a drunkard approached him with a hard tap to the shoulder:

—Comrade, you spoke like a good black man a little while ago.

He took a half minute to burp, then:

—I worked among the Whites: New York, Boston, Chicago. Everywhere a proletarian, which means the oppressed flock. I was not unionized, Comrade, but I did strike. Here (he showed his back), and here, you can touch the souvenir left by repression's baton. Do you know your Marx, Comrade?

Mario signaled that no, he did not know him.

—By the devil, said the man. You accomplished in Cuba what you just said and you don't know the apostle. Do you at least know the revolution of 1905, 1917? No? Damn, that's pretty tough. What do you think then of Soviet Russia?

Mario had a hard time swallowing because he had never encountered all these things Claude Servin wanted to talk to him about.

—Why, then, did you revolt in Cuba? said the man.

Through the alcohol he was burping, Claude Servin's eyes were bright with a solid and stable intelligence. Barely thirty years old. But he had been so oppressed, bullied so much that revolt gushed out of him through all his pores. A sort of literary mysticism had almost skewed his sensibility before, to the point that he recalled having longed for pain, just like in Dostoyevsky's novels. He burped again, while making a terrible grimace, and then repeated his question:

—Why did you revolt in Cuba?

—Because in Cuba, said Mario, the employed Negro and the bull that pulls the cart are the same thing. Except the bull that pulls the cart receives his ration of grass for forty hours of work, and the employed Negro for twelve hours in the field, in the factory, or on the road, his ration of money: $1.00.

—An average of thirty dollars a month, said Servin. But, then, did you think about what your twelve hours of work were bringing to the bosses?—Millions to pay for their Rolls and the Havana empire, Comrade.

Jacques Roumain, Gouverneurs de la rosée (1944)

"Tell me about Cuba."

"It's a country, maybe five times, no ten, no twenty times as big as Haiti. But, you know, me, this is what I'm made of."

He touched the ground, caressed the grain.

"I am this, this land and it's in my blood. Look at my color: it's like the land bled onto me, and onto you, too. This country is the black man's share and each time they tried to take it from us, we weeded out injustice with our machetes."

"Yes, but in Cuba, there is more wealth, you live more comfortably. Here, you have to fight hard with life, and what's the use? You don't even have enough to fill your belly and you have no rights when it comes to the authorities' wickedness. The justice of the peace, the rural police, the surveyors, the speculators, they live off us like fleas. I spent a month in prison, with all those thieves and murderers, because I had gone into town barefoot. And where would I have gotten the money, I ask you, my friend? So, what are we, us, the peasants, the barefoot black men, disdained and mistreated?"

"What are we? If that's a question, I'll answer you: well, we are this country and it is nothing without us, nothing at all. Who plants, who waters, who harvests? Coffee, cotton, rice, sugarcane, cocoa, corn, plantains, provisions, and all the fruits—if not us, who will make them grow? And with all that, we're poor, it's true, we're wretched, it's true, we're miserable, it's true. But, do you know why, my brother? Because of our ignorance: we don't yet know that we are a force, one force: all the peasants, all the men from the plains and the mountains united. One day, when we will have understood this truth, we will rise from one end to another of the country and will have the general assembly of the masters of the dew, the great *coumbite* of workers of the land to clear out misery and plant new life."

Translated by Nadève Ménard

Anti-superstition Laws

President Sténio Vincent

In September 1935, President Sténio Vincent's administration criminalized sacred rituals and the assembly of Vodou practitioners. Ceremonies, dances, the possession of objects, and particularly the sacrifice of animals were placed in the category of les pratiques superstitieuses (superstitious practices). This was part of a longer tradition through which certain political leaders sought to repress popular religious practices as a way of proving to the outside world that Haiti was "civilized" and "modern." This was partly in response to the proliferation, in Europe and North America, of racist and exoticist literature that focused on Vodou in denigrating depictions of Haiti. There had been an explosion of such depictions during the U.S. occupation, notably during the 1920s. The enforcement of this law, in 1935 and especially during a widespread anti-superstition campaign carried out by the Catholic Church from 1940 to 1942, led to the repression of religious practices and the destruction of many religious objects, including drums. Despite their violence, these campaigns did little to alter the religious life of most Haitians, and in their aftermath a process of constant negotiation between the police and Vodou leadership was established. During the 1940s and 1950s, styles of popular dance based in Vodou were celebrated as national folklore and became popular among middle-class North American and European tourists.

Decree-Law

STÉNIO VINCENT, PRESIDENT OF THE REPUBLIC

With regard to Articles 21 and 30 of the Constitution:

Considering that the state has a duty to prevent the performance of all acts, practices, etc. liable to foster superstitious beliefs harmful to the good name of the country:

Considering further that articles 405, 406 second paragraph, and 407 of the Penal Code have been repealed due to the exaggerated application of these laws, to the detriment of the citizenry's rights, particularly the rural peasantry, to have fun organizing dances, according to local customs;

Considering that it behooves us to find ways to curb superstitious practices without hindering the legitimate right of peasants to enjoy themselves in an honest and decent manner;

On the report of the Secretary of State for Justice;
And the opinion of the Council of Secretaries of State.
And after approval of the Standing Committee of the National Assembly.

Decrees

Art. 1. Are considered to be superstitious practices: (1) the ceremonies, rites, dances, and meetings in the course of which are practiced, in offering to so-called divinities, sacrifices of cattle or fowl; (2) the act of exploiting the public by making it believe that, by occult means, it is possible to manage either to change the situation of fortune of an individual, or to heal him of any illness, by processes unknown to medical science; (3) the fact of having in one's residence cabalistic objects serving to exploit the credulity or the naïveté of the public.

Art. 2. Any individual convinced of said superstitious practices shall be sentenced to imprisonment for six months and a fine of four hundred gourdes, such sentence to be given by the Court of Summary Jurisdiction.

Art. 3. In the cases provided above, the judgment becomes enforceable, notwithstanding any appeal or annulment.

Art. 4. The objects used in the perpetration of the offense provided for in Article 3 shall be confiscated.

Art. 5. The present Decree repeals all laws or provisions of laws contrary to it, and will be executed at the behest of Secretary of State for Justice.

Given at the National Palace in Port-au-Prince,
5 September 1935, 132nd Year of Independence.
Sténio Vincent

Translated by Nadève Ménard and Millery Polyné

An Oral History of a Massacre

Isil Nicolas Cour

*Between 2 and 8 October 1937, the Dominican military killed with machetes an esti-
mated fifteen thousand persons, including Haitian immigrants who had been living
for many generations in the northwestern frontier region of the Dominican Republic,
and Dominicans (some of Haitian descent) from this bicultural region. This atrocity
was ordered by the powerful and brutal dictator Rafael Leonidas Trujillo Molina,
who seized power in the Dominican Republic in 1930, the same year that Vincent was
elected. The two heads of state presided over their nations in periods that followed a
U.S. military occupation (the U.S. occupation of the Dominican Republic took place
between 1916 and 1924).*

*As early as 1933, Trujillo and Vincent began meeting regularly to renegotiate the
boundaries of the Haitian-Dominican border. Under dispute was land that included
Haitian communities, which were incorporated into Dominican territory by a 1929
border treaty. U.S. officials, in conjunction with the preceding presidents of Haiti
(Louis Borno) and the Dominican Republic (Horacio Vásquez), produced the 1929
treaty, purportedly to resolve territorial disputes that stemmed back to European ex-
pansionist ambitions from the eighteenth and nineteenth centuries. In 1936, Trujillo
and Vincent ratified a border treaty that redesignated land to Haiti.*

*We will never know with certainty what led to the massacre in the Dominican
frontier. As is often true with large-scale violence, the particular form and extent of
this attack seem to exceed all causal explanations (e.g., the fact that Haitians were
killed even as they tried to flee across the border into Haiti). With few exceptions,
Haitian workers on sugar plantations, which were located elsewhere in the Dominican Republic and mostly belonged to U.S. firms, were not attacked during the massacre. Presumably the Dominican army did not use guns in the slaughter to permit some
shred of deniability—the official story, however implausible, being that the killings
had been the product of a conflict between Haitian and Dominican residents. Because
of the way the killings were carried out, ethnic Haitians who managed to survive by
escaping across the border into Haiti would remember the massacre as "the Slashing"
(Kout kouto a).[1]*

*Isil Nicolas Cour was among the many Haitian-Dominicans who fled to Haiti
during the massacre. The oral history with Cour that follows is one of dozens that
Lauren Derby and Richard Turits collected between 1987 and 1988 with the assistance*

of Édouard-Jean Baptiste and Ciprián Soler. Most of the elderly men and women they spoke with were, like Cour, Haitian descendants who faced assault. Cour and the many others who shared their testimony described fluid, highly integrated, bilingual, and peaceful frontier communities comprising ethnic Haitians and Dominicans (and, needless to say, their bicultural offspring) prior to the massacre. For this reason, as Cour recounted, the killings appeared to him and his neighbors to come out of nowhere.

Cour came from a family of small farmers. Indeed, the vast majority of the frontier population in the 1930s, whether of Haitian or Dominican descent, were independent peasants. Cour emphasized the economic vitality and security of this peasantry, based on their enjoyment of free access to land for farming and an open range for abundant livestock. Cour also recounted how Trujillo himself visited the community in which Cour lived a few years before the massacre. This visit was one of many trips Trujillo made to rural areas in the 1930s to boost small-scale agricultural production among peasants (as opposed to subsistence exploitation of wildlife together with itinerant farming). Cour recalled Trujillo's words on this visit, particularly his explicit disavowal of the existence of any significant differences between Haitians and Dominicans. We all have the "same blood," the dictator proclaimed. Cour also recalled Trujillo's affirmation of land rights for all who cleared and cultivated land in the still-vast untamed Dominican countryside. Notably, too, under regime policy before the massacre there had been no restrictions on immigration from Haiti—though migration was increasingly taxed—and there was frequent back-and-forth movement of residents across the border between the two countries.

The 1937 massacre occurred almost exclusively in the Dominican frontier regions. The military attacked the population of Haitian descent who for generations had resided there and traversed the porous border. Because this genocidal campaign was a regional one, nearly absent elsewhere in the country, it did not lead to any sustained reduction in the Haitian-descended population at large. Indeed, the numbers of ethnic Haitians in the country would increase under Trujillo's rule, as the regime expanded the Haitian migrant labor force in order to obtain needed workers for the increasingly state-owned sugar industry. Trujillo's crime against humanity also had virtually no effect on the overall racial makeup of the Dominican population.

Isil Nicolas Cour's willingness to recount his life history makes a crucial contribution. Cour illuminates a lost and surprising history of Haitian-Dominican relations prior to the massacre. He also documents a state atrocity and act of ethnic terror for which there are not adequate words.

—Contributing Editor: Richard Turits

RICHARD: Where were you born?

ISIL: I was born . . . on the other side, in the Dominican Republic [Panyòl] . . . [in the town of] Cola Grande. . . . A lot of the people here [in Haiti] lived in Cola Grande. . . . I grew up on the other side. That's why I had my godfather [there]. He was Dominican. . . .

RICHARD: What language did you speak as a child?

ISIL: . . . You'd speak two languages there, you speak Kreyòl, you speak Dominican. That is, when you are amid your countrymen, you'd speak Kreyòl. But when you are amid Dominicans, you'd speak Spanish. . . .

RICHARD: Did you have Dominican friends before the Slashing [*Kout kouto a*] took place?[2]

ISIL: Definitely, I had a lot of Dominican friends. That's why I could tell you we lived together, all jumbled together, so much so that even in Haiti, some still come to see us. . . .

RICHARD: What language did you speak with your Dominican friends?

ISIL: Oh, we speak all languages, we speak Haitian, they speak Haitian too. . . . Those who come to see you here, they speak Haitian with you. When it's to your country they come, they speak your country's language. . . .

I did have Dominican friends coming to see us in Haiti [after the Slashing]. They used to come see us right here in Dosmon. That allowed me to see that I had friends among them. If they weren't my friends, they wouldn't come to see me—it's not me they come to see. They come to see my dad and mom, and then they'd see me too. There are a lot who would come see us, a lot of Dominicans.

RICHARD: Did you have any personal experience of any Dominican treating you with disrespect before the Slashing?

ISIL: Dominicans. Well, I went to dances, Dominican dances. We participated in the same ways Dominicans did. And there were never any disagreements. I never saw any fighting, insulting, swearing. . . .

But they, Dominicans, I can't tell you, what factor led them to abhor the [Haitian] people. Because just like that, they came and you found them starting to kill like they were killing ticks.

. . . The section chief[3] got word to my dad not to stay: "Go to Haiti, go to your country." . . . My father said no. He had to find out what was going on [first]. . . . Oh! Well, what it was was knives falling on everyone. They just killed five guys right nearby. And then when they finished killing them, they came, they took my dad and Augustin and another fellow named Clemié. They took all of them and tied them up. . . . All the women started screaming. . . . They killed them with bayonets. It wasn't with knives that they killed those people.

. . . When they came to take my father, to kill him too . . . they said to my dad, "How," they said, "do you yourself like this country, old man?" . . . My father said, "Well, I don't know—I feel good here now, it suits me." . . . "But, look," he said, "what's the matter with those people? They're crying." . . . My dad said, "What's causing them to scream?" . . .

And just then, they let my dad go. They let the men go. They said, "Look. Go get your whole family and get on the way to your country. They can kill people." So they went and took their entire families on the way for their country. . . .

And, then, you know, I can say that the only thing that people took with them was their clothes. But they dug a hole in the ground and put around eight big pots in it . . . cassava plants and . . . ten big goats [etc.]. You have to realize: we didn't know we were leaving forever. We thought we were leaving and then coming back, you see? . . .

Then, my man, people started dying on Monday. . . . I went somewhere called Copey. . . . And they let us store things there. I and two brothers of mine and a cousin they named Arturo.

All three of [us] were holed up there. . . . It was only Tuesday around three in the afternoon that I could get out and come here. After I arrived [in Haiti], people didn't come at all anymore. . . . People didn't leave anymore. Then they killed the people, like that, I could tell you, worse than rats. . . .

Yes, they chopped them up, threw them in a pile, a pile of dead people. And then they asked others, Dominicans to come and to take them and bury them.[4] Understand what I am saying. And then one evening, they set them on fire and buried them. Once they had killed a lot of them, they poured gas on them and set them on fire. . . .

EDOUARD: Did people know [in advance] that they were going to kill people?

ISIL: . . . Did they know they were going to carry out the Slashing up [*Kout kouto a*] of people? We didn't know that. Had we known, we wouldn't have waited a minute [before fleeing].

. . . What they said was that they were killing a few people who were sorcerers, who were bad, like thieves, only they weren't really thieves. . . .

RICHARD: Did Dominicans practice Vodou as well?

ISIL: Dominicans, they all practiced. Dominicans practiced, the same way as Haitians. You understand? But because of the country's laws, they practiced in secret. . . .

RICHARD: When the Slashing began, what did you think? . . .

ISIL: Well . . . this is what I could say, it was because they were demanding, were demanding their country. So they threw you out like an animal, like an animal. Because, for example, you're sitting in a chair there. And perhaps you don't do anything wrong at all. Then you see me passing right by, and I take the chair out from under you. You see that I am engaging in an act of cruelty with you. If you had done something to me, you'd say I was taking revenge. But, no, I passed by, I took the chair from you, you see I'm engaging in an act of cruelty with you. Well, it was like that. We didn't think of anything. And because we saw that, we knew they were carrying out an act of cruelty with us. Everyone, those who had pride, didn't stay. It was no little thing. . . . It's pretty much of a mystery. It's something for us to ask God . . . no?

. . . The Spanish, the Dominicans, they tricked us before the knife was raised up. But this is what they told us. They came, they celebrated, they gathered the whole community, they celebrated. President Trujillo himself came to Dajabón. He said all people are the same. There are no differences between one another. . . . He told us, there are no Dominicans, no Haitians. It's all the same blood. He said if you put Dominican blood in a white dish, and you put Haitian blood in a white dish, there isn't any difference. It's the same blood. . . .

That was before the Slashing, one year, two years before, he came and told us that. . . .

He told us, there is no difference. Haitians and Spanish are not different. It's the same blood that makes us all, he told us. And at that time he brought us some fifteen, twenty, thirty trucks of arms, tools, machetes, hoes, saws, pickaxes, rakes, and more. He said these were for us to cultivate the land. He distributed [them to us]. I alone received three hoes.

Then, he told us, there is no one that owns the land, he is the only one who owns the land, he is everyone's father, and [the land] was there for everyone to farm. "You can take the land wherever you find it, under one condition," he stated. "Each citizen must work productively thirty *tareas*"—anew.[5]

I couldn't do it. I was too young. My father did . . . half, three-quarters of it. . . .

He was a great worker. . . . This wasn't grassland! It was clearing woods—as all the land was then—felling trees, burning woods, cutting down trees all the way to Ouanaminthe [in Haiti] . . . and then setting it on fire. I myself cleared about fifteen *tareas*. . . .

Trujillo tricked us . . . into providing work for the country, cultivating the land, turning the whole place into farms. . . .

This wasn't two or three Haitians. The entire country . . . had been a vast woods. And everyone was slashing trees and converting the land to farms, fully cultivated farms. . . . During this time, [Haitians] weren't being mistreated at all still. And then the knife was lifted. And all that work [that Haitians had done] remained for them [Dominicans].

RICHARD: What had they planted on that land?

ISIL: Peanuts, corn, rice, cassava, plantains, other things . . .

LAUREN: Did your family produce enough food for your whole family? Or was it necessary, did your family need . . .

ISIL: Oh yes, you had enough to eat—and enough to sell, too. We used to go all the way to Santiago to sell peanuts. And we had a lot of animals, cattle, pigs, chickens, goats—there were plenty of those—sheep, all those things, we kept a lot of them. My dad was an important citizen, an important resident [*abitan*]. When he would harvest the crops, we would have . . . three or four hundred boxes of peanuts. . . .

LAUREN: How many heads of cattle did your dad have in the Dominican Republic?[6]

ISIL: A lot of cattle. But that's not something we could have had an account of.[7] My dad had a lot of cattle. . . . A little sister of mine everyone called "Avéfèman," even she had ten cows, a little child, I'm telling you—there was a Dominican who people called "Bètoline," the godfather of . . . one of my little sisters. . . . (You know the woman they call Man Sifran in Ouanaminthe, a white lady—he was that lady's son.) He alone . . . [helped her get] ten cows. . . . They were something we had plenty of! . . .

LAUREN: Were there any arguments over land in the Dominican Republic before the Slashing took place? Maybe there had been some jealousy?[8]

ISIL: No, nothing like that. On the contrary, when we organized a *konbit*,[9] even the section chief would come help. . . . And if he couldn't come, you know what he did? He would buy two or three things, seasonings and other things, so you could provide lunch for and feed the people [working in the *konbit*], he said. My dad would organize a *konbit*. And he [the section chief] himself would come barefoot. He'd tell us, *"Está bien, está bien"* ["It's fine, it's fine"]. That's to show that I am really a friend of yours. I come to the *konbit* without shoes. He came like that. . . .

LAUREN: Did you use to pay the migration tax?

EDOUARD: Were there some Haitians who didn't want to pay?

ISIL: That didn't want to pay? Yes, there were the Haitians . . . [who were] themselves natives there [in the Dominican Republic]. They were born in the country. They were baptized in the country. They grew up in the country, you see. They spoke the language well. They got by well. And they said they weren't Haitian. They denied they were Haitians. The compatriots said they weren't Haitian . . . to retain their money. They said they weren't Haitian, that they were countrymen. . . . They obtained [Dominican] birth certificates, so they were seen as Dominican. . . .

[The tax] was six pesos, six pesos, and you got it easily. . . .

RICHARD: I did have some other questions about the Slashing. Were a lot of Dominican civilians involved in the Slashing?

ISIL: Well, civilians were obligated to be. Even if they were your friend, and they were looking for ways to help you flee, they couldn't look like they were trying to help you. They would kill them too then. If they were open about it, if they'd say this person does not deserve to die, they would kill them too.

If you showed up [at a Dominican friend's house] . . . as long as they didn't see anybody else, they would tell you, "You have to get out [of the Dominican Republic]. You have to get out." They'd hide you somewhere and, after doing that, would quickly help you get to your country and save yourself. But they couldn't appear to be coming to your aid. They couldn't. . . .

RICHARD: Did Haitians born in the Dominican Republic have more opportunity to make a life for themselves than the Haitians who arrived from

Haiti, because they had fewer Dominican friends or they didn't speak the Spanish language?

ISIL: Those born over there . . . the intelligent ones, they went to school, they went to Dominican schools, they used the [Spanish] language a lot, and some even made it into the [Dominican] army on the other side, which means they were not "Haitian" [quotation marks added]. But for people farming the land, able to be farmers, as the majority were, including me, there wasn't any difference, all the same. Whether or not you were born on the other side, grew up over there, it was the same thing. The only exception was if you went to school, you went there, learned the language, you used it, and you weren't seen as Haitian, you were seen as Dominican. And then after that, you didn't have to pay migration [the migration tax]. If you had your birth certificate, you passed . . . under [the law]. . . . That meant you were Dominican, you understand? But you did have to pay the fee for the *cédula* [Spanish word for the Dominican national identity card]. But when the knife was lifted up, my friend[,] . . . it didn't make any such distinctions. No, it was just, "Disappear!" . . .

You had a birth certificate over there but at the time of the Knife, you definitely could not stay. Oh no, "*negro* [black] settlers"—you definitely could not stay! The black color could not stay on the other side.

And even if you were red [lighter-skinned of African descent], even if you were red, they have a question they ask you, to say *perejil* [parsley]. They gave you that [word] to say. They tell you, "Look . . . you can speak Dominican." They told you, you were *atravesado* [crossbred], you hear that? They told you, "*Dice perejil*" [You say parsley]. They told you, "*Dice Gualaguano*" ["You say Gualaguano," a subdistrict not far from where Isil lived]. They were trying to be tricky and mess you up—*Gualaguano* is a *trabalengua* [tongue twister] . . . to get you. *Dice perejil* and *Gualaguano* . . . If you say it and you can't say it the way their kin [*kina yo*] say it, well like that: "*Tu eres haitiano*" ["You're Haitian"]. When they were chasing you, if you were white [they'd ask you to say that].[10]

RICHARD: They did that, in case you were a white Haitian . . . ?

ISIL: Some lighter-skinned Haitians, lighter-skinned. Before the Slashing . . . there even had been a group of people who, when they couldn't pay it, they took them—when I tell you it was cruelty they were practicing—there was a group of people they got and they . . . sent all those people . . . to go work, forced labor. There was a guy they called Océan. They sent him there.

EDOUARD: Sometimes people were imprisoned [under Trujillo]. They took them for [not paying] the *cédula* [both Dominicans and Haitians]. They took them for [not paying] the migration [tax].

ISIL: Yes, they'd serve six months, they'd serve a year. . . .

RICHARD: Were there a lot of Haitians that were quite poor as well?

ISIL: . . . They weren't poor and begging, you realize. But they were, like, hard-working citizens. So they weren't rich. But they had the means to live. Over there, there weren't poor people. There weren't people who couldn't eat. You see, they weren't rich, you know, but they had enough to live. Everyone, you know, had their own cattle, not to mention pigs, goats, raised a lot of chickens. There were people who raised a lot [of livestock]— so you worked a lot too. There were no poor people. It's in Haiti that I first came to see people begging. I had never seen that. It's in Haiti that I began to see that. . . .

RICHARD: Did some people who lived close to the border in the Dominican Republic, did the Haitians who lived closer have more opportunities to save their lives than the people who lived farther away from the border?

ISIL: Well, the people who were closer, who were nearer, many of them died. How do you think they died, if you know? They died because they didn't want to cross the border through the woods. More of them died. It was in Dajabón where they died. They went to pass through Customs there. As they were better off, they were so well off that there were people who carried loads of money. They went on mules . . . [or] they rode horses. They had the means and money. So they do not go through the woods. They went to Customs. So they [Dominicans] see them traveling well. And when they see them, they took all those people, mashed those people up. But otherwise, for the people who didn't go through Customs, many were saved. Many survived, they went through the woods. . . .

RICHARD: From your perspective, what do you think was the cause of the Slashing? Why did Trujillo do this?

ISIL: Me, I can't tell you why, not why. I, I call it cruelty. I call it cruelty *because* I don't know why. . . . When a person could simply [do this to you when] you didn't do anything to him . . . I've never known why, not why, he didn't say why.

RICHARD: Did you ever return to the Dominican Republic after the Slashing?

ISIL: If I went back? I never went back.

RICHARD: Why?

ISIL: I never went back. Principles are principles. I never went back. . . .

RICHARD: Do you have any hatred or disgust for the Dominican people?

ISIL: I don't have hatred against them. . . . They didn't stick a knife in my body. But they did take all my assets. Those were all the assets we had. We lost everything. . . . I don't hate them in spite of that. If on one day they come here, if I have some change, and they show up here, I can't say I'd ever eat and not give them any. I'd pay for them anyway. But I'm not going to look [to make a living] on their terrain. . . . I'm not crossing over. . . . Principles are principles.

Translated by Nadève Ménard and Richard Turits

Notes

1. On the massacre and its most likely causes, along with the history of the northern frontier region, see Richard Turits, "A World Destroyed, a Nation Imposed: The 1937 Haitian Massacre in the Dominican Republic," *Hispanic American Historical Review* 82, no. 3 (August 2002): 589–635; Lauren Derby, "Haitians, Magic, and Money: *Raza* and Society in the Haitian-Dominican Borderlands, 1900–1937," *Comparative Studies in Society and History* 36, no. 3 (1994): 488–526; Lauren Derby and Richard Turits, "Historias de terror y los terrores de la historia: La masacre haitiana de 1937 en la República Dominicana," *Estudios Sociales* (Santo Domingo) 26, no. 92 (April–June 1993): 65–76.

2. The text beginning here through the next seven paragraphs (ending on "fighting, insulting, swearing . . . ") was moved from farther down in the conversation, for the sake of clarity.

3. The section chief was the submunicipal authority, then an important local figure in the Dominican Republic known as the *alcalde pedáneo*.

4. Here Isil is referring to Dominican civilians—as opposed to the armed forces carrying out the killings.

5. A *tarea* is a Spanish unit of measurement equal to approximately two hectares or roughly five acres. Isil presumably is referring here to newly cleared land.

6. This question and Isil's response have been moved up from a later point in the conversation, for the sake of clarity.

7. Most cattle, after being branded, ranged freely in the Dominican countryside. Thus it was difficult to know the exact number one had.

8. This question and Isil's response moved up from a later point in the conversation, for the sake of clarity.

9. A *konbit* is an agricultural work party made up of voluntary laborers from the community.

10. Presumably Isil was recounting here an effort by Dominican soldiers to ensure that possessing light skin did not allow a resident of Haitian descent to pass as Dominican. In the interviews Lauren Derby and Turits conducted, there were multiple accounts of the Dominican military demanding that those captured say words such as *perejil* (parsley), *tijera* (scissors), or various others, generally with the letter *r*. Supposed inability to pronounce these Spanish words without an accent was then taken as an indicator of Haitian identity. This practice appears to have been borrowed from local police who had used it in the past to determine whether ethnic Haitians would be required to pay the annual migration tax (records of birthplace were not necessarily or easily available). Anyone who had pronounced the words like Dominican locals, particularly the *r*'s (a perceived challenge, however the *r* was very weak in most of the Dominican countryside compared with Spanish elsewhere), was presumed to have been born in the country and would not be taxed. In fact, however, as Turits writes: "Ethnic Haitians with deep roots in the Dominican frontier most likely pronounced 'perejil' fluently and often indistinguishably from ethnic Dominicans in the area. Thus, this litmus test was evidently rigged during the Massacre. It served largely as a pretext, a mock confirmation of the presumptions and fantasies of an inherent and radical distinction between ethnic Dominicans and Haitians clung to by outside officials and elites." Turits, "A World Destroyed, a Nation Imposed," 617.

Massacre River

René Philoctète

Poet, novelist, and playwright René Philoctète was one of the three cofounders, with Frankétienne and Jean-Claude Fignolé, of the late twentieth-century aesthetic philosophy of Spiralism. He was also a member of the Haïti Littéraire collective, a small group of politically engaged poets (including Vilard Denis [Davertige], Serge Legagneur, Roland Morriseau, and Anthony Phelps) active in the 1960s, all of whom were forced into exile during the Duvalier dictatorship. Aside from six months spent in Canada, Philoctète remained and wrote in Haiti during the successive Duvalier presidencies-for-life. While his prose fiction works make no explicit references to the politics of his time, they nevertheless present biting critiques of the abuse of state power and the quotidian battles fought in Haiti. In Massacre River, *Philoctète tells the story of Pedro and Adèle, a Dominican-Haitian couple living in a small town on the border between Haiti and the Dominican Republic during the time of the Parsley Massacre, the mass killing of Haitians on the orders of General Rafaël Trujillo during the fall of 1937. The impending massacre is foreshadowed in the below excerpt: Trujillo has issued the order to his military, the Dominican people have tacitly approved—or have raised no protest—and "the beast" has been unleashed. The relative autonomy of the Haitian-Dominican borderlands posed a challenge to the heads of state in both Haiti and the Dominican Republic, given that political dissidents were able to use the fluid territorial region to move between the two states. Consequently, residents of the terrain and, by extension, the nations at large, found themselves in the midst of political conflicts that were unmatched by their daily experiences. In this scene, Pedro heads home to his Haitian wife after a long day spent working in the cane fields, as yet not fully aware of the horrors about to unfold. As he walks, he muses on the common history and culture that profoundly unite the whole of the island, his reflections a stark contrast to the racist and divisive state discourse that prepares the terrain for the unspeakable violence to come.*

The madness will not be unleashed today, of course, but everything is ready. The sealed orders leave no room for doubt. Don Agustín de Cortoba, crammed into his khaki uniform, has seen Don Preguntas Feliz. They have smiled. They have embraced. A fine coupling of cunning and atrocity: Preguntas, the man of laws and subtleties; Agustín, the man of arms and blind anger. The lieutenant was not talkative. Authority in action has no need of words. Harangues, allocutions, proclamations, philippics—these are for elections. And the people rush to the polls. When you elect death, there is no need to vote. Preguntas has pronounced it legal. The lantern has shown what time it is. Trujillo has made his decision. Don Agustín has placed his fat hairy hand on the *alcalde*'s right shoulder. The two of them have had coffee. Have made faces. Perhaps their coffee was . . . ? That's why Adèle was shaking when she watched me uneasily enter the dawn.

"Will you come back, Pedrito?"

"Who can stop me, *mujer*?"

"The beast, of course! Racing across the plains, scaling the mountains, flying over the seas, striding over the towns, that beast is a herald! It has proclaimed the order of the day."

When the cane fields burn, stalks twisting in the flames become so many lighted candles, inviting admiration of the disaster, fostering the acceptance of cruelty. All autocracy has its magic, its seduction: the troops on parade, the bright flags, the thunder of marching feet. And the people, enraptured, approve, forgetting that those who tried to dispel the darkness have been swallowed up in the solitude of dungeons. . . .

Striding through the dew just beginning to burn off, Pedro Brito brushes by a tuft of basil. The air sneezes, somersaults, breaks its nose, all in a daze. Bewildered insects jiggle their mirrors of spinning colors: from saffron yellow to pure violet, from jet black to the pellucid white of waterfalls. Beautiful, beautiful, beautiful, these lands! Both of them together. One high, the other low, with their underground sortileges: the Zemis' gold, the sweat of those wrenched from Africa. The Cacique Caonabo knew Anacaona, the *samba*. The tenderness of Jaragua was dissolved into the pride of the Cibao Valley. Flowers discovered the intoxication of bravery. When the hurricane blows, the teals whirl in circles—a fragile crown in the vigor of the gale.

Pedro Brito crosses a stream in which glitter the last jewels of the sky. In a few hours I will meet with *los compañeros*. Machetes will cut the cane; the sticky juice will cling to the stalks. The muscles of two peoples will work together to bring forth the goodness of the Dominican earth. Ah! The smell of the canebrakes on a clear morning! As if the earth wished to bless the sky. Pedro Brito flares his nostrils greedily, inhaling the life of the island in whiffs of warm air. The land here bears my footsteps, which can surely be heard on the other side. In the other land, my land! The caciques visited the cacique, and their fires burned brightly for a long time, from coast to coast. Adèle understood perfectly when she said: "Is it possible to separate us when I have become flesh of your flesh?"

Pedro hurries a little faster. Dawn has been shipwrecked, strewing noble debris: rims of clouds, corroded stars, mists lost on the violet flanks of foot-hills. A frank and royal early morning sky spans the two lands, the low one here, the high one over there, strangely serene!

Pedro stops walking. Tumbling over the cane fields, the peasants' voices rush to his senses, catch in his throat. He breathes with delight both this direct presence of the earth and this fraternal warmth of honest toil coming to him from beyond the plantations. The sky sets the trees of the Sierra de Neiba aflame, and the breeze arrives to rustle them in a silent shimmering of deep-red gems sifting down through the branches. The Sierra becomes like a clear glowing fire where every wing drinks deeply, every roof gathers radiance, every waterhole takes nourishment. Standing tall, gazing toward the light, Pedro watches the Haitian earth turn rosy in the distance, astonished that the land should be so lovely, wondering at his birth in such a marvel, for both lands are marvelous.

. . .

People were absurd. They wrote on the white walls of municipal build-ings all across the country, in big, black, block letters: *"¡El diablo haitiano!"* They partook of the Eucharist while cursing the men of the West. They orga-nized public meetings at which they distributed tracts against their western neighbors. Along with machetes and the Dominican flag. In military bar-racks, reveille was sounded at intervals, day and night, to keep the troops on their toes. Firing ranges were set up on marketplaces. Men went through the motions of hand-to-hand fighting, the parry-and-thrust of fencing, combats between athletes, fighting cocks, boxers. People devised tactics. Explained strategies. Invoked the spirits of their ancestors.

People went on with their ordinary lives, but felt on the verge of chaos. No violence has as yet led to violence, but everybody spoke freely of violence. In the shadows, imaginations were rising like bread dough.

Despite this public panic, two heads of state, Haitian and Dominican, met at Thomazeau "with a view," they proclaimed, "to strengthening the bonds of friendship" (as the phrase goes) "between the two countries," which (inci-dentally) only the accidents and interests of colonization had cleft in twain.

On the 1937 Massacre

Esther Dartigue

In the following excerpt from Esther Dartigue's posthumously published memoirs, we gain rare insight into the 1937 massacre through Dartigue's firsthand account from the Haitian side of the island. Dartigue was born in Vizakna, Hungary (30 December 1908), and raised from the age of five in the United States, where she lived until moving to Haiti to be with her husband, Maurice Dartigue. The Dartigues met at Teachers College, Columbia University, in New York City, while the two were pursuing advanced studies in rural education.

Maurice Dartigue's travels to study in the United States were part of his early involvement in cooperative efforts between the Haitian government and the U.S. government to use study abroad as a means of professionalizing various aspects of the Haitian state and society. This training led Maurice to occupy several posts including director of rural education (1931–41) and minister of public instruction, agriculture, and labor (1941–46). Dartigue's prominence within the administrations of Sténio Vincent and Élie Lescot gave Esther Dartigue a particularly intimate experience of Haiti's political class during the fifteen years she lived in the country. In 1946, the Dartigues left Haiti for the United States after popular protest and a military coup deposed Lescot from the presidency.

In 1995, Esther Dartigue wrote an account of the 1937 massacre that offers a glimpse into the atrocity from several vantage points: that of foreigners residing in Haiti, working-class Haitians residing in the outskirts of Port-au-Prince, and politically elite Haitians. Her self-reflexive comments reveal someone who attempted to be aware of her own position of privilege within Haitian society.

Maurice and I had come into town from Thorland when news came of the massacre of Haitians in the Dominican Republic. This was in 1937, and we were in the area of Croix des Bossales. It was there that I witnessed my first *kouri*—crowds panicking and running in several directions. It was quite frightening. The rumor was that Trujillo was on the march with an army to attack Haiti. Maurice stopped the car and we watched the vendors throwing their wares back into their baskets, lifting the baskets high, looking for the quickest way out of the square and heading for it. When most of the crowd had left, Maurice managed to turn the car around and we started for Thor-land. We no sooner had arrived when Mildred telephoned to say that the lights were out in town, that we should seek safety as anything could happen. We decided to stay put. We had several oil lamps if the lights should go out. They did not. There was no panic in our area or in Carrefour, a small town farther on.

But for days all was tense. There were more alarms and more *kouris*. Rumors of all sorts were going about. The palace was on the alert for fear of an uprising. I realized that Mlle Vincent would feel deserted, so I decided to go into town to see her. Mine was the only car on the street. The palace gates were shut. I got out and said that I had come to pay my respects to Mlle Vincent. As there were no telephones on the grounds, a soldier had to be sent up to give the message. He returned, the gates opened, and I can still see myself walking up the very wide stairs that led from the driveway to the palace entrance, with guards at either end of each step. I was not afraid. I wanted everyone to see that a friend in need is a friend indeed. I do not remember whether I had considered that as a white and as a foreigner it was easier and safer for me than for a Haitian. In 1946, when it was my turn to be in danger, Mlle Vincent stayed away. I never really forgave her for this sign of cowardliness. Perhaps my gesture was only bravado. Most people stayed at home to see what the outcome would be. President Vincent kept his job. If there was a plot to overthrow him, it did not materialize. Rumors of plots were common. The massacres and their consequences might have put the presidency in jeopardy. Questions arose. Why did Trujillo decide to have the Haitian cane cutters killed? Why had he not rounded them up and had them sent back once the cane cutting had been done? It was estimated that at least fifteen thousand or more people had been murdered.

A few months before this, Trujillo had been in Haiti. He had visited Thor-land in the company of the President and Mlle Vincent, and I had been introduced to him there. Had he come for negotiations? Had they failed?

The massacres did bring out the hostility of the proletariat for the upper class. There was some pillaging even in private homes. I knew of one intrepid house owner. At that time doors were not locked. This tiny frail woman had gone out on an errand. Several women from the poor section of town had worked their way up to Sacré-Coeur. They spotted the open windows of this small house, and not seeing anyone around, they boldly went up the steps and through the door. They were already filling their baskets with odds and ends and enjoying themselves when in walked the owner. Arms akimbo, she gave them such a talking-to, insisted they empty their baskets, and then told them to be off. Without a word, one after the other, off they went and once out of the house ran down the street. The owner called her maid only to find she had hidden herself in a closet, trembling with fear. The maid also received a tongue-lashing, and all she said was, "Madame, you are you, but who am I?"

In the spring of 1941 Maurice was sent as a delegate to the Dominican Republic for a few days. Trujillo invited the group to visit his country home where he showed off his two hundred suits and many horses. Was he trying to make amends in various ways for the massacres of 1937?

Official Communiqué on "Incidents" in the Dominican Republic

Governments of Haiti and the Dominican Republic

This is a joint statement in response to violence on the northern frontier between Haiti and the Dominican Republic by officials from the two countries. The statement describes the violence as "incidents" that must be addressed to preempt "exaggerated commentaries" that would be "contrary to the harmony and cordiality" between the two governments. The document vividly illustrates the stark tension between official declarations of Pan-American amity during the 1930s and a period of tremendous anti-Haitian violence in the Dominican Republic.

The communiqué appeared just a week after Haitian and Dominican officials acknowledged the violence taking place in the Dominican Republic. The tone of the public announcement reveals the extent to which the Vincent and Trujillo administrations held fast to a diplomatic approach to the situation. Having recently regained sovereignty from U.S. military occupation, neither head of state wished to appear politically weak. The communiqué comments on the events as distant and detached from the Dominican state and its leader, Rafael Trujillo, deflecting responsibility to members of the general public. But, as scholars have extensively documented, Trujillo was not only aware of and involved in the massacre, he orchestrated and encouraged it, in conjunction with members of his administration and cabinet of intellectuals. Both heads of state turned to inter-American rhetoric to defend their positions in the situation. To distance himself from the violence and sustain his reputation as a model of inter-American leadership, Trujillo feigned a willingness to cooperate with the Vincent administration's attempt to secure an inter-American investigation into the massacre. For his part, Vincent turned to inter-American rhetoric to muster support from the United States and other neighboring countries, to defend against the aggression.

In order to avoid that some incidents that have taken place on the northern frontier between Dominicans and Haitians give rise to exaggerated comments contrary to the harmony and cordiality that both the Honorable President Trujillo and the Honorable President Vincent strive to create and intensify, inspired by the common destiny, in peace and prosperity of two peoples that are brothers, we make it known that the cordial relations that exist between the Dominican Republic and the Republic of Haiti have not been breached.

The Dominican government has energetically disapproved the incidents that have been denounced to it, and has opened a meticulous investigation in order to determine who is responsible and to apply necessary sanctions, according to the results of such investigation. So that in advance we can affirm that everything will be solved to the satisfaction of the two governments.

May the cordial friendship that has always existed and that currently exists between the Honorable President Trujillo and the Honorable President Vincent constitute the strongest and most effective force to prevent the destruction of the harmony between the two peoples and the patriotic work of their two illustrious representatives, work that by its great spirit of morality and justice has earned the applause of every nation in the civilized world.

Ciudad Trujillo, 15 October 1935
Evremont CARRIE, Extraordinary Envoy
and Plenipotentiary Minister
of the Republic of Haiti
Joaquin BALAGUER, Secretary of State for
Foreign Relations of the Dominican Republic

Translated by Chantalle F. Verna

Vyewo

Jean-Claude Martineau

"Vyewo" is a song by Jean-Claude Martineau, who also goes by the pen name Koralen. The text narrates the plight of two Haitian cane cutters in the Dominican Republic and has been interpreted by well-known Haitian singers from Manno Charlemagne to Emeline Michel to Renette Désir. Although its references to space are specific, it remains vague in terms of time, giving the impression that it could be describing a scene from the past or a reality that is very much current.

In the middle of a cane field near Higuey
In the Dominican Republic
Two Haitians sit in a batey,
Barefoot and bare-chested.
One is talking, one is listening.
They are not loud.
The wind in the cane alone hears
What they have to say.

Vyewo, you who are going to work the land in Haiti,
Here's something to give to my wife for me.
Vyewo, it's "diez peso,"
and a pair of earrings.
When you get there, if she's living with someone else,
You can give them to my mother.

Vyewo went, Vyewo came back
With news that made the heart heavy.
The mother had died
Several years back.
Some people say
She died of sadness.
The wife is still there,
Still holding on,
But the kids are not well cared for.

The first one grew like a horse,
The last one doesn't even remember his father.

In the middle of a cane field near Higuey
In the Dominican Republic
Two Haitians sit in a batey,
Barefoot and bare-chested.
One is talking, one is listening.
They are not loud.
The wind in the cane rushed to erase
What they had to say.

Cousin, I come from working the land in Haiti.
Here's a message your wife sent to you.
Cousin, she says it's time for you to return.
Cousin, even if you have nothing to bring,
When you cross the border,
Don't leave your machete behind.

Translated by Nadève Ménard

Nedjé

Roussan Camille

During the 1940s and 1950s, francophone writers, thinkers, and political leaders gave birth to a global literary movement known as Négritude. Similar to the Indigéniste writings in Haiti produced during the late nineteenth and mid-twentieth centuries, Négritude writings were a response to colonial and racist representations of people of African descent. Aimé Césaire, from Martinique, and Léopold Sédar Senghor, from Senegal, among others, spearheaded the movement, which explicitly celebrated blackness and African culture. Négritude's impact on Haitian literature is visible in the writings of certain authors, notably Roussan Camille, journalist, diplomat, and poet. "Nedjé," his best-known poem, highlights the similarities between the conditions of black people around the world, including the exploitation of young black women. The poem was one of many works translated by the African American educator, scholar, and diplomat Mercer Cook, and published in a collection edited by the African American literary writer and social activist Langston Hughes. Together the two men helped introduce the ideas and writings from the Négritude movement to English-speaking audiences.

Not quite sixteen,
you said you came from Danakil,
you whom vicious white men
crammed with anisette and whiskey
in that smoke-filled cafe
in Casablanca.

Through the narrow window
the dusk was dripping blood
on the burnous of the Spahis
leaning against the bar
and tracing above the desert outside
epic visions
of clashes, pursuits,
defeats and glory.

One bloody evening
which was but a minute
in the eternal bloody night of Africa,
so sad a night
your dance became imbued with it
and made me sick at heart
like your song,
like your glance
blending with my soul.

Your eyes were full of countries
so many countries
that when I looked at you
I saw anew
in their wild light
the dark suburbs of London,
the brothels of Tripoli,
Montmartre, Harlem,
every pseudo paradise
where Negroes dance and sing
for others.

The nearby call
of your mutilated Danakil,
the call of black fraternal hands
infused into your dance of love
a virginal purity
and echoed in your heart
great familiar songs.

Your frail arms
through the smoke
yearned to embrace
centuries of pride,
kilometers of landscape,
while your steps
on the waxed mosaic
sought the highlands and the lowlands
of your childhood.

The window opened on the anxious East.
One hundred times your heart returned there.
One hundred times the red rose brandished
in your delicate finger-tips

adorned the mirage
of the gates of your village.

Your sorrow and nostalgia
were known to all the débauchés
sailors on manoeuvres
soldiers on leave
the idling tourists
crushing your brown breasts
with the vast boredom of travellers.
The missionaries and the fearful
sometimes tried to console you.

But you alone know
little girl from Danakil
lost in the smoke-filled cafes of Casablanca,
that your heart
will find its happiness when
in the new dawns
that bathe your native desert
you return to dance
for your living heroes,
your heroes yet unborn.

Then each step,
each gesture,
each glance,
each song
will show the sun
your land belongs to you!

Dyakout

Félix Morisseau-Leroy

Although Félix Morisseau-Leroy (1912–98) published in both Haitian Creole and French, today he is mostly remembered as one of the pioneers of literature in Haitian Creole, which he used for both poetry and theatrical works. As early as the 1930s, but particularly during the 1940s, Morriseau-Leroy was among the few Haitian educators and artists who lent growing attention to the value of instructing in Creole. Morriseau-Leroy was part of an emerging class in Haiti that benefited from scholarship opportunities organized by the Haitian and U.S. governments in order to develop various professional cadres in Haiti. Thus, in addition to his studies in Haiti, Morriseau-Leroy spent time at one of the foremost U.S. host institutions, Teachers College, Columbia University, in New York City.

After a period of working in Haitian education, Morisseau-Leroy lived abroad. He spent most of his adult life outside of the country, including periods of exile in Senegal, then in the United States. A street in Miami's Little Haiti neighborhood, where he spent his final years of life, was posthumously given his name. His international experiences and connections to political thinkers and activists from the United States, Africa, and the Caribbean who challenged and ultimately helped to usher in the end of European colonial rule after 1945 had a noticeable impact on his writings. Morisseau-Leroy's references to black consciousness, anti-imperialism, and critiques of religion (especially Catholicism), for example, go beyond Haitian history to include Africa and North America.

The untitled poem below is from Morisseau-Leroy's first collection of poetry, Diacoute (1953), a seminal work in Haitian literary history. It is a tribute to the father of the Haitian nation, Jean-Jacques Dessalines. Morisseau-Leroy expounds on Dessalines's importance to him personally, to all Haitians, to blacks in general and to all men everywhere.

Papa Dessalines, thank you
Every time I feel what I am
I say thank you, Dessalines
Every time I hear a man from the colony,
A man who's not yet free to speak
I say: Dessalines, thank you

Félix Morisseau-Leroy
(1912–98). Photo courtesy
of CIDHICA.

Only I know what you are to me
Thank you, Papa Dessalines
If I'm a man
I have to say: thank you, Dessalines
If I open my eyes to see,
It's thanks to you, Dessalines
If I walk with my head high,
It's thanks to you, Dessalines
Each time I look at another man,
I say thank you, Dessalines
When I see what's going on in other places
I say: thank you, Papa Dessalines
When I hear the whites talking
I say Papa Dessalines, thank you
When I hear a few of my fellow black men talking
I say: thank you Papa Dessalines
Only I know what you mean to me
Dessalines the bull
Dessalines, my blood
Dessalines, my two eyes
Dessalines, the heart of me

Only I know
Every man should say:
Thank you, Dessalines
You showed us our way
Thank you, Dessalines
You are our light,
Dessalines
You gave us the land we walk on
The sky that covers our heads
Trees, rivers
Oceans, ponds, it's you.
Dessalines, you gave us the sun
Gave us the moon
You gave us our sisters, our brothers
Our mothers, our fathers, our children
Because of you we're a certain way, a certain manner
We're not like other men
If I look everyone in the eyes
It's you who's looking at them, Dessalines
You gave us water to drink
You gave us food to eat
Thank you, Papa Dessalines.
What's more, you've given us a house to live in,
A place to plant and work the land
You taught us how to sing
You taught us how to say no
They say there are men who say: yes, yes
There are men who say yes, sir.
You taught us how to say: no.
Dessalines showed all men
All men on earth to say: no
Thank you, Papa Dessalines
There are men who want to explain that
Today is not like yesterday
And nowadays
La fraternité humaine
L'humanité, la civilisation
That's all French
Me, it's Dessalines that I know
I say: thank you, my father
You've made me
My mother is your child
My son, my daughter, are your children too

Thank you, Dessalines
My grandchildren are your children
King Dessalines, thank you
I don't even need to mention the flag!
No need to mention *Lakayè*
Or *Gonayiv*!
That's been said already
And who's going to listen to that again?
Requiem mass on October 17th?
Who's going to the cathedral?
Minister's speeches?
Who's going to listen to that?
But what I say here
Is just one word: thanks
Thank you Dessalines, my father
There are people who don't know
I have to tell them
Without you, we would not be here
Thank you, Papa Dessalines
And no more of your Our Fathers,
Monsignor, Dessalines is not dead
Enough of your French, minister
Dessalines will never die
Dessalines is here
Could that man die!
Dessalines is in my heart
Arms at the ready
Dessalines is watching
One day Dessalines will rise
That day, you'll all know
You'll know if 1804
You'll know if Lakayè
You'll know if Lakrèt-a-Pyewo
You'll know if Vètyè
If Dessalines did all that
So little guys could write poems
So ministers could make speeches
So priests could sing Te Deum
For monsignors to give absolution
Dessalines does not need absolution
Everything Dessalines does is good
One day, Dessalines will rise
You'll hear them calling

All around the Caribbean Sea
Where is he
Dessalines has taken up arms
Arrest him
Then you'll hear his voice like thunder
Everybody: cut off their heads, burn the houses
You'll hear them calling all across America
Stop him
Dessalines's voice is already on the radio
Cut off their heads, burn the houses
All over *Harlem*, Dessalines is putting things in order
You'll hear: stop Dessalines
All the way in *Dakar*
All the way in *Johannesburg*
You'll hear: Where did Dessalines get to?
Cut off their heads, burn the houses
Dessalines does not need absolution
Does not need God's forgiveness
On the contrary, Dessalines is God's arm
Dessalines is God's justice
He does not need a monsignor's Our Father
Nor the forgiveness blacks want whites to ask for
Dessalines does not need that
For all he's done, I say: Papa Dessalines, thank you
For everything he will do
I say: thank you, Papa Dessalines.

Translated by Nadève Ménard

Estimé Plays Slot Machine in Casino

Gordon Parks

This 1949 photo by U.S. photographer Gordon Parks exemplifies what scholars have referred to as Haiti's golden age of tourism (1946–56), a period when considerable infrastructural developments geared toward the tourist economy were built by the state or foreign investors. The most visible moment of this era was the celebration of the two hundredth founding anniversary of Haiti's capital city with a World's Fair called the Exposition International du Bicentenaire de Port-au-Prince. That event, and related tourist activities in Haiti, led to the erection of buildings, roads, casinos, and hotels. These developments provided an illusion of national progress by attracting largely North American and European middle-class tourists. At the same time, tourism proved to be one of the factors driving massive migration to Port-au-Prince and other urban areas. This spike in Port-au-Prince's residential population placed a tremendous strain on public services such as electricity and sewage systems. Additionally, the employment opportunities and levels available in Haiti's cities did not match the surge in population levels and costs associated with urban living. Consequently, a strained infrastructure, unemployment, and underemployment were also characteristics of this so-called golden age.

Gordon Parks, *Estimé Plays Slot Machine in Casino*, 1949. President Dumarsais Estimé is pictured on the left of the image, trying his luck at the slot machine. Reprinted by permission of Getty Images.

On *The Voice of Women*

Madeleine Sylvain Bouchereau

Madeleine Sylvain Bouchereau (1905–70) was an important feminist activist in Haiti. She was the daughter of prominent Haitian writer and political activist, Georges Sylvain, and the sister of anthropologist Suzanne Comhaire-Sylvain (1898–1975). She was a strong advocate for the institutionalization of a public education for girls and women, and one of the founders and leaders of the Ligue Féminine d'Action Sociale (LFAS), established in 1934. Over the years, the LFAS included various writers, including Cléante Valcin, Madeleine Gardiner, and Paulette Poujol-Oriol. The league was active for several decades and is the precursor of contemporary women's organizations. Indeed, some of the laws proposed in recent years in Haiti are strikingly similar to those proposed by the LFAS in the 1950s.

The selection below, Sylvain Bouchereau's "Nous Revoici" ("We're Back"), was published on the relaunching of the league's newspaper, La Voix des Femmes (The Voice of Women), in 1947, after a four-year hiatus. At the time, Sylvain Bouchereau was the newspaper's editor and the league's president, and in this piece she reflected anew on women's intellectual, political, and economic contributions to the nation. The essay also provides the reader with an abbreviated history of La Voix. She emphasized that activism in Haiti was part of an international movement of intellectual exchange and debates about gender inequality. In what she called a "new politics of the mind," Sylvain Bouchereau challenged male journalists to embrace women as a valuable component of the nation's intellectual community in order to reengage politicians and citizens in a discussion about democracy in Haiti. Over the next three years, the newspaper chronicled women's struggles as they fought successfully for equal education and full suffrage, which was won in 1950.
—*Contributing Editor: Grace Saunders*

Eleven years ago, in October 1933, "The Voice of Women" was heard for the first time in the Haitian press. Its goal was to defend a noble and just ideal, that of the social, intellectual, and civic emancipation of the Haitian woman that will enable her to take up the role she deserves within the family and society.

For eight years, our journal has fought for the defense of women's interests and also, through the discussion of important social problems, contributed to the awakening of the social consciousness of the Haitian people. . . .

But in December 1943, "The Voice of Women" had to shut down because of the difficulties created by the war and the general indifference with regard to social ideas.

. . .

Now the "Voice of Women" begins again, strengthened by the support of new collaborators. It is not the organ of a party or the defender of a doctrine. It wishes to extend its activities to include everything that concerns women.

It wishes to be the link between all Haitian women who do not know one another. Thus, it will try to connect them to women around the world who, whether free or oppressed, are working for the emancipation of women. It will enable these women to become aware of themselves and to organize themselves according to their affinities, their abilities, their political convictions. . . .

We are interested in literature, art, music, and in the education of our children. But we need to do more, and we will sometimes leave the house to contemplate for a moment the great suffering in these other homes which are also a bit our own, these nests of people which constitute our country's hem of misery. We will, in time, consider the expanded household that is the state, in order to better understand our role in the edification that we all must contribute to, and our place in this nation. . . . We will travel further afield to take a look at women in other countries, in order to work hand in hand for a little more love and harmony in the world.

We hope, gentlemen, that you will come talk to us sometimes, as friends, about the social problems that are wreaking havoc in our country and the world, and that together we will manage to solve them through a "collaboration of both sexes for the good of the country."

Dear Brothers of the Press, we take our place by your side, and want to be regarded by you not as adversaries but as collaborators who want to work with you to uplift our country.

Translated by Nadève Ménard

On Women's Emancipation

Marie-Thérèse Colimon-Hall

Marie-Thérèse Colimon was a feminist activist from Haiti who addressed the First Haitian Women's Congress in 1950. Before an international audience from Jamaica, Puerto Rico, and the United States, Colimon linked the modernization of the nation to young women's access to economic and political power. Colimon was particularly interested in the emancipation of young girls from an elite ideal of womanhood which suggests that women should be more concerned with their social affiliations and marriage than with public service, politics, and professionalization. Colimon's comments aligned with those of other intellectuals of the time, such as Jean Price-Mars, who also challenged members of Haiti's political and economic elite to focus on civic involvement and education in order to strengthen the nation. Colimon would go on to serve as the president of the Ligue Feminine d'Action Sociale through the 1960s, where she oversaw the development of social education programs.

We need to make our peace with the loss of certain ways of life, for we will never return to those patriarchal traditions that some people look on with nostalgia. Isn't humanity marching toward a new ideal, in which the apathy of earlier times is no longer appropriate?

The young woman needs a clear initiation into her diverse tasks, as much as with regard to work as with regard to her social duties and moral life. She is now obligated to be self-sufficient, to participate in public life, to take responsibility, to run the risks of freedom. In our milieu as elsewhere, these have become daily realities. Isn't it important for her to be prepared?

. . .

We demand the young woman's emancipation because this emancipation is the necessary corollary of woman's emancipation. She has to be able to fully exercise her political rights once she has acquired them. We cannot wait for her to change civil status to ask her to prepare and apply herself.

We demand the young woman's emancipation because young women are the vital forces of the nation and the reserves for the future.

We demand the young woman's emancipation because a society that wants to be strong must use all of its elements indiscriminately, regardless of sex or civil status; because the young woman who contents herself with being only a young woman, which means not to be at all, is deadweight and the community cannot drag deadweight around forever, without eventually transforming it into countless radioactive rays.

Because there will be more young female doctors and nurses unafraid of the night when it is a matter of saving a life or of relieving suffering. There will be more educators who are not afraid of the bush, nor of far-flung villages when it is a matter of bringing light.

There will be more women lawyers who are not intimidated by a single gaze in a crowd of thousands when it is a matter of the triumph of justice.

There will be more social workers whose new role is . . . so fulfilling and so productive . . . that no filthy door can repulse them when it is a matter of knocking to bring knowledge and well-being,

There will be more young artists unafraid to express their talents whatever those might be, even if such expression causes endless talk and incurs general disapproval.

There will be more women whose intelligence will not only be on display in salons, as has too often been the case up until now.

Our little country will be much more prepared to fulfill its role as a great nation. It will depend on the young woman, standing on the shore of time and turned toward this future that her hope fills with sunlight, who must not let herself be blinded by mirages and led toward false happiness.

It will be up to her, as active and productive cell of the great human body, to make proper use of the double-edged weapon she will have conquered, to not turn it against herself, to know how to combine within herself our foremothers' charms and the virile qualities of strength and self-respect which she will need to use constantly.

If the education she then receives is adapted to the needs of this new conquest, if the unwillingness of relatives to understand does not collide with her decisions and her struggles, if in her efforts she is helped by the advice of those with more experience, if the law comes to her aid by protecting her from meetings of seduction, the Haitian woman walking toward the future will have completed a new step, and the sons of Haiti to be born and raised will have gained a profound guarantee.

Translated by Nadève Ménard

On the 1946 Revolution

Matthew J. Smith

In this passage, historian Matthew J. Smith describes the remarkable popular up-rising of 1946, which overthrew Élie Lescot and led to the presidency of Dumarsais Estimé. Bringing together a wide range of activists, the movement represented the cul-mination of decades of activism that began during the U.S. occupation and had far-reaching implications for the reconfiguring of Haitian politics. Here Smith describes how a young group of student activists, including the writers Jacques Stephen-Alexis and René Depestre, were able to trigger the remarkable uprising.

In 1946 the political history of Haiti changed course. The overthrow of the Lescot regime that year during what is commonly referred to as "the five glo-rious days," intensified unresolved tensions and fermented a decade-long po-litical conflict. The radical movement born in the occupation and nurtured during the Vincent-Lescot years, matured with incredible force following the fall of the government with the revolution of 1946. More broadly, the revolu-tion was the first popular response against a U.S.-supported government in postwar Latin America and the Caribbean. The triumph of the movement did not lead to the creation of long-term economic recovery from the abuses of the deposed government, nor eradicate political corruption, and only mini-mally improved the material benefits of the country's impoverished majority. It did, however, signal a breakdown in the legitimacy of elite political su-premacy; forcefully asserted radical ideology as a political weapon; gave the black middle class unprecedented political leverage; announced the crucial role of the labor movement as a force in national politics; and strengthened the role of the military. Most symbolic of the major changes in the political culture was the coming to power of the black peasant-born Dumarsais Es-timé in August. . . .

The movement to topple Lescot emerged . . . from the young Marxists in Port-au-Prince. . . . The formation of the Association de Étudiants en Mé-decine, Pharmacie et Art Dentaire (ADEM) in 1945 was an attempt to create a fraternity of students concerned with the state of the profession. ADEM also became an important forum where political ideas were discussed. The president of the association was a brilliant, energetic, twenty-three-year-old black student from Gonaïves named Jacques Stephen Alexis. Alexis's father, Stephen, was a respected military journalist of the twenties and later ambassador to Paris. Alexis's interests extended far beyond the medical profession. In 1945 he was the president of the country's most prestigious intellectual organization, Club Intrepid, a high honor considering his young age. A staunch communist who had been exposed to radical thought through discussion with his father's colleagues, Alexis used ADEM's journal *La Caducée* as an opportunity to express his views on world politics.[1]

. . .

Of the several radical students in the medical school, Gérald Bloncourt, the son of a Frenchwoman and an elite Haitian, was one of the more prominent. In spite of his youth the twenty-year-old distinguished himself in several areas. He was an athlete of some repute and respected artist and director at the Centre d'Art before enrolling in medical school in 1945. On the posthumous release of Roumain's *Gouverneurs de la rosée* that year, Bloncourt, a strong admirer of Roumain, had a fortuitous meeting with a senior medical student and fellow Roumain follower Jacques Stephen Alexis.[2] The two young students fast became close friends and often met after classes and on weekends to discuss current trends in art literature and the international communist movement.[3]

. . .

In April 1945 René Depestre, a nineteen-year-old high school student from Jacmel who had relocated to the capital four years earlier, published a book of poems titled *Étincelles*, which was received with great enthusiasm among the young militants. . . . Like the other students, he was a fervent communist who idolized Jacques Roumain. "Camarade Roumain," wrote Depestre in his ode "Le baiser au leader," "you are our ideal. You are our flame. You are our God. [You] cried a voice and the present choir will respond."[4] For the young radicals, Depestre's work was a reflection of their own political sympathies, and a confirmation that a new generation of intellectual youth was becoming politically conscious. . . . These young men, many of whom were poets, writers, and artists as well as students, agreed that their revolutionary ideas deserved an outlet for expression, and thus decided to start an activist journal. . . .

On December 7, 1945, the first issue of . . . *La Ruche* appeared in Port-au-Prince. . . . The writers often went into the popular areas of Port-au-Prince and read the articles in Kreyòl for the largely illiterate audience.[5] The *La Ruche* writings were often bold, defiant, and idealistic, driven by revolutionary zeal and naive optimism in Marxism. . . . The potent discourse of the *La Ruche* collective was fashioned not only from Marxism but also from French cultural theory. None proved more influential than surrealism. In early December André Breton, the doyen of the surrealist movement, visited Haiti for a series of lectures on surrealism and modern art. . . . The presence of the revered Breton, whose visit coincided with that of Cuban artist Wifredo Lam in Port-au-Prince over Christmas 1945, stirred considerable excitement among the members of La Ruche and their peers, who religiously attended his discussions at the Savoy club and his lectures at the Rex Theatre.[6]

. . .

Emboldened by Breton's presence, the writers of the paper decided that the special edition they were planning in honor of Haitian independence on the first of January would instead be a tribute to Breton. The paper bristles with harsh critiques against dictatorship. The opening of Depestre's front-page article crystallized the exuberance of the youth: "The year 1946 will be a year of profound experiences. . . . January will no longer be called January but Justice, February, liberty, April will be called deliverance, May, union, etc. A new future for man will begin." It was, however, the scathing page-length pronouncement they ran on the second page that proved most incendiary:

> 1946 will be the year of Freedom, when the voice of real democracy will triumph over all forms of fascist suppression.
>
> Down with all the Francos!
>
> Long Live Democracy in Action!
>
> Long Live the Youth!
>
> Long Live Social Justice!
>
> Long Live the World Proletariat!
>
> Long Live 1804![7]

The appearance of that page, which was widely circulated in the city, was the drop that caused the cup to overflow. Two days after the paper appeared, police acting on Lescot's orders stormed the Ruelle Roy headquarters of the newspaper and forced its immediate suspension. Depestre and two other members of the group were arrested and released the following morning. . . . That night at Alexis's house, Raymond Pressoir, Alexis, Depestre, Baker, Chenet, and Bloncourt met to strategize. They agreed that drastic action had to be taken against the government's banning of the paper. The young men reasoned that the best way to demonstrate their anger would be to organize a student strike. . . .[8] A student strike, they averred, would precipitate a social revolution and the overthrow of the regime. For the remainder of the week-end group members busied themselves contacting fellow students in the law and medical faculties of the university and in the high schools, informing them of the plan to strike on Monday morning. The strike organizers devised various coded messages to relate information to the high school students. According to Emerante de Pradines Morse, then a student participant, the students were given a simple question to ask each other in order to determine which of their classmates supported the strike effort: "Are you going to the funeral today?"[9]

. . .

The students hoped to galvanize support from the older Marxists in Port-au-Prince, many of whom were expected to appear at Breton's fourth lecture on Sunday night at the Rex Theatre. On Sunday afternoon, Gérard Bloncourt visited Breton at Mabille's house in Pétionville on behalf of the "Jeunesse Révolutionnaire d'Haïti" and pressured him to dedicate his fourth lecture that evening to freedom, as the next day the country would be in Revolution. As Bloncourt later recalled, "This was the first revolution that had a date and time already set!"[10] A shaken Breton agreed, and under heavy scrutiny delivered a stirring lecture on surrealism and freedom. Capitalizing on the fervor of the moment, Depestre and Baker led a small demonstration in front of Champ de Mars immediately following Breton's lecture. Both were arrested and released later that night, while the other members of the group went into hiding and plotted to continue to strike as planned.[11]

Shortly before ten o'clock on Monday morning, 7 January, the students alerted the press and the U.S. Embassy to the impending strike, which would culminate with the demonstration in the embassy's courtyard. The task of contacting the embassy was given to Depestre. . . . That morning, the strike began in earnest.

The members of La Ruche along with their supporters from the law and agricultural faculties filed out of their classes and congregated outside the Medical School, shouting "Vive la Revolution!" No sooner had they gathered than police arrived and beat the students with batons. Alexis, who was badly beaten, urged Bloncourt to rally students from the nearby all-girls Lycée des Jeunes Filles, where Bloncourt's mother taught. After convincing the female students that soldiers were abusing university students, they entered the courtyard of the medical school and formed a wall around the students forcing soldiers to desist. They marched toward the Champ de Mars, attracting a large crowd of secondary school students and workers along the way.[12]

With clenched fist raised high above head, the students passed through the leading secondary schools, Lycée Pétion, St. Martial, St. Louis de Gonzague, and St. Rose de Lima, singing the Haitian national anthem, "La Dessalinienne." The numbers of protesters grew remarkably as workers and street people joined the khaki-clad students as they marched through the central streets of downtown Port-au-Prince. . . . As the crowds moved through heavily populated slum areas of Bel Air, La Saline, and Croix des Bossales, nearby businesses closed down. . . . Once the protestors arrived at the U.S. embassy, members of the Garde were already on hand and temporarily detained several activists. . . . Several students were severely beaten during the melee. Military intervention did little to dampen the resolve of the protestors, some of whom spent the night hiding in the popular neighborhoods, preparing Molotov cocktails.[13]

Lescot, who clearly underestimated the determination of the students, was shocked at the demonstration. . . . Though he expected the strike to have subsided by Monday morning, he took no chances. As soldiers packed themselves into jeeps and patrolled the deserted streets of the city Tuesday morning, the students put into effect their new plan of attack. A manifesto by Le Comité de la Grève was sent to the leading press, calling for the recognition of constitutional freedoms and international democratic guarantees. Around midday in front of the Henri Deschamps bookstore on Grande Rue, Bloncourt, who had made his way downtown in disguise, attacked an unarmed soldier. Panicked storeowners closed their stores as bystanders began hitting pots on the telephone poles, sending signals of protests throughout the streets. Employees of the Departments of Labor, Agriculture, and Education joined the students. Strong support also came from the Morne-a-Tuf region near the medical faculty, where a student from the community had died from beatings sustained during the protest the previous evening.[14]

By five-thirty later that day, the four-thousand-strong protest that had marched through the main arteries of the downtown streets climaxed on the Grand Rue. . . . Lescot and his family escaped from the palace by hiding in the back of cars belonging to the U.S. embassy and passed through the protestors led by Alexis before arriving at Lescot's manor in Bourdon. From his home that evening, Lescot issued his first statement since the revolt began. Broadcasting on the radio, he urged student leaders to end the protests and warned them that if they continued the Garde would "take the most drastic measure to reestablish public order."[15]

On Thursday the revolt intensified. In the morning, the Comité Démocratique Féminin, a women's movement headed by Jacques Roumain's wife, Nicole, led a march to the Cathedral to appeal for peace, freedom of the press, and the liberation of political prisoners.[16] When a few supporters shouted "A bas Lescot," nearby officers fired into the crowd, killing two young men and wounding two women. In retaliation, large mobs began to spread throughout the city, storming the police headquarters and hurling rocks at Garde officers before dispersing in the streets. The houses and property of leading ministers and their henchmen were ransacked and destroyed and stores looted. In the hillside areas that surround the capital, the sound of Vodou drums and *vaksins* (hollow wooden instruments made from bamboo) reverberated throughout the city as the factories of Gérald Lescot, Gontran Rouzier, and a host of other government officials burned to the ground.[17]

By that afternoon it was clear that the government was unable to deal with the crisis. Over two dozen people were reported killed and many more were injured during the week of *dechoukaj* (uprooting). A wide range of workers, including bus drivers, agricultural workers, bakers, and butchers, went on strike for the first time in the city's history, and the U.S.-run companies of SHADA, Standard Fruit, and the Atlantic Refining Company were forced to close their operations. . . . The movement spread to other departments by the end of the week. In Jacmel, where large numbers of students at the Lycée

Jacmel had received and read *La Ruche*, student strikes on the seventh were augmented by the participation of workers and peasants over the following two days, by which time, according to one participant, "the revolution had conquered Jacmel."[18]

In an effort to avoid overthrow, Lescot agreed to have the cabinet dissolved. . . . In a private audience with Colonal Lavaud, the head of the Garde, a desperate Lescot ordered Lavaud to use all necessary force to break up the mobs. Lavaud refused and Lescot ordered his immediate arrest. The second-ranking officer of the Garde, Colonel Antoine Levelt, instead counseled with Lavaud and U.S. ambassador Wilson to decide the best course of action. In conjunction with the embassy they formed that evening a Conseil Exécutif Militaire (CEM), which demanded and successfully obtained Lescot's resignation once they convinced him his life was in danger if he remained in Haiti a day longer. Petrified, the rest of the cabinet submitted their resignations that afternoon and fled the country. . . . At three o'clock in the morning of 11 January, Élie Lescot and his family huddled in the back of a police car drove to Bowen Field, then boarded a waiting plane to Miami, becoming the republic's first exiled president since the occupation.[19]

Notes

NB: *These notes are in the original publication.*

1. See, for example, Jacques Stephen Alexis, "Les grands problèmes d'humanité générale," *La Caducée* 18 (January 1945): 9–13.

2. Alexis had been a follower of Roumain since he met him in 1942 at a poetry recital he arranged for Nicolás Guillén. See Carrol F. Coates, introduction to *General Sun, My Brother* (Charlottesville: University Press of Virginia, 1999).

3. Gérald Bloncourt, interview by author, 18 June 2001, Paris.

4. René Depestre, *Étincelles* (Port-au-Prince: Imprimerie de l'État, 1945), 20.

5. René Depestre, *Bonjour et adieu à la négritude* (Paris: Éditions Robert Laffont, 1980), 213.

6. Paul Laraque, interview by author, 5 July 2000, New York City; Raymond Pressoir, interview by author, 17 June 2000, Bethesda, Maryland; Depestre, *Bonjour et adieu à la négritude*, 229. Roger Gaillard, "In Memoriam: André Breton et nous," *Conjonction* 202 (April–June 1997): 35. See also Paul Laraque, "André Breton et Haïti," *Nouvelle Optique* 1, no. 2 (1971): 126–138; Michael Dash, "*Le Je de l'autre*: Surrealist Ethnographers and the Francophone Caribbean," *L'Esprit Créateur* 47, no. 1 (Spring 2007): 84–95.

7. *La Ruche*, 1 January 1946.

8. Raymond Pressoir, interview by author, 20 May 2000, Bethesda, Maryland.

9. Emerante de Pradine Morse, interview by author, 23 July 1999, Pélerin.

10. Gérald Bloncourt, interview by author, 18 June 2001, Paris.

11. Gérald Bloncourt, interview by author, 18 June 2001, Paris; Depestre, *Bonjour et adieu à la négritude*, 212; *Les Débats*, 25 June 1946.

12. Details from the protest taken from René Depestre, "La Révolution de 1946 est pour demain," in *Pouvoir noir en Haïti: L'Explosion de 1946* (Montreal: CIDIHCA, 1988), 57–94, and Gérald Bloncourt, interview by author, 18 June 2001, Paris; see also Gérald Bloncourt and Michael Löwy, *Messagers de la tempête: André Breton et la Révolution Janvier 1946 en Haïti* (Paris:

Le Temps des Cerises, 2007), and Collectif du Cinquantenaire, *Haïti, 7–11 Janvier 1946* (Paris: Flèche du temps, 1998).

13. *Le Matin*, 8 January 1946; Emerante de Pradine Morse, interview by author, 23 July 1999, Pélerin; *Le Nouvelliste*, 7 January 1946; Depestre, *Bonjour et adieu à la négritude*, 213.

14. Gérald Bloncourt, interview by author, 18 June 2001, Paris; *Le Matin*, 9 January 1946.

15. Élie Lescot, "Proclamation de son Excellence le Président de la République, le 9 Janvier 1946," Haitian Collection, Moorland-Springarn Research Center, Howard University, Washington, DC.

16. Their manifesto appeared in *Le Matin*, 8 January 1946.

17. W. Abbott to Secretary of State, 11 January 1946, Port-au-Prince, U.S. National Archives II, College Park, Maryland, RG 84, 838.000; *Le Matin*, 10, 12 January 1946; *New York Times*, 13 January 1946.

18. Bonnard Posy, "Jacmel 1946," *Conjonction* 202 (April–June 1997): 59–66.

19. On Lescot's personal reaction to the events, see Élie Lescot to Maurice Dartigue, 26 April 1946, Dartigue Papers, Schomburg Center for Research in Black Culture, New York Public Library, New York.

VI

The Duvalier Years

This section looks at the period from the 1950s through the mid-1980s—a time that follows the "bloodless revolution" of 1946 and culminates in the overthrow of Jean-Claude Duvalier's presidency forty years later. Beginning with Dumarsais Estimé's election to the presidency in 1946, Haitian politics consistently reflected anxieties around "blackness." These phenomena took on tragic proportions during François "Papa Doc" Duvalier's regime (1957–71) and persisted through that of his son, "Baby Doc." Perverting the Afrocentric, pro-peasantry cultural agenda of Indigenist ideology, Duvalier crafted a political platform that combined racial mystification and authoritarianism into a discourse of *noirisme* (Noirism). This doctrine of essentialist black power valorized Haiti's African roots exclusively and posited absolute racial purity as the foundation for an authentic national identity in which Haiti's "black" citizens would be empowered. Duvalier's color-based fracturing of the nation quickly revealed itself to be little more than a means by which wealthy urban insiders could exploit Haiti's majority population. Its discourse of divisive community and racial hierarchy was subtended by a climate of total corruption and arbitrary violence. Targeting religious groups and sports clubs, schoolteachers and priests, Duvalier's private paramilitary organization, the Tonton Macoutes, bullied and brutalized Haiti's citizens. State terror permeated every level of society, and those writers and artists who dared to remain and create in Haiti during the thirty-year regime were harassed, censored, and even killed. No one was exempt from persecution by the state, including women and children, and rape was commonly employed against the wives and daughters of Duvalier's political "enemies," as well as against activist women like Yvonne Hakim Rimpel.

The speeches, essays, poetry, songs, novels, and other texts excerpted here illuminate the politics and aesthetics that marked the period—including the Noirist discourse out of which Duvalier's state emerged, the rise and fall of syndicalism, the triumphs of and obstacles to Haitian feminism, and the political usefulness of popular cultural expression. These materials are, unsurprisingly, concerned with representing the dysfunctional and brutal relationship between the state and the nation. The texts in this section trace the long historical foundations and contemporary expressions of conflict between Haiti's various political and economic constituencies—both insular and diasporic. Several of the excerpts offer portrayals of the harsh realities of rural life and the exploitation of Haiti's peasant population. Others consider the condition of Haiti's increasingly urban demographic, focusing on grassroots organization, syndicalism, and social activism, and exploring the relationship between a transnational economic order and insular political phenomena. Both the corruptions of elite Haitian governance and the predatory practices of the international community are confronted by the intellectuals, artists, activists, and "ordinary" citizens who dared to speak out during this period in Haiti's history. Expressing no small measure of urgency and often produced under real and violent duress, the documents that follow paint a vivid portrait of life within the suffocating context of authoritarianism.

O My Country

Anthony Phelps

One of the founders of the literary group Haïti Littéraire in 1961, Anthony Phelps ranks among the country's best-known and most well-respected poets. In addition to numerous volumes of poetry, he is also the author of several novels. Phelps was heavily involved in theater and produced several films. He enjoyed a long career as a journalist with Radio Canada in Montreal. He continues to live and write in Canada today.

Mon pays que voici is the defining poetic work of its era. In this long narrative poem, Phelps offers an account of Haitian history in verse, from pre-Columbian times through Spanish colonization and slavery, the U.S. occupation, and ending with the Duvalier regime. The poem's overarching theme of resistance makes it one of the most popular among Haitian readers. Within the text, the poet is portrayed as a leader of his people.

Mon pays que voici was first released as a recording in 1966. Within Haiti, many would hide the LP in other record jackets to avoid being accused of subversion during the Duvalier dictatorship. The poem was not published as a written text until 1968, when Phelps was settled in Canadian exile, presumably beyond the regime's reach.

This here, my country . . .

Stranger who walks through my city,
keep in mind that the land you walk upon
is a poet's land
and the most noble, and the most beautiful
because above all, it is my homeland

Our calloused hands are cast iron
and our flesh is painful
from having handled the pickaxe
beneath the commander's rod
But we acquired this haughty stance
these slow gestures
from raising our heads
toward our palm trees and mountains

and the heat of our gazes
is a gift from the blue sky

The time for learning to suffer will come
The time to awaken will come too soon
It will be brutal it will be cruel
Sleep, my child, sleep.

Your small hands are harmless
and your head's voice could not sing
the notes of love and freedom
that our hearts invent throughout the spring
Sleep, my child. Sleep.

Summertime will soon come
when you will say no to modern colonizers
the time to fight for your beautiful country
a sunflower at the corner of your mouth
and words of fire on your pure lips
But not now
Be patient, my son
Sleep, my child. Sleep.

The time will come when we will subjugate
the green god of Yankees
when the dust of the pariahs
and the sweat of the homeless
will be but images with no reality
in the new dawn.

The day will come when the country
will once again find its angle of repose
and the people welded together by love's bonds
will carry the mast's powerful jet to the sky
But, be patient, my son
Sleep, my child, sleep.

The kites' day will come
with the wind that sings of love
on the dual keyboard of color rings
Sunlight's day will come
with flowers on each branch
and in their hands, the golden stalks of the good harvest
But be patient, my son
Give me your frail hand

and your steps in my steps
and your ear on my heart
listen to the beat
listen to the life
of my city and my country
your city and your country

. . .

At the still and burning noon hour
the sun was melting the sky
and in my hands, I captured the blue lava
to bring it into my house
But without a starpoint
how would I attach this small piece of sky
to the ceiling in my room?
And now you are coming toward me,
proud and gentle aborigines
soldiers of the great saga
glorious Cacos who died for naught
now you are coming toward me on a carpet of stars
Take then this hand that I hold out to you with open palm
And may my song that honors you justly
please you

At a time when all cats are gray
I recognize my country's steps
making its rounds
wearing its heroic sandals

I will welcome my land
bastard daughter of Columbus and the sea
my land with a heart of hot star
with fingers of guinea grass
I will welcome my land with the honor of a song
on my doorstep
open to the four currents of the spirit
And bent over the slate of its hands
where everything is written with a hard, clean, precise pencil
I will find the luminous road
leading directly toward landscapes of men.

At the quiet hour
when the fragile flower of the cactus opens
in the midnight of a fragile blue

I receive celestial animals at my table
All of the constellations honor my home
with their scintillating presence
for I interpreted the luminous signs
of the cross-stitch in the sky.

I who possess neither palace nor castle
I reside within a word
a word with neither curves nor curlicues
that pierces upward like a stalk
a word with a straight frank line, no smudge

I reside within the essence of a word
where drop by drop
the parentheses of the past
let filter onto their slopes
the noble history
of black demigods
knights of the virgin forest
sleeping in peace in deep bronze sleep

I reside within the essence of a word,
lain on the water like the horizon
and the splice is without fault
that links my heart
to the star heart of my country

From the depths of ages
your savage heart
sings at midvoice
like before
in the long-ago time of slavery

Your slow complaint
that wrings my entrails
muffled from the shadows
oh, my abandoned country

From the depths of ages
your savage heart
sings at midvoice
O my abandoned country
and my vibrant blood
picks up the rhythm and the message
and spreads them

like before
in the long-ago time of slavery

Knights of the virgin forest men of vast lands
and of wide-open spaces
populated by fauna and raised on sun
I come from you
for the angles of our faces are of the same degree
and I have the memory within me of bushes, amulets,
faces painted in bright colors
and ritual gestures
when within the dense and heavy night
the melancholy and reserved moon rises.

Knights of the virgin forest
men of vast lands
my steps proceed from yours
and my country is a spark of your continent
bridgehead on the Caribbean Sea

Aquatic flower on the Caribbean Sea
this here, my country
you smooth your black petals
your spearheaded leaves
you move and sway slowly
for in the murky water
your floating roots have felt the movement of a submarine current

Rum road leading to woman
Rum road leading to night
And the essence of things

I pour the three ritual drops on the threshold
and I bring to my lips the blue cup of the sky
to get drunk with space and the invisible
and to quench my pores in the wind

. . .

On my face I have drawn the signs of the Samba
and I am slowly climbing, O my country
the bed of your history
among the fire stone and the cut flint
And the acrid odor of powder mingles
with the sweetish scent of apricots.

You didn't know the high priest
with the obsidian knife
who opened the sun road
to the brave warrior

Through the voice of the Butios
the Zemes oracle
governed the land of a hundred caves
and the Chémis, masters of human destiny
shared space
watching over your childhood O my country

But one morning they came by the salt road
spilling terror into your children's hearts
They came with
glass necklaces and silver handcuffs in hand
small pieces of frozen spring

They came with the cross
with the pickaxe and the rod
with their dogs and their hoarse voices

By the salt road
they came on their ships
these Caribs of another race
cannibals in their own way

Over roads of sand
they came on their horses
these conquerors that fell from the sky
They came in search of their God
the pure metal with yellow highlights
and thunder became their accomplice
And I saw the cacique surrounded by his people
hurl the Spanish god into the abyss
to banish the conquerors that fell from the sky

from his shores
But those who copied his sacrilegious act were struck
by the voice of thunder
and it was a terrible thing
and it was a horrible thing
the Spanish god was stronger than the Zemes

Among his virgins
the three hundred women

naked as roses
Golden Flower lulled the cacique
with the rhythm of tambourines
Dressed in the flowers of her caste
in the color of peace
the favorite Samba danced before his queen
And it was song and it was dance
It was the poet's song
and it was festivity beauty
And it was dance
and it was flower
It was the dance of love
and it was the flower of the flesh
And from hands in garlands
rose the new life

But one morning
they came
those Caribs
of another race
cannibals in their own way

And the Samba's voice broke
into a thousand shards broke
like a goblet O my country
The song shattered at the bottom of your throat
Samba of all times
dressed in the color of peace
the Spanish god did not like poets

In the land of great hunts in the land of apricots
the Indian rests naked in his humus hammock
He will not know hunger again
and never again will he be hot
and never again will he braid
garlands of flowers at the mouths of caves
the Indian lying in his last hammock
smoking the eternal peace pipe
For one morning
they came
those Caribs
of another race
cannibals in their own way

For one morning they came
by the salt road and the sandy paths
in search of their god
the pure metal with yellow undertones

And they died O my country
your first sons in the depths of the mines
so that the great ones could have soft beds
and well-rigged ships

Aborigines of great hunts and of the land of apricots
    draped in the sweetness
and the pride of your race
pass down to us your belief
in the paradise of our land.

I continue O my country my slow poet's walk
a chain clanging in my ear
sound of waves and surf
and on my lips a taste of salt and sun
I continue my slow walk into the darkness
for the death ships are in power.

They came in the hold
your new sons with black skin
to relieve the Indian in the depths of the mines
(The Spanish god has no prejudices
as long as his great places of stone and prayer
enhance his presence with yellow undertones
no matter to him the hand
that brings it from the earth's belly)
And the black man arrived
with his strength and his song
He was ready to take the next shift
and ready too for the excesses
His tanned skin defied the rod and torture
His bronze body was not made for slavery
for if he was the color of ebony
it's that he had known
the great burnt plain of freedom

So for the Indian followed by the mute dog
to hunt the songbird in apricot country
with the arrow protected by cotton padding

for the son to know his father
and so that the daughter no longer be
a fountain by the side of the road
and for man to be respected
in his flesh and in his faith
it was the black hole
and in history
the high color gap

O Fathers of the land
Precursor Emperor Builder King Republican
Glorious Fathers that I shall not name
for all have the same right to our love
O Fathers of the land
give us the gift of courage and honor

I continue O my country my slow poet's walk
And I slowly climb the bed of your history
with the nobleness of your children in my memory
The earth had attained its angle of repose
and each stone taken in its clay bed
held the vast choir and the great spurt of the mast
the martial march and the brand new flag

Eleven decades and a year
despite chaos and war noises
the faultless stone of foundations
did not roll out of its clay

Eleven decades and a year
in sorrow or in joy
in disorder or in peace
the clay held the new stone

Yet one morning
the Spanish God
found other adorers
who came
through the moving door
with a starred cloth in hand
and in their mouths an unknown tongue

And one morning of too-bright blood
the great mast fell and the choir fell apart
The incorruptible stone had left its bed

And it was Pierre Sully
And it was Capois Fort
And it was Marchaterre

Charlemagne Péralte was crucified
On a door in vain
and the five thousand Cacos
in vain gave their blood
through all of their wounds

The green god of the Yankees was stronger than the loas

And everything was to start again
according to the rhythm of their life
according to their laws their prejudices

And everything was to start again
for one morning they came
those protectors dressed in yellow
to teach us informants and servitude
with shame

And the lesson was profitable
for in my slow poet's walk
I saw O my country your children without memory
in all the capitals of America
holding out their calabash, having drunk all their pride
knees bent before the paper-god
bearing Washington's portrait

what's the point of this past of sorrows and glory
and what is the point of eighteen-oh-four

O my country
I love you like a being of flesh
and I know your suffering and I see your misery
and I ask myself with rage in my heart
what hand drew in the registry of nations
a little star beside your name

Yankee of my heart
who drinks my coffee and my cocoa
who pumps the sap of my sugarcane

Yankee of my heart
who enters my home as a conquered land
prints my gourde and makes my coins

Yankee of my heart
who comes to my home speaking in English
who changes the names of my old streets

Yankee of my heart
I wait in my night
for the wind to change its air

I continue O my country my slow poet's walk
through the forests of your night
and the North Star's reflection
among the essence and the sap
counting the sapwood's circles beneath the bark
Between the liana and the roots
an entire people plagued with silence
moves within the clay muteness of voids
and inscribes itself within the retina
muffled movement has replaced the verb
Life everywhere is on hold

The sky has rusted love rolled through the mill
Fungus has grown on the stars
and the night smells musty
And our fingers are as sharp as blades
cutting gesture at the base of the skin

Within us: our veins of curdled blood
On us: the poultice of fear
and its sticky warmth
and our withered skin doubled by doubt
like baggy clothing
gaps upon the remains of a man.

Sunday-less week
Corn: dry as stone
Bread: nothing but cutting croutons
Houses closed the streets the plazas
left to the wind
And the resigned faithful
on their knees in the churches

Life everywhere is on hold

Life lived in the country
Life lived in the big city
Life around the tables

Along the springs
Life lived in the shadow of the churches
Life lived in the shadow of the temples
in the mystery and the smoke of rites
Life in the huts
life in the villas
life between the sheets
or on the damp hay
life that lives
this life
the same everywhere
life everywhere is on hold

O my country, so sad is the season
that the time has come for us to speak to each other in sign

The language of eyes becomes richer each day
a gesture of the hand says more than a speech
and to dream my life at the edge of sleep
in the lining of my pillowcase
I would have sewn my most beautiful episodes
but even love is sad
the scars of suffering would chip the dream

Unmoving as a stake staved into sand
I carry within me the density of night
and insects make love on my useless hands

Ah! when will the bud burst beneath the weight of the bee
I want to hear the blood of my land
walk among the coffee plants with white flowers.
I want to hear the murmur of the wounded wind in the canes
cutting are the flowers of the sugarcane

When then will come that time
when we will start up the sun
when the kiss will vouch for our lips

O my country so sad is the season
that the time has come for us to speak to each other in sign

I continue my slow poet's walk
through the forests of your night
shadowed province peopled with the voiceless.

Who dares to laugh in the dark?
We no longer have mouths to talk with
What obscene choir sings in the shadows
that song in my sleep
that song of great maroons
keeping time pressed close to lips

Who dares to laugh in the dark?
We no longer have mouths to talk with
The usual words are rounded
sticky with the honey of resignation
and the muted speech of fear
coils within our padded brains

Who dares to laugh in the dark?
We no longer have mouths to talk with
we carry the world's misfortunes
and birds have fled from our cadaver scent
The day is no longer transparent and resembles the night
All the fruits have leaked we pointed them out

Who dares to laugh in the dark?
We no longer have mouths to talk with
For the keyboard of the Founding Fathers' key words
In the attic of the past is out of tune abandoned
O my country so sad is the season
that the time has come for us to speak to each other in sign

. . .

There is within my throat this love cry soaring
to pierce the clouds' amazement
This song beneath my uvula
to shatter the darkness
And the quicklime of the verb
behind my closed mouth

There are the words not spoken
that we slip to each other through eyelids
The expanseless bodies
Colors with no support
The grain to be shelled
for hope to sprout in open air
And the entire sky to sweep
The holy water to spill
before the magical touch

and there is your name your crucial name
your pivotal name your open sesame name
O this here, my country

I continue my slow poet's walk
for my calling is to be invisible
I am the outsider
in the city of men of my race
I am he who comes from everywhere
and who is not from here
I arrive on the music of my words
on the wing of the poem and the fourteen feet of the line
to teach a new score
to renew the repertoire of plaintive and broken voices
for old-fashioned and perverse choir masters
have reduced the single gesture
to anecdotal dimensions
and intellectuals with thin hands
versed in the art of resounding words
have kept the people
in mystery and ignorance

Bearer of yeast to an entire defenseless people
to an entire people without counsel
talkative people teller of legends beneath the pergola
living in the perpetual prolonging of desire
carefree and good-natured people
going back and forth like ants
fishing at the foot of piers
the foreigner's golden coin
crafting scarves
from the cloth of forty-eight stars
people black as night
(and because the master visited the slave
on her straw bed
some have frizzy hair
and dun color)
and bearer of yeast to an entire unleavened people
I come from the beaches of knowledge
through the moving paths of water
with the mission to preserve
the ardent mouth of thirst
that knot of sand at the border of the tangible

Liberated land with a heart of hot star
Bastard daughter of Columbus and the sea
we are of the New World
and we live in the present
We cannot walk backward
not having eyes at the back of our heads
and the windmill churns the words on our lips
for on the pedestals of memory
in the flour of our words O my country
we shape new faces for you
You need live heroes and not dead ones

My load of gestures and magnetic words
is of good measure and weighs well in the balance
and on the threshold of summer I salute you
in the scarlet blooming of flamboyants
I will spring from you like the source
my pure song will open for you the path to glory
and my cry will pierce the eardrum of your night
for my flint-pointed love
is forever planted in your heart of hot star
O this here my country.

Translated by Nadève Ménard

General Sun, My Brother

Jacques Stephen Alexis

Jacques Stephen Alexis (1922–61) was a political activist, essayist, and novelist born to a middle-class family in Gonaïves, Haiti. Although the date is not confirmed and his death has never been officially recognized, general knowledge fixes the date of Alexis's assassination by government forces as 22 April 1961, in the wake of a failed plot to overthrow Duvalier. Alexis's life and œuvre were grounded in political activism. Many scholars compare him to Jacques Roumain, fifteen years Alexis's senior, also a Marxist, similarly an esteemed novelist, and, like Alexis, deceased before the age of forty. Today Alexis is known primarily for his novels and for his contribution to the conversation on magical and marvelous realisms. His fiction depicts protagonists who are "typically Haitian," from different parts of Haitian society, portraying situations that put into play choices that everyday Haitians have faced, linking the seemingly apolitically quotidian to the revolutionary. In the below excerpt, which figures as a poetic prologue to General Sun, My Brother, *Hilarion, a Haitian who is not of the ruling or bourgeois social classes, is described in the delirium that accompanies hunger. To eat, he commits a crime. Arrested and put in jail, he becomes acquainted with a political prisoner. Once released, profoundly affected by his encounter with the political activist, Hilarion engages in a struggle not only for daily survival, but also for a more general political consciousness that puts the interest of the masses ahead of those of the elite.*
—Contributing Editor: Alessandra Benedicty-Kokken

Hilarion could see through his barely cracked eyelids. A man dressed in white was standing against the wall, dabbing at his right cheek with a handkerchief. Whiffs of alcohol came from his direction to the rhythm of his exhalations. There were both men and women here and there, crouched down, standing, lying on the ground—some fifteen people in all were in the cell. It reeked of urine and vomit—a cocktail of body odors and bacchic effluvia attacked his nose. The sound of tears mingled with snoring, hiccups, murmuring, and hands slapping bodies to crush vermin.

Across the corridor, light oozed out and there were the sounds of laughter and fragments of conversation. The police were probably playing cards. Hilarion stood there, half-conscious and motionless. Two large tears glistened

Jacques Stephen Alexis (1922–61), novelist and poet. Photographer and date of photo unknown.

on his cheeks. He made no sound. Mosquitoes stung his face, hands, and stomach, even through his tattered shirt. Minutes dribbled away interminably through the strong aromas and annoying bites.

Things were insidiously turning strange for Hilarion. One man seemed gigantic, extraordinarily large with a minuscule head. The other people in the cell appeared to be quite small with enormous, grimacing faces. Distraught, Hilarion observed this phantasmagoric scene. He was standing, but he had no feet!

The aroma of a bakery struck his nose. Fresh bread! It invaded his senses and made him dizzy. He was unable either to lie down or to move. The aroma of bread . . . [1]

Then Hilarion turned, emitting a sharp cry that radiated out in all directions and flailing his arms in the air—once, twice . . . He fell down in a heap. Other yells answered his own and everybody in the cell became tense and fearful, with their eyes riveted on him.

His limbs were rigid and there was a frozen grin at one corner of his mouth. He lay stretched out. Light dripped everywhere. His legs began to jerk. Nervous spasms flowed through his entire body to his arms, his hands. His limbs flew out in all directions and his eyes rolled. His face was incredibly black and contorted in a grimace. His head knocked rhythmically against the floor, like the beak of a pecking bird.

A cry rang out: "He's having a seizure!" They all backed away.

Hilarion lay in a pool of urine. A sticky, bloody fluid dripped from a corner of his mouth. His body continued jerking like a chicken with its throat slit. Somebody threw a bucket of water over him. He kept on quivering spasmodically. . . .

His mouth tasted sour, his forehead was burning, and a cold sweat poured from his entire body. He opened his eyes. He had the vague impression that the lights had been cut off. Pain and despair jabbed him all over with their surgical scissors and instruments. His fists were clenched and he had a crazy urge to pound his head against the wall so he could break it and stop the entire machine that was torturing him—to make it be still and leave him alone until all of his suffering disappeared along with his life.

Outside on the ground, the night stretched lifelessly after the terrible struggle between the cocks of darkness and light—they were still crowing their lungs out. The cock of the day, with his sunny comb, was crowing victory for all he was worth and flapping his sparkling fiery wings. If only he could die . . . pound his head against the wall . . . He did not do it. Somebody was muttering close to him. He fell back into a deep sleep, broken by nightmares. The same nightmare each time: a gray snake biting his face. He breathed heavily.

Note

1. All ellipses in this selection are in the original.

Flicker of an Eyelid

Jacques Stephen Alexis

In this passage from Alexis's second-to-last prose fiction work and his last novel, Alexis again deals with the plight of the common person. Flicker of an Eyelid, while not one of his best-known works in decades past, has more recently garnered greater attention from critics and readers. In the novel, Alexis not only stages the experience of the male character, a ship mechanic, El Caucho, but also includes the voice of several women, notably that of the prostitute La Niña Estrellita (Eglantina). Set during the 1940s, the novel resonates with contemporary readers both for its historical reference to a twentieth-century Cold War history and for its ability to deal with complex social issues: racial, religious, and sexual. As noted from the names of the characters, he also gestures toward a pan-Caribbean identity of workers united, rather than a nationalistic one, limited to Haiti.
—Contributing Editor: Alessandra Benedicty-Kokken

Filled with reflections and tension, they fall silent. My God! What if he were to think that she, too . . . Then what? If he questioned her, wouldn't she, too, have some difficult confessions to make? What will she do if he insists on knowing? Lie? Doesn't she have the right to lie so nothing will affect her only treasure, her miserable neurotic love? A man is clear-headedness itself! But what if deception, perpetual duplicity, lies, or even simple mental reservations slowly undermine the feeling that is her guiding light from now on? Isn't that confession beyond her strength? Even if she wanted to, maybe the words won't come out! As for El Caucho, he isn't even thinking about such things. He's thinking about the mutual desire that will have to be allowed from now on. He's meditating on the inevitable hopes and disillusionment ahead. He's considering the difficult social constraints that will undoubtedly affect their fragile communion. He's a conscientious, responsible worker— and he has found her once more after years of separation. Sure, the idea came to his mind that all the women in this bordello are crazy. Eglantina is crazy, too! Will love be able to survive and take root in the depths of their personalities, a little more deeply each day? If love remains simply sexual harmony and shared memories, if the inclinations of their changing personalities don't grow in their hearts, if love remains only what it was at the moment of its crystallization, it will inevitably wither and destroy itself. Every day, with tiny, repeated flicks from all sides, life slowly but surely remolds the hearts of every human couple, their senses, their consciousness, their aspirations, their loves. An abyss tends to appear spontaneously between two people as soon as their respective evolution stops growing in agreement and confrontation. Will she be able to guess . . . Oh! He doesn't ask much of her; he doesn't ask her to change instantly into what he wants her to be, what every human being should be; he only insists on her living, that is to say, changing, moving imperceptibly each day toward a more certain equilibrium, so she will free herself slowly but continually from all that her horrendous life has imposed on her. Without an evolution parallel to his own, not identical to his but parallel, devised and deliberated through intuition, Eglantina's love will soon become inert, a poor crawling thing incapable of renewing surprise, joy, and the poetry of human relations for which people are always searching. A human being demands constant renewal on all levels, going beyond that divine sense of the unknown—that's a law! With the sense of things already seen, known too well, the most beautiful colors become boring! One fine day, love dies from stagnation. If the rose of her eyes loses its insight, if the five intimately linked senses stop learning life's secrets, the attractions of the body fail, pleasure changes to banal perception, indifference, disharmony, opposition, spite, and animosity. If personalities are in disaccord, growing apart, if they no longer commune with one another before the bread on the table each day, a flower, a bird, the springtime, illusion, chimeras, and action, love follows its inexorable path of devaluation and is transformed into repulsion, scorn, hatred. Slipping, sliding, bumping, everything loses its dignity and becomes degraded!

The Sad End of Jacques Stephen Alexis

Edouard Duval-Carrié

In this painting Haitian artist Edouard Duval-Carrié depicts the poet Jacques Stephen Alexis as a martyr to the Duvalier regime. Alexis was killed after being captured as part of a small force that had disembarked in Haiti from Cuba in an attempt to overthrow the Duvalier regime. In Duval-Carrié's rendering he is nailed to the floor of the infamous prison of Fort Dimanche. Watching over his corpse is the figure of François Duvalier, on the right, ironically depicted holding his doctor's briefcase, while on the left a skeletal evocation of the Haitian lwa Bawon Samdi is ready to dig his grave. The nails through Alexis's hands and heart evoke Christian imagery, making of him a specifically Christlike figure. The painting is a spectral reminder of all the lives and possibilities lost through the repression of the Duvalier years.

La triste fin de Jacques Stephen Alexis, oil on canvas in artist frame, 150 cm × 150 cm, Collection des Musée des Arts Africains et Océaniens, France. Image courtesy of Edouard Duval-Carrié.

The Trade Union Movement

Daniel Fignolé and Jacques Brutus

The immensely popular Daniel Fignolé was a chief political figure of the 1940s and 1950s, as well as a journalist, author, educator, activist, and provisional president in 1957. He was above all a union leader, a position that won him respect among the popular classes. Labor unions were virtually nonexistent in Haiti prior to the political changes that followed the overthrow of President Elie Lescot in January 1946. That revolutionary moment led to the rise of the charismatic Fignolé on the political scene and also a serious interest in trade unionism. Although other political groups such as the PSP (Parti Socialiste Populaire), had attempted to organize Haitian workers, it was Fignolé who would come to dominate the labor movement. Called the "Moses of Port-au-Prince," Fignolé's magnetism among the poor majority in the capital ignited opposition from political elites. Fignolé soldiered on despite attempts to silence the movement growing around him. He formed his own party, the Mouvement Ouvriers Paysan (MOP), in 1946. MOP also took on the role of being an umbrella organization for the emergent unions. As leader, Fignolé proved himself an able organizer who pressured employers and the state for improvements in working conditions. Through his newspapers, regular meetings, and activities with the workers, he turned MOP—and the independent labor unions that supported the party—into a major force in Haitian politics. During these buoyant early years of Haitian labor, Fignolé earned renown for his defense of workers' rights. In the following extract taken from his book-length assessment of Haitian labor, Fignolé reflects on the beginning of union activism in the 1940s, emphasizing the state's accountability to workers. Later, in the chaotic election campaign of 1957, Fignolé became provisional president of Haiti. He governed for less than a month before he was overthrown by military forces and exiled from Haiti for three decades. His words in this extract provide testament to the conviction behind his political ideas and his important role in Haitian political history.
—Contributing Editor: Matthew J. Smith

I did not volunteer to speak about the work of the Peasants and Workers Movement (Mouvement Ouvrier Paysan) from a political, economic, and social point of view. My intention was not to show the highly humanitarian actions of citizens who suffered with me in the war I waged against the exploitation of the dire poverty and ignorance of the people. Rather, I call the attention of the reader to the role that I, myself, played in organizing several trade unions. I hold the truth up against the slander and deliberate errors of my unscrupulous adversaries.

Talleyrand, among his incisive thoughts, proposed the following so that men who know how to benefit from their experiences might ponder it.

There is a weapon more powerful than slander . . . the truth.

Paul Valery reminded sociologists of the consequences of incorrectly interpreting the facts.

If there is one thing more treacherous than faulty reasoning, it is incorrectly interpreted facts.

And so I write a page in history, or rather, in the History (with a capital *H*) pertaining to the documents I signed and to my accomplishments while exercising my authority as a member of the Committee of Trade Union Leaders.

My political ideas are well known to everybody: I am a nationalist and a democrat.

I have made statements of principle in my capacity as journalist, trade union leader, chief of party, minister of state, and member of Parliament. I am presenting the facts that sociologists should bear in mind when considering the claims, conquests, and mind-set of large numbers of workers during a particular period.

In speaking of the democratic workers movement, it pains my heart to acknowledge that nothing of consequence was attempted before 1946. Neither the framers of our constitution nor our legislators endeavored to introduce into our way of life and our institutions, the notion of and the conditions for organizing the defense of workers' interests. But we would do well to remember the position of a great thinker: J. B. Dorsainvil. As early as 1912 our eminent compatriot presented the problem as follows:

> Without jeopardy to itself, the state cannot be indifferent to the physical development of its citizens, their material well-being, nor their intellectual and moral evolution. If we think of the importance of labor- and credit-related issues to contemporary society, we will be convinced that, where the fight for existence is concerned, the state has a significant role to play as the regulator of social forces. The state is accountable, not only for providing the people with a means of employment, but also for their professional training, for teaching them to come together, for fostering a spirit of community. The state is also responsible for encouraging citizens by providing dependable and gainful employment.

Now, in any democratic government worthy of its name, the agricultural and industrial sectors must have their own official agencies and organized services, so that the public activity (governmental policy/legal system/public policy) supporting them may be ongoing, regular, and efficient. This policy, which is mainly inspired by the overarching interests of the nation, is deemed to be either national or democratic. Those who have been observing in good faith will concede that the position I have taken and the actions I have carried out have always been in accordance with that great thinker, J. B. Dorsainvil's perspective, whether it be at the helm of trade unions that I have organized, in the executive committees of the political parties I have formed, at the Ministries of National Education or Public Health, in the Chamber of Deputies, or in the National Assembly.

I leave to the conscience of the honest reader the task of extracting from this work the sociological and philosophical teachings of history, as it relates to the facts I am presenting.

Daniel Fignolé
30 April 1954

Writing six years into the dictatorship of François Duvalier, Jacques Brutus provides an overview of the Haitian labor movement from 1903 to 1963. The achievements of labor unions in gaining benefits for workers were a highlight of the radicalism that blossomed after the ending of the U.S. occupation in 1934. Independent labor, however, was constrained in the late 1940s when the state created its own Labor Department. Although the Labor Department drew wide attention to workers' problems, the state also restricted the activities of vocal opponents in the unions. In fact, the labor movement had been politicized as union leaders were involved in national political campaigns. This compromised union interests and increased state suppression, factors that undermined Haitian labor in the period leading up to the election of Duvalier in 1957. In 1961 Duvalier initiated the "François Duvalier Labor Code," which purported to revive the unions. This move raised the optimism of labor leaders and workers alike, a point captured by Brutus's comments at the end of the extract. However, in late 1963, with firmer control of the state apparatus, Duvalier unleashed a harsh repression of the unions. Leaders were arrested or exiled and the state issued a unilateral dissolution of the Inter-Union Association of Haiti (UIH). Few unions remained, and these were forced into supporting the dictatorship. Written on the eve of these actions, Brutus's overview provides a glimpse of the brief yet pivotal years in the Haitian labor movement.

To understand the reasons that gave rise to the trade union movement in certain already industrialized countries in the eighteenth and nineteenth centuries, we must visualize sad towns, enveloped in smoke, narrow streets, lined with infinitely monotonous houses, overrun, morning and evening, with the goings and comings of waves of workers, to and from work. The unsanitary villages, with their dilapidated shanties, were no strangers to hunger; and the towns were abased by insalubrious slums.

In Haiti, the situation was quite different. There were practically no industries, and artisanry was in its infancy, when forty-six workers, working in Mr. Dessources Poveda's workshop, founded the Haitian Shoemakers Trade Union on 24 March 1903. This was an audacious gesture in an environment that was not quite prepared for it, and before long, under the pretext that these pioneers were engaging in politics, they were made to discontinue their activities in spite of several attempts at regrouping.

With the American occupation came the installation of several companies such as HASCO (the Haitian American Sugar Company), Standard Fruit, and the Dauphin plantation, as well as the creation, in 1924, of the Department of Labor. Workers were treated with such suspicion and the police were so wary of the leaders that there were no guarantees for those who were beginning to feel the need for impartial legislation governing employer-employee relations, as well as an adjustment to paltry workers' salaries. The workers swallowed their bitterness in silence and were readying themselves because retrograde regimes do not extend the right to have a voice to the oppressed.

Then came the January 1946 Revolution. The workers' claims were complete, and by the end of February, several trade unions, as among which HASCO's, were declaring their associations' constitutions to the Executive Military Committee and submitting their claims to employers, very often by means of strike action, as was the case of Standard Fruit workers and dockers. The voices of the workers rang out from capital to provinces: they were demanding social justice for themselves and their families. The Department of Labor, whose history was very intricately intertwined with the Haitian Trade Union Movement's history, made every effort to maintain a modicum of balance between the incessant but well-grounded claims of workers and apprehension on the part of employers.

The creation of the Labor Bureau, through the 1946 Constitution and the law of 9 October 1946, regularizes trade union activity, and the government of the late Dumarsais Estimé was beginning to channel workers' claims. The trade unions, for their part, continued their battle and even formed several bodies. The Federation of Laborers and Workers Trade Unions (La Fédération de Syndicats d'Ouvriers et Travailleurs), the Federation of Haitian Laborers (La Fédération des Travailleurs Haïtiens), the Haitian Labor Federation (La Fédération Haïtienne du Travail), the Federation of Construction Workers, etc. . . . And on 25 March 1949, three of these federations came together to form the General Confederation of Haitian Workers (La Confédération Générale des Travailleurs d'Haïti).

From this period onward (1946–1950), the trade union movement registered significant achievements for the benefit of workers. Workers everywhere were demanding (1) more equitable salaries, (2) annual vacations with pay, and (3) and compensation. Wrongful dismissal and compensation discrimination were viewed with disdain. This was no longer the period when governments protected undeserved profits and obstructed equitable allocation of representatives in the Port-au-Prince local government, which was playing an increasingly prominent role in dispute resolution and sometimes intervened inappropriately against workers.

Between 1946 and 1947, the autonomy of the Haitian trade union movement was diminished as a result of political strike action attempts and, subsequently, a systematic organization of the Labor Bureau. Internal strife developed among labor leaders and the trade unions lost their foothold. From 1948 to 1950, the Labor Department organized important events such as the First Labor Congress (1er Congrès du Travail) and Labor Day (La Fête du Travail), during which the driving forces of the nation were invited to reflect on certain aspects of the Labor dilemma or to demonstrate their loyalty to the government.

The real intentions of trade union leaders became evident during the period 1950–56, torn as they were between their political allegiances and the desire for autonomy on the part of trade union members. The movement lost momentum due to a lack of confidence and employers took advantage of this to transform the most modest claims from employees and workers into a political action. Trade union organizations became a laughingstock and were viewed as such because of the stand they took during the 1956–57 events. Political leanings overshadowed workers' requests and uncontrolled and incontrollable strike action punctuated the revolutionary milestones.

When Dr. Duvalier came to power in October 1957, trade unions were at the end of their tether, leaders were exhausted, and most of the workers' aspirations had been trampled underfoot. The task at hand was to establish certain rights, establish limits, and restore worker confidence. In this regard, the Labor Code constitutes an appreciable effort geared toward ensuring employer-employee aspirations, while guaranteeing the interests of capital. The trade unions gradually regrouped to form three bodies: the Inter-Union Association of Haiti (L'Union Intersyndicale d'Haïti), the Laborers' Force (La Force Ouvrière); and the Haitian Federation of Christian Trade Unions (Fédération Haïtienne des Syndicats Chrétiens).

Regional federations were also established in the provinces and, through their activities and claims, were instrumental in breaking down previously impenetrable barriers, removing unjustified benefits, and ensuring that workers were treated with human dignity.

The trade union movement spearheaded a remarkable personal rehabilitation effort, through the organization of evening classes, clinics, leisure activities, and cooperatives. This initiative was worthy of being expanded, especially into the provinces, so as to ensure that the working class was protected against any inappropriate political influences, to increase and protect its autonomy, to ensure a promising future for workers through security measures, and to contribute effectively to a wider effort to develop the country.

Translated by Matthew J. Smith

Speech by the "Leader of the Revolution"

François Duvalier

François Duvalier was a physician, ethnologist, and, from 1957 to 1971, president of Haiti. He played a role in the intellectual circles that emerged among young Haitian students protesting the U.S. occupation during the 1920s, and later gained recognition in Haiti as a public health doctor working to eradicate yaws disease across rural Haiti during the 1940s. Having come to power in 1957 through an election carried out in near–civil war conditions between the working class, the nascent Left, and the military, Duvalier's political imagination fixated on the goal of transcending Haiti's social and political contradictions by taking over and neutralizing them. As dictator, Duvalier sought to infiltrate all realms of civic life in Haiti. He achieved this by assembling a vast patron-client network that spanned all levels of Haitian society and that cultivated various factions within the bourgeoisie as well as the lower and middle classes. The Volontaires de la Sécurité Nationale (VSN)—or Tonton Macoutes—made up the heart of this political system. At once a paramilitary force and informal redistributive network, the VSN frequently attracted volunteers of working-class and urban indigent backgrounds with the prospects of individual social advancement through membership.

He gave the following speech before an audience of three thousand militia members on the Day of National Sovereignty and Thanksgiving, 22 May 1964, announcing the integration of the military, paramilitary, and police forces into a unified chain of command which he would head. This act prepared the ground for Duvalier's anticipated ascension to the presidency-for-life in June 1964. By uniting the armed forces, Duvalier effectively ended the agency of the army, which in years prior had usurped a political role for itself.

In appointing himself "Supreme Commander" over a military and paramilitary force of unprecedented scale, Duvalier looked to Haitian history to justify his actions. In his speech, Duvalier meant to embolden militia volunteers with a sense of common enterprise. He defined their role as a solemn historical duty, a continuation of the nineteenth-century Haitian Revolution of Jean-Jacques Dessalines, who occupied a central position in the liturgy of Duvalierism, the regime's official ideology. The revived historical memory of Dessalines's empire served as a useful medium through which Duvalierism articulated its fundamental ambitions: the construction of a

powerful state, vigilant to foreign incursion, that would redress the historical mar-ginalization of black Haitians.
—Contributing Editor: Allen Kim

Militia of the Nine Geographical Departments of the Nation,

As I have proclaimed, I have decided to take supreme and effective command of the armed forces. I become at this moment the Supreme Commander of the Armed Forces and their effective commander, at the same time as I am the commander of the civil militia and the national police. Now that the command is unified, one heart and one mind will lead the national security forces: the army, the militia, and the national police.

Tomorrow you will accomplish the great tasks at hand under the supreme direction of the Leader of the Revolution. And you must follow exactly the instructions you will have received from me.

There will be, militiamen, a great holiday—a great civil and military demonstration. At that moment I will also present myself before you, having united with the army and united with the police, to receive the military honors appropriate to the high rank I occupy.

The Presidency for Life means something. Now and from today onward, militiamen of the nine geographic departments of the nation, you will receive your orders from me. There is no revolution, no Presidency for Life without gunfire. Stay firm. Anchor your soul in those of our ancestors to understand me, because I am not a sentimentalist. I know what I am doing. And the history you know will not repeat itself under the iron fist of the Leader of the Revolution and the Supreme Leader of the National Security forces. It matters little that you saw my photo showing the Chief of State armed with his rifle; I will not leave you alone to demand respect for that which Dessalines bestowed on us at Butte Charrier, at Vertières, and yesterday and henceforth in Gonaïves.

The nation must be at arms. There is no revolution without gunfire. The nation must be at arms. And the Supreme Leader must always be ready at the side of his troops to demand respect for that which must be respected, that is to say you, that is to say Me.

On 21 and 22 June 1965, Duvalier organized mass rallies to commemorate the first anniversary of his inauguration as president-for-life. Duvalier made the following speech to keynote a march organized by the mayor of Port-au-Prince on behalf of the municipality and representative sectors of Haitian society. While speaking from a position of august authority and as a member of the intellectual elite, Duvalier flat-

tered the humble origins of much of his audience claiming his own integral identity from among the peasantry. In calling for revolution, Duvalier evoked the Haitian revolutionary past, the aesthetic of twentieth-century socialist revolution, and a vision of mid-twentieth-century scientific and technical modernity. This complex of concepts and associations lent Duvalierism an anachronistic quality, anchored as it was in multiple strategies of power and legitimation.

BRILLIANT IMPROVISED SPEECH ON THE OCCASION OF THE GRAND RALLIES
ORGANIZED BY THE MUNICIPALITY OF PORT-AU-PRINCE, THE WORKING CLASS,
THE UNIVERSITY, THE COMMERCIAL AND INDUSTRIAL SECTORS,
AND THE POPULAR MASSES, 21 JUNE 1965

And so, my dear friends, the current chief of state has looked after the masses and lived among them with his father. He has never been ashamed of his origins. For these men of humble origins are the ones who most frequently prove themselves to be competent and lucid and capable of toppling the archaic order of things and invalidating those myths that my old friend André François, former candidate for the National Assembly, just spoke of.

My dear friends, even with all our philosophy, pragmatism, and realism we have never been able to understand what the political animal who guides the destinies of the nation needs. Thus it is that a spiritual cripple dared to say in a conversation with one of the deputies of our people: But Duvalier is the biggest communist we've got. And the deputy retorted: On what do you base such an assertion? And here's the reason: The president always talks about the masses in the back country, of the work he agrees to take up in increasing their standard of life, while among us, the Leader, in addressing those he administers, calls them "My People."

And so, when I speak of my people, I speak of Myself. These are the urban and rural masses of the back country, stagnating in their ignorance, to whom that Country Doctor brought the message of public health so many years ago.

Today as well, I speak in the name of the masses in the different provinces of the country. It is with them and for them that I emerged. I am not content to only be an intellectual; I am rather more of a peasant.

My dear friends,

A great intellectual from Latin America, one of the so-called leading lights of Latin American intellectualism, in speaking of the Haitian OAS delegation, which operates for us under the instruction of the President for Life, reproached us for always giving the key vote to guarantee peace on this continent. Attacking us directly, he claims this behavior is characteristic of countries under dictatorship. And this great intellectual goes on to add that communism is a social reality in his country.

As for us, we are neither Stalin, nor Lenin, nor Khrushchev; we are Dessalinists.

Duvalier is a man of the masses, a man of the provinces. He has conquered and will always conquer. I ask you, My dear friends, to always be disciplined. In order for Me to properly and objectively analyze the international situation, the home front must remain firm. Discipline is necessary for that. Without discipline there is nothing.

Permit Me also to give you some advice. You must follow the advice of the Chief of State so that, like Ataturk, he might be able to manage the nation and make it a volcano of spirituality and morality. And it is through doing this that the man who guides the nation can once again give you great and beautiful things such as the Maïs Gâté Airport.

Haiti finds itself within the context of the Alliance for Progress after having constructed its jet airport all by itself. After having achieved this we can sympathetically examine what is indeed humanistic according to the word of Daniel Rops.

Before deciding, My dear friends, I am going to ask you to observe a minute of reflection in honor of my brave soldiers vulgarly dubbed "Tonton Macoutes." They have been massacred by those who, invading our frontiers, would have sown disorder in this peace-loving country.

Therefore dedicate one minute of reflection to their bravery. They richly deserve it. And it is with these words that I say my farewell to you. I thank you all.

Translated by Allen Kim

The Haitian Fighter

Le Combattant Haïtien

As one of the early Haitian exile newspapers in the United States, Le Combattant Haïtien *(The Haitian Fighter) sought to inform the first wave of Haitian exiles and migrants to New York, Miami, and Chicago about state violence and corruption under François Duvalier's dictatorship.* Le Combattant, *along with Radio Vonvon, was an organ of the Haitian Coalition, a New York–based assembly of nonmilitaristic political exile groups who fought for the end of the Duvalier regime and advocated for the economic and social advancement of Haitians. Despite having less than two thousand copies in circulation, Raymond Joseph, chief editor of* Le Combattant Haïtien *and secretary general of the Haitian Coalition, managed to effectively communicate the coalition's aims to a number of human rights organizations, such as the Inter-American Association for Democracy and Freedom. Although "human rights" proved not to be a popular term until the 1970s, one can argue that Joseph and others emphasized democratic principles and human rights issues in Haiti and in the global arena early on.*
—*Contributing Editor: Dimmy Herard*

There are many methods of fighting. One could choose to go it alone, to climb into one of those ivory towers. But because of the increasing pressure and complexities of underdevelopment and the Cold War, those ivory towers have become useless and precarious habitats. We have chosen, rather, to fight in the open, the path of free discussion and research, faithful to our democratic beliefs; refusing absolute solutions, which always lead to tyranny.

But within the opposition to Duvalier, there remain a few radical groups standing on their balconies, shouting war-whoops that sound like Middle Age trumpets. No one listens to them anymore. They have turned their backs on reality.

For when we look around us, we can measure the immensity of Haitian despair and we realize that the challenge Duvalierist incompetence has posed to all capable and prepared Haitians has become possible only through the unfortunate fragmentation of the opposition in recent years. And we realize that those ivory towers with their ready-made ideologies stand out today like ridiculous anachronisms.

Underdevelopment, we must remember, is a three-headed monster: one is generalized poverty, with an economy that isn't even traditional, the other is an antiquated social order; and the third is political tyranny. If, with Duvalier, this monster has been rejuvenated, the tradition of tyranny and radicalism—a cultural trait well ingrained in the majority of underdeveloped elites (including our Haitian mulatto-black elite)—is responsible. In fact, this disease has burrowed to such depths that it has ultimately reached even those who have been held outside the limits of dignity by blind oligarchies. And that is where, in large part, the multiplicity of ivory towers in Haitian politics stems from.

These towers are already falling into ruins, while we are tapping into a new, "authentic" democracy to retain that which is dynamic, humane, real, constructive and revolutionary. For democracy has ceased being the colonial cliché that some insist on presenting to us at every turn. We have looked for and found within it the fresh new values brought by the second half of the twentieth century. We want to try the experience.

That is why we are here, a group of men gathered together to scrutinize ideas, to sum up data, to take the inventory of the technical and moral values available with one goal in mind—so rare among Haitians—to stick together at all costs. We are certain that as in any democratic group, there will be disagreements about one matter or the other, but we are also certain that finding some middle ground in order to move the machine forward and to maintain harmony is always possible. It is only a matter of accepting it. We submit to a SELF-IMPOSED discipline that turns divergent opinions among our members into bumps on the road during a long, difficult journey. At our destination, victory over Duvalierist mediocrity will find us united.

For there exists among us a marvelous regulator, which we have not invented, but which we have adopted—the democratic spirit—the spirit desperately needed by an abandoned Haiti, a country whose professionals and technicians have fled in favor of Africa, the United Nations or the O.A.S.

It is this spirit that has made the success we have already had possible. It is this spirit that will, in time, destroy the Duvalierist inferno.

It is the spirit of the Coalition.

It is the spirit of Radio New York.

It is the spirit of "Le Combattant Haïtien."

Translated by Dimmy Herard

Atibon-Legba

René Depestre

Jacmelian poet, novelist, and essayist René Depestre (b. 1926) is among Haiti's most significant literary voices. One of the founders of the leftist literary and political journal La Ruche *(The Hive), in 1945 he was arrested by police the next year. News of his arrest began a student protest, general strike, and riots—Haiti's so-called "bloodless revolution" of 1946. In 1947, due primarily to his communist affiliations and his popularity as a rebel leader, Depestre received a scholarship to the Sorbonne, which became his ticket to lifelong exile from his "native land." He returned briefly in 1958 only to be exiled again in 1959, when he left for Cuba, a country in full revolution. After twenty years there, he left for Paris in 1979 to work for* UNESCO. *Since his retirement in 1986 he has lived in Lézignan-Corbières in the south of France.*

Depestre wrote his most powerful poems while in Cuba. Once in France, Depestre turned almost completely to writing novels and short stories. These works of what he deemed "the marvelous Haitian real" (his tweaking of "magical realism") remain widely read. The poem excerpted here, "Atibon Legba," is taken from the section entitled "Epiphanies of the Vodou Gods" in Depestre's long revolutionary poem Un arc-en-ciel pour l'occident chrétien, *his "Vodou mystery poem." Moving through slavery, brutality, and suppression, Vodou continues to offer a resilient means of adaptation and change. A common assumption is that it is an old system imposed on a new world. And the unfortunate and frequent use of the term "primitive" suggests that the practice is fixed, backward, and regressive. But Vodou keeps reforming itself in response to the impositions and vicissitudes of modern life. Its gods still carry with them a bewilderment and tentativeness that recalls the plight of the ancestors transplanted in chains to a strange land.*

Depestre's belief in the positive revolutionary force of Vodou inspires the voice of the gods, especially that of Legba, master of the crossroads and interpreter of the profane to the sacred. Legba leads the poetic procession of the lwa, *the spirits or gods of Vodou, and he must be invoked first in every ceremony: "Legba Papa, I wish to pass. Papa Legba, open the gate. I will thank you on my way out." In Dahomey, Legba loomed as the procreative energy of all things, symbolized as a heap of earth surmounted by a phallus. But the Haitian "Legba-of-the-Old-Bones" signals the great loss suffered by his people. Suffering and aged, he looks for the remnants of his old world in the new. "Atibon-Legba has come to the gate. How old he is! Papa Legba* has come to the crossroads." Depestre retells Legba's story in this militant epiphany. Here Legba begins the journey of the gods to a judge's parlor in Alabama, "the violent Dixie-pit," and initiates the ceremony of revolt, by announcing the transformation of his old pipe, bamboo cane, and large hat into swords. Age-old suffering and spiritual promise become his weapons, and as his strength is renewed he takes revenge against racism and oppression.

—Contributing Editor: Colin Dayan

I am Atibon-Legba
My hat comes from Guinea
So does my bamboo cane
So does my old suffering
So do my old bones
I am patron saint of the gatekeepers
And of the elevator-boys
I am Legba-Wood Legba-Reef
I am Legba-Signangnon
And his seven brothers Kataroulo
I am Legba-Kataroulo
Tonight I plant my sanctuary
The great tree of my soul
In the earth of the white man
At the crossing of his roads
Three times I kiss his door
Three times I kiss his eyes!
I am Alegba-Papa
The god of your doors
Tonight I am
The master of your small paths
And of your white man's crossroads
I the protector of the ants
And of the plants of your house
I am the chief of the gates
Of the human body and spirit!
I arrive covered with dust
I am the great black Ancestor
I see I listen to what happens
On the paths and on the roads
Your white man's hearts and gardens
Have very few secrets for me
I arrive exhausted from my travels
And I thrust my great age
Over the tracks where

René Depestre, Havana, 1961. Photo courtesy of CIDHICA.

Your white betrayals slither!
O you judge of Alabama
I do not see in your hands
A jug of water or a black taper
I do not see my *vêvê* traced
On the floor of the house
Where is the good white flour
Where are my cardinal points
My old bones arrive at your house
O judge and they do not see
The altar to rest their sorrows
They see white cocks
They see white hens
Judge where are our spices
Where is salt and pepper
Where is peanut oil
Where is grilled corn
Where are our stars of rum
Where are my rada and my mahi
Where is my yanvalou?
The devil take your bland dishes
The devil take white wine
The devil take apple and pear

The devil take all your lies
For my hunger I want yams
Malangas and small pumpkins
Bananas and sweet potatoes
The devil take your waltzes and your tangos
The old hunger of my legs
Asks for a crabignan-legba
The old thirst of my bones
Demands the virile steps of Man!

The Festival of the Greasy Pole

René Depestre

The Festival of the Greasy Pole *was first published in 1975, in a longer Spanish version, during the two decades Depestre lived in Cuba as an exile from Duvalier's Haiti. Beginning in the late 1960s, Depestre had become disillusioned with Fidel Castro's socialist government and was vocal in his critiques of Cuban socialism. Consequently, he found himself relegated to the ineffectual position of lecturer at the University of Havana, where he taught non-credit-bearing classes to students hand-selected by government authorities. Written just a few years before his definitive departure to France, the novel tells the story of one man's struggle to resist the repressive violence perpetrated by a predatory state—ruled by President for Life Zoocrates Zachary and his National Office for the Electrification of Souls (NOFES)—against its terrorized nation. The novel places elements of a "carnivalesque" Haitian folk reality within a Marxist political framework to produce a thinly veiled allegory of the arbitrary and absurd reality of life in a totalitarian state. The Vodou religion functions prominently—if ambivalently—in the tale, portrayed as both a cynical political tool of the oppressive government and a support system for the hero Postel in his transformation from "zombified" victim into revolutionary agent of his own destiny and that of the wider community. The excerpts below narrate Postel's reflections as he makes the decision to enter the state-sponsored Greasy Pole competition rather than flee the country into permanent exile. Apparent here are Depestre's commitment to a Marxist politics, whereby the enlightened individual serves as an example to and leader of an alienated collective, as well as his belief in the importance of local resistance in Haiti as it might reflect, albeit perhaps obliquely, global sociopolitical realities.*

Postel started off for home. He was thinking about what was going to happen on the opening day of the games. It was dawn on Thursday. They would start on Friday afternoon, 21 October, and end at the latest by Sunday evening, 23 October. Thursday would be devoted to the erection of the pole, to the decoration of the Square of Heroes, and to discussion of the tournament on radio, television, and in newspapers. Since he hardly ever read the NOFESian press and didn't listen to the radio either, he didn't know whether this propaganda had already started or not. The event will undoubtedly be televised. This will be the first time pole climbers appear on a television screen. The entire government will doubtless take its place on the Tribune in order to see him work for his "salvation." His mind reeks of everything he has avoided like the plague since his adolescence. He will knead his life into the dough of his action! His arm wrestling with Moutamad did him some good. He wasn't at all repulsed by squeezing the crook's hand. It had even seemed like a warm, human hand. Shit, there must be some honest people with cold, flabby hands and some evildoers with a passionate, decisive grip. Such thoughts won't help him climb. What you've got to do is rediscover the innocence of sports competitions when you were young. Not even a week remaining to burn the fat off his body. At least his arms have remained vigorous. He has always been proud of his arms and also of his calves. His years of sports will help him now. The noise, dust, flies, ever-available tafia, heat, filth, have gotten the better of his creative years. Now, you're going to have to climb as the man they've made of you. Win or lose, of course, there won't be any emergency meeting of the UN Security Council to consider your case. No chapter entitled "The Crisis of Tête-Bœuf" in any history book. Your pole may be anything, except the navel of the world or the axle of your destiny. It is not one of the "hot points" of their Cold War. It's not that well-known bridge where one man alone was able to hold back an enemy army. Not a parade in which a handful of blacks try to stop the advance of this century's Persians. Nothing but a fucking magic pole! If you just had a bit of time! If what you're going to do has more than one meaning, the city's imagination will be able to decipher it. Your role is simply to climb. You haven't been given a mission to write some allegory in the sky over the city nor to play a new Postel for thousands of spectators. Your bitch of a life is no spectacle. You're neither a collector of solitary virtues nor one of those impotent intellectuals lost in a crowd and endlessly dabbling in symbols and fables of the moral conscience. You're going to work for your people, and with them. Are they as debased as Ritson thinks? If you could just keep quiet for these few days. No unnecessary thought or word. Always thinking, dreaming, talking too much. A bunch of words and thoughts out of the blue have ruined you.

Raising his head, he saw that he was within several meters of his house in Tête-Bœuf. He had followed the whole road back simply by his sense of direction. The neighborhood had its predawn odor: the Saint Joseph Bakery, the sweaty donkeys humbly carrying market women to town along with the delightful aromas of the country—fresh milk, vegetables, fruits, stalks of bananas, and the aroma of the first coffee being brewed in the neighborhood.

Masked dawn was approaching the noises, dust, flies, the diurnal rats, October's blinding reverberation, the miserably bestial electrification—degrading, haggard, reopening the thousands of fatal little wounds of the day.

He already had the key in the lock of his door when he saw a ray of light through the wall of Master Horace's place. He hesitated, then decided to knock on the shoemaker's window.

"Who's there?"

"Henri."

"Henri Postel?"

"Yes."

The astonished face of the shoemaker appeared in the window right away.

"Couldn't you leave, Chief?"

"I changed my mind. I'm not going to leave."

"What good news. I didn't close my eyes all night, you know. This very instant, your departure was on my mind. Didn't it work out? Come on in, Senator, I've just made some coffee."

Postel stepped over the enclosure of the meager garden and went into the shoemaker's by the rear door. Master Horace was wearing shorts and his torso was covered with a mended old undershirt. His face was haggard, his forehead was waxen black, his cheeks hollow—he looked like a Sancho Panza from the underdeveloped nations receiving his Don Quixote on the dawn of an uncertain campaign.

"You seem exhausted," said Master Horace, looking right into the eyes of the ex-senator in the pallid light of the lantern.

"I've been up since I left you yesterday."

"What about your departure?"

"It went as planned. I was supposed to stow away on a Canadian freighter. I changed my mind. I'm going to take part in the coming Tournament of the Greasy Pole."

"Good heavens! Don't do it, Chief, leave! When I talked about action, I had something completely different in mind. The greasy pole is no matter for a man like you."

"You doubt my strength, too?"

"Why would you climb up a tree cadaver along with the worst thieves of the city? Get out, Chief, I beg you! I'd rather never see you again than stand there with my arms cut off watching your perdition on the greasy pole."

"It's definite, I'm staying. That pole is my point of no return. Later in the day, if you want, we'll go into the practical aspects of the operation. For the moment, I'm dead tired. You're sleepy, too. See you later, Master Horace."

"As you say, Chief."

Postel went into the Ark, washed his face, arms, and hands, took off his trousers and shirt, lay down on his stomach on the cot. He fell into a deep sleep right away. He woke up eight hours later. He felt good.

Dance on the Volcano

Marie Chauvet

Born in Haiti in 1916, Marie Chauvet is one of Haiti's most important twentieth-century voices. Author of the allegorical play La légende des fleurs, *as well as several masterful works of fiction—*Fille d'Haïti *(1954),* La danse sur le volcan *(1957), Fonds des Nègres (1960), Amour, colère et folie (1968), and Les rapaces (published posthumously in 1986)—Chauvet was a courageous social critic who laid bare the unjust, long-historical workings of race and class in Haiti, paying particular attention to the consequences of these injustices for Haitian women. The excerpt below is from* La danse sur le volcan. *Set in late eighteenth-century Haiti, the novel follows the extraordinary career of real-life historical figure Minette, a "mixed-race" opera singer whose immense talent affords her great privilege despite the constraints of race and class in the colony. As her star rises on stage, however, Chauvet's Minette becomes increasingly aware of the untenable social order that governs her life and the lives of those she loves. Forced to confront, and ultimately inspired to intervene in, the politics of the pararevolutionary moment, Minette becomes a tragic heroine in the literal theater of revolution that was Saint-Domingue. This scene from the very first pages of the novel in many ways sets the stage for the narrative that follows. It provides a window onto the subtle, illusory, and crucially important distinction of race and class that determined the parameters of women's lives at the time, introducing Minette against the backdrop of this fraught colonial world.*

On that June day, all of Port-au-Prince was at the harbor, joyously anticipating the arrival of the new governor.

For the past two hours, armed soldiers had been keeping order among an immense crowd of men, women, and children of all sorts. The mulatto and Negro women were gathered a certain distance away, as was the custom; they had pulled out all the stops to rival the elegance of the white Creole and European ladies. Occasionally the freedwomen's calico skirts, striped or flowered, brazenly brushed up against the white women's heavy taffeta skirts and diaphanous muslin gaules. Everywhere you looked, breasts barely covered by flimsy, see-through bodices attracted the delighted gaze of the men who, despite the horrendous heat of that summer morning, were dressed in velvet, with ruffled blouses, fitted coats, and vests. Beneath their curly wigs

Marie Chauvet in her library. Photo courtesy of Anthony Phelps.

they were sweating more than the slaves. What bliss for them, then, whenever the ladies played flirtatiously with their fans! The jewels adorning the toes of the mulatto women—whom a new law had banned from wearing proper shoes—just made them all the more fascinating and desirable. Seeing their diamond-shod feet, the white women regretted having called for the new regulation directed at "those creatures" who had dared to imitate their clothing and hairstyles. Having complained to the governor about the inexcusable offense, they had called for justice—without admitting, of course, that their real desire was to punish and humiliate these rivals who had become far too appealing to their own husbands and lovers. As always, society's laws were powerful. The white women had easily won their case against the freedwomen, products of the despised slave caste.

However, doubtless to get their revenge, at present "those creatures" were decorating their feet with the jewels their white lovers had given them. This was the height of insolence. No one could deny that they were utterly charming, coquettish, and captivating. They were without equal in the art of showing off their arched waistlines, the uniquely provocative curve of their breasts, their generous and supple hips. The combination of the two so vastly different blood strains had created the most prodigious beauty in these women. So in this regard, nature herself was responsible.

The officers in their sparkling uniforms—desired by all the women, be they white or mulatto—made no attempt to hide the lustful looks they were giving to the beautiful Negresses with their hair done up in madras scarves as sparkling with jewels as their feet. Their breasts half exposed, they smiled, and their perfect teeth traced a flash of light across their dark faces. From time to time, they broke out in great cascading bursts of laughter. But this noisy gaiety was by no means sincere, for their eyes were full of contempt, hatred, and provocation.

Among the women of Saint-Domingue, the rivalry had produced a fight to the death that was in fact at the heart of all relations in the colony: rivalry between white colonists and low-class whites; between the officers and the government officials, between the nouveaux riches, with neither name nor titles, and the great nobles from France; rivalry also between the white planters and the freedmen planters, between the domestic slaves and the field-workers. This state of affairs, combined with the discontent of the freedmen and the silent protestation of the African Negroes who were treated little better than animals, had created a state of perpetual tension that produced a strange heaviness in the atmosphere.

Because of all this, and despite the vibrancy, the laughter, and the elegant clothing and wigs, a sort of menace hung in the air. Yet nothing was visible on the surface. As with all such days of great public celebration, rows of six-horse carriages, covered wagons, and closed carriages lined the road. The officers and colonists' opulent getups, the gold-trimmed cars, the women's elaborate hairstyles, makeup, gloves, and flowers—together with the trees, the insolent blue of the sky, and the radiant sun—created a marvelous tableau. People lingered, laughing, in front of the jewelers' and the perfumers' windows, and the women gave suggestive looks as they accepted gifts from the men. Groups of slaves in chains passed by, led by their masters, and from time to time one could hear the snap of a whip lashing a naked torso.

All of a sudden, an immense clamor arose from the crowd; the long-awaited royal vessel had just appeared. Immediately, the bells rang out, the cannons resounded. The clergy, bearing banners and crosses, ornaments and incense burners, waited beneath a dais for the governor, newly appointed by the king.

A hundred men went out in rowboats to greet him. Upon his arrival, the crowd applauded with cries of "Long live his majesty the King of France," and accompanied him to the church. Curious young children struggled with those trying to push them out of the way. A few of them protested loudly. The women seized the opportunity to shout insults at their rivals. A young mulatto woman met the gaze of an officer who had been looking her over. There was a blond woman on his arm, totally absorbed by the spectacle of the governor's welcome. The mulatto woman took a bouquet of flowers from her bodice and threw it to the man, who caught it smilingly. The blond turned around immediately.

"Foul Negress," she screamed, "if you're looking for something to cool your fire, I'm sure there are some slaves who'd be more than happy to oblige you!"

Without responding, the mulatto woman turned her head toward the soldiers.

With all those uniformed men surrounding her, there was no way she could return the insult to that white wench! Ah, if only there hadn't been so many soldiers, she would have gouged out her eyes. After giving it some thought, she decided it was best to shrug her shoulders with an impertinent smile.

She wore a long white cotton skirt trimmed with red flowers and, gathered tight at the waist, a chambray bodice so transparent her breasts were all but exposed. A light wrap thrown carelessly over her shoulders came to a point on her back and revealed the low neckline of the bodice. Her madras scarf, adorned with costume jewels that sparkled in the sun, was set high atop her head, half covering her right eyebrow. With a slow, steady gait, in harmony with the swing of her hips, she went off in the direction of the crowd, sending flirtatious and seductive glances as she passed.

Someone shouted out to her, calling her "Kiss-Me-Lips." She smiled, turned around and, with a sweeping hand gesture, shouted in Creole: "But where are you? What, I can't see you anymore?"

A man joined her—a white man in a jacket and cotton pants, wearing neither wig nor shoes with buckles.

"You're still being cuckolded, and yet you're not looking for a shoulder to cry on?" she asked, bursting into laughter.

"I'm resigned to being cuckolded," responded the man, taking her arm. "Come, 'Kiss-Me-Lips,' let's have a drink at the nearest cabaret. I know someone who makes a perfect rum punch . . ."

"Rum punch . . . if that's all you've got to offer! . . ." "All right, come on— you can choose whatever you like." "A sweet Bordeaux, that's what I want." They went off in the direction of the central square as the crowd dispersed. In the streets, carriages manned by Negroes rolled along to the noisy clip-clop of hooves.

Two little girls, one twelve and the other ten, walked along holding hands.

Shabbily dressed in faded calico skirts and bodices modestly held together with pins, they were barefoot and their hair was left loose. With their golden skin and long tresses, they looked at first like two little "poor white" girls. But on closer inspection, one could see that they were in fact "mixed-bloods," for their black blood had added that extra spice—that slight note of originality—that any white person could detect at first glance. The elder one in particular, with her sensuous lips, her black eyes pulled slightly toward the temples, and her rebellious locks, was a perfect specimen of the mestive. They walked holding hands with a modest air that contradicted the gleam of curiosity in their eyes.

Interview of Jean-Claude Duvalier: Duvalier's "Liberal" Agenda

Jon-Blaise Alima

François Duvalier's transfer of power to his adolescent son, Jean-Claude Duvalier, via constitutional amendment marked a further mutation in twentieth-century Haitian politics. Jean-Claude Duvalier's installation as president-for-life on 23 April 1971 represented a subordination of the principle of elected governance and effectively ushered in a dynastic era. Outside observers quickly noticed factions evolving within this small universe: François Duvalier's wife Simone Ovide Duvalier and several old-guard Duvalierists or "dinosaurs" on one end, and Jean-Claude and his cabinet of young technocrats and administrators on the other. Rumors circulated attesting to Jean-Claude's susceptibility to the influence of his mother and later his wife, Michèle Bennett, whom he married in 1980, to the disapproval of the Duvalier family.

Riding on an initial wave of public goodwill, Jean-Claude used the temporary political stability afforded him to announce a top-down program of economic modernization and liberalization. He announced his new direction in a slogan he would repeat through the duration of his presidency: "My father made the political revolution. I will make the economic revolution." In tune with neoliberal transitions elsewhere in Latin America and the Caribbean, Jean-Claude Duvalier focused on attracting investments from multinational corporations and international financial institutions. Haiti became a haven for subcontract manufacturing enterprises that profited from Haiti's large population of unskilled and meagerly paid laborers.

As part of his modernization program, Duvalier also made mild concessions to civil liberties and independent political activism. The government allowed for a measure of free expression, erratically issued reprieves to political prisoners, and grudgingly allowed a small number of non-Duvalierist candidates to run for public office. In April 1978, Duvalier attempted to co-opt and channel these tendencies through the creation of CONAJEC (Conseil National Jean-Claudiste), a civic forum designed to steer public opinion. Despite his efforts to stage-manage liberalization, an unanticipated groundswell of independent journalism and local political activism threatened the integrity of the Duvalierist regime. In 1980–81 Duvalier responded by unleashing his paramilitaries on these emerging pockets of independence, thus beginning an er-

ratic cycle of liberalization followed by repression that dominated the next five years of the regime's existence. Up to the very moment of his exile in early 1986, Jean-Claude failed to resolve the contradiction latent in his government: seeking new legitimacy through fostering increased civic participation and public opinion on the one hand, but ultimately relying on repression to remain in power.

The following interview by Jon-Blaise Alima, a journalist for the Franco-African journal Jeune Afrique, *was conducted on 22 April 1978, just weeks after Jean-Claude's creation of* CONAJEC. *Duvalier most likely scheduled this interview to coincide with the creation of* CONAJEC *to showcase his liberal agenda to an external audience. Duvalier fields probing questions that highlight the political impasse in Haiti: the lack of meaningful bodies for political participation, allegations of external political influences, and the ever-present signs of military repression across the country.*
—*Contributing Editor: Allen Kim*

JEUNE AFRIQUE: Were you intimidated by the power you assumed when you succeeded your father?

JEAN-CLAUDE DUVALIER: Not really. I have to say that my father prepared me for it. But I knew Haiti was a difficult country and that Haitians—like the French—wouldn't be easy to govern. It was because of that that I initially refused. But eventually, I had to give in to the will of my father.

J. A.: It seems that you're under the influence of his companions and your mother?

J. C. D.: Let's just say I have friends who advise me. My mother does not play a mystical role that some would ascribe to her. She doesn't directly exert pressure on me. The exercise of power has certainly given me experience. And if there's talk about a feud between the ancients and the moderns, it's precisely because I had to separate myself from my father's collaborators who were spending their time devising all sorts of maneuvers to safeguard their own interests. I had to rely on friends who frequently happened to be young like me. In fact, I eliminated those elements who were going against the current of history. Even if no one wants to admit it, I am convinced that this action will serve the cause of liberalization.

J. A.: Why haven't you attempted a politics of national reconciliation with the exiled opposition?

J. C. D.: The door is open to all those who for one reason or another left Haiti. For that matter, those who have returned have not been harassed.

J. A.: There has been the impression nonetheless that the country exists in a certain psychosis of fear. It is striking to see police guard posts installed at the entrance of every city.

J. C. D.: Those are the products of a history of violence, which you certainly know about. We harbor no illusions about the difficulties we have had to surmount. Only consider that our country has had to repel thirteen invasions since the advent of Duvalierism. Liberalization must not exclude vigilance.

J. A.: Political activities are not authorized in the country. And the party created by your father and predecessor remains dormant.

J. C. D.: The party, it's true, hasn't been reorganized. It has remained silent, awaiting the right moment to create a united party in which all sides can have their say.

J. A.: How do you explain the inability of the first black republic in the world to foster sustained relations with the Third World?

J. C. D.: We would love to open embassies in several African countries. But that's not possible at the moment. It's a question of means. We hope to have them one day. Each problem carries its own priorities. First, we must above all concern ourselves with stemming the hostility of our powerful neighbors before reaching out to the Third World, which supports us. We have been happy to receive a number of African chiefs of state such as President Léopold Sédar Senghor of Senegal and Kenneth Kaunda of Zambia. Recently I also received a visit from Mr. Ouattara, the representative of the Organization of African Unity (OUA) to the United Nations. We envision sending a Haitian delegation to observe a summit of the OUA.

J. A.: Do you consider yourself a continuation of François Duvalier's politics?

J. C. D.: Each person has his own style, his own temperament. I am not thinking of deviating from the schemas he (François Duvalier) traced even if I situate my action on other grounds. My father won the political battle. I will win the economic battle.

Translated by Allen Kim

On the Saut-d'Eau Pilgrimage

Jean Dominique

In the early 1970s, the journalist Jean Dominique attended and made audio recordings of the religious pilgrimage of Our Lady of Mount Carmel, which takes place every July at Saut-d'Eau, Ville Bonheur, in central Haiti. The famous waterfall and the village of Ville Bonheur are held sacred by Vodouisants, who bathe in its waters, make sacrifices, and pray to the saints and the spirits; the village is a holy site for followers of the Catholic faith, as well. At the time of Dominique's visit, Haiti was under the Duvalier dictatorship, which had for two decades engaged in systematized repression of the Haitian peasantry, seizing land throughout the country and distributing it to local Duvalierist sympathizers and strongmen. François Duvalier had appropriated, distorted, and exploited the Vodou religion to serve his ideological and political ends, while the practice of Vodou itself remained marginalized and stigmatized in many sectors.

For these reasons, Jean Dominique's reportage on the Saut-d'Eau pilgrimage was revolutionary. He described the rituals and beliefs of the Haitian masses not as superstition or folklore, but as strength: resistance to the political powers that sought to crush them and co-opt those very beliefs. But Dominique, like other members of the independent Haitian press during the Duvalier years, had to be careful. He could not say this outright. He had mastered the art of pale andaki, speaking in subtle and cloaked ways. In 1991, five years after the fall of Duvalier regime, on a special broadcast celebrating Radio Haiti's fifty-sixth anniversary, Dominique recalled the Saut-d'Eau pilgrimage as a formative moment in his own understanding: "I got to the front of the church, cassette in hand, I started to record, and there I discovered a great truth. That truth . . . ! I realized—and I said all of this on the radio in a report that caused an uproar at the time, because it was the first time that listeners had heard such things. And we were under Jean-Claude Duvalier, we were under [high-ranking Macoutes] Luc Désir, Jean Valmé, Luckner Cambronne, and company! We were under the tigers! The people opened their arms in front of the pilgrimage site, they looked toward the church, and they described their misery. They described their oppression, how the life was squeezed out of them [peze-souse]. They described how everything was being destroyed [kraze-brize]. They spelled it all out. They described it in a litany, for hours. For days. And . . . when I arrived under the palm tree, I heard something else: 'Those who do evil cannot set foot in Saut-d'Eau.' Big words! When you got *up to the water, they said the same thing. I said, 'Hmm! Listen to what the people are saying. The people are using the spirits to reveal their enemies.'"*

The original broadcast, interspersed with clips of the ceremonies, songs, and prayers of the Saut-d'Eau pilgrims, was part of Dominique's ongoing series on haïtianité —on what it means to be Haitian. Part of the audio also appears in Jonathan Demme's documentary about the life of Jean Dominique and Radio Haiti, "The Agronomist." —Contributing Editor: Laura Wagner

The Original Broadcast, July 1974

Saut-d'Eau, City of Joy; Saut-d'Eau, City of Mystery; Saut-d'Eau, City of Misery

Fifty thousand pilgrims were at Saut-d'Eau this year. Fifty thousand Haitian people, one Haitian in every hundred.[1] A thick cloud of beggars assail you at the entrance of the church, crippled, hobbled and lame, half-blind and afflicted. Four hundred trucks over fifteen days, kilometers upon kilometers of ornamental cord in blue, purple, yellow, and red, thousands of pigs turned to *griyo* [fried pork], millions of gallons of *kleren* [undistilled sugarcane liquor], liters of rum, tons of dust swallowed night and day, pestilential clouds of human excrement, cow dung, horse manure, pig manure, hundreds of cooking pots on the ground cooking how many thousands of *akra* [malanga fritters], *marinad* [savory dough fritters], fried plantains, fried sweet potato, whole roads engulfed in smoke, candles, the melted ends of tallow candles, and the persistent hum of the water in the canal carrying all the town's waste, where men, women, children, horses, cars, trucks wash and from which they drink, a water so crystalline and abundant despite all the vicissitudes of its journey, and amid the chaos of this derisory eight-day festival: a song of the misery and false hopes of man, the tragedy and the terror of a people.

This human tide, cacophony of cries and lamentations, an incessant coming and going amid the clattering of the trucks, tears running down a face daubed with magic powder, songs of joy at the passage of the Virgin on her day of glory, amplifiers roaring with *merengue* and *konpa* music, dice rolling on tables near the front porch of the church: this and more still is Ville Bonheur, city of joy, city of mystery, city of misery.

Saut-d'Eau, City of Miracles

Dozens of trucks traversed a narrow stretch of mountain this year, and yet there were no accidents. Fifty thousand people slept wherever they could: under trees, on the street, *anba tonèl* [under small open-air shelters], in the entryway of the church, in the courtyard, in trucks, on porches. Fifty thousand people thus installed, any which way, and yet there were no epidemics, no dysentery, no diarrhea or anything of the sort. People drank the water from the canal, filled with all manner of trash, vegetable peelings, waste, even excrement, and still nothing happened. How to feed all these people? How did more children not die? How were there not more collisions in these over-crowded streets, or elderly people suffocated by the crowd, or houses collapsed under the weight of people and things, or trucks overturned into the chasm? Saut-d'Eau, city of miracles . . . miracle of disorganization, miracle of good-natured anarchy, with neither formal committee nor plan nor organization. How many doctors and nurses, how many hospital beds, how many tons of medicine, of first aid? None of any of that, no hospital, no doctor, no nurse—and despite it all, no catastrophe was reported. Everything played out with loose Haitian informality. Saut-d'Eau, miracle of Haitian anarchy. Saut-d'Eau, city of miracles. Miracle of a lush waterfall in the Artibonite, an oasis of green in a country stripped bare by erosion.

Loneliness before the Gods amid the Crowd

July 16, the festival of the Virgin of Saut-d'Eau: a lesson in *haïtianité*, a lesson in deep physical, material, moral, and spiritual suffering. One finds in Saut-d'Eau in that month of July the largest concentration of one-handed people, one-eyed people, stutterers, people covered in lesions, the shriveled and shrunken, the lame and legless, dragging themselves on the ground, that Haiti has ever seen assembled in one place. It is yet another proof of Saut-d'Eau's miracles that contagion did no further harm, but the sense of physical suffering unleashed by the spectacle is unbearable to those with more delicate sensibilities. The misery begins even at the entrance to the church, where the clusters of beggars have an almost-surreal look to them, as though you are entering some *cour des miracles*, or better still delving into some mad dream, some version of Luis Buñuel's *Ascent to Heaven*. Physical ugliness, the discomfort of the human gaze: one feels coveted, carved up, stripped naked, torn to pieces every second. Suddenly in the crowd, a whirlpool begins to form around a particular point. A woman in the modest blue dress of a penitent, her waist encircled by ritual cord, tosses a handful of loose change, and the swarm of beggars clusters around her well-cut skirt, her freshly shaven black legs, clinging with hooked fingers. She looks away, her gaze confident and firm, searching the mêlée for her three well-attired sons while two guards or two militiamen clear the area for her, eliminating the troublemakers with lashes of their leather whips. Who is this mysterious and powerful penitent? Some rich local peasant girl, the wife of some commodities speculator from the Plaine du Nord, member of a Vodou congregation under strict orders to wear only blue embroidered with the symbol of Zaka, a strict and discreet costume that nonetheless does not stand in the way of the latest fashion.

Eighty percent of the pilgrims to Saut-d'Eau have barely enough to pay for the trip. They arrive, crammed into trucks as tightly as sugarcane in one of

HASCO's railway cars;[2] they disembark, eyes wild and bodies white with dust and ask the first person they see directions to the path to the church. You find them lying in the open air in the entryway of the church by the hundreds, whether on thin sisal mats, or on straw pallets, or on rags, covered with earth, or spat upon in penitence; they are scattered by the hundreds throughout the wasteland under the sacred mapou tree,[3] around the first slopes of the valley; they invoke Saint John the Baptist at the foot of a palm tree, the place the first apparition took place,[4] and from whence this legend was born. They arrive, as well, by side roads and byways, by donkey or by horse or on foot, climbing at last toward Ville Bonheur after a year of expectation and suffering. Who are they? Peasants, mostly, and their entreaties to the Virgin carry with them the smell of the land, an ungrateful land, a sterile land—or a stolen land. Their cries to heaven often have the heartbreaking tones of sacrificial animals: they had to sell a cow, perhaps, slaughter some pigs, goats, or sheep to pay for this voyage, in order to recite these very prayers.

Two kinds of people are drawn to Saut-d'Eau: those who come for pleasure, and those who come out of necessity. The ordinary people of the countryside and the town, what are they asking for? Against whom, or what, are they struggling? Malicious neighbors, unscrupulous loan sharks, jealous rivals, abusive mistresses, abuses of power, both legal and illegal. It is a rule of Saut-d'Eau, stricter than any of the Ten Commandments: no visitor to Saut-d'Eau can ask for harm to come to another, otherwise it is death unto them as they depart this town. But one asks for the alleviation of pain and hardship, and it is a great clamor that rises with every step, a great and sorrowful clamor . . . deafening. . . . The traveler too is moved to cry: *mercy, mercy on these penitents; mercy, mercy on these wretches; mercy, mercy for this suffering; mercy, mercy for these people, for these fifty thousand pilgrims.* . . . One in every hundred Haitians was at Saut-d'Eau this year.

All the individuals in this crowd of fifty thousand are isolated in their own pain, walled off in their own expression. The invisible wall surrounding each person allows everyone, without the risk of being overheard by eavesdroppers, to recount their life, to proclaim aloud to the Virgin, to the Ginen spirits,[5] to the saints, to the angels, and to ask for miracles. . . . The lamentation of fifty thousand solitary souls, fifty thousand people possessed, no one to hold on to as they stumble into a mystical haze.

Erzulie and St. John the Baptiste

The tragic isolation of the woman with her face powdered white, staring into the unknown. Her eyes well and two tears streak through the ritual makeup of Damballah. Alone amid the crowd in the church's entryway, she prays to the Virgin. She is alone before Heaven, she is alone with her sorrow, alone with her mottled heart, her pockmark-scattered heart.

In the church, among the mats, burlap sacks, coarse sacks woven of sisal or palmetto fiber flattened on the ground, in the swarm of women crouched or stretched out, the intoxicating sight of thousands of small kerosene *tèt gridap* lamps, burnt-out candle ends, Catholic prayers, rising in smoke. Ti Jean,[6] Grand Bois,[7] or Mistress Erzulie[8] step over the torpid bodies, wending their way through the jumble of entangled worshippers. The woman who, this morning, under the brutal weight of the waterfall, had been transfigured, mounted by her protector *lwa*, now prostrates herself and offers up her pitiful lamentation to the Virgin. The angels and the saints, the Vodou spirits and the Virgin come together under the blue-and-white pointed arch of the sanctuary—where the priest led which prayer? to which saint? Is he indifferent to this sacred blend, to this blending of the sacred?

In the valley, the Catholic church gives way to the religions of magical trees, Damballah's mapou alongside Saint John the Baptist's palm.

A Happening for the Children of the Enslaved

For three or four days, Ville Bonheur is at every moment a spectacle, an immense happening against a backdrop of gray distress, where hymns suddenly surge forth, shouted over a *yanvalou* beat.[9] An ongoing spectacle of penitents in *vèvè*-adorned robes moving in pairs,[10] holding out their calabash bowls to the passersby. Groups adorned in the white garb of ritual beggars come from all the Vodou temples and other mystical places throughout the country to atone for sins committed against the *lwa*. To be redeemed, they must beg. They must also give alms to the true and false beggars to appease the wrath of heaven. A curious tableau of ritual begging, in addition to the collective suffering in which Ville Bonheur holds a special place. Such is the importance of the festival.

And there is also pleasure. Voyeurs, drunkards, carousers, libertines, revelers, and tourists wander through the dusty streets, haunting the gambling rooms, prowling around the roulette wheels, waiting to be fleeced by those sellers of dreams and illusions. Or to revel under the massive tent as it unleashes a flood of electrifying music, while nearby a makeshift generator purrs. The jokes fly, beneath the trees, around tables laden with bottles, some of which have been knocked over by drunkards. Coarse laughter mingles with the liturgical thrum. There is no clash between this profane laughter and the sacred fervor of those in need. Saut-d'Eau: beyond all desecration.

The End of Folklore

What a trove of information this celebration is for the ethnologist! A wealth of material on rites, beliefs, myths, and folk traditions. But how to preserve that cold and distant observer's gaze in the face of such profound alienation?

The heart of the matter is the expression of unbearable human suffering. How could one still regard this as folklore? This ugliness, this filth, this profound solitude, relates to the deep bondage of the Haitian caught in a jealous net of mystical fears woven of destitute poverty at the very limits of what is livable. In the streets, in the church courtyard, at the roots of the sacred trees, the heart of our people, the heart stippled and dotted like that of *Ezili je wouj*,[11] Erzulie of the red eyes, the heart of our people, beating with the rhythm of our despair. This ugliness and filth so disgust people of delicate sensibilities that they conflate misery with folklore, alienation with national culture. And everywhere they go, they preach the gospel of the gas stove, the French language, the tractor, electronics, believing that this gospel alone can bring about the end of misery—and too bad for tradition, too bad for the culture of the people! If the roots of our national culture possessed only the formal beauty of Philippe Auguste's verdant paradise,[12] what would be our reward for defending that culture, for desiring its betterment, for wanting it to be respected and admired?

One can endeavor to pit *haïtianité* and modernity against one another, threatening to sacrifice the former, with all of its incumbent suffering, on the altar of the latter and its promises of a better life. But why should the tractor drown out the brotherly song of the *konbit*? It is easy, on the other hand, for visitors from the Christian transistorized West to become enamored of the "noble savage" and see nothing of our land beyond the primary colors of naive art and our recipes filled with the flavor of yesteryear. Nothing is wholly beautiful, and that utterly Haitian expressiveness that gushes from each droplet of the Saut-d'Eau waterfall and from the cry of each pilgrim writhing in pain within their ritual cords, is, as we know, the expressiveness of the alienated. Putting an end to that alienation requires the uncompromised strength of the entire people, of every single person in his entirety. Changes to the material condition can only come about if the true people of this land retain their soul and preserve their true self. To enjoy, at long last, all that they have been bequeathed: land and river, soil and plants, the ground below and the fruits it bears, the water and the sun . . . men and gods, life and dream.

Revisiting Saut-d'Eau, July 1976

In 1976, Jean Dominique returned to Saut-d'Eau and was disheartened at first by what he saw: the spirit and energy of the festival, in all its pain and ecstasy, was seemingly dampened and subdued. Duvalierism functioned in large part by dividing Haitian society, alienating and isolating people so they could not unite in resistance. But just beneath this apparent tepidness, change was brewing. Earlier that year, the Artibonite had seen the first collective revolt of peasants from Bocozelle against Zacharie Delva,[13] a powerful Tonton Macoute in Gonaïves. And so, Jean Dominique wit-

nessed something powerful unfold that year in Saut-d'Eau. Relegated to the margins of the town, banished from the church, people revived their sense of community and collective faith. Just as they had in 1791 at Bois Caïman, the Haitian people drew upon Vodou to come together and resist those who would oppress them.

In July 1976 Radio Haiti aired the original report from Saut-d'Eau (above) interspersed with Dominique's updated observations (below). For the sake of clarity, the two texts are presented separately.

Is it Ville Bonheur that has changed this year? For it rained, and the church-yard was overrun with mud. . . . It seemed to me this year that the flavor of this town, beset for eight days by fifty thousand pilgrims, no longer contained that same fierceness, that harshness, that wild and haunting faith that I knew two years ago. And so I speak to you today of Saut-d'Eau, Ville Bonheur, city of joy, Saut-d'Eau, city of mystery, Saut-d'Eau, city of misery.

I had counted roughly fifty thousand pilgrims last time. Has the number truly dwindled, or is it only that the vehicles are fewer? The entryway to the church teems as ever it did with a world of beggars, people limping and lame, hobbled and infirm, the deformed that assail you among the pilgrims clad in penitents' garments, or the curious tourists who have come out of pleasure. Still others are drawn here out of necessity: they have come to implore, driving their lamentations unto heaven and screaming their prayers.

Was it the rain alone that cooled the atmosphere and mired the churchyard? Or was it, perhaps, the result of a new protection measure laid out by the young priest, and the order to limit access, shutting the faithful out of the church very early? Whatever the cause, still I felt a tepidness in the supplications of the crowd, clinging desperately to the Virgin as their last and only hope.

At the church this year, there were no straw mats, no coarse sacks of sisal or woven palmetto flattened on the ground, no women crouched or stretched out, no intoxicating sight of thousands of small kerosene *tèt gridap* lamps, no burnt-out candle ends, no Catholic prayers rising in smoke. This year the church sheltered no penitents. It had been cleared of people sleeping, of all those people weary and exhausted by their travels, of all the handicapped. Though it remained dirty, it was only mud tracked in on shoes and sandals, and only a handful of women in prayer and a few men offering candles could move freely, quietly, without so much as stepping over anyone's body, without so much as making a baby whimper. Is this the reason for the half-heartedness I observed? The church that had sought to distance itself from syncretic prayer? The penitents of Erzulie and Zaka, in their sacred fervor, were expelled from the churchyard and relegated to the area of the palms, which are also called St. John the Baptist. The Virgin of Mount Carmel no longer mixes with the African gods, as we saw last year. A young priest has restored proper order to such syncretism. But in the people's hearts and in their prayers, in their supplications, is not that marriage still alive?

Among the palm trees, to which those who serve Ti Jean Gran Bwa, Zaka,[14] Loko Atisou,[15] and Ogoun[16] were seemingly driven back, one notes a curious phenomenon. The fervor once possessed by each individual within the crowd in the churchyard has transformed into a collective faith. Groups of penitents form again, in the *lakou*, on narrow patios, and beneath the sacred trees, and it is together, in that group, that they can at last freely express their faith. Some twenty-odd members of a congregation, surrounding an *oungan* or a *manbo*,[17] a few *ounsi kanzò*,[18] a handful of faithful, a smattering of the curious: and thus the true, original altar is rebuilt again, and thus once more the festival convenes. . . . Oh, the drum was left in the village? Never mind! For these hands know how to beat out the shape of the heart, and this choir can sing the rhythm of the drumbeat.

Translated by Laura Wagner

Notes

1. In French, *mystère* means "mystery." In Haitian Creole, *mistè* refers to the *lwa*, the Vodou spirits. The title, then, might equally be rendered as "City of the Spirits."
2. The Haytian-American Sugar Company, which transported sugarcane harvested in the countryside to Port-au-Prince via railway for processing.
3. The mapou (ceiba) tree is sacred in Haitian Vodou; spirits reside within the tree and ceremonies are performed there.
4. The Virgin of Mount Carmel, who is associated with Erzulie Dantor, is said to have appeared on a palm tree at Saut-d'Eau.
5. In Haitian Vodou, Ginen is the mythic land across the sea, where the spirits (*lwa*) live, and where souls return after death.
6. Ti Jean is a fiery Petro *lwa* associated with St. John the Baptist.
7. Grand-Bois, or Granbwa, is a Petro *lwa* associated with trees, plants, and herbs.
8. "Mistress Erzulie" refers to Erzulie Dantor or Ezili Dantò.
9. The *yanvalou* is a traditional Vodou rhythm and dance associated with the serpent *lwa* Damballah or Danbala.
10. A *vèvè* is the ritual symbol associated with each *lwa*.
11. Ezili Je Wouj is a vengeful and wrathful manifestation of the spirit Erzulie. Erzulie's *vèvè* is a dotted heart with a dagger through it.
12. Philippe Auguste was Haitian painter known for his idyllic landscapes of lush jungles filled with gentle exotic beasts.
13. Delva was also an *oungan*, a Vodou priest—another example still of how the Duvalier regime co-opted and distorted Vodou for its own ends.
14. Zaka, or Kouzen Zaka, is the patron *lwa* of farmers.
15. Loko Atisou, or Papa Loko, is the *lwa* associated with trees, plants, and healing.
16. Ogoun is a warrior *lwa*.
17. An *oungan* is a Vodou priest; a *manbo* is a Vodou priestess.
18. An *Ounsi kanzò* is a Vodou initiate who is fully married to the *lwa* they serve.

Dreams of Exile and Novelistic Intent

Jean-Claude Fignolé

.

One of the three cofounders, with Frankétienne and René Philoctète, of the late twentieth-century aesthetic philosophy of Spiralism, Jean-Claude Fignolé was among the relatively few Haitian writers and intellectuals who remained and continued to write in Haiti during the successive Duvalier regimes. In addition to writing essays and several novels, Fignolé has been a journalist, an agronomist, and a political personage in the small southwestern commune of Les Abricots, near his hometown of Jérémie. As with the excerpt below, Fignolé's writings are all pointedly anchored in the physical, geographical space of Haiti and are infused with testaments to both the failings and the potential of Haitians as they are placed or place themselves in the wider world. In this reasoned, if caustic, denunciation of the "tragedy" of exile under François Duvalier, Fignolé reflects on what is lost to the individual in seeking to escape—or, to use his expression, "desert"—Haiti. Casting a critical eye on several canonical works of Haitian literature, he considers the themes of exile and rootedness in a variety of prose fiction and theoretical texts. He argues that much of the country's literature and several members of its literary elite are marked by a profound alienation that reveals itself in a desire to identify with and be accepted by more powerful countries and their cultures. The excerpted paragraphs make plain the author's passion and despair as he censures the misguided departures of Haitian writers and intellectuals to various First World "elsewheres."

Words of desertion punctuate so many of our itineraries. The taste for travel and desire to move around other spaces betrays a longing to flee—to flee oneself—that is common among the characters of our novels. (If only this were just a literary phenomenon.) I seek myself in an elsewhere that I believe to be my own, in order to accommodate dreams that actually belong to others. I suffer my own history by adjusting to a sense that I am somehow different, persuading myself that nothing (the constant posturing, the bloodiness of Carnival, tyranny, abjection, corruption) has anything to do with me because it is all just the work of uncivilized people who look like me but who I don't know at all. I invent for myself a way of being that I cannot really master. My aspirations have no legitimacy except in their ludicrousness. And when, to my own astonishment, I give them some political force, it often results in carnage.

. . .

I am also speaking about—though in a different way—movement toward an elsewhere. Being other(wise) and no longer (my)self. I feel the rapturous pleasure of being possessed by that which fascinates me. By contrast. By complex. I feel diminished by what I am. All the more so because that which possesses me today long ago got me to accept the idea of my inferiority. And because of this idea I long ago accepted, albeit painfully, I now present my daughter (or my wife) as an offering, to be bedded. Once she is accepted (never out of love, always out of self-interest. Despised), I deny the shame by pretending that she has somehow been uplifted. But of course no one can possibly believe in a liberation that happens on one's back.

"Ah. Only a German man is good enough for our daughters."

I call such an escape illusory. Here always subverts elsewhere. Especially when elsewhere is disdain—pitying to boot—for here. Monsieur Henger [from Fernand Hibbert's satirical novel *Séna*] has the gall to wish for Haiti's progress. I fervently evoke the hypocritical irony, as he knows full well that one of the conditions for this desired progress would necessarily be taking away from him any possibility of exploiting my country so shamelessly.

The fascination for elsewhere is accentuated by the conceded or imposed presence of elsewhere smack in the middle of here. I evoke my backwardness (undoubtedly, I allow my own growth to be stunted) as a pretext for soliciting the Other. I give myself to the Other so that he might assume the burden of saving me. Of developing me (this term, recent and magical, always sounds great). Alcibiades sniggers: "of enveloping me." Giving my self freely, a generous offering, I forget that whatever I offer to an elsewhere deprives me of the right to possession of myself.

Who, then, will free me from my obsession with the foreigner-savior?

. . .

The desire to flee ensures the permanence of the novelistic intention. One travels outside of oneself in order to be transformed. With the certainty that one must change the world around oneself. But one's perspective varies from one project to the next because it is differently inscribed in the desire to flee.

I go elsewhere because I imagine that over there everything is perfect. I go elsewhere because I convince myself that here nothing can ever go right. IRREDEEMABLY

I can choose to better myself so as to return and make things better. I can choose also, out of disgust for this place, to live elsewhere definitively. The desire to flee calls on, for its confirmation, the act of desertion. Disingenuously, I take a stand against fighting. At least in this place. I call for a fight elsewhere, insolently imagining that the fight for elsewhere is also a fight for myself. A fight for my country. I let myself be persuaded that a change of scenery will force me to take root in my personal landscape. The confusion is formidable. I call it mystification. Intentional mystification by an intelligentsia that, having come up short, seeks to legitimate its flight, its resignation, with quibbling explanations. The confessor of souls, in clear bad faith, finds in my weakness a surrogate for his own cowardice. He, who—exiled from a God nevertheless bearing the reputation of a fighter, ferocious warrior with his legions of avenging archangels—preaches resignation and submission to the order of an elsewhere that might very well be his own home (why doesn't he go somewhere else to free his own country?). I refuse the notion of a universal homeland that serves as an excuse for everything.

Translated by Kaiama L. Glover

Dezafi

Frankétienne

Hailed as the first novel written in Haitian Creole (rewritten in French in 1979), this Spiralist narrative offers a thinly veiled allegory of rural life under François Duvalier. Rooted entirely in the Haitian popular imaginary, the novel tells a story of enslavement and revolution that resonates both backward and forward in Haiti's political history. Undergirding the novel is a deployment of the legend of the zombie. According to Haitian folk mythology, the zombie is a being without essence—lobotomized, depersonalized, and reduced through magic to a state of total impotence. A partially resuscitated corpse that has been extracted from the tomb by an evil sorcerer (a bokor), it is an animate being, but without any recollection of its past or hope for the future. The zombie represents the lowest creature on the social scale—a thingified nonperson reduced to its productive capacity. The "zombie" narrative, the post–American occupation Hollywood rescripting and dissemination of the crazed, bloodthirsty monster compelled to hunt down humans and feast on their brains, is a degrading misappropriation of the figure's Haitian roots. In Dezafi, Frankétienne reclaims this narrative with a tale recounted from the perspective of the zombie itself. Gone is the image of the slow-moving, flesh-eating, lifeless monster. Instead readers are drawn to empathize with the zombie, whose struggle is not just a metaphor for that of the Haitian people but also for those everywhere who struggle with oppression. In this excerpt, readers are introduced for the first time to the zombie and their master, Sentil, in a scene that clearly illustrates the brutality and inhumanity with which the zonbi are dealt—a concept that has rarely been explored with such pathos.
—Contributing Editor: Wynnie Lamour with Kaiama L. Glover

Full belly. Empty belly. Twisted insides. Thirsting for water. Thirsting for love. Longing for sunshine. Longing for light. Dreaming of stars. Dreaming of sweet women and the marvel of sparkling disco balls spinning at a party. Dreaming of the Sea Goddess's[1] voyage as she makes her way through the oceans unknown. Imagining the ways of the rainbow on a faraway island.

Dress handsomely. Dress in rags. Asleep with a scowl. Awake with a happy heart. Grinning. Flying a kite in the early morning. Banging the drum to a stiff *konpa*[2] beat. Dancing with no inhibitions.

Celebrate in the nude. Wrapped in rags. Amazed by love. Limitless, boundless love. Buried in a carnival of frightening masks. Buried in the violence of death. Who among us is truly living? Who?

So many people, of all kinds, swallowed up by the burden of troubling excuses. Living souls tossed around in a dream, eyes wide open, with neither inside nor outside. A long-playing dream with neither head nor foot. A dream smeared with terrible, treacherous creatures. A pageant of the macabre, the ugly and the awkward. Noise, confusion, and disorder of scandalous proportion.

Chameleons. *Boulinò*[3] snakes. Three-headed lizards. Flying scorpions. Mongoose. Thousand-legged insects. Spiders. Owls. Hawks. Deafening thunder. *Koukou*. Ugly. *Chanwan*. Fetid, dirty. *Lasigwav*. Ancient, evil. *Madanbrino*. Vibrant. *Chaloska*. Grotesque. Monsters of yore and myth. Masked bearers of death.

We are lost on roads that cross and crisscross. We fight to walk straight but we set off crooked. We're babbling, consumed by the nonsensical and paralyzed by hardship.

There are moments we spin and spin, turning in never-ending circles. We set off one by one, limping aimlessly, heads down. What are we searching for?

There are even moments when we break out running, legs splayed, crazed, and worse than a stray dog startled by pounding storm winds and the crack of thunder, sharp like the sound of a whip on its back. Kote nou prale? Kibò nou vle ale? Where are we going? Where do we want to go?

Day and night, we mumble to ourselves. In front of the mirror, we speak and our words are turned inside out and upside down in a mélange of calico. Who hears what we say? Who tries to understand what we want to say?

They would rather declare that we're crazy. They would rather call us names. Disgusting. Blabbermouth. We don't know how to remain quiet, giving away secrets. Instead, they rush to shut our mouths closed.

The days go by and the nights pass as the seasons play a never-ending game of tag. They rise, then fall. Seasons of lies. Turbulent seasons. Seasons of torment. Masked, disturbing, and disgusting seasons. Seasons of the macabre. An ugly, violent motley of seasons.

We fall asleep drunk.

We awake senseless.

We understand nothing. We grimace under a deck of double sixes. We've become entirely bewildered, stunned stupid under the heavy weight of the burden we bear. We swallow the potion in a long dream smeared with evil spirits, a dream torn apart by a cacophony of rusty knives, sharp machetes, and broken glass.

Rupturing winds. Sheaths of lightning. Deafening thunder. Quarrels fill the night. We shake ourselves a little. In a waking slumber, we open one eye. We remember the dream. We forget the dream. We remember a little. But we forget a lot.

Tangled branches deep in an old yard where living souls are rarely found. Rocks and grains of sand cover the ground. Twisted insides. Pangs of pain. Rita struggles to work, the whole morning long, with no food. In the house,

Jedeyon paces back and forth, grumbling to himself. In the middle of the night, a piercing scream stabs us awake, bursting our eardrums. Our blood curdles. Our stomachs growl. Our hair stands on end. We quickly arise.

Sentil squares himself against the armchair, a herd of zombies kneeling beneath the *peristil*.[4] To his right, Siltàna is sitting on a straw chair. To his left is Zofè, standing stiffly and holding a whip. Three big, baleful candles are lit beneath the *potomitan*.[5] Sentil begins to shake his *ason*.[6]

—Siltàna, my child!

—Yes, Papa.

—Listen well to what I'm about to tell you.

—Yes, Papa.

—You are the only one in charge of feeding the zombies. Never forget, that salt is poison! Never forget that, my child.

—Yes, Papa.

Sentil shakes the *ason*, recites a ritualistic chant, and turns to the left.

—You, Zofè!

—Yes, Master.

—Shave the zombies tomorrow. Shave them bald before the sun comes up, before they go to work in the swamp.

—Yes, Master.

—If one tries to disobey you, here's what you are to do: slice his skin off, ground the meat on his body, destroy his bones, break his head, until he becomes dust. Then, drink his blood. Don't play favorites with anyone! Everyone gets the same treatment!

Sentil arises just as Siltàna does. He shakes the *ason* once more, approaches the *potomitan*, then takes a step back. He grabs a bottle of rum and spills three shots on the ground. He tips back the rest of the bottle in his mouth and finishes it off.

—You, band of zombies!

—*Wi wan! Wi wan! Wi wan!*

—Lower your heads when I speak to you!

—*Wi wan! Wi wan! Wi wan!*

—You're here as punishment for your impertinence! For having dared to defy me!

—*Wi wan! Wi wan! Wi wan!*

—I'm the only one in charge here! The only head honcho in this land!

—*Wi wan! Wi wan! Wi wan!*

—I never repeat myself to anyone!

—*Wi wan! Wi wan! Wi wan! Wi wan! Wi wan! Wi wan!*

—Here, in this *lakou*,[7] you have no right to taste salt! You can only receive food from Siltàna! Only Siltàna's hands can provide you with drink!

—*Wi wan! Wi wan! Wi wan!*

—Remember, the dead never rise. You're all finished, forever! Nothing will ever change for you. You have nothing. When I give, when I want to give, that is when you will have. These are the rules of the game. All you zombies must tread softly and remain silent.

. . .

Rugged voices.

Gruff voices.

Rolling sticks and waving wands. Horses tied to their posts. Stamping, pawing at the ground. A wildcat making its way over the cactus fence. One avocado tumbling to the ground. Up in the rafters of the house, a heavy voice yells out: "I'm falling!" On the ground, they respond: "Go ahead and fall, just as long as you don't get hurt!"

A cluster of dreams, dreams of all colors, in our heads. A cluster of ideas, ideas alit in our minds, trying to figure out, which leg can we use to dance?

We neglect the garden,

Weeds grow.

We turn the key,

Owls fly out.

We stick our index fingers right into the lightning, and it hurts us deeply, down to the bone. We place bets in our sleep. They raise us with our eyes wide open.

Tree branches tangled deep in an old yard where living souls are rarely found. Arms flailing, reaching out in all directions. We take strong strokes, fearful of drowning, fearful of being burned by the flames.

And yet Life wounds us anew. Love afflicts us deeply. And Death taunts us.

We have to beware of the two-faced, backstabbing creatures, as they unexpectedly circle our homes.

Our minds have become flashes of lightning as they shoot stiff sparks in the pitch-dark of a blackout. Frantically, we search for something, anything, to light our way.

We probe our way through a complicated, entangled darkness but lose ourselves in the profundity of the magic. We ask for passage.

Not a single person responds.

Not one person speaks.

Tongue slices tongue.

Disjointed jaws.

Words of ashes, words of betrayal.

Bloody words, words to the wind.

Words scattered in the rebound of commotion. Frequent stumbles rupture our insides. They tease us and they taunt us, spewing nonsense and mockingly calling us names: Stupid. Demonic. Dumb. Diabolic. Straining through the rocky terrain, we dislocate our bones.

We're incapable of being still: we sit, we stand, we lay down, we crouch down. We move slowly, struggling to find a position. We end up curled up on our sides, arms and legs pulled up to our chests. Fetal position. Still, no one can tell us on which leg to dance. During the day, we speak by ourselves. At night, we speak to ourselves. We misspeak. Our words are mismatched. We rush to shut our mouths closed.

. . .

Several days go by. We remain weak, depressed, chins resting in the palms of our hands. We're listless, beaten down. Lifeless under the cursed weight of our woes.

Wands wave, werewolves fly. Bravely, shamelessly, children spin and spin at the corner. They jump up and down, taking pleasure in celebrating. They curtsy, as performers do, to announce their presence; thrusting sharply as they dance a dance of seduction and elegance. They turn their hips in a circular motion, reminiscent of *gedezarenyen*, the spider spirit of death and *gedemazaka*,[8] the powerful peasant spirit. We watch them and we shake our heads. At times we shake our bodies in place. Lightning strikes. Thunder grinds. Rain falls. The flood descends. Despite all this, the *rara*[9] band comes out to play on the roadways.

We make moves to stand up. But, if we are to really enter the ring, how can we fall in step if we know not on what foot to dance?

Our skin is stripped.

We're scarred to the bone.

Two countries. Two yards. Two pennants. Two languages. Two sounds. Two pastures. Two neighborhoods. Two tragedies, for a reality that refuses to change. Which side does the truth lean toward?

Translated by Wynnie Lamour

Notes

1. Lasirèn is the *lwa lanmè*, or the spirit of the sea.
2. *Konpa* is popular Haitian music.
3. Bouli (Nord) is a town in Burkina Faso.
4. The *peristil* is the roofed court of the *hounfò*.
5. The *potomitan* is the center pillar in the *peristil*, which represents the center of the universe.
6. The *ason* is the ritualistic rattle used in Vodou ceremonies by the *oungan*, or Vodou priest.
7. A *lakou* is a yard around which houses from a particular family or lineage are built.
8. The Gede are a family of *lwa* or spirits that rule the realm of the Dead.
9. *Rara* is a type of music associated with big groups singing and dancing in the streets. Usually led by those playing a long, flute-like instrument called a *vaksin*.

And the Good Lord Laughs

Edris Saint-Amand

*Edris Saint-Amand's realist novelistic style is a direct expression of his political com-
mitment to improving the condition of the lower classes, particularly the rural Haitian peasant community and members of Haiti's urban underclass. An activist in
Haiti's midcentury trade union movements, Saint-Amand was engaged explicitly in
struggles for social justice in his country. His turn to prose fiction marks his strong
belief in the power of literature to expose truth and thus impact the social order. A
crucial text of the 1950s,* Bon Dieu rit *(And the Good Lord Laughs) recounts the
degradation of Haiti's rural population faced with the encroachment of the global
imperialist system in the Caribbean. Describing the particular details of rural life, the
novel offers a collage of highly detailed vignettes that evoke the quotidian hardships
experienced by Haiti's exploited peasantry. While much of the narrative centers on
the poverty, disenfranchisement, and cultural alienation of the rural population, it
also relates the small joys that sustain communities of the most marginal in Haiti.
Rich with traditional songs, proverbs, jokes, and folktales, the novel has a documentary quality that ultimately gives voice to the least powerful members of Haitian society. The below excerpt describes the goings-on during market day in a small Haitian
community. Abuse, misery, and injustice are prominent themes; so are solidarity,
generosity, and joy.*

To tell the truth, the case of Madame Prévilien presented some difficulties.
Indeed, it is well known how cruelly she'd been beaten by Octave Cyrille.
Yet she wasn't worried in the slightest. She'd taken some medication. She'd
gotten some massages. Since then she hadn't had any pain. She had no reason
not to tire herself out. She said: "I've got things to sell in town. Up to the day
before I give birth I'll keep going down to Saint-Michel. And if I stay put here,
when I need a dress, where will I get one? Décimus, my first-born, when he
needs a shirt, how will I get one for him? Prévilien is a boy. It isn't his job to
go down to the market. That's my job!" The days went by. And the challenge
of meeting her family's most basic needs always swept up Asséfie with the
same worries, as easily as a river would sweep up a leaf. But she didn't even
seem to notice that she was being swept up, so natural it was. And that's how
she came into her ninth month.

It was a Friday. That day, the market at Saint-Michel resonated with a thousand voices. From a distance, it sounded like a great humming beehive. People had gotten there early, on foot or trotting in on the backs of donkeys, from neighboring hamlets and even from some faraway villages: Batt'sault, Lhermite, Diguaran, Latalaye, Lacidras, Platna, Biarou. Marmelade, etc. They'd brought poultry and all manner of fruits and vegetables. Some had even arrived late the previous night so as not to miss out on a single sale. They'd spent the night under the arcades among all their baggage and food-stuffs. They stuffed their *macoutes* (sacks) and their *haleforts* (bundles held together with straps) to the brim. The poorest among them had come with huge baskets on their heads, making their necks sink into their shoulders. What a marvelous scene market day was! What a party! Some people would head back home with a dress, a pair of pants, a hat, a shirt, a pair of old shoes! Isn't that what everyone had been slaving away for? Stubborn hearts and backs had fertilized the earth. The flower had blossomed, and the ripe fruit was born of the docile tree, like a child on its mother's breast. And today man says: "That's just as it should be. I want to taste the fruit of my labors."

The market people don't arrange themselves any old way. Each person has his place. There are rows organized in accordance with the type of mer-chandise: the row for those selling charcoal, one for those selling herbs, food, cloth, hardware, the row for butchers . . .

The market was set up almost in a circle, right in the middle of the town, and closed off on four sides by boutiques and stores. A few old archways look on vaguely, as if surprised: they seem like so many vestiges left over from some great disaster. And as soon as the sun begins flaming overhead, here, among all the people coming, going, screaming, arguing, fighting, smiling, belly laughing, speaking, shouting, suffering, insulting each other—here, shouting, are huge masses of dust that assault the eyes and that sometimes fly right up into the air, taking a hat or two with them. These whirlwinds are the worst! Because the whirlwind, as we've known for a long time now, it isn't wind. It's two "spirits" who come together to fight one another. Sometimes a donkey brays, its head thrown back. . . .

The day was going now at full steam. The sun beat down directly on peo-ple's heads, and the people were sweating out all the water in their bodies. Asséfie, seated on her *macoute*, which was laid out on the ground, had laid out her eggs, spices, sugarcane, and peas. A thousand other little market women like her had spread out their products on large handkerchiefs, pieces of cloth, and woven mats. It was never easy to make one's way through this abun-dance of eggs, oranges, lemons, cane stalks, bananas, meat, brooms, peas, rice, charcoal, buyers, sellers, hardware, chickens, cock crows, and beggars. From the arches hung sides of beef on which buzzing flies deposited their germs.

Not far from there, two market women were chatting:

—Truly, my friend, sales are down today! I still haven't sold a thing! To tell the truth, I've just arrived. I was caring for one of my children, who's fallen ill. I just don't know if the Good Lord is going to help me sell anything! What's more, we barely break even for our foodstuffs, while everything at the store gets more expensive every week! Truly, we "locals" are killing ourselves for nothing!

While one spoke, the other, disgusted, nodded her head in agreement:

—Everything you're saying is true, my friend! There's no money anywhere in this country! It's as if the Good Lord has turned his back and forgotten all about us! . . .

A local official arrived on the scene:

—Madame, where's your card? . . . Show it to me!

The unfortunate woman, as timid and well-behaved as a child, begging even:

—Sir, I can't pay just now. I only arrived a moment ago! I haven't sold anything yet! This is exactly what I was just saying to this woman here. It's the God's honest truth. . . .

The official furrowed his brow; his dignity was offended:

—Madame, I don't have time to waste this morning. I'm not here to joke around! Pay me, or I'm seizing your bananas.

—I'm telling you I've haven't sold anything yet, Sir! I have to sell before I can pay you. Otherwise, where would I get the money?

—Goddamn it! Pay me so I can get out of here.

The woman stood up, imploring him:

—Well, then! Sir, if you think I'm being dishonest and holding back the money from you, go ahead and search me!

Fat, shortish, with bloodshot eyes, the man went for the corn and the bananas in order to confiscate them. And trying to stop him, the woman held on to her merchandise and was pushed back so brutally that she fell on her bottom. A mob formed quickly. People were screaming: "Restrain that man! Restrain that man! He's going to kill that woman!" People tried to separate the combatants. The poor woman, her nose bloodied, was still fighting for her merchandise. The official punched her. She then sank her teeth into the neck of the representative of law and order. Another punch sent her flying.

A guard came forward. He roughly seized the unfortunate woman, whose face was covered in blood.

—Arrest her! Arrest her! screamed the official.

—Again he tried to strike the peasant woman, but the guard kept him back. The woman let fly words of pain, anger, despair along with her tears. She was brought, with her provisions, to the police station. A few days later, the justice of the peace pronounced her sentence: a fine of seven and a half gourdes and a month in prison.

Asséfie had remained quietly in her spot. Fearing she'd be knocked down, and given her state, she hadn't wanted to get mixed up in the hubbub to go see the battle that was transpiring. She still had to stay at the market for a while. By the middle of the afternoon she'd gotten rid of almost everything. She only had a few pieces of cane and some peas left. A good day! She'd already sold enough to make five gourdes! But despite the discomfort she felt under the burning September sun, she'd resolved not to leave until she'd sold all of her provisions. And the market kept up its same humming rhythm. The market is truly a human beehive. Peacefully seated, a few market women were eating their lunch of cassava, corn, or sugarcane. Some people were leaving, others arriving. A one-armed young man came by, as he did every time he saw her, to hold out his *coui* (small earthenware bowl) to Madame Prévilien. He was granted a yam. Asséfie knew him well. It was Altéus, a young man from Diguaran who, having left behind an arm in Mr. Octave Cyrille's mill and been rendered unable to work, had been forced to migrate to Saint-Michel to beg for his sustenance.

Suddenly, Madame Prévilien felt sharp pains in her stomach and realized she was perhaps about to give birth. She only had enough time to let out a single cry before toppling over, felled by the pain in her abdomen. People ran to her side. Gathered around her. A woman placed a *macoute* under Asséfie's head. Now the crowd was pouring in like a river. Madame Prévilien whimpered. She tried to explain that she was in labor. It didn't take long. She gave birth to the infant on her own—a fat little boy. He was received in an old mat and some rags. The guards arrived, but having ascertained that everything was in order, they, too, were happy to just look on. The umbilical cord was cut with the butcher's machete, still red with the blood of some animal . . . Delivered! Now everything was over. The newborn's mother sat up. The same rags were used to keep her from losing too much blood. A market woman lent her an old skirt to wrap the little one in. The crowd began to disperse, but there were a few latecomers. And just like that, life went on—life, that unstoppable force. Someone who knew Madame Prévilien's mule went to get it from the communal park. The *macoute* was filled with what was left of her provisions: a few pieces of cane and some peas. A little kid took advantage of the commotion to pilfer a few bits of cane and then fled the scene, laughing and cursing. The mother of the newborn straddled the mule. The baby was placed in her arms. Then, thanking everyone profusely in her most tender voice, she whipped the mule, and it set off at a slow trot. . . .

If there was one person who'd dance for joy, it would be Prévilien. Shirtless beneath the *quenepier* tree in the courtyard, he was hollowing out a tree trunk to make a trough with his axe when his wife appeared.

The newborn let out a cry. Prévilien was startled:

—Ha! Asséfie, it would seem you've had a baby!

Asséfie couldn't reply, but she made a sign for him to come help her down from the mule. The father took the child in his arms, anxious to see if it was a boy or a girl. And then he began gesticulating.

—Oh, the Good Lord truly loves me! The little one is a policeman. (He knew not to say it was a little boy, for then he ran the risk of losing the child.)

Then he did a little dance. Décimus, his first boy, was there and shouted: "I have a little brother, I have a little brother!"

Everything happened within the space of a minute. The woman entered the hut to rest. Prévilien sent Décimus running out to spread the good news. Prévilien hadn't been that happy for a long time. That afternoon his heart was as simple and true as a little flower.

Visitors began arriving in great numbers, among whom, of course, were Madame Prévilus, Marilisse, and Big Lésida. Everyone was thrilled, smiling and offering kind words. But as soon as she arrived, Big Lésida stamped her foot and shouted:

—Asséfie, Prévilien, you see what's happened! Christ has spared you, otherwise you'd have lost the child! In any case, what you've seen today is the last warning! Repent, for I'm telling you, the end of the world is nigh! Prévilien, I repeat, you've got to leave behind all this Vodou business. If you don't listen to me, you'll be struck with the worst misfortunes!

Translated by Kaiama L. Glover

Letter to the Haitian Refugee Project

Various Imprisoned Haitian Refugee Women

In the early 1970s Haitians began to flee Haiti for the United States aboard small, often overcrowded and dangerous boats. These so-called boat people claimed to be escaping political persecution and violence in Haiti and were seeking asylum in the United States. American immigration officials categorized the Haitians not as political refugees, but as economic migrants who were thus ineligible for asylum and unauthorized to be in the United States. Since they were classified as illegal immigrants, the Haitians were, throughout the 1970s, subject to imprisonment and deportation. After his election in 1980, President Ronald Reagan introduced the "interdiction" program, designed to intercept Haitian "boat people" attempting to reach the United States and return those deemed ineligible for asylum before they could reach U.S. shores, while also intensifying efforts to jail and deport undocumented Haitians already in the United States. This letter from fifty-seven Haitian women refugees imprisoned in Alderson, West Virginia, to the Washington, DC–based advocacy group, the Haitian Refugee Project, was sent as the refugees launched a twelve-day hunger strike to protest their prolonged incarceration. While this action and other well-publicized hunger strikes by imprisoned Haitian refugees in the same period generated sympathetic media coverage and support from allies, it did not result in their immediate release nor any substantial change in U.S. policy toward the refugees. The letter illuminates the Haitian refugee experience including the reasons the refugees fled Haiti and the fears they had if forced to return, the refugees' understanding of the motives underlying their imprisonment and poor treatment, and the conditions that drove them to initiate their hunger strike.
—*Contributing Editor: Carl Lindskoog*

Appeal to the People of the United States

From the fifty-seven Haitian women imprisoned in Alderson, West Virginia, since October 31, 1981—written as they began a twelve-day hunger strike to protest their five to ten months of incarceration, first in Florida, then in Alderson—incarceration without bond, trial, or representation, separated from their families—for the crime of seeking freedom from the Duvalier dictatorship.

Sick, confused regarding their legal status, yet consistently pressured to submit to Immigration Department proceedings while isolated from potential support systems, they are held hostage as the latest victims of a ten-year practice of racial and ideological discrimination in our refugee policy.

The hunger strike has ended, but five women remained hospitalized, including one who has twice attempted suicide; another has Bell's Palsy; and others require special diets not available at the prison. All have family or sponsors prepared to help them. Despite all this, their faith keeps them going, but their sense of hope diminishes.

"'After ten months of unlawful confinement in a harsh environment,' Judge Carter ruled, 'Justice demands swift remedial action.' Head and heart, he is right. Let them go" (*New York Times*, April 19, 1982, editorial).

April 2, 1982

We are pleased to have you receive our words and wish to bring you up to date about our lives in here—our lives which are becoming more and more aggravated.

Here in West Virginia we now face a very black life. They treat us like animals for no reason at all. They give more importance to a garbage can than they do to us. We face a terrible situation. They treat us like crooks. Which is exactly why we are now going days without any food. Our reasons:

The schedule they give us for eating meals is at 8 in the morning, noon, and 3 P.M. in the afternoon—and then we eat again only in the morning. What is awful is that the food we get for the first two meals is so bad that we sometimes can't eat it. Often, it is only at the 3 o'clock meal that we can find something decent to eat. From 3 P.M. until the next morning is a long time to wait, though. In view of this sometimes we would take something to drink back to the dorm for dinner. The guards, though, locked all our doors (and us inside) and would go from one to the other to search our bodies to see if we had taken anything. If they found food on us, they would take it and throw it into the garbage can. That just goes to show that the trash can is more important than we are. If they had put the food in a place we could have taken it from, we could have said it was on reserve that they placed it there. But no, they had to throw it in the garbage. They treat us like we are thieves. Why such an insult?

From this we can see that they are playing with our personalities—just for a little bit of food.

There are among us those who are seriously ill. The doctor tells them that the INS will not pay for the medicines they need to cure them.

What do we do in such a situation?

Do they have the right to bother us like this? There is one woman among us whom the guards came to bother and knocked her whole head against the walls of the prison and then took her away and locked her in solitary and she hadn't done anything wrong.

Why all these abuses?

Why is it only in Virginia that they act like this? And in the other prisons they free the women. Isn't the life of a human being worth a lot?

That which tears us apart even more is that we understand we must have hearings here in West Virginia. Why don't they include us in the larger hearing? Why do they make us have another?

We would like to know why—among all nations it is only we that they practice this on. How many among all the other countries have had to have a hearing of this kind and have had to be put in a federal criminal prison just for setting foot illegally on U.S. soil?

We all have families who can help us. We the Haitians, our family links are very long. The family is not only composed of mother and child; aunts, uncles, cousins are also very much a part of the family.

We can say that we fled because of the Macoutes, thinking all the time that we would find help. But it seems that we were mistaken. We find Macoutes here as well. We don't know what to do or where we should go.

Because we have no hope any more, given the fact that there is only one death . . . and so . . . we await death because we see that this life has no more meaning for us, no importance, we dedicate ourselves to death.

Watch out. They tell us in the scriptures that if we don't forgive our neighbors, we will no longer be forgiven. . . .

In the hope that you will take pity on the Haitians who suffer in all these jails around the country.

And so, it will be exactly the same for us with the "motherless and fatherless" if we go back. We think that the life of a human being has great importance. It is absolutely impossible for us to go back there. Instead of going there to find death and have our relatives not even know where we are killed, we prefer to die here.

Oh mediator, the INS wants to lead our minds astray about deportation. It is for this reason that we decided to let you know what's really going on here with us in West Virginia.

I hope our letter finds you in good health and that you understand perfectly clearly our situation.

Our best wishes to you.
The imprisoned Haitian refugees
of West Virginia

P.S. We, the refugees of West Virginia, for the past six months they have held us in bondage which is worse for us than for all the others and where they treat us like animals without reason and play continuously with our personalities.

Our misery is becoming worse and worse each day. They give more value to a garbage can than to us. They put us in this place only in order to feed us with lies. Does the life of a human being only depend on food? We, the Haitian refugees of West Virginia, we would prefer to die instead of living only for food.

Friends, consider the facts. Put yourselves in our place and study well our situation. Everyone can see how they're toying with our personalities. You understand well the value of human being's personality because you too have one. We are like all other human beings. We take life from the same blood; we were created by the same God. The only defect we have is that we are black. Is it because of our color that you treat us like this? The difference in color does not mean that we aren't human.

The majority of us are young. In the other prisons they freed the pregnant women, and later those women who have children. But they keep locked up still all the young people. What do you think about the future of young people who suffer all this time in prison? We would like to know if one man is willing to accept the responsibility of ruining the lives of all these young people. Because . . . there are many among us who have decided to kill themselves and who have already tried.

They put us in a place in order to kill us with a slow fire. There are among us many suffering horribly from all sorts of sicknesses: ulcer attacks, eye disease, acid. . . . Others have fractured their feet and have to use crutches. Others have liver illness. They gave us all sickness; when we arrived here we were in perfectly good health. All these illnesses are a result of indigestion, lack of food. That which is awful is that the doctor says he can do nothing for us because INS won't pay for it. Now we feel so humiliated we are simply resigning ourselves to death, and we are awaiting it. The INS told us that President Reagan talked to Duvalier and that if we continued to refuse to go back to Haiti, Reagan could do whatever he wanted with us. We would also like to know if Reagan was the one who ordered the abortions of those women who were pregnant. There were several women among us who were pregnant and they took their babies from their stomachs with pills and injections, telling them that the babies would prevent them from obtaining their freedom and their right to stay in this country.

Are we not human beings like all other human beings? Just because we fled our country to the U.S., is that why we are not considered human?

Or is it because we're black? Don't we have a personality like all other human beings? What did the Haitian refugees do that was a crime so they would get treated in such a way like this? They don't treat refugees from other countries like this.

The only crime we have committed was that we fled from Haiti and landed on American soil illegally. It's not only we who have done such a thing. Many people from other countries come to the U.S. illegally too. We had good reasons for doing what we did. We did it because of the injustice we found in the Haitian government.

Since 1957 the Duvalier regime has been in power. Since this time the government placed at the head of the country a group called the Ton-Ton Macoutes, or the "motherless and fatherless." This group of persons crushed with their feet the people's rights. Since this time we have lost our free will. The only thing this government does is commit wicked acts. We find only disappearances of people—which take place in a blink of the eye. The "motherless and fatherless" don't make any exceptions for anyone, man or woman. Anyone can disappear.

We who are refugees now, seeing how distressing the situation was, could no longer resist the torture, the assaults of the country, the tribulations becoming too difficult to bear. We simply couldn't stand them anymore. Because of this we felt it necessary to take airplanes and to risk our lives on the cruel sea in order to find safety, safety like that we thought existed in the U.S. We knew that that was the country that did not tolerate injustice.

Once we got here, the INS arrested us, and put us here and there in jails around the country, telling us that we did not have worthy political reasons for staying in the U.S. And then they told us the president of the U.S. talked with President Duvalier, and Duvalier said that if we didn't want to return to Haiti, Reagan could do whatever he pleased with us.

Those of us in Virginia, we know the significance of this prison in which we are locked up, and so we lead a very black life. If we could return to Haiti, we would not have to undergo all these catastrophes in prison; misery is not pleasant. What human being would put his/her personality in jeopardy for no good reason? We have let our hearts be tormented by all sorts of misery instead of returning because we know that if we go back we will disappear within the blink of an eye. We have two clear examples of that already.

A couple named Mr. and Mrs. Celix de Jean who could no longer endure the stress in prison finally accepted to go back to Haiti. And now they have been back since November. Until the present time their relatives continue to write them in the prison, even though they are no longer there.

Where is this couple; they are no longer in the U.S.?

2) Also among us there was a young woman named Anoncia Leclerc. She went back to Haiti in January (under pressure to sign voluntary departure forms) and until now her family in Haiti writes her in the prison.

Where is she if she is supposedly in Haiti and no longer in the U.S.? They told these people too that they didn't have a valid political reason to stay here.

Immigration

Tanbou Libète

Tanbou Libète was an activist cultural group launched in New York in the summer of 1971. The group was led by Michel-Rolph Trouillot, who would go on to become a prominent scholar; members included his siblings Évelyne and Lyonel Trouillot as well as Guy-Gérald Ménard and others. The group's official name was Òganizasyon Kiltirèl Revolisyonè Tanbou Libète (Liberty Drum Revolutionary Cultural Organization) and was divided into a performance troupe and a workshop. They produced a total of three records with songs that referenced the sociopolitical realities of Haitians at the time. They performed their music and plays, organized rallies, and tried to raise awareness about the Duvalier regime in order to help bring about its downfall. Although their music is no longer available commercially, several of their songs now constitute part of Haiti's musical patrimony. The best-known version of "Immigration" is perhaps the one later sung by popular folk singer Manno Charlemagne, which became part of his repertoire. The song references various foreign figures involved in Haitian history over the years, from the Spanish to the French and Germans, ending with the Americans. "Immigration" juxtaposes the ways that foreigners have asserted themselves as masters in Haiti with the treatment afforded to Haitian migrants in the United States.

Damn immigration officer
Grabs me by the collar,
Says "You're not a citizen"
He says "Where is?"
I say "What?"
He says "Your alien card."
They stole and they pillaged,
They installed Duvalier,
That's why I ran away.
Today I'm on Broadway
They all cry "Catch him!"

Tell me, my friends,
When the Spanish showed up,

Joseph Emmanuel "Manno" Charlemagne (1948–2017). Photo courtesy of Jacqueline Charles.

And the Indians were forced back
Did Christopher Columbus have an alien card?
Tell me, my friends
When the white Frenchmen came here before 1804
Did Sonthonax have an alien card?
Tell me, my friends,
When they soiled our flag with Captain Batsch's shit
Did the German ships have alien cards?
Tell me, my friends,
During the occupation, when they killed Péralte,
Did the Americans have alien cards?

At home, they tear our skin
Here, they break our backs
Everywhere, they're sole kings.
We're not the ones leading the bull,
It's the bull who's leading us.
But one day small fry
Will become the fat cat.
For another 1804,
Machine guns will crack
And Americans will step back.
Then, in the cemetery, there won't be any alien cards.

Translated by Nadève Ménard

Gender and Politics in Contemporary Haiti

Carolle Charles

The twentieth century saw a wide range of struggles for women's empowerment and equality in Haiti. In this excerpt, Carolle Charles focuses on the politicization and the consequent victimization of Haitian women under Duvalier. Exploring the phenomena of indiscriminate violence and repression as generative of political being, Charles unpacks the means by which the Duvalierist state ironically transformed women into more politicized, albeit more vulnerable, citizens. She traces the changing notions of womanhood that emerged under Duvalier and notes the ways in which women in Haiti were at once targeted and elevated as "equal" citizens. The essay also evokes the rise of women's feminist activism in the Haitian diaspora as a direct response to the new political challenges facing women in the Duvalierist state.

Authoritarian regimes, economic deprivation, poverty, disease, human rights violations, and corruption are not new to Haitian history. Yet the Duvalierist state was a novelty because of the level of state corruption and the degree to which state violence was institutionalized. The Duvalierist state also targeted women in a systematic way, redefining forms of gender oppression. In contrast to other dictatorial regimes of Latin America that appeal to the image of the suffering, self-sacrificing, patriotic mother who has no place in the political arena, the Duvalierist state focused on a "patriotic woman" whose allegiance was first to Duvalier's nation and state. Any woman or man who did not adhere to these policies became an enemy subject to political repression. Duvalier always proclaimed: "My only enemies are those of my country." Ironically, the gendered politics and ideology of the Duvalierist state created a paradox, the increased politicization and raised consciousness of women and their transformation into political agents of social change.

Violence and force always constitute a central feature of any state, yet strong civil societies limit and codify its use. In societies like Haiti where authoritarian regimes have always been part of the sociopolitical landscape, the limits to state violence have tended to be defined by cultural codes. In Haiti, women, children, and old people were defined as political innocents. Because women, in particular, were viewed by the state as being dependents, they had the "privilege" of not being subjected to state violence. Under the

Duvalierist state, however, systematic repressive policies undermined the prevailing conception of women as passive political actors, devoted mothers, and political innocents.

For all political sectors, the coming to power of the Duvaliers marked the entry of ironfisted policies. All political and social organizations were outlawed. Opposition newspapers were shut down; unions were disbanded. More importantly, the Duvalierist state began to use gender as a central element in asserting power and domination. In a country where the ideology of women's weakness was strong, the regime's indiscriminate use of violence against women and children was also a negation of the previous paternalist discourse of the state and a violation of the cultural codes of Haitian patriarchy. Women began to be detained, tortured, exiled, raped, and executed. Ironically, state violence created, for the first time, gender equality.

One of the first actions taken by the Duvalierist military force, the "Tonton Macoutes" (at the time known as "cagoulards"), signaled this departure from past policies. In July 1958, the feminist editor and anti-Duvalierist activist Yvonne Hakime [sic] Rimpel was kidnapped, beaten, and raped. This event—transgressing traditional patriarchal standards—sent a chill through both the political and the journalistic communities. Thereafter, the gender of those in the opposition did not prevent repression or torture. As many women refugees and political exiles testify, women were held accountable not only for their own actions but also for those of their relatives.

The Duvalierist state would restructure and redefine gender roles and representation with two constructed categories of women: a reappropriated historical gender symbol represented by a rebellious slave woman, Marie Jeanne, who as a new constructed category, was transformed into "une fille de la revolution" [sic] (daughter of the revolution) and became an integral part of the state paramilitary forces; and, parallel to the new "Marie Jeanne," another woman—the enemy of the state and the nation. Women who were not loyal to the Duvalierist cause were defined primarily as subversive, unpatriotic, and "unnatural."

Paradoxically, the creation of the category of "Marie Jeannes" gave access to social mobility of [sic] a few women in the black middle class. Yet this form of "state feminism" had a morbid side. For instance, Duvalier nominated a woman as commander-in-chief of its [sic] notorious paramilitary forces, the Tonton Macoutes. Abuse of women by women was the common form of torture for suspected political opponents. . . . All the Duvalierist congresswomen were prominent members of the Tonton Macoutes, giving them access to wealth and privileges.

The Duvalierist state could manipulate gender categories and ideologies for its own political purpose. Silencing women as political citizens, it also appealed to their patriotism. The relationship of the Duvalierist state to gender relations shows how gender role and identity is not static in its social production and representation. What is also important to note is how the state could use gender symbols and discourses as a central element in asserting power and domination.

The level of repression during the dictatorship left no space for the development of an autonomous women's movement. Up to 1965, a few women belonging to leftist organizations continued to mobilize women's sections of these organizations; however, the majority of their activities focused on the national liberation struggle. Similarly, up to 1963, some women trade unionists were still active. Because of the systematic use of state violence by the Duvalierist regime, Haitian women became increasingly aware of their role and were able to situate themselves within the political framework of the struggle for democracy. Yet this new self-definition and sense of having a role to play in the political life of the country could become possible only with the massive immigration of Haitians and creation of many Haitian diasporas in Europe and the Americas.

It is mainly in the Haitian immigrant communities in North America that women were able to reorganize their movement and feminist struggles. In that new political space, Haitian female activists who participated in the struggles against the dictatorship could claim that they too had paid their dues in the struggle against the dictatorship and should gain political recognition. This new consciousness was a form of empowerment that would favor the growth of feminist groups among Haitian women, in particular in the various communities of North America where the new Haitian women's movement often emerged against the resistance of male-controlled political organizations.

VII

Overthrow and Aftermath of Duvalier

> Port-au-Prince is completely bald
> In the street,
> The street that turns right for left,
> Two lone rocks,
> Stones for rainwater
> Streaming down in tatters
> My country is out of control
> Where life gets old
> In chains
> Like a dog
> —Georges Castera, "Lari Pòtoprens"

"Port-au-Prince is completely bald," writes poet Georges Castera in "Lari Pòtoprens" ("The Streets of Port-au-Prince"). Published in 1990, in the aftermath of Jean-Claude Duvalier's exile and the repressive rule of the Conseil National de Gouvernement (CNG), Castera's poetic phrasing highlights the barren economic and political landscape of the nation, its capital city and the intimacy of its streets. Castera's Haiti of the mid- to late 1980s faced some major financial, social, and political challenges. More than half of its citizenry experienced the hardships of extreme poverty and low literacy rates and life expectancy. Stagnant agricultural and manufacturing sectors increased the importation and price of indispensable goods and also exacerbated the already dire unemployment and underemployment situation. Moreover, more than 50 percent of Haiti's urban denizens did not have access to clean drinking water and only 45 percent enjoyed the benefits of electricity. After the dissolution of Jean-Claude Duvalier's executive power, a cadre of international aid organizations and financial regulatory institutions such as the International Monetary Fund, the World Bank and USAID doubled down on their neoliberal economic policies of free market trade, which increased the role of private sector investment and decreased the role of the state in "areas where markets work, or can be made to work." Many scholars of the Caribbean and Latin America argue that this neoliberal approach to underdevelopment ac-

In the wake of Jean-Bertrand Aristide's return to Haiti after a U.S. invasion in 1994, this street artist questioned his political and economic relationship to the United States. Image of 1995 mural reprinted by permission of Pablo Butcher from *Urban Vodou: Politics and Popular Street Art in Haiti.*

celerated class and social inequality in Haiti and in the region, and further exposed the political tensions of a mercurial Haitian government since Duvalier's exile.

The last few lines of Castera's poem paint a picture of the political turmoil that the nation faced from 1986 through the election and fall of President Jean-Bertrand Aristide. "My country is out of control / Where life gets old / in chains / like a dog," writes Castera, who bore witness to the ascendancy of the CNG and subsequently their dependence upon violent and corrupt paramilitary apparatuses similar to the Tonton Macoutes to silence, threaten, and inflict bodily harm on supporters of democracy, free speech, and widespread reform that would aid Haiti's most marginalized groups. Yet despite Castera's reference to Haiti's bare life, its head shaven and exposed to the elements, one can also analyze into this bleak reading of the balding of the Haitian state and nation the need to prune and shear regressive institutions and policies, in addition to the politically inept, so as to foster new growth. The movement of various organizations and coalitions such as Comité National du Congrès des Mouvements Démocratiques (CONACOM) or Komite Nasyonal Kongrè Mouvman Demokratik (KONAKOM) and Blòk Inite Patriotik (BIP) proved to be a formidable counterweight to the regressive approach of the CNG. Their activism helped to pass some of the most progressive reforms of the Haitian

Constitution, such as making Creole an official language of the state and prohibiting Duvalierists from holding public office.

Haitian journalists, such as Jean Dominique, whose peasant advocacy and political life were beautifully captured in the well-received documentary *The Agronomist* (2003), actively critiqued the CNG and military power, which further cemented the power of the press as a cogent and robust venue for dissent. The democratic opposition also included the "radicalized ecclesiastical community" widely known as the Ti Legliz movement. Ti Kominote Legliz embraced a liberation theology approach that seeks to confront and abolish the systematic, capitalist exploitation of the poor by capitalism by centering the teachings of Christianity's messiah, Jesus Christ. Ti Legliz's crowning achievement with the help of the Haitian poor and the country's significant youth population was the election of its most popular leader, Jean-Bertrand Aristide, in 1990. Although Aristide's election came with a groundswell of support, hope, and international recognition, his presidency and his progressive politics proved ephemeral. In September 1991 a coup d'état was organized by Michel François, a major in the army. Subsequently, in October 1994, Aristide returned to power, but had become a proponent of neoliberal principles, which had proved dubious in the 1970s and 1980s.

The post-Duvalier decades, a period of *dechoukaj* (uprooting), provides a lens on Haiti from the street level—where grassroots organizations, Carnival participants, local activists, the Haitian press, and *rara* groups pounded the pavement to amplify their causes and ensure their voices were heard.

Jean-Claude Duvalier
with a Monkey's Tail, 1986

Pablo Butcher

Between 1983 and 1986 Jean-Claude Duvalier's despotic regime had significantly lost its footing. Critiques from Haitian Catholic clergy centered on social and economic injustice. School closings and rising food costs in key cities like Cap Haïtien, Port-au-Prince, and Gonaïves prompted organized public protests. These protests and political objections demonstrated that Jean-Claudisme was an unfulfilled idea of development and that violent tyranny could be openly challenged. Furthermore, much-needed aid from the United States was sidelined in 1984 and 1986 due to the Haitian state's brutal response to impoverished Haitians' political and economic demonstrations. By 1985, Duvalier implemented policies that lacked any real substance. However, state repression gave Duvalier the confidence to publicly remark that his authority was "stiff as a monkey's tail [rèd kou yon ke makak]." When Jean-Claude Duvalier was forcibly exiled in February 1986, graffiti appeared around the capital city soon after with a monkey whose tail had been severed. This image exemplified the fragility of his regime and the courage of activists, students and laypersons who fought to dismantle more than twenty-five years of Duvalier authoritarianism.

Port-au-Prince wall painting, 1990. Artist unknown. Reprinted by permission of Pablo Butcher from *Urban Vodou: Politics and Popular Street Art in Haiti*.

Four Poems

Georges Castera

Georges Castera (born in 1936) is one of Haiti's best-known and most respected con-temporary poets. He first began publishing poetry in the pages of Port-au-Prince's newspapers during the 1950s. His writings thus span several decades. Castera has written from exile (in Europe, then in the United States) as well as from within Haiti, where he now resides. His poems in both French and Creole often reflect the country's political and societal turmoil. Georges Castera is known as a militant leftist and was active in organizing political and cultural resistance to the Duvalier regime during his years in New York. Since his return to Haiti in 1986, he has been very active in the literary sphere, as a speaker, a mentor to younger writers, and a literary critic.

Recurrent themes in Castera's poetry include the city of Port-au-Prince, love, the craft of writing, nature, ecology, and workers' rights. Several of his poems have been put to music. The four poems below were translated from Creole and published over a span of fifteen years.

BLOOD
Let's go watch the bleeding,
Honey.
For once in our lives,
It's not a person bleeding.
For once in the streets,
It's not an animal bleeding.

Let's go watch the bleeding,
Honey.
The sun is setting.

STATE BISCUIT
Like beehives in the sun,
Here we are, hear the screaming.
Soon as night falls, cocks all over the country
Jump up, pecking the sky.

Soon as day breaks, at the corner,
A yellow dog sucks his teeth.

Misery all over the country
Like a strike-anywhere match.

The neighbor says, ever since yesterday, it's weird,
The kids have been playing with rocks.

Soon as he says that,
A sudden shout.

A little skinny one jumps up
Heaves a rock and says:

Some days, standing around,
I'd throw a fucking rock at the state.

PROLETARIAT
Going around taking,
Going around giving,

Washing our hands,
To wipe them on the ground,

Dying for pennies,
In front of grinding machines,

Answering present,
Here and there

With peasants slipping
On sweet potato peels dropped by
Land grabbers

Picking up off the ground,
dividing equally

Fighting to understand,
Fighting nonstop,

We, proletariat,
Are the only class standing.

THE SEA AT PORT-AU-PRINCE

I like to watch the sea come in,
all torn up at the city's feet;
free and unmeasured,
a crazy person, hair standing on end.
I like to watch the delirious sea
barreling like peeled sugarcane.

Huh! A Port-au-Prince sea,
a sea with trash beneath its feet,
a sea arrested for being filthy.

The sea at Port-au-Prince,
a rheumatic grind.
I would let loose with a *rabòday* drum,
the drumbeat of a breastbone falling on its ass
to make it shake its hips
for me,
so at last, it can live up to the name
sea.

Translated by Nadève Ménard

Liberation Theology

Conférence Épiscopale d'Haïti

Though mostly associated with Central and South America, nowhere in the world did liberation theology and the related Catholic "base church communities" have a greater concrete impact than in Haiti. Galvanized after the Second Vatican Council (1962–66) by the Latin American Episcopal Council's reinterpretation of the Gospels at conferences in Medellín in 1968 and Puebla in 1979, liberation theology proclaims that the social mission of the Catholic Church is to exercise a "preferential option for the poor." This inspired the creation of small prayer groups of lay Catholics throughout the region that promoted human rights and protested the injustices of their societies unlike ever before in Church history. In Haiti, the first of these was founded in the rural northeastern town of Mont-Organisé in 1974, and by the early 1980s there were over five thousand throughout the country, a captivating social movement that would come to be known as Ti Legliz (Little Church).

To commemorate the centennial of the Virgin Mary's deliverance of Haiti from a devastating smallpox epidemic, in 1982 the Haitian Catholic bishops organized a Eucharistic and Marian Congress. Another of the Congress's stated goals was "the promotion of human integrity," which in effect bolstered Ti Legliz. With the Congress theme declaring, 'it is necessary for something to change here,' the Duvalier regime quickly realized that the movement posed a serious threat to its dictatorial rule and thus acted to crush Ti Legliz, shutting down its radio broadcasts and persecuting its lay leaders, like Gérard Duclerville, who was arrested and tortured in late December 1982, and its most outspoken priests, like Jean-Bertrand Aristide, whose preaching against the regime resulted in exile abroad, attempts on his life, and the wanton murder of his parishioners.

This was the turbulent social and political context in which Pope John Paul II delivered his influential homily in Port-au-Prince on 9 March 1983. Early on in this sermon, the pope pointed out that all the bishops in Haiti were now "indigenous," that is, Haitian rather than foreign. This was the result of a Duvalierist policy that in the 1960s replaced the French priests and bishops who had long populated the church in the country, but it had in some ways made possible the activism of the church against the regime. The pope celebrated Haiti as "the first in Latin America to proclaim itself independent" and claimed that it was therefore endowed with a "special" calling to develop a social project that made it possible for the people of the country not to have to flee the country seeking work they should be able to find "in their homeland." Some of the pope's strongest lines came in his description of the problems in Haiti, which he suggested had to be addressed by the Catholic Church: "the division, the injustice, the excessive inequality," along with "misery, hunger, widespread fear," and of the struggles of "peasants unable to live from the earth" who therefore headed into overcrowded cities.

The pope's homily was soon be followed by the Haitian Catholic bishops' most assertive statement on human rights, their 11 April declaration entitled "Les fondements de l'intervention de l'Église dans le domaine social et politique" ("Fundamentals of the Intervention of the Church in the Social and Political Domain"). In this speech Haiti's bishops agreed with Pope John Paul II's demand that the Church demonstrate greater concern about the poor. This declaration offered both a powerful critique of the situation in Haiti and a charter for action. "Every violation of human dignity is an offense against the Creator," it announced, and it went on to declare that only when the "common Good" was assured could the "dignity of the human person" be "fully realized." It was, furthermore, impossible to discuss human dignity without "speaking of political society." The bishops, therefore, announced their "right" and "duty" to "intervene in social and political affairs." They also noted that their own political involvement was part of a broader social transformation in which, through radio, movement between rural and urban areas, and the "work of conscientization" among Catholics, "even the most isolated peasant" had become politicized. Their list of what was wrong in Haiti built on that offered by the pope, identifying "deprivation," "all forms of exploitation," and torture and arbitrary detention as evils that had to be protested and challenged.

The speech sent a message to the Ti Legliz and liberation theologians like Father Jean-Bertrand Aristide that the Church would not challenge Catholics opposing the Duvalier regime. Joining forces with a swelling anti-Duvalier student movement, Ti Legliz drew much inspiration from the pope's exhortation that "it is indeed quite necessary for things to change" and from the bishops' declaration, and just three years later indeed they did change: the dynastic Duvalier dictatorship was finally toppled in 1986 after nearly thirty years of presiding over some of the worst brutality and injustice ever orchestrated by a state power in the Americas. And a few years later, Father Aristide was elected president of Haiti in a landslide.

—Contributing Editor: Terry Rey

Homily of Pope John Paul II at the Closing Mass of the Eucharistic Congress of Haiti, 9 March 1983

Dear Brothers and Sisters,

I am here with you in Port-au-Prince, in this country of Haiti that I have long wished to visit, and this grace has finally been accorded to me, to you just as to me, so that together we may worship. . . . Together and with joy, we participate in this feast, me the successor of Peter and pastor of all the faithful, visible principle of the unity of the Church, your bishops, all of whom now are indigenous, and you, men and women, young boys and young girls, infants and the elderly, sons and daughters of this noble Haitian people. Meanwhile, I know well your affinity for the feast and for prayer. I notice it right here thanks to your songs and your enthusiastic responses. I am happy to be part of this occasion and for this I praise God.

But there is more. For the first time during my visits to Latin America I am able to be present in a country in which the majority of the population are people of color, in particular blacks. I perceive in this a sign of great importance, for this has also brought me directly in relation with the third component of the civilization of the peoples of Latin and Central America: people from Africa, profoundly integrated with other indigenous American civilizations and those from Europe. . . .

This country was the first in Latin America to proclaim itself independent. It is thus called, in a special way, to develop, in a climate of liberty, with its own means and through the efforts of all, an endeavor of social and human promotion such that all sons and daughters can readily find work without feeling the necessity of looking for it abroad, and often in oppressive conditions, which they really should be able to find in their homeland.

I thus salute you all and I invite you to prayer and reflection together on the two mysteries that we celebrate today: The Eucharist and Mary.
. . .

You have chosen as the theme for your Congress: "It is necessary for something to change here." And, well, you find in the Eucharist the inspiration, the strength, and the perseverance to engage in his process of change.

It is indeed quite necessary for things to change. In preparing the Congress, the Church has had the courage to face up to the harsh current realities, and I am sure that this is so for all men of goodwill, for all those who deeply love their country. For sure, you have a beautiful country and abundant human resources. And one can speak here of your innate and generous religious sense and the vitality and popular character of the Church. But Christians have also noticed the division, the injustice, the excessive inequality, the degradation of the quality of life, misery, hunger, widespread fear; they have thought of peasants unable to live from the earth, of people overcrowding, without work, in cities, of dispersed families, of victims of various frustrations. For all of this, they are persuaded that there are solutions in solidarity.

. . . Be dignified in your divine relationship with Mary and all that links her to you! Having accepted to renounce sin and to place your faith in Christ, with Mary, lift up your heads and recognize with her the preference of God for the meek, the hungry, and for those who practice love.

I confer you to her, each and every one of you. . . . I ask her to inter-
cede for you before her Son so that a truly peaceful and dignified life
may be granted to you. I also invoke for you the protection of Saint Peter
Claver, the great black saint, glory of your race. . . .

Haitians everywhere, I am with you. I bless you with all my heart.
Courage! Hold Firm! God is with you. Jesus Christ is your brother. The
Holy Spirit is your light! And Mary is your mother!

I supplicate God to bless you, in the name of the Father, the Son, and
the Holy Spirit.

Amen.

Haitian Bishops' Conference, "Fundamentals of the Intervention of the Church in the Social and Political Domain," Port-au-Prince, 11 April 1983

Gathered as the Conference of Bishops, the day after the symposium and the
celebrations of the Eucharistic and Marian Congress, the bishops of Haiti, in
communion with all the Haitian people of God and in response to the call
made by Pope John Paul II in Port-au-Prince in his message of 9 March 1983,
reiterate the principles that govern the intervention of the Church in the social and political domain.

Christ, Light of nations, announces and establishes the Kingdom of God,
Kingdom of Truth and of Love, of Justice and of Peace. In Him, all men have
life and life in abundance. The Church, sacrament of Christ, is "a sign and a
way to carry out the intimate union between God and the unity of the entire
human race" (*Lumen Gentium*). . . .

The first of these principles is that of the dignity and the primacy of the
human person. Created in the image of God, redeemed by Christ's death and
resurrection, the human person has an unsurpassed value, and is superior to
all things: his/her rights and duties are universal and inviolable. . . .

Every violation of human dignity is an offense against the Creator. Every
injustice against man is an affront to Christ himself.

The dignity of the human person is only fully realized to the extent that
the common Good is assured. . . . The Church considers this common Good
"as the first and last law of society" (Leo XIII), and "the soul of every State
of whatever form is the intimate and profound sense of the common Good"
(Pius XII). Those who work in good conscience and honesty for the common
Good engage in an activity of a very high moral standard. They must therefore "keep in mind the needs and the legitimate aspirations of others and
more so of the common Good of the entirety of the human family" (*Gaudium
et Spes* 26, 3).

We cannot treat the question of human dignity and the priority of the
common Good without speaking of political society. . . . These three enunci-

ated principles constitute the major fundamentals of the intervention of the Church in the social and political domain. They likewise justify its engagement in the defense of human rights. . . .

By serving the cause of human rights, the Church promotes the respect of every man as a brother and responds to its mission to be a welcoming place of reconciliation and communion.

It is in this spirit that we intervene in social and political affairs. And we hope that henceforth our Haitian brothers will understand why we have the right and the duty to do so. This intervention of the Haitian Church—which is not, meanwhile, something new—is a response to the aspirations of the Haitian person. These aspirations emerge from a notable change in mindset. Even the most isolated peasant has now become more open to political questions. This new mind-set is due to the mass media, the journeys, and the work of conscientization. . . .

In light of the words of the Holy Father and of the social doctrine of the Church, we exhort you to avoid everything that is counter to the rights of man, in particular:

— all forms of affronts to the eminent dignity of man and woman;
— all forms of illegal deprivation of peasants and town dwellers;
— all forms of exploitation, wage theft, and bribery;
— all forms of usury and illicit enrichment;
— all forms of violation of justice;
— all forms of torture or physical and moral oppression;
— all arbitrary arrests without warrants and of illegal detentions without just cause;

It is also quite apparent that all rights imply duties and, among the principal duties of all members of a community, we underline:

— the respect of the right to life of all human beings, from his/her conception, by avoiding the use of anything that is contrary to his/her development. . . .
— the respect of the right to "an honest and reasonable regulation of births" via the justice system, insofar as divine law approves (*Humanae Vitae* 72);
— the embrace of professional responsibility and conscience;
— the embrace of participation in the promotion of the common Good through social and economic initiatives designed to aid the most needy;
— the spirit of welcoming and sharing;
— the spirit of reconciliation and forgiveness. . . .

This declaration, which will be followed by a Charter of human promotion, is addressed to all of our Haitian brothers and sisters in and out of the country, to the political authorities, to our brothers and sisters of other churches, and finally to all those who work on behalf of the Haitian people.

It is an enormous task. May Our Lady of Perpetual Help, Patroness of Haiti, help us to accomplish it with confidence and courage!

Translated by Terry Rey

On the Movement against Duvalier

Jean Dominique

In this essay, based on his work as a radio journalist and his involvement in the anti-Duvalier movement, Jean Dominique describes the various forms of protest erupting at the time, especially in rural areas. The essay provides a glimpse of the rich forms of organization and mobilization that ultimately toppled the Duvalier regime the following year. His insights into the ways in which religion, both Christian and Vodou, played a role in the opening up of spaces of contestation and liberation are particularly important.

In May and June 1984, cries of "Down with Duvalier" were shouted by angry demonstrators confronting the Haitian dictatorship's police in Gonaïves, in Le Cap, in Hinche, in Bombardopolis. Since then, the popular revolt has kept going. The lifetime presidency, the symbol of the dictatorship, feels directly challenged by the popular masses.

This event is of massive importance, because before now, during twelve years of popular struggle—at first stifled, then open—this question has never been posed. The revolts that took place between 1978 and 1980 in the North and in Artibonite did not openly contest this symbol of absolute power in Haiti. We have entered a new stage.

A new element of the crisis besetting Haiti is emerging from the depths of the country. It is, in fact, the key element. Paradoxically, no one in the "political class" seems—for the time being—able to use this key to the doors to a future without extortion. Everyone—in the middle classes and the bourgeoisie, in the motherland, within the opposition, in the diaspora—walks around repeating: "We are at an impasse."

We are indeed stuck at the level of the political use of this contestation. But meanwhile, it is on the move. . . . It is developing a strategy. Do we understand it? Can we find inspiration in it?

We should have, during the past years, followed the path taken by this rebellion: its origins, its physical and social geography, its stages, its tactics and successive objectives. In fact, though, people have done the opposite: they have ignored, or have wanted to ignore, the fact that for the past twenty-five years our people have been fighting against an ossified social structure.

Jean Léopold Dominique (1930–2000), agronomist, activist, and radio host. Photo courtesy of Michele Montas and Laura Wagner.

We'd rather talk about "food riots" or "spontaneous explosions," or about the "boat people" as a "fleeing population."

In fact, however, what is going on is something totally different. We are seeing the direct intervention into our political life of social classes that have been kept on the margins for sixty years—indeed, for 175 years.

The Appearance of the Maroons

Sixty years ago the last Caco shot his last bullet against the U.S. Marines. Since then, poor peasants—some tenants of small parcels of land, others landless—along with the poor population of the towns have turned in on themselves, indifferent to the political life of a country that excludes them. It was a return to the historical pattern of political marronage.

We know, indeed, that since 1804—silent, mute, gagged, in the fields, in their garden plots, in the slums—the poor, popular classes have been ignored by politicians. They have watched the games, the jousts, the quarrels of the powerful. . . . Everyone claimed to speak for them, only in order to steal from them. They were only able to intervene on extremely rare occasions: Acaau, the Piquets, Salnave, the Cacos. And each intervention brought cruel reprisals against them.

Since the beginning of this century a social project, and a perpetual debate, have agitated the political class. The poor, popular class, the suffering majority, was to be—it was claimed—its ultimate beneficiary. But the result of this endless debate has been the installation in the country of a regime that has systematically organized the pillage, exploitation, spoliation, and dispossession of this popular class in the countryside and the towns. The macoutization of the popular neighborhoods and the backcountry has exposed the final spaces of marronage to the cupidity of the coalition of those in power. The only thing the poor can do is to flee or fight.

For more than fifteen years, without delegating their speech to anyone, instead seeking places to circulate and amplify this speech, the maroon has opened his mouth to say: NO. In 1984, these mouths shouting their rejection of the dictatorship are those of the poor who, slowly, carefully, but resolutely, have conquered—scrap by scrap, a space of protest. . . .

Grénadié alaso

. . . Soldiers have testified about the behavior of the prisoners when they are brought to the garrisons. Under the ropes that trap their arms and legs, though beaten by their guards, they sang old revolutionary songs: "Grénadié alaso, saki mouri zafè rayo . . . " "Charge, Grenadiers, too bad for those who die." . . .

Class Warfare and the War of the Gods

. . . Christian churches have been the backbone of revived popular contestation. To understand this convergence, one has to understand that it marks the crossroads of two different paths. On the one hand priests, preachers, and informed laypeople have carried out a rereading of the Scriptures, of the Bible, a rereading illuminated by the sufferings of the population at the hands of the powerful in this world. Through this rereading, the liberation theology of these Catholics encourages the taking up of political positions alongside the poorest. On the other hand, in their daily life the poor in Haiti have also experienced a cruel alliance between their exploiters, their executioners, and "magical and maleficent" powers.

The enemy, for the peasants of Artibonite for instance, had sneakily and astutely placed what is called "the left hand of Vodou" on its side. Zaccharie Delva, like his master François Duvalier, made himself feared as much through the power of his automatic weapons held by his henchmen as through his aura and mystical terror, carefully maintained through legend, but especially through the network of ritual organization over which he exercised his power. These networks, traditionally clandestine in the Haitian countryside, and which were called Champouèls, Zòbòpes, Vlindbindingues, etc., subjected the peasant to a constant surveillance in his village, at the market, in his *lakou*, but especially in his very soul.

To understand the peasant awakening, to carefully follow the itinerary of its spiritual contestation, we have to understand this moral reversal that he had carried out inside himself, in the face of the pressure of the social, political, military, and mystical forces that exploited and terrorized him.

It is not by chance that, at the time of the revolts in Artibonite, venerable sanctuaries such as Nan Souvenance or Nan Campêche began flourishing once again. It is not by chance that a new fervor carried tens of thousands of pilgrims to Saut d'Eau, the Ville Bonheur, each year. Saut d'Eau, known as the Vierge Miracle, is the town that accepts only those who do no harm to others. A language of popular contestation circulated in all these sites of pilgrimage. Ritual songs and liturgical speech transmitted very different messages from those spread by the Macoutes. Injustice, the exploitation of man's courage, the pitiless cruelty of maleficent powers against disarmed workers—in other words, evil—were all stigmatized, cautiously but constantly. Sometimes sneakily, sometimes openly, allusive *chanson-pointes*[1] carried out a reversal of mystical values, designating the enemy, subtly posing the question: how does one confront the Devil?

It is therefore not by chance that, for the past few years, the voices of the suffering people have found in religious spaces, both the traditional sanctuaries and the Christian churches, a space of liberation. There has been, there too, an upending of the sky. The Macoute high clergy had sought to place God in the service of Duvalier. But today the Church is being slowly subverted through popular contestation.

Translated by Laurent Dubois

Note

1. *Chanson-pointes*, or *chante pwen* in Creole, is translated as a "pointing song." It is a song that makes critical commentary on the nature or personality of an individual or group, often in a parodic or castigatory manner.

Interview with a Young Market Woman

Magalie St. Louis and Nadine André

After Jean-Claude Duvalier's departure in February 1986, Haiti entered a period of intense political struggle. Members of the grassroots democratic movement sought to uproot what remained of the dictatorship, while those opposed to such thorough-going change, including Duvalier loyalists among the business elite, law enforcement, and the military, attempted to rein in the popular uprising, often by using violence. Between September and November 1987, as Haitians were preparing for the first national elections since the end of the almost thirty-year dictatorship, opponents of the popular movement and Duvalier loyalists unleashed a wave of violence which left more than twenty people dead and many more wounded. One week before the scheduled election, individuals identified as macoutes (a term referring to Duvalier's personal militia, the Tontons Macoutes, but also used broadly to refer to those seen as supporting the continuation of "Duvalierism"), attacked the Marché Salomon in Port-au-Prince. More violence on the eve and morning of the vote ultimately led to the election's cancellation. In the campaign of repression market women were targeted because they were known to be key supporters and members of the grassroots movement. This interview, one in a series conducted by journalist Nadine André, provides a firsthand account of the preelection violence of November 1987. It also sheds light on the experience of market women and their families as well as the role of women in the movement, which toppled the Duvalier dictatorship and sought to replace it with a democratic alternative.
—Contributing Editor: Carl Lindskoog

Magalie St. Louis is the seventeen-year-old daughter of a *marchande*, or market woman, who lost everything in the Macoute arson which destroyed the huge Marché Salomon the Sunday before the elections. I had met Magalie the morning before the interview, as relief money raised in New York was being distributed to market women from Marché Salomon. Priests at St. Jean Bosco Church complex in the slum of La Saline organized the distribution. Twenty-nine thousand dollars had been raised, and each woman received thirty-two dollars. I talked with Magalie as her mother waited inside the church for her share. Magalie told me then that the two women had been forced to leave her seven brothers and sisters at home with no food.

NADINE ANDRE: Can you tell me the story of what happened in Marché Salomon? And tell me your name and how old you are?

MAGALIE ST. LOUIS: My name is Magalie and I am seventeen years old.

N. A.: Were you born here?

M. S. L.: Yes, Port-au-Prince is where I was born. What happened at Marché Salomon, well, people came and beat people up and went inside to start the fire. They forced people to go outside the market. They pushed people. People fell down and then ran away. There was a little child, three years old. They told him to say "Viv l'Armé." He couldn't say "Viv l'Armé," he said "Viv l'Arma." Maybe that's why they cracked his skull. They put a big hole in his head.

N. A.: Where were you at that time?

M. S. L.: I was at my house. But when we went in the morning, the people who were in the market, who slept in the market, told us everything that had happened.

N. A.: Where was your mother then?

M. S. L.: She was at home too. She doesn't sleep in the market.

N. A.: But she left her things in the market.

M. S. L.: Yes, she left a lot of things in the market.

N. A.: The market was burned down on Sunday night, right?

M. S. L.: Yes, Sunday night or early Monday morning.

N. A.: And did you find out right then that it had burned down?

M. S. L.: No, not until the morning. There was a man who went around and made everyone wake up, saying "Get up! Fire, fire!" That's probably the reason the fire didn't burn down the people's houses.

N. A.: Do you live near the market?

M. S. L.: I live nearby, but it's still a good distance. But this man went around in his car shouting "Fire, fire!" And people who heard him got up. But we still didn't know where the fire was. It was in the morning that we found out what the fire had done. When it happened there was a woman who began shouting. And there were two policemen standing with—rifles—the army. She ran off. If she hadn't run off, they would have killed her. Because they were the ones who started the fire. So many people lost all their money. So many lost so much. There were some who lost three thousand dollars. Because there were some big merchants in the marketplace. So many people lost their things. Well, that's as much as I can tell you.

N. A.: What did your mother do when she heard that the market had burned down?

M. S. L.: When my mother found out the market had burned down, she was in shock. She started crying and screaming: "What am I going to do with these children? How are we going to live?" And what was she going to do to pay back the debts she owed since the market burned down and all her money was inside? What is she going to do? This was a big blow.

N. A.: How much money did she lose in the fire?

M. S. L.: About five hundred dollars. Money that she had borrowed.

N. A.: And how does that work, *l'escont*, when you borrow money?

M. S. L.: You can borrow $100 for $150. You can also borrow $200 or $300.

N. A.: And where do people borrow the money?

M. S. L.: From a person who has a lot of money. That's what they do for a living.

N. A.: And where are these people?

M. S. L.: Right here in this country, but they have money. That's what they do, they lend money. And that makes them even richer. You borrow it just to get by, but whatever you borrow you have to give much more back.

N. A.: So your mother lost five hundred dollars. What does she sell?

M. S. L.: She sells Fabnack, sandals.

N. A.: About how many sandals did she lose in the fire?

M. S. L.: Many bags of sandals.

N. A.: And where does she buy the sandals?

M. S. L.: She buys them from someone who has gone to the Dominican Republic, because she doesn't have enough money yet to make the trip herself. She buys them from a person who has just made the round trip.

N. A.: When she buys them, how much do they cost?

M. S. L.: I don't know, because when she buys them, she buys a whole lot of them. She's the only one who could tell you how much they cost.

N. A.: And when she sells them, how much are they?

M. S. L.: Some sell for two dollars, some sell for three dollars. Both those prices. And some others cost three, six, or seven gourdes.

N. A.: And how many can she sell in one day?

M. S. L.: Sometimes she'll sell forty dollars' worth in a day. If it's a good day, she can sell sixty dollars' worth. But if it's not a good day, she may sell thirty dollars' worth.

N. A.: And what does your mother do in the morning? What time does she have to get up?

M. S. L.: To go sell? She gets up at six in the morning.

N. A.: And do you go with her?

M. S. L.: When I heard that the market had burned down, I went with her to see it.

N. A.: And what did your mother say to you when she saw it?

M. S. L.: She screamed and asked what would become of her, with all her children who have no father. She cried. It really hurt her.

N. A.: A lot of other women were crying too?

M. S. L.: Yes, a lot of other women were crying. They put their hands on their heads and spoke on the radio, asking for help, asking how they could get by in this country with so many problems, where they receive such blows? And it wasn't anyone else, those men were the ones who committed these sins. They know that this country is no good, but in spite of that, they have no mercy. They keep on causing trouble.

N. A.: And your father? You said that he had died?

M. S. L.: Yes, my father died last January 4th. He had a stroke. He was sick with high blood pressure. He'd had it twice before. The third time they took him to the hospital, and he died. His body was still strong. He died without becoming thin or sickly.

N. A.: How old was he?

M. S. L.: My father was forty-two.

N. A.: And how many brothers and sisters do you have?

M. S. L.: I have three sisters and four brothers. Altogether my mother has eight. I'm the oldest. The next one is fifteen.

N. A.: So what can your mother do to get by with all her children?

M. S. L.: So far she hasn't done anything, because she doesn't want to borrow money again and add to what she already owes.

N. A.: And how will she be able to pay back what she owes?

M. S. L.: God is the only one who knows what a person can do. Because we don't know.

N. A.: And there are many other women in the same situation, right?

M. S. L.: Yes, some people lost their money, but others lost money they had borrowed.

N. A.: And the market isn't being used?

M. S. L.: Just on the sides, people come to sell things on the ground.

N. A.: And what does your mother do now?

M. S. L.: Now she doesn't do anything. She can't sell because she doesn't have any money.

N. A.: And what do you do to get food for all the children?

M. S. L.: What we do, for example—we might go to a priest and explain the problem, and he might give five or ten gourdes (one or two dollars). Or he might give fifteen or twenty gourdes. But if we don't get that, we just stay as we are. We borrowed money, but we couldn't get any money to pay it back. We were forced to sell the few things we had when the fire killed us. We were forced to sell things. For example, if we bought something for fifteen gourdes, we have to give it to someone else for five gourdes.

N. A.: What did you sell?

M. S. L.: What we had. When my father died, he left a radio. My father bought it for one hundred dollars. We sold it for forty dollars. Because life has become harder for us. Because when you have something, you sell it even though you're not sick. It's not your fault. You might have a gourde (twenty cents) one day, and the next day you have a gourde but you can't stay like that, the whole rest of your life, hungry.

Seamstress outside in Jean Rabel, northern Haiti, 2003. Photo courtesy of Noelle Théard.

N. A.: Do you rent your house?

M. S. L.: Yes.

N. A.: And how much is it?

M. S. L.: One hundred dollars.

N. A.: Each month, or each year?

M. S. L.: Every six months. And when the six months are up, we still don't know where we're going to go, because it's not long before it's up. Because you can only be fifteen days late after six months, or they'll put you out.

N. A.: And who's the owner of the house?

M. S. L.: Just a person who owns it. But as soon as the six months are up, you only have fifteen days afterward to figure something out before they close up that house and then rent it to someone else.

N. A.: And all the children, none of them are sick?

M. S. L.: No, thanks to God.

N. A.: So, what hope do you have for Haiti?

M. S. L.: My hope is that this country will change, that there will be a president who understands us, who understands the misery of the poor people, who understands what needs to be done for us. Because things are really bad for us. We need someone who can understand, who has pity, who's conscious, so that the country can improve. If that's not what happens, everyone is without hope.

N. A.: But what are all of the market women from Marché Salomon saying now, after the elections?

M. S. L.: Everyone is praying to God for a good president, to give them back what they lost and rebuild the market. And when there's a president they'd like to receive the money that they lost.

N. A.: You told me that women were part of all the activity around February 7th.

M. S. L.: Yes. A lot of women were part of the demonstrations around February 7th, they were in the front. Some of them died. And women also had their own demonstrations, separate from the other ones, by themselves. And when there were meetings, the women had meetings and rallies, they marched, and they died too. Because they were fired on too.

N. A.: How did that make you feel?

M. S. L.: It makes you stronger when you see others who died. You become stronger, more solid.

N. A.: Are you proud that Haitian women are standing up like that?

M. S. L.: Yes, yes. They're standing up like that because they have the hope that they will be free, and they're not afraid of dying.

N. A.: And they don't want men to dominate them?

M. S. L.: No, they don't want that. They want women to have the same rights as men, for women to be treated the same as men. The same way a man can be president, a woman can be president too.

N. A.: And it's women as well who have to change things.

M. S. L.: Yes, change this situation.

Nou vle

Ansy Dérose

This 1987 song by legendary Haitian crooner Ansy Dérose contains a wish list of what Haitians wanted for their country at the end of the Duvalier dictatorship. It criticizes several flaws of Haitian society and proposes some solutions to recurring problems. Released prior to the presidential elections of 1987, "Nou vle" quickly became one of the most popular songs on both radio and television. Indeed, in the contemporary period, whenever elections are on the horizon in Haiti, "Nou vle" can be heard on the radio.

We want
We want, we want our country to
Change, change with dignity.
Why, why should we copy
What other places have rejected?
We want, we want our country to
Be beautiful, be sweet for its children.

I
We're not just speaking French,
Or speaking empty words.
We want to work, to grab our freedom.
We don't want politicians using us
To get rich—for their own glory, their own purposes.
Our country is sick, it's taken to bed; we have to bring it back to life.
We can treat it with patience and knowledge.
We don't want a bunch of demagogues coming to bluff us,
We want technicians who know how to use their hands.
Together, together we'll bury all our bad habits.
Together, together we'll clean the dirty consciences.

II

All those who are waiting, who are discouraged,
All those who are afraid to fight, all those already in the fight,
For us to save ourselves, we have to sit and think
To measure the length of our chains.
We have to find a way to break free.

We want, we want our country to
Change, change with dignity.
Why, why should we copy
What other places have rejected?
We want, we want our country to
Be beautiful, be sweet for its children.

III

We've decided the face of our country must change
With faith, with courage, with our own strength.
The time has come for us all to pitch in:
We have to empty our sacks
To show what we've brought, what we know how to do.
We don't need a dictatorship that's destroying lives,
Nor anyone who thinks he's God.
The respect we have for each other will bring all hands together—
No weapon, nor evildoer can withstand us.
Together, together we'll bury all our bad habits.
Together, together we'll clean the dirty consciences.

IV

Jean is a candidate, Joseph is a candidate, Émile is a candidate:
They all want to be president.
There is no one who can save us.
Putting heads together is the first remedy.
If we put our heads together, we'll find a way.

We want, we want our country to
Change, change with dignity.
Why, why should we eat
What other places have thrown away?
We want, we want our country to
Change, change for its children.
We want, we want our country to
Change, change with dignity.
Why, why should we copy

What other places have rejected?
We want, we want our country to
Be beautiful, be sweet for its children.
We want, yes we want our country to change.
We want, yes we want our country to change.

Translated by Nadève Ménard

The Constitution of 1987

Government of Haiti

The 1987 Constitution of Haiti was produced directly after the overthrow of Jean-Claude Duvalier, and in many ways its goal was to create a political order that would resist and reverse the previous thirty years of dictatorship. It included several provisions directly undoing Duvalierist policy, notably changing the flag back to blue and red (François Duvalier had made it black and red) and outlawing the "cult of personality." Politically, it substantially reduced the power of the executive, while also articulating the need for a broad range of social rights including access to education and efforts against environmental degradation. It was produced in two languages, French and Creole. Following a process started in 2009, the 1987 Constitution was amended in 2011, most notably to allow for dual citizenship, although to hold certain high offices, such as president, minister, deputy, or senator, one must only be a citizen of Haiti. The amended constitution also establishes a quota of 30 percent of women in the public services.[1]

Preamble

The Haitian people proclaim this constitution in order to:

Ensure their inalienable and enduring rights to life, liberty and the pursuit of happiness; in conformity with the Act of Independence of 1804 and the Universal Declaration of the Rights of Man of 1948.

Constitute a socially just, economically free, and politically independent Haitian nation.

Reestablish a strong and stable State, capable of protecting the country's values, traditions, sovereignty, independence, and national vision.

Implant democracy, which entails ideological pluralism and political rotation, and affirm the inviolable rights of the Haitian people.

Strengthen national unity by eliminating all discrimination between the urban and rural populations, by accepting the community of languages and culture, and by recognizing the right to progress, information, education, health, employment, and leisure for all citizens.

Ensure the separation and the harmonious distribution of the powers of the State in service of the fundamental interests and priorities of the Nation.

Set up a system of government based on fundamental liberties, and the respect for human rights, social peace, economic equity, concerted action, and participation of the entire population in major decisions affecting the life of the nation, through effective decentralization.

Title I: The Republic of Haiti. Its Emblem and Its Symbols

Chapter I: The Republic of Haiti

Article 1: Haiti is an indivisible, sovereign, independent, cooperatist, free, democratic, and social republic. . . .

. . .

Article 5: All Haitians are united by a common language: Creole.

Creole and French are the official languages of the Republic. . . .

Article 7: The cult of the personality is categorically forbidden. Effigies and names of living personalities may not appear on currency, stamps, seals, public buildings, streets, or works of art.

Chapter II: Basic Rights

SECTION A: RIGHT TO LIFE AND HEALTH

Article 19: The State has the absolute obligation to guarantee the right to life, health, and respect of the human person for all citizens without distinction, in conformity with the Universal Declaration of the Rights of Man.

Article 20: The death penalty is abolished in all cases. . . .

SECTION C: FREEDOM OF EXPRESSION

Article 28: Every Haitian (man or woman) has the right to express his opinions freely on any matter by any means he chooses.

Article 28-1: Journalists shall freely exercise their profession within the framework of the law. Such exercise may not be subject to any authorization or censorship, except in the case of war.

. . .

SECTION F: EDUCATION AND TEACHING

Article 32: The State guarantees the right to education. It sees to the physical, intellectual, moral, professional, social, and civic training of the population.

Article 32-1: Education is the responsibility of the State and its territorial divisions. They must make schooling available to all, free of charge, and ensure that public and private sector teachers are properly trained.

Title VI: Independent Institutions

Chapter I: The Permanent Electoral Council

Article 191: The Electoral Council is responsible for organizing and controlling in complete independence all electoral procedures throughout the territory of the Republic until the results of the election are announced.

. . .

Article 197: The Permanent Electoral Council shall rule on all disputes arising either in elections or in the enforcement or the violation of the Electoral Law, subject to any legal prosecution undertaken against an offender or offenders before the courts of competent jurisdiction.

. . .

Chapter V: The University—the Academy—Culture

Article 208: Higher education is free. It is provided by the University of the Haitian State (Université d'État d'Haïti), which is autonomous and by public and private institutions of higher education accredited by the State.

Article 209: The State must finance the operation and development of the Haitian State University and the public institutions of higher education. Their organization and their location must be planned from the perspective of regional development.

Article 210: The establishment of research centers must be encouraged.

Article 211: Authorization for the operation of universities and private institutions of higher education is subject to the technical approval of the Council of the State University, to a majority of Haitian participation in terms of capital and faculty, and to the obligation to teach primarily in an official language of the country.

Article 211-1: The universities and the private and public institutions of higher education provide academic and practical instruction adapted to the trends and requirements of national development.

Article 212: An organic law regulates the establishment, location and operation of university and public and private institutions of higher learning in the country.

Article 213: A Haitian Academy shall be established to standardize the Creole language and facilitate its scientific and harmonious development.

. . .

Article 215: Archaeological, historical, cultural, folklore, and architectural treasures in the country, which bear witness to the grandeur of our past, are part of the national heritage. Consequently, monuments, ruins, sites of our ancestors' great feats of arms, famous centers of our African beliefs, and all vestiges of the past are placed under the protection of the State.

Chapter I: Economics and Agriculture

Article 245: Economic freedom shall be guaranteed so long as it is not contrary to public interest.

The State shall protect private enterprise and shall endeavor to see that it develops under the conditions necessary to increase the national wealth in such a way as to ensure the participation of the largest possible number of persons in the benefits of this wealth.

Article 246: The State encourages in rural and urban areas the formation of cooperatives for production, processing of raw materials, and the entrepreneurial spirit to promote the accumulation of national capital to ensure continuous development.

Article 247: Agriculture, which is the main source of the Nation's wealth, is a guarantee of the well-being of the people and the socioeconomic progress of the Nation.

Article 248: A special agency to be known as THE NATIONAL INSTITUTE OF AGRARIAN REFORM shall be established to organize an overhaul of land tenure and to implement an agrarian reform to benefit those who actually work the land. This Institute shall draw up an agrarian policy geared to optimizing productivity by constructing infrastructure aimed at the protection and management of the land.

. . .

Article 251: The import of foodstuffs and their by-products that are produced in sufficient quantity in the national territory is forbidden, except in the event of force majeure.

. . .

Chapter II: The Environment

Article 253: Since the environment is the natural framework of the life of the people, any practices that might disturb its ecological balance are strictly forbidden.

Article 254: The State shall organize the enhancement of natural sites to ensure their protection and make them accessible to all.

Article 255: To protect forest reserves and expand plant cover, the State encourages the development of local sources of energy: solar, wind, and others.

Article 256: Within the framework of protecting the environment and public education, the State has the obligation to proceed to establish and maintain botanical and zoological gardens at certain sites in its territory.

Note

1. We have reproduced the version available at Political Database of the Americas, George-town University, http://pdba.georgetown.edu/Constitutions/Haiti/haiti1987fr.html, but have made some corrections to the translation.

Rara Songs of Political Protest

Various Groups

On 11 September 1988, a notorious act of political violence took place in Haiti. A band of about one hundred youths armed with rocks, machetes, and pistols ambushed the St. Jean Bosco Church during Father Jean-Bertrand Aristide's Sunday mass. They slashed their way through the pews in search of Aristide. They killed thirteen people and injured seventy, including a pregnant woman, but Aristide escaped unharmed. It was soon revealed that Port-au-Prince mayor Frank Romain, with the complicity of the ruling Conseil National de Gouvernement (CNG), had employed youth groups from the shantytowns to carry out the attack. The following day the most prominent youth leader, Gwo Schiller, appeared on national television with five of his accomplices to boast about the crime, and a week later CNG leader General Henri Namphy visited the assailants to publicly congratulate them. The horrific crime and shameless perpetrators shocked the nation, and the CNG leader General Namphy was ousted in a coup on 17 September 1988. Soon this song became the battle cry for exacting revenge on Gwo Schiller and his accomplices. Crowds from the shantytowns tracked down and killed Gwo Schiller and six accomplices, burning their bodies in front of the church. The song has endured as a sign of the power of the popular movement for democracy in Haiti. Sung in the streets, this song was not recorded or distributed commercially. Chelsey Kivland recorded the following version during fieldwork with musicians in Bel Air in 2013.
—Contributing Editor: Chelsey Kivland

> The Schiller Family
> If you're there
> Schiller will die
> It's in the plan
> Tomorrow at 4 P.M.
> Come with the patriots
> Go before St. Jean Bosco
> You'll find Schiller

"Rara band in Fermathe, Haiti, 1993." This Holy Week *rara* performance in the village of Fermathe is called La Belle Fraicheur de l'Anglade. Image courtesy of Elizabeth McAlister.

In the fall of 1994, the United States and its allies finalized plans to return President Jean-Bertrand Aristide to power following his ouster in a military coup d'état on 30 September 1991. Twenty thousand U.S. troops began landing in Port-au-Prince on 20 September 1994, and soon thereafter rara groups in Bel Air, La Saline, and other poor districts in the capital began taking to the streets with this song. It called on General Hugh Shelton, who led the UN-authorized Operation Uphold Democracy, to arrest the de facto government's leaders and soldiers who had, since 1991, killed thousands of residents in these pro-Aristide neighborhoods. Prior to the intervention, the United States had negotiated lenient treatment for the de facto leaders, and this song condemned the troops' willingness to cooperate with what residents perceived as a criminal regime. The song proclaims that the foreign troops should, like residents, demonstrate fearlessness because the de facto soldiers—including a Bel Air officer known as "the man with the grenade"—were panicking. By October, Operation Uphold Democracy escalated its efforts to dismantle the de facto regime, and they restored Aristide to the presidency on 15 October 1994. This street song was not recorded or distributed commercially. Chelsey Kivland recorded the following version during fieldwork in Bel Air in 2013.

We call them, the UN
Captain Shelton, arrest them
We are not afraid of the army's big guns

We will still arrest them
The man with the grenade panics
We call them, Captain, arrest them
Those who aren't Lavalas are panicking
We call them, Titid
Arrest them, Signor

Translated by Chelsey Kivland

Haitians March against an FDA Ban on Haitian Blood Donations

Richard Elkins

Within a sea of blue and red placards and flags more than fifty thousand people, mostly Haitian and Haitian American, marched across the iconic Brooklyn Bridge in New York City on 20 April 1990 in response to a February ruling from the U.S. Food and Drug Administration that banned Haitians and sub-Saharan Africans in the United States from donating blood. Chanting "Down with the FDA" and singing the Haitian national anthem, among other songs, protesters demonstrated their disgust for a policy that unjustly and unscientifically targeted a nation and its people and further stigmatized them. During the 1980s and early 1990s Americans faced a serious public health challenge with the rapid spread of HIV and AIDS. By January 1990 more than 120,000 U.S. citizens were battling with the virus and the disease, along with the stigma of being infected. The HIV and AIDS epidemic made many fearful and caused hundreds to postpone necessary surgeries, avoid giving or receiving blood, and/or vilify those who were infected. Specific groups were zeroed in on by the Centers for Disease Control (CDC) in 1983 and perceived as transmitters of the disease—homosexuals, hemophiliacs, hypodermic needle users, and Haitians—"the Four H group," or "the 4Hs," became a popular term of the day. According to several health reports, by 1990, Haitians and Haitian Americans in New York City who contracted AIDS amounted to 550 cases out of more than 24,000. Additionally, the World Health Organization documented that Haiti ranked ninth out of forty-four nations in AIDS cases, but the top eight countries were not excluded from donating blood in the United States.

The Brooklyn Bridge march and the smaller yet still significant protests in Miami, Boston, and the Grand Army Plaza area of Brooklyn, New York, where from a few hundred to eight thousand people rallied, amplified growing concerns about how the FDA policy would impact already fragile Haitian lives in the U.S., Canada, and Haiti. The effects were widespread and exemplified how fear drove actions across sectors and groups: Haitian domestic workers in the suburbs of New York City were fired. Bus drivers in Broward County, Florida, wore latex gloves out of fear of being infected

Demonstrators assemble in front of the New York City Department of Health building to protest an FDA ban on Haitian blood donations. Photograph by Richard Elkins, 1990. Reprinted by permission of the Associated Press.

while collecting bus transfers from passengers. Young Haitian students in elementary schools endured constant harrassment and epithets. Yet due to overwhelming pressure from Haitian groups and key public figures who challenged the legitimacy and soundness of the FDA policy, the ban was officially lifted a few months later in December 1990.

The Peasants' Movement

Tèt Kole

These two selections, "Peasants' Movement Holds News Conference" and "Further on Peasants' Position," both from July 1990, reflect some of the major tendencies within the popular movement, dynamic campaigns by both the urban religious and agriculture-based working poor for political and economic change. They reflect the decentralized nature of the movement. The selections are based on a news conference by Tèt Kole and transcribed by the Foreign Broadcast Information Service. The meeting by Tèt Kole pou Tabli youn Mouvman Ti Peyizan (Tèt Kole) provided speakers from throughout the various communal sections of Haiti with a space for discussing the historical exclusion of the "people" from political processes, and their current marginalization. Tèt Kole, and the peasant movement more broadly, represent one element of the popular movement that eventually became Lavalas. The movement also included the various popular organizations, committees, and vigilance brigades being organized in the bidonvilles of Port-au-Prince.

The decentralized nature of the movement goes hand in hand with its rejection of traditional social and political institutions. The name "Lavalas" did not initially refer to a political party. Instead it was a symbolic term used to reflect the coming together of impoverished and working-class people to challenge and "wash away" the traditional institutions of power and privilege that had oppressed them for centuries. It was an acknowledgment of the power that the majority had once mobilized to move toward a common agenda.

In this instance, the common agenda was to organize against elections not directed by the interests of the people. Tèt Kole argued that the majority of the population was being ignored, both by the traditional political parties and by the international community. They rejected being dragged into elections that existed to further others' interests and not their own. They viewed the democracy being clamored for by the Haitian elite and the international community as a democracy that went against the interests of the people; a democracy where the people had no voice. Instead, the peasants, like the other sectors of the popular movement, called for the direct participation of the poor and working classes in decision-making processes. Tèt Kole called on the poor masses to organize themselves across Haitian society, to establish true popular organizations that they controlled in order to push for their own interests, while also calling for a single course of action guided by the Haitian people's demands for a people's alternative.

—Contributing Editor: Dimmy Herard

The democracy that people wish to establish in Haiti will remain a sham, for the peasants are not being listened to. That is the conclusion reached by the association known as Tèt Kole pou Tabli youn Mouvman Ti Peyizan (Solidarity with a View to Establishing a Movement of Small Peasant Farmers).

The spokesmen for this movement, which today has thirty-five thousand adherents, condemned at a news conference this morning the shunting aside, in connection with major national decisions, of the class that constitutes a majority of the population of Haiti.

Tèt Kole also feels that the existing lack of consensus among the different sectors has caused Haiti a great deal of damage.

The speakers, who come from Haiti's different communal sections, also spoke harshly of the meddling by foreign powers in the nation's internal affairs. Tèt Kole also advocated forming people's tribunals to judge and condemn all those who have contributed to leading the country into its current state of lethargy. The association feels not a single one of the serious trials being demanded today is possible. The association also believes that the holding of elections absolutely will not change much in the situation of the peasants throughout Haiti.

[Begin Recording] [FIRST SPEAKER] People have never sat down, never reached a consensus, with the masses to see what they want, to hear their demands, so we can arrive at a real, true liberation. They continued, and we saw on 17 September, saw a battle fought to oust Namphy. Avril took power, but things continued exactly the same. This resulted in 13 March, just the other day, with the population still on the outside looking in, never participating to really know that what the people decides is what must be done. We in Tèt Kole notice that the reason all this happens is because big interests are being defended, and the interest of the masses do not lie in the same direction as those of the big shots and of other big countries. And if the Haitian people were to come and set in place a government that was in its interests, this would mean many other interests would be threatened. That is why they always avoid, brush aside all the people's demands, as well as the population itself.

In that same document, we also discuss that situation. . . . If we do not wage a proper battle against the Macoutes, we will always have to continue to fight, because we will never manage to "get" the enemies we have in the country. . . . For example, we peasants have the big landowners and the section chiefs, who are still there, giving us problems. We also have the big countries, which are supporting a corrupt bourgeoisie and which are putting governments in power that smash, destroy, the country and the population.

[SECOND SPEAKER] We already understand that elections, for us peasants, will always be something that is organized up in the air above our heads. . . . I mean, they make us go and say yes to something they already had all planned out. Thus, things leave us cold. . . . Thus, the way peasants see things, elections are never to our advantage! . . . However, peasants who are beginning to become aware of what the situation is really like, are taking a stand to show that elections are not going to change anything for them. [End Recording]

Another subject brought up at this press conference by Tèt Kole: the repressive role of the section chiefs in the countryside. Tèt Kole announces that an important document on the section chiefs, who sow terror among peasants, is going to be published soon.

Regarding the commemoration of the third anniversary of the Jean-Rabel massacre, Tèt Kole invites the peasants throughout Haiti to reflect and to mobilize.

Further on Peasants' Position, 18 July 1990

For as long as can be remembered, and to this day, political decisions . . . have never gone the way the Haitian people seek. This was the conclusion of Tèt Kole after reflection and an analysis of the current juncture in Haiti.

According to Tèt Kole, Haiti's political, economic, and social crisis has now become a great battle to the death, with the presence of the Macoutes, who are doing everything they can to take back political power totally and finally. There is a big threat of death hanging over the head of all the nation's true popular organizations and of the Haitian masses which are struggling to liberate the nation from all forms of repression, exploitation, and domination that Haitian big shots and big foreign powers have established here. All that is to protect such parties' own interests against the will of the Haitian people.

Tèt Kole feels the Macoutes' plan cannot be uprooted as long as they allow big shots, politicians who are in bed with the Americans, French, and Canadians, to drag the Haitian masses into the battle along their own path—the path of such people's own interests and own ideas.

[BEGIN RECORDING] . . . The democracy they want for the Haitian people is a democracy that goes against that people's interests, one in which the Haitian people themselves do not really participate, in which they are not really allowed to speak up. . . .

We feel that certain big countries encourage such a democracy, especially elections for the kind of democracy they want us to have. There are also other sectors in the country, such as the church, the merchants, and the bourgeoisie, who support such a democracy because such a democracy is not in the interest of the Haitian masses. The Haitian people are alone in their struggle. . . .

Tèt Kole also talked about next 23 July, the third anniversary of the big Jean-Rabel peasant massacre, and took advantage of the opportunity to ask peasants in the four corners of Haiti to rise up resoundingly in protest during the week of solidarity beginning 23 July. He said they are counting on the solidarity of all other serious organizations, so that the current juncture will not smother the cry for the justice they are demanding for other peasants who are being victimized.

Tèt Kole encourages the poor . . . to organize themselves even better: to set up all kinds of organizations of their own in their neighborhoods, on the estates they live on, and everywhere. The true popular organizations are our own organizations that we ourselves control and guide in our own interests and in the interests of the entire Haitian people, organizations that do not take orders from any phony, crooked wheeler-dealer democrats, and that are not in cahoots with any such people. Never forget that all forms of protest that we may organize should be effected using a single compass, a single guide: the Haitian people's fundamental demands. Do not let any politician, any chameleon that changes color every day, play in your heads.

Furthermore, the Macoutes control the nation's judicial system. . . .

Tèt Kole asks that you denounce, and rise up against, all forms of meddling in Haiti's affairs by foreign governments and embassies. They will take advantage of the confusion created by crooked wheeler-dealer big shots and politicians in Haiti to trample underfoot the independence of the Haitian people.

Tèt Kole ends its declaration by saying: Cooperate everywhere, all over Haiti and at all levels, with all truly popular organizations so we can, in proper meetings, reach agreement on a single watchword, a single course of action. That is the true path that will lead us to the proper conditions that will allow us to attain our own alternative, a people's alternative. To really attain this, we must never forget that our only force is truly popular organizations.

Aristide and the Popular Movement

Jean-Bertrand Aristide

In the following transcriptions from radio programs aired in September and October 1990, Jean-Bertrand Aristide (popularly known as "Titid") discusses why he decided to take part in the elections as "the people's alternative." While he rejects the notion that these elections can be a panacea for Haiti's problems, he presents them as an opportunity for the popular movement to offer a unified agenda and present its demands. These pronouncements showcase the ways in which Aristide used vivid images and metaphors, along with nicknames and layered cultural references, in making his political arguments. They also give us insight into how he believed change in Haiti would happen: not through the bargaining and negotiating that occurred in legislative bodies, but rather through popular pressure placed on the powerful by the people organizing themselves and presenting their demands on the streets.

In the first interview, which took place before Aristide announced his candidacy, he criticized the actions of groups he considered were aiming to make sure the election did not allow for the expression of the popular will, vividly describing one political group as a champwèl, *or secret society, group that was doing evil to the country: "They have stolen, plundered, and committed so many crimes." They were doing so, he went on, because they were in the "pay of U.S. imperialism." Using a Creole nickname, he mentioned the U.S. ambassador at the time, Alvin Adams, as someone with clear power over the elections who had to be pushed to negotiate through popular participation. The army, he further argued, was complicit in political killings and was the "flunky" of the U.S. government and Ambassador Adams. He summed up the forces arrayed against the popular movement: "Little bosses are the flunkies of the big bosses, and the big bosses the flunkies of the big imperialists."*

In his 12 October pronouncement, Aristide issued a call for unity, which he argued could make the people "an avalanche." "A fork cannot be used for drinking soup," he declared. And the people had to either "take over the elections," making them truly into an expression of democracy, or else reject them entirely. As he argued in his 25 October pronouncement, issued just hours after he had declared his own candidacy for president, the goal of the Macoutes who were seeking to maintain an authoritarian regime was to organize "their kind of elections," which "they will later describe as democratic" but which would not allow for true participation and would only bring in "the same criminals, the same Macoutes, this time in disguise." Haiti was at a

"crossroads," and there was an opportunity to use the elections as part of a "struggle to build a true democracy." He also celebrated Cuba as a place that had shown that it could "stand up to the world with dignity" and pursue "social justice" and equality. Ultimately, he declared, there was an opportunity to fight the imperialism of the United States and the legacies of older imperialism, and for Haiti to "demand a little of what has been taken from us from the period of colonization," as well as through "the colonization that today is portrayed as democracy."
—Contributing Editor: Dimmy Herard

Father Aristide Holds News Conference, 7 September 1990

Father Jean-Bertrand Aristide held a news conference yesterday [6 September] during which Titide announced maneuvers aimed at breaking up the Provisional Electoral Council. Here is Marcus Plaisimond's report.

[Plaisimond:] . . . He made strong statements regarding the second anniversary of the Saint Jean Bosco massacre, insecurity, and the nation's political situation.

Paying homage to all those who have fallen over the past four years, particularly journalists, the head of the popular church declares he harbors no hatred against the perpetrators, much less against those who issued the orders. He even admitted that two of the members of the Armed Forces who entered his room after the massacre acted decently toward him: former Colonel Leone Qualo and Major Renaud Simbert, now deceased. This does not, however, absolve the FADH for the acts for which they are directly or indirectly responsible, added Aristide. Speaking on the elections, Father Aristide denounced ongoing maneuvers aimed at sacking two institutions and holding elections similar to those of 17 January 1988.

[ARISTIDE:] The forces of evil, and Ertha,[1] who is wearing a red dress, and not a white one like she is in the habit of claiming, are like a *chanpwèl* group.[2]

I say these people are like a vile *chanpwèl* group in the sense that they have stolen, plundered, and committed so many crimes . . . .
The way I see it, Ertha is heading this group, wearing her red dress. They are going to try to do away with the current CEP and ignore the State Council, and hold elections without the CEP and without the State Council, sort of saying to the people: Come and get it. You do not want it? Well, then leave it! And if the population should snarl, what they [. . .] might try to do is to replace Ertha with someone else; maybe someone the population does not want

. . .

Regarding the rally held by the National Alliance for Democracy and Progress in Saint-Marc, Father Aristide noted that extreme poverty and hunger have led people to think that elections will be held with dollars. Nevertheless, there's something positive for the population did not go along with it.

The big political parties are not great in size, as President Trouillot claims. Rather, they are big in the sense that they are in the pay of U.S. imperialism.

[Plaisimond:] Father Aristide also expressed his opinion on the initiative launched by the Unity Committee for the Respect of the Constitution.

ARISTIDE: The organization that launched the alternative has made an effort, a very good effort. I think that if they continue along that same line, and manage to trigger a popular mobilization that takes up the alternative as its own and does not allow anyone to give it an alternative in which it did not participate, we will then be able to detour off the path of death known as elections by appointment. We will be able to divert the plan for elections held by means of dollars, as is being done, and this will lead to a different alternative, an alternative in which the population will feel it has participated. And, I would say, this is what is going to provoke a change in "Loaded Donkey."[3] At that point, Adams will be obliged to negotiate, just as he negotiated in connection with the population's mobilization against Avril.

For example, as far as the masses are concerned, the Constitution can be summed up by Article 291, which says that there must be no Macoutes in the game. As soon as the Haitian people overrun the government apparatus, the necessary cleanup will automatically take place; and from then on, you will see that the Constitution will be strictly adhered to by the population.

In my opinion, it is the Macoutes who are preventing the Constitution from being applied. If the Haitian people overrun the government apparatus, they will make them respect Article 291, and respect for the rest of the articles will follow little by little.

You can see, however, that the moment the Haitian people get behind the steering wheel, there will immediately be a cleanup.

[Plaisimond:] Aristide says the nation is currently in a situation more serious than that of 1987, especially because there are not many candidates willing to join the sector that acknowledges that Ertha Pascal Trouillot cannot go on being chief of state. The existing division gives the Macoute sector greater force, says Father Aristide.

Aristide also discussed the CEP's meeting with the Army and the arrests made by the police within the framework of the climate of insecurity.

[ARISTIDE:] As far as I am concerned, the fact that the Haitian Army is allowing *zenglendos*[4] to go around killing people means that the army is in complicity with them. Because the army allows section chiefs to repress the peasants, I consider the army responsible for the repression. As long as this continues, all promises of security are worth nothing, worth zero. I am convinced of this. If the army wanted to prevent the insecurity and the killings, it would have. There might be a sector of the army that would like to. [Passage omitted] However, I also know that, basically, the Haitian Army is the "Loaded Donkey"'s flunky. It is the U.S. government's flunky. It takes orders from them. I mean, little bosses are the flunkies of big bosses, and big bosses are the flunkies of big imperialists. The current agenda is also the agenda of the U.S. imperialists. I mean: Let the *zenglendos* sow fear and cause insecurity to prevent the Haitian people from holding free and democratic elections. They do not want there to be such elections. That is the agenda that the Haitian army is to carry out, now.

Father Aristide Urges Unity during Elections, 12 October 1990

Since 7 February 1986, we have learned that alone we are weak; together we are strong; tightly united we are an avalanche, a powerful, driving force. Those who want to serve the people must listen to the people. Only by listening to the people can they learn that the fork of division cannot be used to drink the soup of elections.

The presidential candidates are divided, and they divide the people. As long as candidates are successful in dividing the people, the elections will be ineffective. A fork cannot be used for drinking soup. Presidential candidates standing alone should be left alone. Candidates working together will join with the people to become an avalanche that will take over the elections completely. . . .

If candidates refuse, ignore all of them. If they all abandon us, ignore them all completely, and thus reject the elections completely. Such elections are not for the poor people; they will not do the poor any good. Such elections would give rise to an alliance that would work with the Macoutes. If the elections cannot be elections of the people, they must be rejected totally. That is, the people must take over the elections or reject them altogether. . . .

Before Jean-Claude Duvalier took a plane, an avalanche was launched. Before Prosper Avril took a plane, an avalanche was launched. Before the criminals take that same trip, an avalanche must be launched. Before the high cost of living can go down, an avalanche must be launched, launched with the one program that the people will build, one leader that the people will choose, one power that the people will establish. Because alone, we are weak, together we are strong, tightly united, we are an avalanche.

Aristide Outlines Campaign Strategy, Objectives, 25 October 1990

REPORTER: Father Aristide is one of the most popular leaders in the Republic of Haiti. Aristide decided to register as a candidate to the highest office of this Caribbean country in the past few hours. Father, why did you decide at the last minute to register as a candidate to the Presidency of Haiti?

ARISTIDE: I have always said that I was not a candidate, but I have also said that I want to conform to the will of the people, because in the theological area, to do the people's will is to do God's will. So, since the people have asked me to do this, I have obeyed, and in obeying, I feel at peace with my conscience.

Haiti's reality is presented today as a crossroads at which the antidemocratic forces, the forces of the Macoutes, want to wipe out everything that we have tried to do in order to build democracy in Haiti. They do not want any democratic elections. . . . They want to organize their kind of elections, which they will later describe as democratic, but which in fact would not be democratic, and we would see a new government with the same criminals, the same Macoutes, this time in disguise.

That is why, although we have always felt that in a country where there are corrupt structures, only a revolution, and not elections, can bring solutions. We believe that in today's Haiti, it is necessary or possible to choose a strategy of participating in elections, but with one condition: that we be the majority in those elections; that we represent the people itself in those elections. In this way, we—the active forces of the country—will clearly be a lot stronger, and by playing this strategic game, using what we could call a tactical alliance, we said yes to elections, but to elections that can be democratic under those conditions. Why? Because our votes, the votes of the majority will be cast. And, if along the way they try to deceive us, of course since we will be, and are already the majority, we can stop at any time. And if we stop, it will not be possible for them to tell international opinion that they have organized democratic elections; that the Haitian people have chosen a Macoute, that they want a Macoute government.

In the crossroads that I have mentioned, we the Haitian people are trying to establish conditions of struggle, a struggle to build a true democracy. That is why I speak of elections in those terms.

REPORTER: If Father Jean-Bertrand Aristide assumes the highest office in Haiti, what would be the first measures he would take as the constitutional president?

ARISTIDE: If one is not the voice of the people, one kills the people. Well, the people know this. That is why the people's power makes me the voice of the people, one who will have to lead the people. With the United States, for example, it is a matter of seeing a people, the Haitian people, negotiating with respect, negotiating without provocation, without lowering themselves to their knees. Establishing a relationship of equality, in which through dialogue, it will be possible to create what we might call new relations, not the relation of a boss faced with a person on his knees, but of two equal countries.

REPORTER: You have spoken on the international level of Haiti's relations with the United States. What about the other Latin American countries?

ARISTIDE: Of course, to me Cuba is a country that I love, because I love the Cubans. Throughout the course of history, they have shown—not just with words, but with deeds—that they can stand up before the world with dignity, trying to build a country in which men and women can eat, go to school, can have what they need when they are ill; a country in which there is an attempt to provide social justice to the Cuban people. Of course, when we in Haiti have seen what has happened in Cuba, we cannot close our eyes and believe that we can give the United States a gift by showing them that we Haitians will try to distance ourselves from Cuba in order to say that we are on the side of the United States. No. In the United States, there are men and women. In Cuba, there are men and women, and the relations that we want to have with the United States, as well as with Cuba, are above all, human relations that are balanced, relations as equals, as men talking with other men without demeaning themselves.

With the other Latin American people, we are of course waging the same struggle; the struggle for justice, the struggle to defend ourselves, not to beg for what the United States would have to give us as favor, but to take the paths along which, with dignity, we can demand a little of what it has been taken from us in the period of colonization; even today, through the colonization that is portrayed as democracy, when it is actually a democracy for a small group.

Well, the time has come in which our country is saying, and will continue to say, to all Latin American countries: United, we will be able to struggle for the total liberation of the Latin American territory. We have the human resources, and through those resources comes the light to open the way so that there will be new men, new women, on both sides who are trying to build a new land with relations of justice for all, respect for all, and work for all; in other words, a true democracy.

Notes

1. At that time Ertha Pascal-Trouillot was president of the provisional government overseeing the elections.
2. The *chanpwèl* are secret societies.
3. "Loaded Donkey," or "Bourik Chaje" in Creole, was a nickname for U.S. ambassador Alvin Adams.
4. A Creole term used to describe violent criminals.

My Heart Does Not Leap

Boukman Eksperyans

Headed by husband-and-wife duo Lòlò and Manzè (Théodore Beaubrun Jr. and Mimerose Beaubrun), Boukman Eksperyans is one of Haiti's most prominent and influential rasin *or roots bands. These bands find their inspiration in the rhythms of Vodou and other Afrocentric belief systems. Indeed, Boukman Eksperyans is named for Boukman Dutty, credited with launching the Haitian Revolution at Bwa Kayiman. Although the band began playing live in the 1980s, their first album,* Vodou Adjae, *was not released until 1991. It contained their hit Carnival song, "Kè m pa sote," which literally translates to "My Heart Does Not Leap."*

The song marked a turning point in Haitian Carnival, which had until that point been dominated by konpa *music. It also points to the various ways that music and politics intersect in the Haitian context. Created for the Carnival celebrations of 1990, the song makes several covert references to the military government in power at the time and their exploitative and abusive use of power. This practice called* voye pwen *is a staple of Haitian Carnival music. "Kè m pa sote" remains popular today.*

Oh, Samba, it hurts
(I'll scream, Samba, I'll scream)
Oh, Samba, it hurts
Look what they did to me
Samba, I'm bleeding
They gave me the load to carry, I can't carry it
The load is heavy, I'll roll it
The load is heavy, I can't carry it. I'll roll it.

(I'll scream, Samba, I'll scream)
Oh, Samba, it hurts
It hurts way down in my heart.

Oh, Samba, it hurts
Look what they did to me
Samba, I'm bleeding
They gave me the load to carry, I can't carry it
The load is heavy, I'll roll it

The load is heavy, I'll roll it
The load is heavy, I can't carry it, I'll roll it

Oh, Samba, we're calling on Samba
Samba, yeah, we're calling Samba
Don't you dare talk in people's business
Don't be all up in people's business

(I'll scream, Samba, I'll scream)
Oh, Samba, it hurts
It hurts deep in my head

Oh, Samba, it hurts
Look what they did to me
Samba, I'm bleeding
They gave me the load to carry, I can't carry it
The load is heavy, I'll roll it
The load is heavy, I can't carry it, I'll roll it

I'm not afraid
I'm not afraid this year, Boukman's in the Carnival parade
I'm not afraid

Better not mess around
Better not mess around this year, Boukman's in the Carnival
Better not mess around

Keep moving, don't get violent in the crowd
Move

I'm not afraid
I'm not afraid this year, Boukman's in the Carnival parade
I'm not afraid

Better not mess around
Better not mess around this year, Boukman's in the Carnival
Better not mess around

(What is it?) Boukman!
My God, man, it's Boukman
Boukman
Balenndjo, no poisoned food can kill Balenndjo's horse
Balenndjo
What's your problem, then? (Bunch of hustlers)
What's your problem, then? (Bunch of talkers)
What's your problem, then? (Bunch of fools)
What's your problem?

Keep moving, don't get violent in the crowd
Move

What's your problem?
What's your problem, then? (Bunch of fools)
What's your problem, then? (Bunch of hustlers)
What's your problem?
Balenndjo, no poisoned food can kill Balenndjo's horse
Balenndjo

Don't you dare talk in people's business
Don't be all up in people's business

I didn't know you; now I know you very well
Don't you dare talk in people's business
Don't be all up in people's business.
It's because I didn't know you, now I know you well.

Translated by Nadève Ménard

On Theology and Politics

Jean-Bertrand Aristide

In Theology and Politics *President Jean-Bertrand Aristide reflects on the central role of liberation theology and its relationship to his political outlook and Haitian activism from the late 1980s through his ephemeral first presidency. For Aristide, liberation theology was a tool to empower and educate Haitians, primarily the Haitian poor, and to understand how biblical teachings could further illuminate the causes and consequences of injustice and inequality propagated by the state and foreign powers. In this excerpt, Aristide discusses how a person's alliance with reforms that uplift marginalized peoples allows him or her to fully appreciate the capability and greatness of the human. Additionally, Aristide believes that it is this support of the poor and actualization of liberation theology that inspired the Haitian resistance to Roger Lafontant, former head of the Volontaires de la Securité Nationale (VSN), a repressive paramilitary group, and Duvalierist supporters who forged a coup d'état against Aristide's fledgling administration on 6 and 7 January 1991.*

God, we believe, as aforementioned, does not exist "elsewhere," He exists in us. He does not come from somewhere else. Our presence reveals His. The linguistic concepts used to speak of His presence may let us perceive an "elsewhere," a distance, a place where He might come from. Philosophical categories may open a whole debate around this present absence or this absent presence. The terminology used in determining His presence does not matter. What is important to us is to understand that He cannot but be in us as a place of revelation, a primary theological place.

We are men and women, we are black, white, poor, weak, strong, we are exploiters or exploited. Such are the binomial concepts which underline differences: differences of essence, essence of God that can be found sooner in this one than in that one. The biblical world unveils a God represented by the poor, making them the primary place of His revelation.

From the Old to the New Testament, we continuously encounter this God at the heart of the lives of the poor. In 1991, the God of Jesus Christ continues to appear on the human scene through the poor. In the cave of Bethlehem, the eyes of the believers discovered Him. Poor woman, Mary; poor husband, Joseph; poor baby, Jesus. A fulfilling poverty, rich in transcendental values.

Such is the value and the greatness of a poverty which goes beyond a material wealth, though not fleeing the material aspect. God comes to us, the poor, to meet all of us and each of us. He comes to us, the poor, to salute the rich He also loves. God appears through the man who gives himself out of love for Him. The poor man inhabited by God becomes rich. The rich man who gives himself to approach the poor becomes even richer. This closeness allows him to understand the greatness of the human through the poor. And the poor person who opens himself to the spirit of God becomes light for any man or woman swathed in the thickness of economic wealth.

It is a thick material wealth that prevents the eyes of the rich from seeing through the material to discover the spiritual. To be sure, we do not want to establish any dichotomy between material and spiritual, but we are convinced that the materialist who does not weigh the pros and cons of his belief will not grow as will the poor who, by opening himself to the values of justice, freedom, love, becomes richer in a different way. The sacrifice to make is to acknowledge one's limits, accept oneself as a limited being to catch the voice of God through the poor. Blessed are those who are in communion with the poor because they transform the sacrifice in their deeds.

It is the joy of this celebration that shines in the mobilization of the poor, in their uprising, because the sacrifice of the poor is entirely different when they give themselves to transform their land and thus act in the name of their God. They go from Good Friday to Easter Sunday. The poor person who feeds at the spring of this spirituality does not stop growing richer. His suffering cannot rise as a wall stopping the march of history. Instead, living in the faith of this God of life, the suffering derived from his sacrifice projects him toward a future, without keeping him in a sterile past.

Up to here we have tried to embrace the spiritual depths that energize the reality of the poor, to better immerse ourselves in the theological depth from which the historical strength of the poor arises. We have to remember the difference between sacrifice and holocaust. When the blood flows on the altar and grease is burned, the flesh shared between the priests and the men who offer the sacrifice, the biblical world speaks of a sacrifice of peace. . . .

United, we launch ourselves on the political scene, defying death. The night of 6–7 January 1991 came. While the Haitian people were already exploring the paths leading to the 7 February 1991 celebrations, they got the bad news that a coup had taken place. What to do? How to react? Should we expose ourselves? Should we sacrifice ourselves? Sacrifice for whom, for what? The spirituality which had always fed the roots of the people became a strength: they woke up, they went into the streets, they went from door to door to unleash a collective awakening, a national uprising. From north to south, from east to west, during the night, the population invaded the streets. They built barricades around the towns, notorious *macoutes* were taken care of, an enormous and spontaneous movement on a countrywide scale. Everywhere: Democracy or Death! was on everybody's lips. If Lafontant had counted on the *macoute* terror to keep the population at home, he had miscalculated very badly. . . .

The prisons of fear were attacked by this force. Death no longer posed a threat. The weapons of Roger Lafontant and his accomplices were of no use in scaring the people. No, in the twinkle of the eye, in the middle of the night, the people rose up. Who could stop them? Who could take them into the lap of fear? Nobody! Their uprising was linked to their convictions, the fruit of a theological maturity. Because we are poor, poor in money but rich in spirit of freedom, we go beyond the fear to lose our life for the sake of the other. *Blessed you the poor, God's kingdom is yours* (Luke 6:20). Yes, the poor are happy and God's kingdom is theirs.

On the night of 6–7 January 1991, the poor of Haiti did not choose a kingdom of God to explore in the other world, when they will have left the earth. On the night of 6–7 January 1991, the poor of Haiti did not sit and wait for this kingdom. The night of 6–7 January 1991, the poor of Haiti did not wait for an order to go out in the street and declare war on death. Inhabited by the Holy Spirit, they assumed their responsibility as Christians to plunge themselves in the situation, in spite of the night, and thus protect their future.

What about those who do not share Christian faith? We will not hesitate to assert that Christian faith could not transform the poor into believers far from a reality of hunger, injustice, and exploitation. Christians, Catholics or Protestants, Voodooists, believing in God or not, atheists, for us religion is experienced entirely differently, for experience has shown that, in the world of the poor, misery does not have religion, nor does injustice and exploitation even less. As long as we fight against these evils, we find ourselves on the same road, going in the same direction, the one that necessarily gets to peace.

We must welcome the freedom of the poor which enables them to respect the freedom of the other, thus avoiding the strategies of religious domination. The ecumenical world appears when we manage to unite beyond religious faiths to fight against all subhuman conditions. Blessed are you the poor, God's kingdom is yours, but wretched are you the rich, you have your comfort, adds Jesus to verse 24 of the same chapter 6 of Saint Luke.

Which rich people are we talking about? Would they be those swathed in gold but whose heart suffers from fighting with the poor against hunger? Absolutely not! Rich is the one who owns a lot. A lot of money, a lot of love, and therefore he is no longer miserable. Wealth becomes a source of poverty when one closes oneself to stop vibrating to the suffering of the other and does not share with him. Wretched are you the rich, you have your comfort. Blessed are you the rich if you share your comfort.

This implies a sacrifice. Just as the poor do, we too learn to give up a little of our ambitions, a little of our interests, to offer a little more every day as a sacrifice and be in communion with the sacrifice of the poor. With the poor one becomes rich. The more one accepts the leadership of the forces of this spirituality, the less one contributes to increase poverty. Of course, politics, which is always a balance of forces, is enough in some cases to offer the poor the means to fight their poverty, and the rich the means of human and social growth. For us, in Haiti, the balance of forces takes place in a context that is both theological and political. The political structures crush the poor and weaken them. The theological values energize the poor and favor their fulfillment. Where politics isolates, theology unifies. Unity is strength, Lavalasian strength, a strength which erupted in the night of 6–7 January 1991.

Shrewd observers would not have hesitated to observe the political reality in light of this verse from the Apostles Acts 17:7: *All these individuals act against the decrees of the emperor, they claim there is another kind—Jesus.* If we talk about the emperor's decrees, we are fully into politics, and it is the biblical context that obliges us to recognize it. The text continues: they claim there is another king. There is another concept which links us to a political reality: king. But at the same time, the last word of the verse on the side of king is Jesus. Here are two more concepts: political king and theological Jesus. But we make a king out of Jesus. The theological thrust goes toward politics.

Is there a fusion between politics and theology? In fact, if we compare our people who, in this night of 6–7 January 1991, historically rose, we must recognize that, in the past, Christians were accused of making Jesus a king. Today the poor recognize in Jesus a political king. It is because of Jesus that they chose a priest as a candidate, because they saw in him the image of their king Jesus. We must, with much humility, realize this.

Instead of letting ourselves be carried away by conceit or hypocritical humility, we accepted this theological perception; that is, Jesus, king of the poor, greeted by Haiti's poor, and the image of the candidate, reflecting the one of Jesus, necessarily fascinate this Christian people. For us, it is not a question of an accusation, but rather an observation.

If these people left political leaders aside and chose a disciple of Jesus, it is precisely because of their deep Christian spirituality. If this people came together as one and became a historical force, it is thanks to the power of their Christian spirituality. They acted against the *macoutes* and their accomplices, they acclaimed their king Jesus by agreeing to go out unarmed in the streets where the enemy's weapons were circulating.

Some had their machetes, others had stones. What happened to the uprooting operation they started? This is a profoundly Christian understanding, where the poor are driven to use this strategy of uprooting. Uprooting is part of the philosophical thrust linking cause to effect. It is the expression of the victims when dealing with aggression: they express themselves with the help of the words and actions. Acts of active nonviolence in the face of terrorist violence. To the Romans, chapter 13, Paul will say: "*Every man must obey the authorities who exercise power for there are authorities only from God and those who exist are set up by Him."* The text is not rejected by the Christian people. The Holy Spirit illuminates Haiti and allows the poor to distinguish political power from theological power.

Lafontant symbolized a political power of death. Therefore, the people did not submit to his authority. We will even say: if authority only comes from Above, Lafontant does not have authority. The people have a political authority, their elected president. Because he wanted to steal his authority, Lafontant lost everything. Paul continues in verse 2: *"He who opposes authority rebels against the authority of God and rebels will call condemnation upon themselves."* In the context of 6–7 January, the rebels are not the ones who rose against the political power crystallized by Lafontant, but Lafontant himself became a rebel to the divine authority set up in the people, a people who had become an authority for having freely chosen their president.

Such is the power that is not limited to one person. Such is the collective authority, precisely because it follows collective demands. It emerges as a force, it imposes itself as the voice of the majority, the majority of the poor. Also animated by this force, authority becomes the prolongation of this choice, realized thanks to the force of its beginnings. Because they had this force thanks to their spirituality, they gave birth to this authority, and authority becomes force because it is the prolongation of the moving force.

In brief, the historical uprising calls on all and each of us to deepen our spirituality in order to find ourselves on the side of the poor. Throughout biblical history they have inhabited a political universe that they have not stopped directing toward justice for the advent of peace. Today they still energize the present time to live not as absent beings but in the present.

Street of Lost Footsteps

Lyonel Trouillot

Originally published in 1996, Street of Lost Footsteps *is renowned novelist Lyonel Trouillot's third novel. The three principal narrators, a madam, a taxi driver, and a post office worker, tell the story of a population caught between the clashing forces of the dictator Deceased-Forever Immortal and the Prophet, culminating in the "night of the abomination." In the following excerpt, the taxi driver narrates driving through the streets of Port-au-Prince as chaos erupts.*

I haven't changed. . . . Look, kid, Rue Paul-Robeson, it's double rate, double fare. A good buy that old Toyota, my buddies had given her just until my daughter was due and then till the twins were baptized. Not only did she make it to the baptism, but she took care of their mother and her illness as much as the doctors could. When she buried Mathilde no one could figure it out anymore. Fortunately for us she was there. What would I have done with those little guys? I'd already had hard luck with their mother, a flighty and fragile girl. At the time of the events the Toyota was running slower and the engine conked out now and then but on the Day of the Dead we weren't riding some nag to go see Mathilde in the cemetery. Rue de l'Arsenal, basic rate, standard fare, if the client agrees to get out at the corner, at this hour the street is already heaped with trash, you'll get blowouts in your rear tires from the glass shards and nails. Rue de la Réunion, an easy trip, I used to like the look of the lions at the entrance to the Hall of Justice, they gave the place a certain dignity. As for what went on inside, not much has changed, but with all these jobless people hanging around the Ministry of the Interior day and night you'll pick up a few fares. Wave at them. Sometimes it's the taxi that hails the passenger. There's timid ones who'll never make up their minds on their own. General headquarters, yes sir, *mon commandant,* no charge, *mon commandant.* Don't be afraid of using *mon commandant, monsieur le professeur,* it helps them be patient if you hit delays on the way. Rue Paultre, no thanks, those steep streets, they burn too much gas, you're going to have to think about changing these tires after all, I'll go haggle some up tomorrow, used of course, that's where you get your margin of survival. If we could, we'd even buy used food, recycled meat for skinny budgets, synthetic popcorn, but the

Americans haven't invented that stuff yet, if it takes them too much longer there's some around here that soon won't be eating anything at all, lots of them are already trudging up Empty Belly Street and that's what makes your murderers. I don't like putting myself forward, kid, but you already know that after the truck was sold I spent the year without a job running all over Port-au-Prince. It's nice to have conversations in your head while you're driving. At the time of the events, when I was working, I chatted with the Toyota, or I talked to myself. The extension of Chemin des Dalles, no, last week a colleague got mugged there, why do so many people have to live on these dreary streets with their ominous names—Martyrs' Cross, Iscariot—plus my back's been after me to change jobs, but what else would I do, I just drive people whenever they want to go, well almost, the Rue des Pas-Perdus, oh no, not you, with your mess of maps and constellations, if you can pay for the ride, I'll be glad to take you to the asylum, general headquarters, again, that's the third time this evening, at your service, *mon commandant*, basic rate, standard fare, thank you, *mon commandant*, you say I've got ten minutes to get home again, after that it's watch out civilians, uh-huh, thank you, *mon commandant*. When an officer tips you off to head home and tips you his change besides, chances are it's already too late. Ten minutes, kid! My old Toyota was a fine machine. I'd been offered good prices, but I'd preferred to keep her. I'd overhauled the engine, repaired the radio, passengers they like to listen to music *I'm still that boy from out of town* I mean, a car in great shape! She appealed to everyone, even the upper class who fuss over things like cushions, but ten minutes, no way. I'd already made it to the airport in twenty minutes for a woman looking to catch her husband taking off with his mistress, to the public hospital in record time for pregnant women and sick children, so I knew the best routes. But when soldiers take over the streets without warning and you hear gunfire even before you see them, when patrols are popping up at every corner, there is danger on all sides, no route is safe. The streets were already crawling with patrols. Rue des Remparts, they'd gotten out of their cars and taken up positions in groups of four. Rue Oswald-Durand, they'd occupied the square, jeering at the fleeing doves. Rue Cadet-Jérémie, I'd turned off my headlights, and the night was coming toward me, dense, metallic. . . . A tank! They'd called out the tanks! Back up, turn off to the right, I knew there was shooting, but I didn't hear the bullets, only this voice in my head telling my foot on the accelerator you're going to die, I want to die, you're going to die, I don't want to die. Rue Paul-VI, two bodies lying spread-eagled, back up, shit, they're already dead, and the voice insisting you're going to die, I don't want to die. And the soft thump of the bodies beneath the wheel, Rue des . . . But what the fuck did I care about the street names, I was in the corridors of a huge barracks, a labyrinth of machine guns, my fear was driving any which way, peeing, crapping, weeping, clinging to the walls of my stomach, talking, singing, yelling—*I haven't changed*, communiqué, you're going to die—cackling with glee. I was certain I knew that laughing voice, an acquaintance from another world, a mask that had already laughed in my face, stop talking behind my back, don't laugh like that, they'll hear us, shoot at us, don't laugh, just gather up all your fucking old papers, North Pole, South Pole, they'll think they're leaflets, while the others kept on singing, screaming, the madman's voice bored into my ear, not a thing I could do, it was me hiding behind me, you've finally found that Rue des Pas-Perdus, basic rate, standard fare, all roads lead to death.

Let's go home, kid. You've learned enough for one day. And I could sure use a drink. These memories wear me out.

VIII

Haiti in the New Millennium

Within a year of Jean-Bertrand Aristide's presidential oath many Haitians quickly understood the domestic and international obstacles that thwarted effective leadership from the executive office, including a U.S. embargo, and systemic malfeasance within the ruling party and at varied levels of legislative and economic control. As President Aristide struggled to maintain control in light of a growing and aggressive opposition to his reelection and the success of his political party, Fanmi Lavalas (FL), in local legislative elections, his administration became more rigid and autocratic. During the three years of Aristide's second term as president, some armed groups known as *chimès* attacked FL opposition, specifically members of the Convergence Démocratique and Group 184. There remains much debate about the events that led to the overthrow of Aristide in 2004. Alex Dupuy argues that by not reining in these forces, Aristide "failed to create the social and political conditions necessary for the consolidation of democracy."[1] The political missteps of Aristide along with the combative civilian tactics of the Revolutionary Front for the Advancement and Progress of Haiti (FRAPH) and the Gonaïves Resistance Front for the Overthrow of Jean-Bertrand Aristide weakened the Haitian state and led, in 2004, to the president's controversial exile.

Throughout the late twentieth century and to the present day, Haiti has endured constant intrusion by multinational military forces, most notably the United Nations Stabilization Mission in Haiti (MINUSTAH), and some friction by numerous nongovernmental aid organizations and international election observers. For more than a decade, global discourses of militarism, humanitarianism, international cooperation, and political intervention and notions of security have exacerbated asymmetrical political, social, and financial relations within both the nation-state and the region. In 2004, MINUSTAH's objective was to subdue militant oppositional groups and to work to rebuild local communities and political alliances. However, there were a number of cases of violence, including sexual violence, against Haitian citizens by peacekeeping soldiers, in addition to a festering resentment by the masses toward the well-funded occupying force, whose $500 million budget could have immensely benefited Haitians during the food riots of 2008. Two years later a

UN humanitarian mission found itself wedged between the benevolent work of aid ten months after the 7.0 earthquake, and the truth that their contingent was a significant factor in the cholera outbreak at the Mirebalais MINUSTAH camp. As of 2016, cholera had killed close to ten thousand people throughout the country.[2]

In light of the tremendous wreckage, loss of life and deprivation caused by the earthquake of January 12, 2010 (or *Goudougoudou*, as many Haitians have referred to the seismic event based on the sound heard at the time), many Haitian officials and foreign aid institutions made economic and infrastructural proposals that echoed the common refrain to "build [Haiti] back better." An international recovery effort produced close to $9 billion in aid. However, 59 percent of the funds went to UN agencies, international NGOs, and private contractors, 40 percent went to the donor countries' civil/military entities, and 1 percent went to the Haitian government. Foreign aid agents, much like NGOs in weak states, typically circumvent the state largely because of distrust, which further impairs an administration's efforts to build state capacity and improve the lives of its people. One maddening example is the 2015 report by ProPublica and National Public Radio that the American Red Cross raised $500 million in aid but built only six dwellings.

Despite the diminished capacity of the Haitian state, the U.S.-backed president Michel Martelly, who emerged in 2011 as the winner of highly contested elections, adopted an "Open for Business" policy. The approach was more reactionary than visionary and replicated capitalist modes of development that have historically produced structural underdevelopment and inequality in the Caribbean. The opening of a South Korean industrial park and manufacturing plant in Caracol, an area in northeast Haiti unaffected by the earthquake, displaced hundreds of Haitian farmers, utilizing arable land. The plant was praised for providing fifteen hundred jobs (initial estimates were sixty thousand) by the Interim-Haiti Recovery Commission, headed by former U.S. president Bill Clinton. However, the South Asian corporation, Sae-A, receives the typical perks: tax exemptions, duty-free ports, and cheap labor. The question of how Haiti benefits from foreign investment and other outdated modes of development proves critical as more reports about the discovery of an estimated $20 billion worth of gold and silver deposits by Eurasian Minerals Inc. are published. What percentage will the Haitian government receive? How it will be managed? And will the various mining companies invest in training Haitian workers and paying them a living wage?

Clearly Haitian people want jobs. They want to work and live and to participate in the prosperity of their communities with dignity. In situations of questionable leadership and exploitative measures from internal and foreign actors, Haitian workers and farmers may embrace the idea of self-management. Yet the *moun andeyò* (people living outside the mainstream, and most notably outside circles of economic privilege) are fully cognizant of the increasingly connective commercial and ideological tissue of this interconnected world. As scholar Jennie Smith documented with peasants in her study of southwestern Haiti, "If they [peasants] fail to gain the respect of those outside their communities, their hopes for a better society are in vain." So if one can argue that many Haitians have good reason to harbor a healthy distrust of the state, the U.S. government and Western NGOs, then who can they build alliances with, if any? Is there precedent for nonstate cooperative ventures? Would intra-Caribbean or racial-historical/cultural bonds within the Americas or on the African continent that highlight people sharing the same dream of prosperity with dignity be a more viable possibility? What are alternative ways of thinking about prosperity and implementing better living conditions in the Haitian context?

In the future, Haiti, as other states with limited economic and political power, will face arduous times and unstable moments, particularly within the realms of environmental and economic calamities. But Haitians have proven themselves courageous, defiant, and resourceful in this age-old fight against the binary politics of center vs. periphery and despotism vs. sovereignty. Policy continues to change toward improving women's social life, the press remains free and open, the cultural spheres—music, visual art, literature, and cinema—are still vibrant, and authoritarian rule is a dangerous option for any new president. This may continue to help to nurture alternative and radical ideas, songs and calls that challenge inequality and ease internal and foreign tensions.

Notes

1. Alex Dupuy, *The Prophet and Power: Jean-Bertrand Aristide, the International Community and Haiti* (Lanham, MD: Rowman and Littlefield, 2007), 163.
2. "Cholera Cases Expected to Rise in Haiti," Partners in Health, 4 October 2016, www.pih .org/blog/cholera-cases-expected-to-rise-in-haiti.

The Agronomist

Kettly Mars

This 2002 short story by Kettly Mars, one of the country's foremost fiction writers, captures the tensions that have traditionally existed between urban and rural dwellers in Haiti. There is often misunderstanding on both sides. Haitian history demonstrates that residents of the countryside have good reason to be wary of initiatives taken by those who inhabit the city, whether government officials, NGO workers, or urban businessmen. Most national services and programs are centralized in the capital and other urban centers. The bulk of the Haitian population lives in rural areas, although the disparity is not as stark as it once was. When urbanites venture into the countryside, they are often viewed with suspicion.

No. You couldn't die beneath such a sun. It would be a sin, sacrilegious, a crime of lèse-majesté. You'd be cheated, like when you're going to throw down your last ace to make a clean sweep and a treacherous wind comes and mixes the cards on the table. It would be like the glass of cool water taken away from you just as you are about to quench a cruel thirst, a forgotten password at the door to the treasure. It would simply be too stupid to go away when the sun caresses the banana leaves until they beg happily for mercy, while the earth is crying out its delight with scents that leave you light-headed. It was a much too beautiful day to die, the weather was too sweet. The weather was one where you are forever twenty years old, that's how much your blood rejoices in life, a time to share complicit laughter, amid the fat odor of cow dung, a time to eat milky corn and smoked sweet potatoes. It was a time for rivers and springs, for fresh water, waterfalls, horseback rides, for hands slipping under blouses. It was sunny enough to warm you to the point of fever. A time for summer vacation, the very start of summer vacation, when you feel like it will last your whole life. It was like the moment when, crazy in love, you will finally be with the woman you are desperately craving. A woman who wants you too and tells you so, her eyes in yours.

And yet death was there, it had the agronomist surrounded, cornered him more and more tightly, trapping him, paralyzing him. Insidious death, infiltrating the insistent odor of anise, wild sweet basil and lemongrass. Death became a terrible thing, shapeless, colorless, with no rhyme nor reason; it dried up his saliva and injected his entire body with a glacial wind, an anesthetic that muddled all understanding, all logic. Death separated from shadow, its twin, its namesake, the time it took to snatch a breath. Each one of the men, the women, and the children surrounding the agronomist wore the face of death. They became death-givers like others became shoe shiners, government workers, street sweepers, accountants. They blocked out the sun. Each of the stones they held at arm's length was already covered in the agronomist's blood, to which were stuck his hairs and remnants of his skin.

They didn't know why they had to kill him. It wouldn't be the first time they meted out death together, that they would carry out the killing ritual. A collective climax that freed them from fear. They had to defend themselves against everything: political enemies of the people, fake friends, governmental vultures, rivals, land conflicts, strangers. So said the Prophet. If this practice didn't bring them any good, they weren't any worse off for it. A danger was perhaps averted. Who knew? No later than last week, the next village over had been besieged for two days by a small group of pillagers, two days of hell during which these men's folly spared nothing, neither property nor virtue. So they remained on the defensive. Life was no longer worth anything, true, but they still clung to it. Hope springs eternal. They only knew that this unnamed man, still holding a notepad and pen, had to die because he was threatening their lives. All strangers were a threat to their lives. All strangers were voyeurs, shameless people coming to ogle their misery. Trust had ceased to exist a long time ago. A crazy word, "trust," a grave error in judgment that had led many of them to an early grave. The *compère* no longer trusted the *commère*, the father no longer confided in his son, the man doubted the mother of his children. Too much misery, too much hunger in their stomachs. Since the time they'd been forgotten in the depths of these mountains, what was this man who arrived in a jeep, at high noon, wearing a pith helmet doing here? Even worse, he was asking questions, a bunch of questions about the land. The land, their private life, their intimacy, the land they worked with their fingernails, that they watered with the sweat from their brow. How much was the can of fresh red beans? The sack of peanuts? Does the French plantain grow better here than bluggoe plantains? At what time of the year did they reap okra, radish, leeks? Where did they get the vegetable seeds, the fertilizer? When was the last coffee harvest? And he carefully wrote all of it down in his notebook. Nonsense! Grandstanding! Parasites had devoured the last two coffee harvests. Who gave a damn? He must not know, the stranger. The land gives almost nothing anymore, they are dying of hunger. How could they know that all this wasn't some kind of staging? Or an elaborate scheme? That this gentleman from the city wouldn't come back at nightfall, with others, to burn their huts, rape their women, ravish the land?

They hadn't yet touched the agronomist, but already he felt their blows. They were all looking at him intensely. They were hitting him with their hatred, spitting it in his face. One by one, they came closer. A silent, tacit, terribly irreversible movement. A sense of urgency and the call of blood to be let bound them together in an instinctive and animalistic brotherhood, the time of a killing. Even the women scented blood, from afar. He didn't understand anything, the agronomist. Angry outbursts wounded him. Bursts of hatred crippled him. Everything came to him in confusion, a drone of voices, blurry faces. He must surely be dreaming. But the fear was precise, acute, devouring. It suffocated him. The light fell straight onto him, a cylinder of light that already excluded him from among the living. His life depended on one stone, the first that would be thrown. He tried with all of his mental might to hold it back. The first stone . . . the one that starts the avalanche.

He heard himself saying words, the agronomist. He talked about a mission, a study, cooperation, international organization. Gibberish! Biased jargon to lull suspicion. . . . He showed them his badge, with his picture. Trivial words, useless gestures. Already the agronomist no longer existed. The words flowed from his lips because it was necessary to talk, to know that he was still alive, to hold on to minutes, to seconds. But for them, he was already dead. Because trust was gone from the mountains. Good morning, *compère*! Hello, *compère*! How's the body? Dirty hypocrite! I'll never turn my back to you, your dagger is watching me from beneath your shirt. The Prophet had asked them to defend themselves. Each man for himself. . . . They would defend themselves against everything and everyone. No discrimination here. The agronomist asked to see the authorities for the hundredth time. I don't mean you any harm; you see I don't have a weapon on me, nor in my car. I am doing a job, an agrarian inspection, nothing more. He no longer recognized his own voice, it came from afar. We're the Authority here, the Prophet says so. And your words, your notebook, we don't get them at all. The circle was closing. The amplified voices dizzied the agronomist. He needed air. A man with lips ravaged by white rum held an enormous rock above his head. He balanced it like a suspended sun. All the sun in the sky burned in that rock that blinded the agronomist.

They didn't know why they had to kill him. Maybe because it was Tuesday, market day, and that the foodstuff didn't bring much anymore after the handling fees, the transportation by truck to the capital, because the bad alcohol flowed freely and that messes up empty heads and stomachs, because a strange fever was killing off their poultry, because the day before there had been fraud in the Santo Domingo lotto, because . . .

But you can't die like that, at the market on the main road, in the crisp mountain, smelling cassava and rapadou, under such a blue sky, with lots of stains of color everywhere, in front of these kids electrified by the imminence of death and the mutt dog weaving in and out between the legs of all these men busy killing a man.

Translated by Nadève Ménard

Poverty Does Not Come from the Sky

AlterPresse

Haiti has long been associated with natural disasters in the global imaginary. There was the devastating earthquake of January 2010, and more recently Hurricane Matthew, which struck the country as a Category 4 storm in October 2016. Indeed, historically, tropical storms and hurricanes have been much more frequent on the island than earthquakes, periodically taking numerous lives and causing great damage. Hurricane Hazel in October 1954 was the first natural disaster to prompt wide-scale international humanitarian aid. Other notable storms were Flora (1963) and David (1979), which was immortalized in a song by legendary musician Ti Manno. The impact of these natural disasters is exacerbated by deforestation and poor living conditions in the country.

In 2004, Jeanne hit the city of Gonaïves as a tropical storm on 17–19 September, killing around 3,000 people and leaving close to 300,000 homeless. Four years later, Gonaïves and the surrounding areas were again hard hit by a series of four storms in close succession: Ike, Fay, Gustav, and Hanna in September 2008. In 2016, Hurricane Matthew devastated Grand'Anse, Haiti's most verdant department, as well as other cities and villages throughout the country's southern region.

The following editorial was published on 27 September 2004 by AlterPresse in Haiti, which reprised it from the French publication Convergences Révolutionnaires. *It emphasizes the fact that natural disasters are exacerbated by man-made situations and places Haiti's natural disasters in historical context.*

Already 1,650 dead, 800 missing, and 300,000 homeless: such is the heavy toll of the devastation caused by Tropical Storm Jeanne's passing over Haiti according to reports, which are unfortunately only temporary. Gonaïves, the country's third-largest city, was completely devastated: 80 percent of houses were destroyed, and several neighborhoods are still under water and mud. The residents have no means with which to clear out the mess. They have nothing for shelter and nothing to eat, no potable water. Famine is growing, and epidemics—cholera, typhoid, or others—threaten to emerge.

The rich countries, in spite of some media hype, have refrained from using extraordinary means to come to the aid of the Haitian population. Food aid is almost nonexistent; indeed, it is so paltry that the principal activity of

This stamp issued by the Haitian postal service in 1955 was part of a series meant to raise money for the victims of Hurricane Hazel, which devastated the cities of Cayes and Jérémie in October 1954, killing over one thousand people and leaving many more homeless. Coffee, cacao, and banana crops were all destroyed by the storm, which had a long-term impact on the Haitian economy. Various organizations including the International Red Cross, as well as the U.S. military, were very involved in the post-storm relief efforts. A U.S. Marines helicopter is represented in the stamp. Photo credit: iStock/ecliff6.

the UN's blue helmets consists of trying to come between meager stocks of food and thousands of famished people. The UN helicopters are apparently too small to transport provisions, they can only serve for reconnaissance missions. As if the great powers had not shown that in emergencies they are able to mobilize troops, provisions, terrestrial, or aerial materials around the four corners of the earth . . . when it is a matter of imposing their law and putting governments beneath their thumbs!

Which doesn't stop any of them from shamelessly bragging about their charitable spirit, and France is not the least of them, while hundreds of homeless are thus abandoned, while the number of victims can only grow in the weeks and months to come.

Only four months ago, torrential rains had already caused hundreds of deaths on the island. These repeated dramas are not due to the fatality of a tropical climate. Poverty is the principal cause: a few days earlier, Hurricane

Ivan, despite being of much stronger intensity, caused many fewer victims on the coasts of the United States. But Haiti is the poorest country in the Americas and one of the poorest in the world. A majority of Haitians survive with less than a dollar a day, and the life expectancy barely passes fifty years. Deforestation worsens the effects of hurricanes: soil erosion makes it impossible to absorb strong rains. It is poverty that forces inhabitants to cut trees to make charcoal, the only accessible source of energy to cook their food. The lack of roads, the extent of shantytowns, the negligence of a state apparatus in the hands of armed gangs, everything contributes to transform any unexpected climatic event into a catastrophe.

But this poverty does not come from hurricanes itself. The French colony of Saint-Domingue, ancestor of Haiti, rich and green, was transformed at the end of the eighteenth century into a huge forced labor camp: hundreds of thousands of slaves had been imported from Africa to produce sugar on the plantations. Commerce of human beings, exploitation and plundering: such were the methods used by the French bourgeoisie to build its economic power. A slave revolt two hundred years ago allowed the Haitian population to conquer its independence after a hard struggle. But Haiti rapidly fell into the clutches of the wealthy countries, notably the United States, which via several interventions took care to maintain dictatorships and continued to profit from the free exploitation of Haitian workers. For the great powers, no economic development was possible, and a parasitic local bourgeoisie continued to pump Haiti's riches. It is the workings of the capitalist economy that continues to dig an even deeper trench between rich and poor countries across the world.

The current intervention of the great powers does not go beyond their principal concern: reestablishing order to preserve their economic interests and to keep the poor population from revolting. They have reason to worry, for if the injustice of their society plants poverty, they might also harvest the anger of millions of the exploited and oppressed.

Translated by Nadève Ménard

Pòtoprens

BIC

The rap kreyòl *movement started in the 1980s, spearheaded by Master Dji (Georges Lys Hérard), but did not become part of the mainstream urban Haitian music scene until the late 1990s and early 2000s. Today rap artists perform in traditional venues, are regularly given promotional gigs, and constitute some of the biggest draws during Carnival, especially with rivalries such as the one between Barikad Crew and Rockfam.*

Roosevelt Saillant, who goes by the stage name of BIC *(Brain—Intelligence—Creativity), emerged onto the Haitian hip-hop scene in 2000 as part of the group Flex before launching a solo career as rapper, singer, and songwriter. He quickly became known for writing and performing songs that reference Haiti's cultural and social realities. In "Pòtoprens," a song about the Haitian capital,* BIC *reflects on the degradation of the city, evoking poverty, prostitution, and violence, among other themes.*

Port-au-Prince
If you're not in a hurry,
Let's have a little chat.
I'm sitting here looking at you—
Seems like times are really tough.
Port-au-Prince, how are you doing?
Tell me about Main Street:
Jean-Jacques Dessalines Boulevard.
How is the oceanfront?
Tell me about Lasalin.
Good God, Port-au-Prince.
Do guys to this day
Still piss on Madan Kolo's[1] feet?
Are we still up the creek without a paddle
Whenever there's a little drizzle?
Are kids still sniffing cement in jars?
If that's the case, we're not normal yet.
Port-au-Prince: capital
Port-au-Prince: headache

Painting Toussaint Louverture in preparation for Port-au-Prince bicentennial, 2004.
Photo courtesy of Noelle Théard.

Port-au-Prince: hot coals
Port-au-Prince: Kosovo
Port-au-Prince: mafioso
Port-au-Prince: pile of trash
Port-au-Prince lagging behind
Port-au-Prince in agony
Port-au-Prince plucked bald
Port-au-Prince getting worse
They tell me there's a problem,
Too many kids with matches.
I have to ask:
Does this country have no keepers?
Port-au-Prince, we have to talk.
They tell me there's a brass band,
Violence is its maestro.
Guns are singing in Dolby stereo refrain.
Good God, Port-au-Prince.
Do little girls still lie down
For a plate of food?
Is the youth still
A loaded gun?
Are brothers and sisters

Still crossing swords?
If that's the case,
We need to change.
Port-au-Prince: capital
Port-au-Prince: headache
Port-au-Prince: hot coals
Port-au-Prince: Kosovo
Port-au-Prince: mafioso
Port-au-Prince: pile of trash
Port-au-Prince lagging behind
Port-au-Prince in agony
Port-au-Prince plucked bald
Port-au-Prince getting worse
You sit with your head in your hands,
Sucking your teeth at life.
All your dreams have dried up
Since way back when the bearded dudes were president.
Who would have said
Port-au-Prince would be what it is today?
I hear your screams.
I smell you.
Have courage, I'm praying for you.
Port-au-Prince: capital
Port-au-Prince: headache
Port-au-Prince: hot coals
Port-au-Prince: Kosovo
Port-au-Prince: mafioso
Port-au-Prince: pile of trash
Port-au-Prince lagging behind
Port-au-Prince in agony
Port-au-Prince plucked bald
Port-au-Prince getting worse
(repeat)

Translated by Nadève Ménard

Note

1. This line refers to a well-known fixture in the Bel Air neighborhood: the statue of Madan Kolo, a woman believed to be a French colonist. It is said that she is the sole original inhabitant of Port-au-Prince.

Political Music from Bel Air

Rara M No Limit, Bèlè Masif, and Blaze One

In fall 2004, residents from the Port-au-Prince community of Bel Air and other popular neighborhoods waged a militant movement against police and UN peacekeepers who attempted to quell unrest after Jean-Bertrand Aristide's second ouster from power on 29 February 2004. The movement, called Baghdad, went on for several months and resulted in countless deaths and a mass exodus of residents.

Both songs below, attributed to the group Rara M No Limit, were sung as battle cries among neighborhood militants fighting for Aristide's return. The song "Le Police" articulates the emergence over the previous years of a local, informal security force composed of baz—*a complex term denoting the militant social groups who claimed to defend residents against political and personal enemies. Using the French articles* le *and* la, *the song distinguishes between* la police, *the official security forces who were viewed as assaulting residents, and* le police, *the fearless local* baz, *who were seen as protecting the population and its political cause. There are two additional double meanings worth highlighting. The term* asayan *refers not to any assailant but to former army soldiers in particular, and the reference to those who are* pi frajil *implies not fragility or weakness but, rather, impulsivity and therefore danger. The second song acted as a warning to outsiders not to enter the neighborhood unless they lived there and could claim membership in a* baz. *This song remains very popular in the area as a sign of the residents' militancy and political pride. Neither clandestine song was recorded or distributed commercially. Chelsey Kivland recorded the following versions on the streets of Bel Air in 2010.*
—*Contributing Editor: Chelsey Kivland*

LEPOLIS
There is *la police* and *le police*
And I hear you, "You can't die?!"
Assassins [former military] do not rush forward
For the ones that remain are more dangerous

462

Protests against Jean-Bertrand Aristide, 2004. Photo courtesy of Noelle Théard.

UNTITLED

If you don't live in Bel Air
Don't come to Bel Air

If you don't have a *baz* in Bel Air
Don't come to Bel Air

The rap group Bèlè Masif unites several rap artists from Bel Air. Their songs speak from and about their impoverished district, primarily addressing young male residents, whom they want to educate about the area's predicaments, enter into their fan base, and convert to their worldview. Their lyrics offer a view into the marginalized and deteriorated "ghettos" of Haiti's neoliberal democracy. The artists identify as ti nèg, or black and poor, and racism and poverty are their primary objects of denunciation, which aligns their movement with hip-hop in the United States, the greater Caribbean, and elsewhere. (The Haitian Creole word nèg is usually translated as "man," but in this particular context, it is opposed to both woman [fanm] and white [blan]. Therefore, it is here translated as "black man." The expression ti nèg [little black men] is often used to distinguish ghetto residents from wealthy and powerful gwo nèg [big black men]). They also identify as men who perceive women of their generation as more integrated into the economy and less victimized by crime, politics, and police abuse than their predecessors. Their lyrics often express an aggressive masculinity cultivated in acts of militant defense, drug and alcohol use, and the domination of women and revilement of queer identities. Their music thus relays the destructive forces that young, unemployed men use to survive amid insecurity. Furthermore, it is reflective of a culture that is largely unsupportive of the social and economic ordeals of the LGBTQ community, despite constitutional (1987) assurances that all Haitian citizens are protected under the law. Vodou practitioners, in spite of the more common disdain for queer identities, are more welcoming and supportive of people who identify as LGBTQ. However, amid their masculine boasting, Bèlè Masif also illustrates respect for many of their fellow citizens. Ultimately, they leave an impression of their neighborhood as the place where "the life is all right" and where one finds talented, smart men who long for peace and respect.

Bèlè Masif's songs are performed collaboratively, with each member of the group contributing vocals. In this transcription, the rappers' names appear before their respective sections. The group recorded this song in 2006.

STIL BÈLÈLÈ

YAKUZA: What we lay down is a good beat. It's what it is, with rap we're married. Each rhyme we marry with our vibe. Leave all who say it doesn't make the grade. Those who rule the streets are hot, burning your clothes on you.

That is the Bel Air style. All people say, "Yeyeye!" They say what time?, for the masses in Bel Air platinum. They all remain silent, they're high, near the corner of Pè Nene. . . . It's Bel Air for Bèlè Masif platinum, hey. Pot, take a hit, blow it out, smoke fades, hey.

H. JAY: Bel Air, we got more respect than all the other blocks. We have style. We have fresh air, so why are they most afraid of this block? All who say we are *chimè* [pro-Aristide militants] it's garbage they are saying. They have nothing important to do. Every day it's booze they swallow. During Operation Baghdad we never lost form. Bèlè Masif stayed in action so that we could serve as an example. We made *gaye pay* [dance style] on the plateau with RaraM deployed on the concrete. Zapzap will contend on the deck. It's us they seek during the season.

DEF: We believe in our motto that *l'union fait la force* [Unity Is Strength: the motto on the Haitian flag]. Analyze the jokes and it's division that makes us horrifying. We must not listen to contempt. Come now, for us to do it with strength. Our mission is to care for the city. Come now, for us to make a new approach. Only this area has more echo than you know. Already it's this area that is the first among all the ghettos that you know. It has its own customs and traditions. Bèlè Masif, the platinum. The only thing you can say: the strength of the area is all connected. Now we have come to give you respect.

FLU: With the beat, we valorize our block. We go and rise up so we can give them a hit. All my bloods, brothers. All of you can embrace it if you want. Taking money to make us "hot," we put it out of sight. It's a matter of "one love." We put it on high, not daring to be frustrated. A zone of pleasure. I'm flush, baby. My money I give you, and we say it. They give us a peace prize. Aren't they trying to flatter us? All those we hate, you must see it's war. Believe that what we spit, what we say, brothers see that's what happens. To the critics, you are shit!

KAMELE-1: Bel Air is *yayayaya*, *rara* parades, the reign of Blada. Bel Air is Frank, Frankétienne,[1] Edner Day[2] who yells, yells, "You must stop!" Bel Air is ka, Kamele-1 [name of rapper], ka, Cameroon, ka, Cathedral, for Marielala la. Bèlè Masif platinum on CD-Rom. We make you dance like Mariela on top of the pole at Sans Fils,[3] and if you take the wire, you feel chill with all the children of Madan Kolo,[4] to the drum of Ti Roro.[5]

KALAMITE: Bel Air is my block, for all the bloods, it's there that life is all right. Bel Air is my zone, where all the bloods came to set up. Bel Air is my block over all other zones. Each day we take a platinum medal for the people of Bel Air it's a phat zone. Say, "Yeyeye!"

YAKUZA: Bel Air is hot, we're smart, on our track, give you a thwack. We're back. Make your choice if you're weak, don't say, "Woy." Each of us is a Glock, we can give you a shot. Bel Air is not a conflict zone anymore. They gave us a peace prize. They gave us a gold plaque. Come give "hardcore" to the mass with too many faults. We beat them again. It's more than a record, the entire street agrees. Open all the eyes, it's a bolt of lightning. In all areas, the Bel Air men on the bottom rebel. One in the area who is never at the bottom of the label makes all the fakes afraid. Make all of them believe we are high level.

I SHOT: We have only one objective: it's to play music. Despite the critics, we find several ways to make a big drumbeat. We play several rhythms: RaraM does level no limit, ZapZap gives the Titanic ship. But understand this: it takes more than a little talent to learn that. We make poetry on beats, always work to hit the street. There's no time to lose. We give ourselves platinum, yes. We are the masters of the zone, men of the zone. We believe in Jah, that's what makes us masters of the zone.

DOG-TOM: A platinum for freedom that does not depend on anyone. A platinum for the masses in Bèlè Masif that depends on hip-hop, for poetry we wake up. All the crazies we blow-up for our pleasure. In B.L. Club, we are busy drinking booze. We have more to give you . . . , we're not for one side more than another. We dance with peace, we clench teeth at *pede* (slang for homosexuals). Our style is not to drink alcohol for hardness (erection). . . . M.O.G. (a local *baz*) makes me unafraid. That clan will make you beg for mercy in Bel Air.

The music of rap artist Elysé Sénora, better known as Blaze One, chronicles what he calls "the history of the ghettos." His songs detail the major figures that have shaped life in poor districts in Port-au-Prince since 1986. In line with rap music in black communities in the United States and elsewhere, his songs shed light on the structural inequalities, political corruption, and gang violence that perpetuate misery and insecurity among the urban poor. He pays particular attention to the perpetual conflicts that pit local gangs (baz) and residents against state agents, politicians, and police. The song "Istwa Bagdad" focuses on the period of unrest leading up to and following Jean-Bertrand Aristide's ouster in 2004, which the rapper refers to as a coup d'état. It offers a nuanced interpretation of the multiple forces that shaped the conflict. Blaze One's portrayal of baz leaders as struggling to defend their communities but as also susceptible to criminal rackets and police corruption complicates any partisan analysis of this political history.

ISTWA BAGDAD

Yeah! The History of Baghdad, yeah! Haitians, they think they can walk all over us. Make us fight each other. We must unite!

Refrain: [Cité] Soleil makes Baghdad, Baghdad. Bel Air makes Baghdad, Baghdad. The men of Grand Ravine, men of La Saline all make the life of Baghdad. Martissant makes Baghdad, Baghdad. Fort Touron makes Baghdad, Baghdad. A lot of crying, a lot of wailing when there was Baghdad. The president makes Baghdad, Baghdad. The police makes Baghdad, Baghdad. The private sector and the journalists, all of them make the life of Baghdad, Baghdad. There are those who become rich in Baghdad, Baghdad, those hiding out in Baghdad, Baghdad. A lot of crying, a lot of wailing when there was Baghdad.

The history of Baghdad began before the coup d'état, the big shots would bring ammunition because they knew power comes from the masses, where there is misery, where there is the life of tribulation. They made the police stand and fight against the people, those who are there to serve and protect. But it was never like that. GNB[6] protesting Rat Pa Kaka,[7] the mouse can't cross the street or else you'll be shot.

Refrain: Baghdad, yeah! Yo yo! Yo yo!

Aristide left. Now everyone is about *dechoukaj* (uprooting). They finished uprooting the stores. The *boujwa* (bourgeoisie) is thinning out. The Ministry of Justice wanted to tie up those who made the trouble. Most of the ghettos rallied together to cause bedlam. Dread MacKenzy got started, then later, he fell. That's what caused most of the soldiers to leave the battle. Every day the Rats turn the city upside down, the mouse can't cross the street or else he'll be shot.

Refrain: The History of Baghdad, yeah! Yo yo! Yo yo!

Haitians I need to know: are we waiting for the messiah? A black leader or a white leader? Tell me who are we waiting for? At a certain level, all the talk says we're not a country. We can never find an understanding even though Haiti is perishing. . . . They say, "Blaze One, you're digging too deep." Those guys invest money in insecurity. Every time they're handling their business, it's the people who suffer. Downtown people take bullets, assassins become cannibals, kidnappings cause scandals. Inside the ghetto it's dirty things. Those guys live off division. They act on our short-sightedness, and we always pay the price for our illusions.

Refrain: Baghdad, yeah! Yo yo! Yo yo!

Translated by Chelsey Kivland

Notes

1. Celebrated author Frankétienne was raised in Bel Air.
2. Edner Day was prefect of Port-au-Prince during the Duvalier regime. He is reported to have ordered and supervised the torture of numerous citizens during his tenure, especially in the Bel Air neighborhood.
3. Mariela was a young adolescent girl (her age is usually given as twelve) who in the 1970s climbed to the top of the tallest telecommunications tower (about one hundred meters) in Port-au-Prince at the time and danced. A crowd gathered to watch her, and firefighters tried unsuccessfully to bring her down from the tower. She eventually descended on her own.
4. A statue of Madan Kolo, a colonial woman symbolic of Port-au-Prince, is located in the Bel Air neighborhood.
5. Celebrated Haitian drummer Raymond Ballergeau went by the stage name Ti Roro.
6. GNB, or Grenn nan Bounda (ones who have balls), was a loosely organized group composed of different individuals and groups who opposed Jean-Bertrand Aristide, his administration, and his supporters.
7. "Rats Don't Play" was the name given to those who supported Aristide and took up arms to defend him. They engaged in various forms of violence. They were previously called *chimè*.

Strange Story

Bélo

Born in 1979 as Jean Bélony Murat, Bélo is a songwriter, singer, and guitarist whose career took off when he won Radio France's Prix International de la Découverte in 2006. "Strange Story" features on his first album, Lakou Trankil *(2005)*, and was reprised on his second one, Référence *(2008)*. It explores the reasons behind Haiti's high rate of external migration, citing poverty and unemployment.

This is the story of five young men who took to the sea,
To see what life has to offer.
These guys were tired of poverty.
They had to leave, leave their families behind.
They didn't even have a destination.
They're on the water in the care of the waves and the wind,
These guys had only one vision,
To leave Haiti, let their kites catch wind and fly.

Oooo
They left
Oooo
Days going by,
The guys are on the water,
Flooded by despair.
There's no food, not even water.
They're in the clutches of fear.
One of them said, he'd rather
Throw himself to the sharks
Than return.
He's young, he's in his country, he has two hands
Each day the sun rises, to find him doing nothing.
Ooooo
Complaining wife
Ooooo
Complaining kids.

These guys are just like us,
They loved Haiti a lot.
They were always suffering.
Life was not easy for these guys
They had to leave
Poverty and high prices sent them on their way.
Peasants leaving
Artisans leaving
Students leaving
The country's best have gone.
Guys from the ghetto are leaving
Guys from the top are leaving
People selling water leaving
Even the little birds are leaving
The proletariat is leaving
Teachers leaving
City dwellers leaving
The musicians have gone.
Ooooo
They've all left
Ooooo
The country is broken
This is the story of five young men who took to the sea,
To see what life has to offer
These guys were tired of poverty
They had to leave us far behind
They didn't even have a destination
They're on the water, in the care of the waves and wind
They had only one vision,
To leave Haiti, let their kites catch wind and fly
Ooooooo
They've all left
Ooooo
They were tired
Ooooo
They had to
Ooooo

Translated by Nadève Ménard

Faults

Yanick Lahens

In this nonfiction piece, award-winning novelist and short story writer Yanick Lahens reflects on post-earthquake Haitian society and the ways it is in fact a direct continuation of pre-earthquake Haiti. While evoking the changes in the country's landscape after 12 January 2010, she pays particular attention to the cleavages between different segments of the population, as well as how they are intertwined. She also evokes the role of the international powers in maintaining the status quo in Haiti. The faults referred to in the book's title are not geological but, rather, the ones that form the very foundation of Haitian society.

On both sides of the street, men, women, and children are on the move. Carrying a bag, a bundle, or a mattress on their head, plastic basins, a cooker, a few utensils. A shriveled, skinny old man is carried by two strong men. These images have already been seen on television, in magazines or at the movies. It's crazy what you can read, see, and store with magazines, television, or the movies. It's crazy how similar the world's misfortunes are.

I can't know what form this movement of the population will take, exodus toward the provinces, of course, but within the urban spaces, I don't know. What I am sure of is that these women and these men left along the road have an intuition, an instinct all their own. It's been two centuries since they no longer believe in governments nor in the promises made by politicians, not those made by economic powers or those made by intellectuals, not by me, not by you. When they did happen to believe, they were always quickly disenchanted. Today, defiance is rampant, structural. And for good reason. It's been two centuries since they've learned to move forward in history on their own. Without anyone to hold their hand or show them the way. It's been two centuries since they have been dodging all governments, all politicians, all of the powers, even before those governments, those powers or those men can ignore them. That is the head start that they have which means that they always manage to catch them unaware.

Today, they can no longer be caught by any government, any international body, or NGO. They slip out of all reach. This intuition is much more than a posture, more than a strategy, it is knowledge.

The sophistication of this particular knowledge has nothing to do with what is taught at Harvard, the ENA, Oxford or what is analyzed at the IMF or the World Bank. It has nothing to do with the revolution of the socialists, Guevarists, Maoists, or Trotskyites either. Because this knowledge doesn't depend on any hope in powers or in brighter tomorrows. Its first postulate is precisely that hope is not the only answer.

If exclusion has led to the results that we all know, can this knowledge be a way out today?

I don't know.

. . .

The camps or the end of a system?

The camps are really being formed. Upon hearing this word, we imagine the Palestinian camps or those of the Darfur refugees. But I know that what is shaping up here is at once the same thing and something different. It is a new spatial distribution of the haves and the have-nots. The have-nots were more or less hidden, either behind the houses of the haves, or in the shanty-towns that surround their neighborhoods. Today a large part of the have-nots are in front of the houses of the haves, or in what remains of the public squares in the city and its outskirts.

Anthropologists and sociologists have designated by the respective terms of "Bossales" and "Creoles" the have-nots and the haves. The Creole is a mulatto (fruit of a union with a white colonizer or a white-skinned foreigner during the nineteenth or twentieth century) but can also be black-skinned (the descendant of a free person of color in colonial times or of blacks having acquired a fortune and/or Western education over the years). The Bossale is black (aside from a few pockets in the rural areas of trace residues of long ago mixing with the descendants of Caribbean Indians or with whites descended from the Polish who had joined the cause of the black insurgents during the war of independence). A Haitian sociologist, Jean Casimir, established this fundamental dichotomy in his work *La culture opprimée.*

. . .

I don't know of a greater historical and social fault line than that one in Haiti. It's the one that has been producing exclusion for two centuries. It cuts through all of us, Bossales as well as Creoles. It structures our way of being in the world. It shapes our imaginary, dictates our fantasies about skin color and class. It locks our society into two insurmountable molds: master and slave. Feeds our frustrations. Nourishes our illusions. It silently crushes us as well. Having said that, we have said the most important, but we are far from having said it all. We would first have to nuance the monolithic character of the two groups, then nuance the complete impermeability between the two groups, and also take into account obvious recent mutations. Finally, simplifications based solely on racial, color, or social categories often fail to render the global nature and the complete coherence of individual or collec-

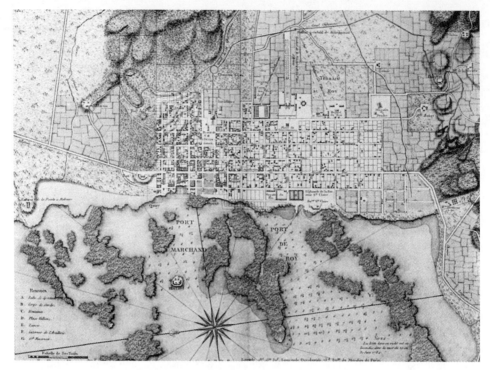

This map from the late eighteenth century reveals a version of Port-au-Prince that contrasts greatly with the contemporary capital as described by Yanick Lahens. Today the general metropolitan area of Port-au-Prince includes neighborhoods which were once considered separate towns, and the population in the capital continues to increase at a steady pace. Image courtesy of CIDHICA.

tive behavior. They are especially dangerous when used as easy shortcuts to clichés or ideological banalities.

But let's keep going anyway. Our way of inhabiting the urban areas (that the presence of the camps is arranging in a new way ever since 12 January) is no stranger to this Bossales/Creoles dichotomy. In fact, the haves and the have-nots have been playing a real game of tag for almost half a century as far as the occupation of space is concerned. The haves settled in the heights of Pacot, Debussy, Pétionville, but with the accelerated rural exodus were eventually caught and surrounded by the have-nots. The haves then climbed even higher or into enclaves they thought were inaccessible, before being caught again by the have-nots, who again silently surrounded them. So the haves continue to climb and to flee farther, toward Laboule, Thomassin, and even Kenscoff. At this rate, the haves as well as the have-nots risk finding themselves in the Dominican Republic, since the territory is not infinitely expandable. Except if? Except if we all finally decide to live together on this territory with mutual respect. In common decency. Absolute lack is itself an indecency, ownership in such a context ends up being one as well. Are we a nation in the sense of a citizenship sharing common references and values? Certainly not.

Will the camps render this game of tag obsolete? Blindness and mistrust suicidal? There again, I don't know. In any case, it is the system as a whole that has done its time. Privilege eventually becomes ugly, but misery cannot be beautiful. How then to live with dignity? Camus gave us an indication in his own way: "Man is not only the slave against the master, but also the man against the world of master and slave."

. . .

The Decline of the Middle Class

That night, I didn't expect to chat with a friend on Yahoo. She's a manager at a private bank. Her spouse is a self-employed professional. The conversation wasn't a true one, since my words often missed their mark, as always happens when we're faced with a despair for which we can provide no way out.

When her message pops up on the screen, I answer:

ME: F, how are you? Are you hanging in there?

F: What do you think? Not at all.

ME: What's going on?

F: I'm still staying with friends with L. and our youngest. My oldest son is staying with a cousin. Our house collapsed.

ME: Do you have any prospects?

F: To soon find myself on the street. You know, people welcome you for a few days or a month, but after that it's no longer possible. You're a nuisance.

ME: What do you plan to do?

F: I'm supposed to be the strongest one in the family.

ME: Yes, I know about the Haitian woman as *potomitan*,[1] but no one expects us to be strong all the time. That's not written anywhere.

F: Well, there's no longer any *poto*. I'm broken. Like the house.

ME: . . .

F: You see, in all these reconstruction stories, people like me will be left behind.

ME: Why?

F: Because I'm part of that middle class that continues to fall into precariousness.

ME: . . .

F: In this much talked about recasting/reconstruction, the rich will get richer. They've already put themselves in position to do so with the help of the government and the international. I hope for the poor that their situation improves. But for us, nothing.

ME: . . . Measures will be taken.

F: Do you really think so? I don't at all. Listen, I have a car that I finished paying off three months ago. I have six years left to finish paying for my house, which now no longer exists. But the debt still exists. And to own a Hyundai and a small house is to be rich in the eyes of the foreigner and in the eyes of Haitian demagogues.

ME: In any case, democracy can't be built without the middle class, nor can an economic rebound take place without it.

I know that by writing those words, I am spouting a purely theoretical fiction, but I do it as though to convince and reassure myself.

"But you haven't understood anything," replies F. "Absolute poverty is their moneymaker. And the image of the poor is a useful cliché. I'll be driven to sleeping in my car and really become poor. Then, maybe someone will pay attention to me."

ME: Think of the kids.

F.: My eldest is a third year medical student at the State University and it's been almost a year since classes have been held. My youngest son attends St. Louis de Gonzague. The school was damaged on January 12th and the yard is filled with tents of homeless people who for right now have nowhere to go.

ME: Force yourself to consider some prospects.

F.: No. Because in any case I belong to the category that people don't see. The country's managers and executives keep leaving. And all of the policies undertaken by national and international actors are so that we go elsewhere. I wanted to stay and I'm paying dearly for my nationalism.

ME: . . .

At the time that I'm writing the memory of this dialogue, her son's university has still not reopened; the possibilities for evacuating the yard of her second son's school are at a standstill. But even better, an internationally recognized NGO is making the argument that it's a bourgeois school and a big Los Angeles daily is stating that a thousand students who don't go to school is no big deal, because there are three thousand needy people in the tents. Why, instead of exacerbating the conflict, don't they first try to find an outcome that would be beneficial to both parties, as they would have done in their own country?

Those thousand kids are far from being bourgeois children. It's already been more than three decades that Saint-Louis de Gonzague educates children of the middle and lower middle classes. Children from the bourgeois classes attend international schools that NGOs and journalists cannot stop from functioning.

But, even better, I received in my inbox propositions from no fewer than three Canadian agencies to emigrate to Canada. A whole wave of professionals once again made the leap. In a few months, I'll read in the international reports, including those from Canada, that Haiti is worrisome. That it cannot absorb the aid, nor organize itself, due to its lack of professionals. They take away with one hand what they give with the other. A way to keep us in the same state and to continue politics as usual. It's logical from start to finish.

We are sinking, we are sinking! F., how right you are . . .

Translated by Nadève Ménard

Note

1. The term *potomitan* originates in Vodou, indicating literally the center pillar of the temple. A common Haitian saying is that women are *potomitan*.

Everything Is Moving around Me

Dany Laferrière

In this layered collage of evocative fragments, diasporic Haitian Canadian writer Dany Laferrière offers a tableau of the richness of Haitian life before, since, and despite the January 2010 earthquake in Haiti. Laferrière, who received his most notable recognition when he became one of the few non-French citizens inducted into the elite Académie Française in 2015, writes of how the earthquake served as a revelation—revealing both the conditions under which the Haitian people have long struggled to assert their humanity within and outside the country and the limits and prejudices of the international community. Laferrière does this from the powerful perspective of firsthand witness. Having traveled to Port-au-Prince from his home in Canada, the author was present during the earthquake and in the days immediately following. Laferrière reflects on the notion of Haitian "resilience" against a rich sensory backdrop; the precise sounds and smells of the postapocalypse are there alongside bigger-picture musings on his personal relationship to the island and on Haiti's history. Laferrière's writing is marked by a tone of incredulous outrage faced with the veritable crisis of extra-insular representation that has long reduced Haiti to an assemblage of unflattering stereotypes. He counters by juxtaposing the tragic seminal moment of this natural disaster with the man- and woman-made triumph of the nation's revolutionary past.

The Crowd

The city, during that first night, is occupied by a disciplined, generous, and discreet crowd. People milled about endlessly with a strange determination. They seem indifferent to the pain they're carrying around along with the elegance that brought such universal admiration. The planet is already glued to its TV screens so as to bear witness to this strange ceremony where the living and the dead get so close to one another that you can barely tell them apart. If, on the eve of his death, Malraux came to Haiti, it was because he felt that the painters of Saint-Soleil had intuitively discovered something that rendered futile any struggle against death. A secret path. It seems incredible that people could have spent such a long time under the rubble without drinking or eating. It's because they're used to eating very little. How can one take to the street and just leave everything behind? It's because they possess so few things. The fewer objects one possesses, the freer one is, and I'm not trying to romanticize poverty. It isn't Haiti's misery that so moved the rest of the world. It's that this disaster made appear before our very eyes a people whose gangrenous institutions had kept them from blossoming. It was ultimately necessary that these institutions disappear from the landscape in order for a people at once proud and discreet to emerge from a downpour of dust.

. . .

The Rhythm

One arrives in Pétion-ville. I count tens of collapsed homes. Perhaps there are others. I can only see those lining the street. Pétion-ville seems to be holding up. I can breathe a little. People are chatting in small groups on the sidewalk. I was expecting a crowd beaten down by sorrow, but life was already imposing its rhythm. Even misery isn't able to slow down the incessant daily activity of these poorest regions of the world.

. . .

The Semantic Battle

From a question posed to me by a Canadian television journalist on the Port-au-Prince airfield, just before taking off, I understood that a new qualifier had been affixed to Haiti. For a long time, Haiti had been seen as the first independent black republic in the world, and as the second American republic after the United States. This independence was not granted to us over a couple of martinis, a few hypocritical smiles, and some pompous speeches on a confetti-strewn lawn. It was conquered after a high-pitched battle against Europe's greatest army, that of Napoleon Bonaparte. My childhood was filled with the lullabies about slaves who had no other weapons than their desire for freedom and foolhardy courage. My grandmother told me stories in the evening about the exploits of our heroes who had to acquire everything from their enemy: as much the weapons as the strategies of war. Even the French language was a "spoil of war." And then suddenly, toward the end of the 1980s, people started speaking of Haiti uniquely in terms of poverty and corruption. A country can't be corrupt—only its leaders can be. The three-quarters of the population that, despite an endemic impoverishment, manages to hold on to its dignity should not be subject to such despicable affronts. When the word *Haiti* is pronounced, they are implicated. And when Haiti is insulted, it's still them—and not the wealthy—who are targeted. Poorest country—that's true enough; the numbers tell the story.

But does that erase its history? We're accused of trotting that out too often. But not more than any other country! When, for example, French television wants to fill its coffers, it puts out a series on Napoleon. There's no shortage of books on the history of France or England, or even on the Vietnam War, whereas there's not even a single film on the greatest colonial war of all times—the battle where slaves turned themselves into citizens by the sheer force of their will. Yet now I see there's a new label hatching that's getting ready to bury us completely: Haiti is cursed. There are even a few confused Haitians who have begun to use it. You've got to be pretty desperate to accept the disdain of others for oneself. This term can only be resisted at its source: in Western opinion. My only argument: What has this country ever done to merit this curse? I know of a country that has provoked two world wars in one century and proposed a final solution, yet no one says it has been cursed. I know a country completely insensitive to human suffering, that has never ceased starving the rest of the planet from its powerful financial centers, and yet no one says it has been cursed. On the contrary, it presents itself as a people blessed by God. So why should Haiti be cursed? I know that some use the word in good faith, not having found other terms to account for this avalanche of misfortunes. But that's not the right word, especially not when one can see so clearly the energy and dignity that this people has manifested in the face of one of the most difficult ordeals of our time. But every day that goes by makes this task even harder. It only takes one person to use the word "cursed" on the airwaves for it to metastasize like a cancer. Before we start talking about Vodou, savagery, cannibalism, people who drink blood, . . . I think I still have enough energy left to fight.

The Pivotal Moment

It's an event whose repercussions will be as important as those of Haiti's independence, on 1 January 1804. At the moment of independence, the Western world turned away from this new republic and left it to savor its triumph in isolation. Such was the fate of this people that had just managed to make its way out of the long, dark, and slimy tunnel that was slavery. The West has always refused to recognize this arrival into the world. Both Europe and America turned their back on Haiti. And, crazed by solitude, these newly free peoples turned on one another like animals. And ever since, the West has used Haiti as an example to any peoples seeking to liberate themselves from enslavement without permission. A punishment that has lasted for centuries. You will be free, but alone. Nothing is worse than being alone on an island. And so it is that today all eyes are fixed on Haiti. Like an immense door turning slowly on its hinges of light and darkness: the pivotal moment. In the last weeks of January 2010, Haiti was seen more than it had been in the last two centuries. It wasn't because of a coup d'état or one of those bloody tales of Vodou and cannibalism—it was an earthquake. An event no one could control. For once, our misfortune wasn't exotic. What's happening to us could happen anywhere.

Translated by Kaiama L. Glover

We Are Wozo

Edwidge Danticat

Afro-Haitian American novelist, short-story writer, memoirist, essayist, and editor Edwidge Danticat was born in Port-au-Prince, Haiti. When Danticat was two years old, her father migrated to New York to seek work and to escape the constraining political reality of life under President-for-Life François Duvalier. Her mother followed two years later, leaving Danticat and her brother in the care of her aunt and uncle. Danticat's aunt is an important character in her first novel, Breath, Eyes, Memory *(1994), and her uncle is the subject of her family memoir* Brother, I'm Dying *(2007). In 1981, at the age of twelve, Danticat moved to the United States to join her parents and two U.S.-born younger siblings, who lived in a Haitian American community in Brooklyn, New York. She very quickly became aware of the class and cultural differences that separated her and her family from "real" Americans. There was great stigma attached to being from Haiti in the 1980s. It was the period during which waves of so-called boat people, fleeing Duvalier's Haiti, were landing on the shores of Florida—and the period during which the U.S. Centers for Disease Control designated Haitians as* HIV/AIDS *carriers and subsequently banned all Haitians from giving blood. As a teenager, Danticat suffered acutely her "immigrant" status; the linguistic marginalization, social exclusion, and cultural conflict she experienced as an adolescent would subsequently inform all of her writings.*

Danticat's reflections in this article for Essence *magazine's online publication emerged in response to a series of texts written in and about Haiti and circulated throughout the literary and cyber spaces of the global "First World." The article is an intervention into a "post-earthquake" debate among women researchers and journalists regarding the representation of Haiti and, especially, women living in the tent cities. Addressing a specific U.S. woman reporter's unauthorized exposing of a Haitian rape survivor's story, Danticat condemns the irresponsible ways in which black female victimhood is mobilized for ostensibly progressive agendas. Her article moves from the involuntarily public trauma of one Haitian woman to a consideration of the ethics of storytelling in a hierarchically raced and gendered world. Danticat, a well-respected and celebrated writer, gives space in this essay for the woman in question to be heard—in her own voice—well beyond the boundaries of the Haitian camps.*

In this way, Danticat's essay evokes and transgresses the geopolitical borders that circumscribe the bodies and the voices of the world's most marginalized.

At the risk of prolonging a contentious debate concerning this essay by *Mother Jones* magazine reporter Mac McClelland, I would like to add another voice to the conversation.

Earlier this year, I met the woman that Ms. McClelland has called both Sybille and K* in her writings.

I met her at a meeting for rape survivors in Port-au-Prince. She is a twenty-five-year-old mother of three children. She has a beautiful singing voice and often sings in talent shows to inspire other rape survivors.

This incredibly brave and talented woman speaks Creole, French, and Spanish. She learned Spanish while traveling between Haiti and the Dominican Republic to buy grocery items, toiletries, and nonperishables that she would then resell in Port-au-Prince. She lost the father of her older children to illness before the earthquake and lost the father of her youngest child on January 2010, during the earthquake. She also lost her home, which is how she ended up living in the camp where she was raped.

In her essay, Ms. McClelland writes that K*'s trauma led in part to her own breakdown. Nevertheless, during Ms. McClelland's ride along with K*, on a visit to a doctor, Ms. McClelland, as has been reported elsewhere, live-tweeted K*'s horrific experiences. The tweets put K*'s life in danger because they identified the displacement camp where K* was living—with details of landmarks added—her specific injury, her real name, and suggest that she is a drug user.

When K* found out about Ms. McClelland's tweets, even before Ms. McClelland's original *Mother Jones* article was published, K* wrote a letter to Ms. McClelland and *Mother Jones* magazine asking that Ms. McClelland not write about her. Her lawyer emailed the letter to them on November 2, 2010.

The full text of the letter in K*'s own handwriting is attached and is written in Haitian Creole. It says:

> You have no right to speak of my story.
> You have no right to publish my story in the press
> Because I did not give you authorization.
> You have no right. I did not speak to you.
> You have said things you should not have said.
> Thank you

Ms. McClelland has stated on this same Twitter account that she had K*'s permission and K*'s mother's permission to ride along with them, but she certainly—according to K*'s lawyer, and the driver on the ride along, and

K* herself—did not have K*'s permission to tweet personal and confidential information about her. And even if Ms. McClelland in some way thought she had K*'s consent, the attached letter should have made it clear that it was withdrawn and that she had, as the letter states, "no right" to write about K* anymore, especially in ways that her previous tweets had made K*'s and her location easily identifiable.

I have K*'s permission to publish this letter and to talk about K* because she is angry at the way Ms. McClelland has portrayed her in the tweets, has ignored the wishes of her letter and continues to make K* part of her story.

This week, K* wrote me an email from Port-au-Prince saying, "I want victims in Haiti to know that they can be strong and stand up for their rights and have a voice. Our choices about when and how our story is told must be respected."

She closed her note by adding, "Se wozo nou ye," citing an irrepressible reed which grows, in spite of impossible conditions, on the side of Haitian rivers.

"We are wozo," K* writes. I agree.

Many have applauded Ms. McClelland's courage, while showing little consideration for K*. However, faced with extraordinary obstacles, to which one should not add other types of exploitation, K* and Haiti's other rape survivors have had to be more than courageous. They've had to be wozo.

Haïti pap peri

Jerry Rosembert Moïse

Recurring images of young children and granmoun *(elder men or women) spray-painting the words "Haïti pap peri" (Haiti won't perish) appeared in key neighborhoods of the capital city, Port-au-Prince, days after the January 2010 earthquake and the ensuing weeks when the aftershocks provoked heightened levels of uncertainty and peril. Celebrated visual artist Jerry Rosembert Moïse conceived and painted this piece along with a myriad of other powerful murals on untrustworthy cement and stone walls, which illuminated the hardship, the aspirations and the mundane in everyday Haitian life. The depiction of the spry children and the old yet spirited man—the future workers and leaders of the republic and the enduring citizens working together to broadcast to the survivors that they and their country will withstand the devastation and create anew—articulated a poignant and necessary dispatch circulated since the moment of Haitian independence. However, given the promises and challenges that faced the nation at the turn of the twenty-first century—the reelection of Jean-Bertrand Aristide (2001)—and the transformative moment of the earthquake, "Haïti pap peri" becomes an adage that forces the viewer to ask critical questions. What are the material and ideological components that will help the nation-state to feed, educate, and secure the dreams of its citizens? What role do foreign powers have in Haitian economic, social, and infrastructural development? Given the legacy of Haiti's standing at the periphery of global capitalism, how and in what institutions does one anchor his or her hope?*

"Haiti Will Not Perish," 2010, mural, Port-au-Prince. Moïse became famous for this declaration of strength and survival in the wake of the 2010 earthquake. Image by Jerry Rosembert Moïse, photograph courtesy of Lena Jackson.

"Birds and Water," 2010, mural, Port-au-Prince. In a city where access to clean water is a struggle for much of the population, Moïse evokes the joy that access to the resource would bring. Image by Jerry Rosembert Moïse, photograph courtesy of Lena Jackson.

"Girl Reaching for Cherries," 2010, mural, Port-au-Prince. Here Moïse incorporates a tree generously growing over a wall from a private home to offer its fruit into his artwork. Image by Jerry Rosembert Moïse, photograph courtesy of Lena Jackson.

"Girl Dreaming of Justice," 2010, mural, Port-au-Prince. Moïse depicts a young girl hoping for a more just political and social order. Image by Jerry Rosembert Moïse, photograph courtesy of Lena Jackson.

"Pakistan and Japan," 2011, mural, Port-au-Prince. Here Moïse expresses solidarity on the part of Haitians with those elsewhere in the world suffering from similar natural disasters, particularly (in the detail, top) the floods in Pakistan and (in the detail, bottom) the earthquake and tsunami in Japan. Image by Jerry Rosembert Moïse, photo courtesy of Lena Jackson.

The Cholera Outbreak

Roberson Alphonse

In the fall of 2010, just months after the earthquake, a cholera epidemic began in Haiti. Investigations traced the source of the outbreak to a camp of UN peacekeepers who were part of the MINUSTAH mission in the country, but the United Nations denied responsibility until August 2016. To this day, they deny legal liability for the cholera outbreak and resulting deaths. This article by Roberson Alphonse of Haiti's daily newspaper Le Nouvelliste *was one of the earliest detailed reports about the outbreak.*
—Contributing Editor: Claire Payton

"There it is!" Brows darkened, a woman with faded clothes pointed toward "Camp Annapur" of the Nepalese blue helmets in Meye, a locality of Mirebalais. "There it is, I'm telling you!" she insists before disappearing through a field under the bright sun of Tuesday, 2 November 2010.

Following the deaths of more than thirty people in Mirebalais and its surrounding areas and the hospitalization of a thousand more infected since the beginning of the month of October by *Vibro cholerae*, the cholera bacteria, this military facility has become a curiosity to ordinary people and the media. It was constructed in 2004, a few steps from national route number 3, on the banks of a tributary to the Laterme River, which flows into the Artibonite River.

More than fifteen days after the identification of the first case, public opinion continues to attribute the spread of the epidemic to parts of the Nepalese battalion that is stationed in this camp, a claim which is virulently contradicted by MINUSTAH. But not just anyone can freely enter into this supposed "hotbed of cholera." "No, you cannot enter here without an express authorization from the commander of the military forces. This is a high-security facility," kindly explained an officer in the shade outside the camp, close to one of the four sewage disposal drains leading to the river.

Are there soldiers who were sick with cholera here? How do you carry away human excrement? "No, I cannot respond to these questions. There are communication officers appointed to do that," he responded with reticence and the courtesy of an officer. "Where is the sewage dump located?" A smile. Nothing more.

Some five hundred meters from "Camp Annapur," some men are working on a piece of land that serves as an unauthorized dump for excrement and detritus, where turkeys and guinea fowl peck alongside fat pigs wallowing in the mud. The discharge of feces is not a septic tank and is located less than 150 meters from the river below. "I only know that someone closed the dump," one of the workers drops laconically. Have the inhabitants of Meye been infected? "No," responds a young man, visibly annoyed.

At the CDI in Mirebalais

Contrary to the young man, nurse Tulmé Marie Millande, an epidemiologist, confided that one of the first to die in a hospital was from Meye. "Rosemond Lorimé, twenty-one years old, is the first hospital death. He died on 17 October 2010, shortly after he was admitted to the CDI [Integral Diagnostic Centers]. His sister, two of his brothers, and two other people from the same house, located one hundred meters from the Nepali camp, had acute diarrhea, vomiting, abdominal pain," added the epidemiologist. She explained that she collected six stool samples from the infected and sent them to the national laboratory for examination, along with samples of water taken from the river that were sent for analysis at CAMEP on 19 October, two days after the death of Rosemond Lorimé.

"In principle, as an epidemiologist I should continue to research active cases, take samples and work on prevention. But after three days, I was told to no longer run tests because in the city of Saint-Marc it was confirmed that it was cholera, even though nothing had been determined for Mirebalais," explained the nurse. She also underlined the decline of the number of those infected with cholera received over the last few days at the CDI of Mirebalais. "The awareness campaign, the distribution of oral serum, gave satisfying results. To date, the CDI has identified 10 hospital deaths, 21 community deaths, and 1,572 people infected," she said.

In the Footsteps of the Hospitalized Death

Returning to Meye, on the left side of national route number 3, some two hundred meters from "Camp Annapur" and less than fifty meters from the bridge to Mirebalais, Pierre André Fleury, seventy-one years old, grandfather of Rosemond Lorimé, explains that his wife and young twenty-four-year-old son Jonas Fleury had been hospitalized. "We contracted the illness. My wife almost died," laments the man. "We have always drunk water from the river and nothing happened to us," added the sexagenarian. He complained that he had to pay off the debts contracted by him and his family to pay for the funeral of Rosemond Lorimé, who had lived in a shack without a latrine or sanitary facilities. "Other people from the neighborhood have fallen ill. Now we only drink well water that has been treated with bleach and Aquatab," continued Pierre André Fleury.

Mirebalais and Saint-Marc, the First Recognized Hotbeds

According to Dr. Jacques Boncy, the head of the national laboratory, "the first hotbeds identified are Mirebalais and Saint-Marc. There are investigations underway into the origins of the patients and the collected water samples." What are the results of the stool samples of Lorimé and the river water collected by Tulmé Marie Millande?

"It's the investigative commission of the MSPP [Ministère de la Santé Publique et de la Population] that must collect information about this affair. However, you must understand that we cannot reveal the results of the tests. They must be communicated either by the investigative commission of MSPP or by the doctor of these patients. The results of the examination belong with the patient, not to the public. This is ethics," added Dr. Jacques Boncy.

Asian Strain

A MINUSTAH press release made public on 2 November 2010 reported that according to the conclusions of the analyses done by the National Laboratory of Public Health (LNSP) in Haiti and the Centers for Disease Control and Prevention (CDC) based in Atlanta, in the United States, the strain of cholera responsible for the epidemic in Haiti is identical to the strain found in South Asia.

"However, in light of the speed of the movement of the strains of cholera across the world—transmitted by food, contaminated water or by infected people—health specialists underlined the difficulty, or even the impossibility, of determining with precision the manner in which cholera came to Haiti," underlined MINUSTAH. "Tests on water samples collected from inside and around the military base near Mirebalais as well as from the banks of the river were conducted Friday, 22 October, and Tuesday, 26 October, and the results were all negative. At the insistence of the Force Commander, additional tests were conducted on Wednesday, 27 October, in the interior of the camp and between the camp and the river. These tests have been analyzed by an independent laboratory and have also proved negative," reminded the UN mission. Amid suspicions that authorities have tended to simply overlook the origin of the contamination, the investigation continues. In the meantime, the epidemic is subsiding. The last report released recorded 442 deaths, of which 193 were deaths in the community and 6,742 infected.

Translated by Laurent Dubois

On the Politics of Haitian Creole

Various Authors

Any mention of Haiti or its people invariably leads to a discussion around language. Do Haitians speak French, Creole, Kreyòl, Haitian Creole, or just Haitian? Many prominent linguists studying the Haitian language are currently engaged in a heated debate surrounding the political and social implications of what one should call the language of the Haitian people. Other important questions include: Why is the language that is spoken by the vast majority of the Haitian people glaringly absent in so many parts of the public sphere, most notably in government correspondence and legislation? Who is responsible for creating a space in which the Haitian language can serve as a propellant for progress rather than being portrayed as a deterrent? In an October 2000 interview linguist Emmanuel W. Védrine explores some of these questions and reflects on the role that language can play in lifting Haiti out of "isolation." His attention to Haitian Creole is rooted in the notion that language is a tool that can be used not only to identify Haiti's problems but also to help solve them. Védrine encourages those focused on Haitian Creole research to shake their "colonial mentality" and be less self-serving by producing more texts in Creole.
—Contributing Editor: Wynnie Lamour

SICRAD: What major walls must come down in order for use of Kreyòl to spread?

E. W. VÉDRINE: Well, I see that you mention "major" that means what would be the most important one? Here, it would be politics, a fragile area to touch in Haiti. It is the government that has supreme power everywhere in the world. So, what is the power of the Haitian government here? Are there some international organizations that are there secretly, manipulating the issue so that Kreyòl doesn't spread? Talking about the "government," you encounter the legal aspect here also (that the state should have taken into consideration) and, globally speaking, we can point to the 1987 Constitution that declares two official languages: that is to say, everywhere that French is present, Kreyòl should be present also.

The second wall would be with people who had the opportunity to go far in school. Whether they are living in diaspora or in Haiti, they are still Haitians. They should get rid of all the bad colonial mentality within themselves in order to feel that they are a nation, that they have their own language and culture, and they should learn to appreciate that. In this second group, you can see professionals in all domains: they are the ones who should be models for the young generation. We have already mentioned the press; it should take its responsibility and do its part around the communication issue. We need more people who write in Kreyòl. Most Haitian authors write in French; they should start learning how to write in Kreyòl. Most Haitian linguists don't publish in Kreyòl, apart from some rare ones such as Yves Dejean, who makes a difference. If linguists who do research on their own language can't write or publish research in their native language, that turns into a comedy, a whole circus in this sense of analyzing the extension of colonial mentality. You can ask yourself this question: Are they doing and publishing research for the advancement of the Kreyòl language in Haiti or just to make foreign universities talk about them as "great researchers" who are writing on Kreyòl in a foreign language but who don't and can't write anything in Kreyòl? As polyglot myself, I am not against the fact that they are writing and publishing in the language of others; on the contrary, the more one can speak other languages, the better it is for that person. But, we (especially linguists), should have a commitment toward the native language and we should serve as models for the generations to come.

SICRAD: In a time where there is much talk of "globalization" and where the English language is the dominant one in the world, how can the Kreyòl language serve to pull Haiti out of her isolation?

E. W. VÉDRINE: Well, we can't deny the reality of the English language in terms of "globalization" and everything related to it. English has become a second language almost everywhere in the world. First, we can see how English predominates already in the domain of technology, science, and commerce in general. Latin enjoyed such privilege at a certain time, but don't regard that in a negative sense. I see it more at a "communicative" level. So, it would be an error if schools in Haiti don't put emphasis on the English language in their curriculum; we should start teaching it very early in school (as they do in the Scandinavian countries). Not only would every student like to pass the English portion in the Bakaloreya Exam, but there is a reality: many universities in the world (where English is not the language of these countries, including Haiti) use English textbooks in a range of subjects and in Haiti the English language would appear as a third language. So, there is nothing wrong with encouraging its teaching early in schools.

We have a generation of Haitians in the diaspora for whom English is the dominant language. For many of them, Kreyòl would be a second language, or they would not speak it fluently, but many are proud to say they are Haitians or that their parents are Haitians. Language doesn't isolate us; rather, we isolate ourselves. At the age of ten, I was already bilingual (speaking Kreyòl and French), and I started learning Spanish and English through music and books. Nevertheless, I blame myself for being able to speak only six languages; I had the opportunity to master more. If you see any problem of isolation related to Haiti, please don't think it's caused by Kreyòl or French. It is true that stereotypes exist between the two languages, but at the same time let's try to not make them responsible for Haiti's problems.

Language is not just a medium and a means to communicate. Language is also a tool, but it depends how we use it. There is only one country in the world that speaks Japanese; there aren't two or three. Does the Japanese language serve to isolate the Japanese? Let's look for the real cause of Haiti's problems, and talk about them to see what exactly would isolate us: Is it politics at home? Is it leaders that we don't really have? Is it Haitians who don't believe in their potentiality to meet challenges? Is it the colonial trap that compels us to not take our responsibility as adults? These are several questions that call for reflection.

While Védrine briefly mentions the power that the government can have in shifting the role of language in Haiti, Jacques Pierre, a Duke University–based linguist, takes it even further in an open letter to President Michel Martelly in May 2011. Pierre plainly indicts the Haitian government in its failure to implement the law of the Constitution of 1987, which states that "Kreyòl se sèl grenn lang ki simante tout pèp ayisyen an," or "Haitian Creole is the only language which binds all Haitian people." Writing in the language for which he is advocating, Pierre urges Martelly to continue engaging with the Haitian people in Creole, as he did during his presidential campaign. Pierre goes on to clearly outline the need to create a communications team that would allow the Haitian people critical access to Martelly's administration not only in French but also, more importantly, in Creole. Both Védrine and Pierre were speaking truth to a stark reality in Haiti: the persistent linguistic hierarchy, which creates an environment of exclusion, preventing the full participation of monolingual Creole speakers in the growth and progress of their country.
—Contributing Editor: Wynnie Lamour

President Michel Joseph Martelly:
On behalf of all the Haitian people, I congratulate you for your great victory, according to the official results of the Provisional Electoral Council on 20 April 2011. President, in the speech you gave on 5 April 2011, you said that you were the president of all Haitians, so I hope your administration will work to improve the lives of everyone, and will respect the rights of all Haitians and those of everyone living in Haiti.

Myself, a linguist and an educator, too, I will take advantage of this occasion to tell you that a fundamental right of the Haitian people that deserves unflinching respect[1] is their linguistic rights. All Haitians born and raised in the land of Haiti, we all speak Creole. It's true that there is a handful of people who speak French also; but Creole is the only language that all Haitians can use to speak to one another without any problem. Article 5 of the 1987 Constitution states that "Creole is the one and only language that brings together all the Haitian people." We are thus asking you to respect the linguistic rights of the Haitian people during the five years you will spend in power. It would be a great victory for you if the Haitian people could see Articles 5, 24–3, 40, and 213 of the 1987 Constitution implemented during your mandate.

President, I would like for you to set up a communications team to create a website in which all Haitians can find information in Creole and French on what the presidency is doing. It is also important for the country's official newspaper, *Le Moniteur*, to publish all of its information in Creole and French. Similarly, all official state documents should be released in both languages, and all state employees should speak Creole with all Haitians in need of services from government offices. Lastly, I would like your administration to create an Office of Translation at the Secretariat of Literacy in order to translate documents from the previous centuries that exist only in French. If an Office of Translation already exists, I hope you will provide it with the support to get work done because there are many documents that need to be translated into Creole. While the Office of Translation is translating these older documents, I hope that all documents published from day one of your administration will be made available in Creole and French. Mr. President, I believe there are enough resources to make all of this happen; now the question of will is in your hands.

Mr. President, in all the areas and remote places you visited while you were campaigning, you spoke frankly in your mother tongue. This is how the people were able to understand you without any problems: Creole is spoken, Creole is understood. I hope you don't push the people to the side on 14 May. I hope you do not give a speech in French, a language that the majority of the population does not understand. Also, to speak your mother tongue is to speak with all of the Haitian people, it is to invite all Haitians to reflect and comment on your speech, to give their own opinions. I hope that the 14 May speech will not be a speech with a few short phrases in Creole with the rest in French. If that is the case, it will show that truly when someone becomes a leader in Haiti, they no longer need the people. They do not speak for the people to understand because although the people's vote counts, their voice does not. I would like to see the people's vote and voice become one so that we can stand Haiti on its two feet with the participation of the entire rural population.

President, there are people who think you should give your speech in French so that diplomats and people in the international community can understand you. But the diplomatic missions have interpreters. And if there are some who don't have interpreters, your government can find people to interpret for them. You should not use an interpreter to translate for the majority of the people. If you did not do so during your campaign, why would you want to do it now? Therefore, it is important to show from the first day that your administration will not continue with the linguistic discrimination that has existed in this country from its inception.

Mr. President, I wish you to work well. We know the work is not easy. I invite everyone to work with your government, because if you fail, then the whole country fails too. It is clear that all serious-minded Haitians, whether they voted for you or not, do not wish the country to become any worse than it is because worse than this would be death for us all. So, I am asking all other professionals who have expertise in other domains to come together to critique and propose solutions they think will help the government when they have taken a false step. In order for this to happen, it is important for the presidency as well as the Office of the Prime Minister to create a website which has a space where all groups of professionals can give their opinions and make proposals with order and discipline, without anyone attacking the personality of the people running the country.

Long live a Haiti where no one can use language as a barrier to keep us from discovering the good ideas each individual Haitian has in his/her mind. In that way, everyone can participate in the country's reconstruction. Many hands make the load lighter.

With great respect,
Jacques Pierre

Translated by Nadève Ménard

In 2014, the Haitian Creole Academy finally became a reality after a protracted legal and political process. Although the Constitution of 1987 declared the existence of the Haitian Creole Academy, it took almost thirty years for the institution to exist in concrete terms. Haiti's State University and its vice rector for research at the time, Fritz Deshommes, spearheaded the effort to make the academy a reality. The process included establishing a committee to choose the academy's thirty-three founding members, a vote by the Senate in December 2012, a vote in the Chamber of Deputies in April 2013, and finally the publication of the official decree in Le Moniteur *on 7 April 2014. President Michel Martelly was slated to officially inaugurate the academy, but never showed up to the ceremony. Jean Vernet Henry, rector of the State University at the time, presided over the inauguration ceremony on Thursday, 4 December 2014.*

The following excerpts from the law establishing the Haitian Creole Academy give an idea of its overall mission. Although the decree in Le Moniteur *was published in French, the law itself was written in Haitian Creole.*

Chapter II: Status and Mission of the Academy

Article 3—The Haitian Creole Academy is a state institution. It is independent and covers the entire country. It is administrative, cultural, and scientific in nature.

Article 4—The Haitian Creole Academy is a state institution having jurisdiction to work on the Creole language as required by the amended Constitution of 1987. It is to guarantee the linguistic rights of all Haitians in all that concerns the Creole language.

Article 5—The Haitian Creole Academy is the reference for the Creole language in Haiti, whether oral or written, in state and private institutions.

Article 6—The Haitian Creole Academy will:

> Take measures for all state institutions to function in the Creole language according to the principles, rules and development of that language;
> Take measures to encourage institutions and people producing in the Creole language to follow its principles and rules;
> Take measures to help the Haitian population find all the services it needs in the Creole language;
> Take measures to help and encourage all state offices—whether belonging to the executive, legislative, or judicial branches—to respect the Constitution in linguistic matters;
> Serve as a reference for the Creole language in everything having to do with the language's standardization, whether within Haiti or in other countries where Haitians have settled;
> Do all that is necessary for Haiti to play its role as leader in the creolophone world.

Article 8—The Haitian state must provide all financial means and resources necessary for the Haitian Creole Academy to function.

Article 9—The Haitian Creole Academy has the right to look for funds and to receive all other types of resources it needs to function.

. . .

Article 11—The Haitian Creole Academy has a mission to:

> Do all that is necessary to encourage production in the Creole language
> Encourage the people's experiences in discovering, creating, and producing in Creole, whether oral or written production
> Do all that is necessary so that Creole can have genuine influence and

prestige in the eyes of the Haitian population and in the eyes of the
other populations

Work toward and foster well-balanced relationships in terms of how
institutions are using the languages in society

Work so that the state institutions apply the Constitution by
publishing all official documents in the Creole language

Make proposals as to how people can use the Creole language in
public communication within the country

Encourage work on the development of tools such as grammars,
dictionaries, lexicons in all areas

Encourage work on programs of technical training for all sectors that
need advanced training in the Creole language

Perform inventory of everyone working on the Creole language and
specialists in all subjects who are producing in the Creole language

Perform inventory of production in the Creole language and
production on the Creole language within the country and outside
of it

Encourage and propose genuine research on the Creole language

Work so that regional institutions can use the Creole language to
integrate the creolophone populations.

Article 19—"Academician" is an honorific title. People having the title "Academician" do not work for money, have no salary, as required by Article 214
of the amended 1987 Constitution.

Article 20—For someone to earn the title "Academician," he/she must:

Be Haitian, woman or man

Be at least forty years of age

Enjoy all civil and political rights, have no problems with the law

Be someone who works, who researches in or on the Creole language;
who produces quality work in or on Creole that has important
value for the advancement and development of the Creole
language;

Be someone whose work the society already recognizes as promoting
the advancement of the Creole language.

Article 21—The number of Academicians in the Haitian Creole Academy is
a minimum of thirty-three and a maximum of fifty-five.

. . .

Article 25—A person is an Academician for life; all Academicians are members of the Academic Council. An Academician loses his/her title when he/
she loses his/her civil and political rights, when she/he does not abide by the
ethical principles established by the academy.

. . .

Article 42—The Haitian Creole Academy will create a publication called the *Creole Academy Bulletin*. The *Creole Academy Bulletin* will serve to publish the body of dispositions, resolutions, and decisions taken by the academy with regard to the Haitian Creole language.

. . .

Article 44—The Haitian Creole Academy is a transversal institution; that is why it must establish collaborations with all ministries that have roles to play in the academy's work.

Translated by Nadève Ménard

Note

1. Here Pierre uses the term *tèt kale* to convey "unflinching." He employs the expression throughout the letter to emphasize various ideas. Michel Martelly often used the expression himself—he was a member of the Parti Haïtien Tèt Kale (Tèt Kale Haitian Party).

Stayle

Brothers Posse

During the 2012 Carnival season President Michel Martelly attempted to ban the popular Haitian music group Brothers Posse from performing their celebrated song "Stayle." The song, which employs language and themes from Rastafarian tradition and Jamaican dancehall, is layered with symbolism of political resistance and serves as a critique of the Martelly administration and the UN Mission for Stabilization in Haiti (MINUSTAH). Brothers Posse lyricist Antonio Cheramy, a.k.a. Don Kato, Haitianized the Jamaican patois word stylee—meaning "stylish"—by turning it into stayle, which evokes putting on false airs and showing off. Historically, Caribbean musical and visual expressions during Carnival showcase biting assessments of domestic governance and social life. "Stayle" is emblematic of that narrative of public criticism; in particular, the song's use of sexuality is one important lens through which to read about popular civic commentary on pre- and post-earthquake violence, particularly allegations of sexual violence by UN soldiers, exploitative state practices, and international relations.

President Martelly eventually extended a formal invitation, a float, and the customary $20,000 stipend to the band after polls showed the Carnival song was the most popular that year. However, during Haiti's Carnival in 2013, Martelly, a noted singer and lyricist whose own songs critiqued past presidents such as Aristide and Préval, censored the group. In January 2016, Antonio Chéramy was sworn into the Haitian Senate.

—Contributing Editor: Alice Backer

> There are those who come and go
> There are those who sit still
> But BP always chills
> From dirt roads to Cavaillon
> We send strong vibes
> Young or old
> In the cities or on farms
> Fans can't get enough of Brothers
> Let's put our voices together and sing
> Brothers Posse is our pillar

Voices in unison to sing to humanity
Wake up to speak the truth
Voices in unison the rastamen have arrived
Wake up and shake the dreads please

Jah will never give the wicked power over his faithful children
He will not suffer us bowing our heads to Babylon
Today the ghettos are suffering for their conviction
But we have learned to resist just like Papa Dessalines
Ghettoes united in love and peace say "Long live Ayiti Cheri
    [Beloved Haiti]"
Wide awake without violence to pray for them

Voices in unison to sing to humanity
Wake up to speak the truth
Voices in unison the rastamen have arrived
Wake up and shake the dreadlocks please

Bend down low to hear Kato's sacred word
Which says the people's victory is hidden in the castle
Fake promises, breaking the law
Empty words on loudspeakers
That's always how it goes but not this time
The people are upside down
Nowhere for the boss to hide
Our young brothers turned licky licky
Our pretty girls turned sicky licky
UN brought cholera chi chi licky
Government burning through cash like liquid liquid
Limp duds showing off acting freaky licky

Haiti won't be divided
It won't be divided
The ghetto won't betray
It won't betray
The dreads won't get cut
They won't get cut

Put your hands in the air!

Dread for dread
Rasta for Rasta
Dread for dread
Samba for samba
Dread for dread

Brother for brother
Our people for our country
Our country for our people

That's how we play
That's how we roll
A *stylee* president
That's how we play
That's how we roll
A stylee UN army
(*Previous two stanzas repeat*)

Haiti rise up to stand up for our rights
All the bad sense they've brought, we're gonna chase away
UN soldiers after our rear ends, we must see they're chi chi
We're trying to save our asses so they don't take them away
Chase them away! Fight!
Tell them to get lost! We will never deal with them! No!
(*Stanza repeats*)

Dessalines's country is not for the UN
Brothas betta watch your rear ends
They have weapons, they have bullets
They are chi chi and fabulous
(*Stanza repeats*)

Haiti won't be divided
It won't be divided
The ghetto won't betray
It won't betray
The dreads won't get cut
They won't get cut

Dread for dread
Rasta for Rasta
Dread for dread
Samba for samba
Dread for dread
Brother for brother
Our people for our country
Our country for our people

That's how we play
That's how we roll
A *stylee* president

That's how we play
That's how we roll

Dessalines's country is not for the UN
Brothas betta watch your rear ends
They have weapons, they have bullets
They are chi chi and fabulousssss
(*Stanza repeats*)

That's how we play
That's how we roll
A *stylee* president

Dread for dread
Rasta for Rasta
Dread for dread
Samba for samba
Dread for dread
Brother for brother
Our people for our country
Our country for our people

That's how we play
That's how we roll
A *stylee* president
That's how we play
That's how we roll
A *stylee* UN army

Translated by Alice Backer

To Reestablish Haiti?

Lemète Zéphyr and Pierre Buteau

The editors of the collective volume Refonder Haïti?, *published at the end of 2010, gathered texts from over forty Haitian academics, journalists, writers, and policy makers to insert a sampling of Haitian thought on the post-earthquake situation into a landscape dominated by foreign pundits. In addition to emphasizing the diversity of Haitian voices, the editors aimed to "interrogate . . . the mechanics of exclusion, the systematic reproduction of inequalities, the cultural issue, the city/country dynamic, the status of the peasantry, class relations, the forms and effects of dependence, the conditions of wealth and poverty production." They aimed also to contextualize the January 2010 earthquake and its aftermath, especially with regard to Haitian history.*

The two excerpts that follow are both written by professors at Haiti's State University. In the first, linguist, translator, and pastor Lemète Zéphyr shows how a profound crisis in leadership aggravated the aftermath of the January 2010 earthquake. In the second, Pierre Buteau, a historian and former minister of education, traces the path that has led from Haiti's emergence as an independent state in the nineteenth century to its crippling dependence on foreign entities at the dawn of the twenty-first.

Lemète Zéphyr, "Let's Build a Leadership That Can Live Up to Our Challenges!"

The Biggest Obstacle to Haiti's Development:
A Predatory Leadership Holding the State Hostage

On 12 January 2010, . . . I took up "humanitarian work," searching here and there for which victim needed transportation to the hospital, which pressing need remained unsatisfied, which emergency had not been followed up on. . . . Like many Haitians of goodwill who had been proud up until that point, I was forced to agree with the president of the Dominican Republic, Leonel Fernández: "The Haitian state does not exist." I looked everywhere for signs of some public power. I listened to the radio in my free time or while at the wheel to find out about the state's big decisions, about instructions given to the population, strategies to manage the catastrophe.

In short, I expected a reassuring and visionary speech from the state. On the contrary, just like the special correspondents from Radio France Inter (RFI), I was forced to observe that the "lack of a state in Port-au-Prince," "the absence of structures," "the sluggish political authorities" constituted the biggest difficulty paralyzing the foreign missions that came to help save the victims. More than once, RFI used phrases like "this little bit of island," "this cursed island," "the only LDC [least developed country] of the Americas," "the most corrupt country in the world," etc., to complete the picture.

It took several days before the rescue process could begin. On Thursday, 14 January, in my presence, Mrs. Nadine Anilus, one of my former students at the Haitian State University, reported her failure to radio hosts from Radio Caraïbe after spending the day searching for a justice of the peace to authorize action at the site of the DGI [the Direction Générale de Impôts, the country's tax service] on Paul VI Street to help the civil servants, certain high-ranking, who were still alive beneath the debris, of whom she cited the names and positions. According to one of the radio presenters, the judge had just left the radio station. He had lost his cell phone. It was impossible to contact him.

The survivors of the School of Applied Linguistics reported that Professor Pierre Vernet, who was by their side, at first tried to comfort them, saying that help would come soon. But he must have regretted the inefficacy of the state before passing away. Worse, the survivors and the corpses freed during the first four days that followed the catastrophe were freed by students from the institution, whom the neighborhood rightly called heroes.

These cases are used here as examples to illustrate "the absence of the state" RFI was talking about. If the state could not relieve nor even assist citizens of goodwill who were trying to save the civil servants of an institution as important as DGI, across the street from the National Palace, even if the latter was partially destroyed, what state are we talking about?

Yet it is through institutions such as the government, the legislative power, the judicial power that the state manifests itself. The entire state apparatus serves the interests of a handful of supposed authorities to the detriment of the population that they are supposed to serve. A predatory, monopolizing leadership is holding the state hostage. That is the principal obstacle to Haiti's development. It is this absence of a state that got us the takeover of Haitian institutions by the international community, through the voluntary suicide of Parliament that sanctioned the emergency law, of which one of the immediate consequences was the creation of the powerful Interim Commission for Haitian Reconstruction, which in practical terms, replaced what was left of the Haitian state.

The Short- and Midterm Solution to the Current Chaos:
Evacuate Port-au-Prince to Rebuild It and/or Displace the Capital

The current situation requires short-, mid-, and long-term actions. Many people are surprised to see that six months after the earthquake that had drawn the world's eyes to Haiti, almost a million citizens are still living beneath tents that cannot deceive the sun. The majority of cleaned private properties are the result of their owners' actions. Unsanitary conditions, precariousness, promiscuity, hunger are in full swing. Several months after 12 January, the state has not kept its promise concerning the payment of school fees for all children in order to facilitate the return to school. The hurricane season has already shown, if it was necessary, the population's vulnerability.

All of this places great pressure on the environment, already put to the test by the country's accelerated desertification. What needs to be done immediately? If everyone is talking about reconstruction or reestablishment, the most astute cannot help but ask this basic question: where is the plan for land development, which is a prerequisite for all physical reconstruction? For it is physical reconstruction that is at stake in the action plan for the recovery and the development of Haiti proposed (endorsed) by the Haitian state.

The more time that passes, the more the direction of this reconstruction becomes precise in the discourse. The first stone of the Ministry of the Interior and the territorial collectivities has already been placed at the old site of the French Institute of Haiti. We are talking less and less about the reconstruction of the country when we are talking about Port-au-Prince.

Taking into account the critical reality of Port-au-Prince, where all the services are concentrated, the Haitian state should seize the opportunity of 12 January to develop the provincial cities, to evacuate the shantytowns where anarchic construction reigns, to develop social housing projects and infrastructure outside of Port-au-Prince at the same time in order to encourage massive investment and modernize organization of the land.

Such an approach would reduce the pressure on Port-au-Prince, thanks to job creation and access to all the services necessary for the smooth functioning of any modern city in the world, and would allow time for those responsible to either conceive of and build a modern capital from a cohesive urban map in a restored environment, or to establish the capital in another department, the Central Plateau, for example, far from the various currently known fault lines.

We now have the opportunity to define a global framework for action, by activity sector and by region, to which all NGOs present in our territory or who want to come help support our efforts should have the obligation to submit, according to our real needs, along with indicators of measurable results. Any request to be recognized or to take action that does not conform to the state's framework should be denied.

A Leadership Freed from Unhealthy Dependence Syndrome

It is a fact that independence does not have the same meaning today that it did when the slaves of Saint-Domingue decapitated the colonizers and burned down their residences in 1804. The globalized world in which we live forces us to reposition ourselves. Nonetheless, a state worthy of that name should be able to take sole responsibility for its territory, the security of its borders, the feeding, protection, education, health, the housing of its people. . . . Since the first U.S. occupation of Haiti (1915–34), the country has become weaker and weaker, more and more dependent on multilateral aid to finance even its operating budget. This extreme weakening has opened the door for all sorts of actions by foreigners, who are more comfortable in our home than we are. Thus follows the proliferation of NGOs, foreign charity institutions, the overpresence of American and UN armed forces at every crossroads of our history. Haitian authorities have shamelessly developed an unhealthy dependence syndrome. They do everything they can to sell the people's misery to foreigners at a profit. Fighting poverty, improving the lives of the masses, strengthening the local population, attracting investments, etc., is on everyone's lips without the slightest action toward sustainable development. For they know that the international community will take advantage of any excuse to "fly to the rescue of the poor Haitian people." Consequently, it is out of the question to try to end this vicious cycle, since it is a comfort zone for the leaders.

The history of humanity can offer no example of a state that has developed sustainably through foreign aid, without a local development plan, with no management capacity. Foreign interventions at regular intervals give the illusion of a fast solution while intensifying the causes that rendered them necessary. Where is the logic, for example, in the fact that the Haitian state refuses to reconstitute its army or to re-create one, according to the dictate of the 1987 Constitution, yet we have several foreign armies on our territory to "assure a minimum of security"? Because our army has always been seduced by political power? Or because all armies are budget-hungry? A mere glance at the functioning of the little countries that are our neighbors and at the budget of the UN forces present in Haiti is sufficient to deconstruct these fallacious arguments. We need a leadership freed from the unhealthy foreign dependence syndrome; a leadership ready to get on with the task of restoring the country's nineteenth-century sense of pride through the elaboration of a sustainable development plan over at least twenty-five years, with the participation of the key local actors from the outset so that there is a real sense of ownership, followed by a search for external aid to complete our own investment budget. It is the condition *sine qua non* to reduce the country's dependency little by little and develop this conscience of what is possible without which there can be no state. . . .

It is time, more than ever, for us to involve the Haitian youth, that mass of the unemployed eager to contribute, at all levels of the process: cleanup, brainstorming, tailored training, reconstruction. It is absolutely urgent to combat the wait-and-see attitude that is so stressful and so disenchanting. All reconstruction undertaken without a significant Haitian contribution is doomed to fail from the start. For no one can develop anyone. And were this reconstruction to succeed without us, its effects would be short-lasting insofar as it would symbolize eternal shame to us and would diminish us in the eyes of the whole world.

Renewing Leadership by Reestablishing the Haitian Education System on the Basis of Inclusion and Haitian Identity

To take advantage of the current opportunities, Haiti needs another type of leadership, a leadership that is ready to serve, concerned with the collective well-being, visionary and imbued with a culture of results.

. . .

Where will we find this type of leader today? Do we have the time to create them? It is up to the nonsubservient civil society, to astute university community members, to the institutions that are still standing, to take this country's destiny into their hands and to dismiss the predators in the near future. The weakening of the Haitian state that facilitated the foreigners' stranglehold on our national sovereignty happened because of the incapacity of state structures to fulfill—even in mediocre fashion—their role of protecting citizens against banditry, against natural catastrophes aggravated by the environment's vulnerability, and of offering minimal services to the population: health services, basic education, electric energy. . . . Added to that the psychological insecurity created by the alienating character of the Haitian education system, which brings our leaders to idolize that which is foreign, to demonize their political adversaries and to ignore the capacities of their fellow citizens, their rights, and their needs in order to blindly lean on the foreigner.

. . .

Why weren't men and women like Lesly F. Manigat, Gérard Latortue, Michèle Pierre-Louis, among the very best of the country, able to successfully install a new order in Haiti? Why did Jean-Bertrand Aristide and René Préval, who came to power with real legitimacy and up until now have been the most popular presidents at the start of their terms, eventually espouse the traditional approach, which consists of dividing to conquer and forgetting hardship, social injustice, in short, the legitimate claims they were supposed to take on in their management of power?

Many arguments could be made. But, to my way of thinking, the fundamental reason remains their common worldview, fashioned in a traditional society that prepares its best elements by means of a traditional school that reproduces the system of social inequalities instituted right after national independence through the distribution of privileges to high-ranking officials who fought the European enemy and the maintaining of the masses in the status quo. Jean Price-Mars's *La vocation de l'élite* (191[9]), a series of conferences pronounced during the first U.S. occupation of Haiti, seems relevant to us as we perpetuate that worldview born of slavery that he was already denouncing. The rebuilding of Haiti necessarily entails

> social education, a discipline to which each individual must submit and which is apt to bring him to his fellow [citizen] in order to achieve together the ideal of peace and reason outside of which there is only violence and lack of leadership.

This social education must entail the reestablishment of the Haitian education system at all levels (basic education, the new secondary school, technical training, professional and higher education) basing it on another system of values such as solidarity, generosity, inclusion, tolerance, equity, responsible citizenship, healthy management of the environment, the spirit of service, etc., which will model the Haitian child's character and predispose him to "achieve together the ideal of peace and reason."

This new school, based on an awareness of the failure of suicidal individualism, will develop team spirit within the young Haitian with a view toward finding the common good, the ability to negotiate, the valorization of the Haitian sociocultural heritage and popular wisdom (Haitian Creole, arts and crafts, oral and written literature from yesterday and today), the use of positive elements from all the cultures we're exposed to, critical thinking, a moral sense, transparency, in order to get rid of the cultural alienation transmitted by school, among other things, generation after generation, and which predisposes us to submit to the foreigner against our common interest and to disdain our compatriots.

This new school will eventually produce another type of Haitian, modeled from childhood according to a design that pools energies in order to free us from the tendency to exhaust ourselves in inglorious struggles for power which weaken us before foreigners and give them free rein on our future, against our collective interest.

This new society will put to use what all of its children, without discrimination, carry within themselves in terms of primary materials for the production of human and economic development, political renewal, environmental restoration, etc. The leaders that come from this school will value everyone's collaboration to serve everyone and will put collective well-being above individual interests. These leaders will reform our dying institutions through the modernization of the judicial system, the application of the law, decentralization and deconcentration, planning the national territory, etc. Of all the proposed "plans" analyzed during the Forum on National Reconstruction organized by Haiti's State University, only the Strategic Plan of National Rescue/Intergenerational Pact for Shared Progress and Stability proposed by intellectuals, politicians, and individuals from civil society seems to me to be close enough to this ideal.

Pierre Buteau, "Why Reestablish?"

What is to be reestablished? The term reveals itself to be ambiguous and suspect because it is a direct attack on this country's personality and that of the beings it comprises. It is brutally offensive to what we can call Haiti's idiosyncrasy, its profound nature—that is to say, its historical individuality: its signature date, 1804, its beliefs, its myths, its traditions, its population's way of life. Can we then reestablish what had been previously founded, on symbolic but also material bases, . . . as fragile as these foundations—which have never been as solid as when the country first emerged on the international scene as a free and sovereign state—may seem? Would we have the right to reestablish Rome, the eternal city, while leaving aside the legend of Romulus and Remus nursed by the Wolf? France, while silencing Providence's message to the devout Joan of Arc? Has Japan turned its back on its traditions, did it betray its institutions when it rebuilt itself after the harsh tremors of the Second World War? As for the promoters of the Marshall Plan, they definitely did not question the civilizational foundations of Western Europe to facilitate the Glorious Thirty. Why, then, the desire to reestablish a country that is barely emerging from a shock, terrifying, yes, but having only concretely hit three departments, even if one of them, the West, has since the end of the U.S. occupation of 1915 imposed itself as the center of the country's economic activity and political decisions? Can we reinvent a country built over two centuries ago? Why is the almost general tendency to guide it toward a path both unique and radical? At what moment did Haiti attain the critical threshold, so critical that most of those concerned about it invite it to rethink itself? We seriously believe that this critical threshold deserves to be evaluated in order to question the moment from which the country began an accelerated process of material and spiritual degradation, forcing everyone to seize on the earthquake as an excuse to reestablish it.

A complete overhaul often invites one to undertake a history of beginnings. That of this land, of the men and women who have inhabited it, who died for it or have been vanquished by its nature, by that of its gods. That of its beliefs, of its traditions, of its foundational myths like the Bois Caïman ceremony, where Catherine Flon sewed the flag snatched from the French with a strand of her long hair. The Haitian people and the Haitian state, in their fusion, present themselves as a difficult mixture of the religious and the political. If the religious has cemented this people by gathering all the ethnic groups that came from Africa into an almost homogenous whole, the political was not able to completely accomplish the job of organizing. This country, in spite of everything, was able to manage and maintain for two centuries a delicate balance between the needs and the material possibilities offered by the conditions of production. This balancing act was only interrupted by untimely civil wars and an awkward and catastrophic American occupation, that of 1915–34. That did not destroy Haiti, however, and the illusion of success was able to be maintained under the administrations of Estimé (1946–50) and Magloire (1950–56). This country still managed, in spite of Duvalierism, which messed everything up, to maintain up until beyond 1970 a certain measure of self-sufficiency with regard to food.

. . .

Well before the fall of Jean-Claude Duvalier's government, a set of transformations occurred that strongly impacted people's mind-sets. Children began to no longer want to be like their parents. The Haitian way of life once again underwent profound changes. The bourgeoisie multiplied its secondary residences here or there in order, perhaps, to mitigate the threat of the slums and continued to place its increasing capital in more secure places abroad, thereby undermining the material basis of its existence, especially by the weakening of a national market still under construction. Among the more privileged, the middle classes also changed; they became more bourgeois. With unimaginable stunts (measures to obtain residency or citizenship in Canada or the United States, delivering babies abroad, etc.), they showed great ingenuity for putting as much distance as possible between themselves and their place of origin in order to offer their children another type of knowledge, no doubt for their security, but with no real effect for the production and continuation of a cultured knowledge within the country. For over almost three generations now, we've realized that the products of these privileged social groups have practically never attended an authentically Haitian school. The most underprivileged classes, for their part, have turned away from working in the fields and small jobs. Thus, is it possible to wonder, not without some anxiety, but with a degree of relevance, about the existence today of an ethnic Haitian compared to a Dominican, an Argentinean, a Canadian, a Frenchman, or an American? It is against such a backdrop of sociocultural mayhem that the Duvalier dynasty collapsed and that the democratic transition developed with the objective of modernizing the Haitian political regime.

Duvalierism, in its totalitarian path, carried out an upheaval of the country's institutions. After having neutralized them, his regime totally folded them into his project. From Haitian, they became Duvalierist. Duvalier did not destroy these institutions; rather, he perverted them. One of the greatest weaknesses of this democratic transition resides in the fact that those responsible mistook the true nature of these institutions and neglected or ignored the democratic institutions that had been functioning since 1930. They could very well have salvaged them and adapted them to the necessities of the time, but they did not understand, or refused to understand, that Duvalierism had subjected all of the institutions (the army, the tobacco company, the state store, the techno-administrative personnel, the national radio and television stations, the national phone company, etc.) to its totalitarian goals. All of the state's components managed to function, sometimes regularly, sometimes with the utmost rigor, but always primarily in the regime's interest. Thus, the section chief and the dew breaker, to cite only the bottom rungs of the army, guaranteed a minimum of administrative support such as recording births and deaths or delivering passports to the herdsman for the ordinary and regular flow of cattle; the Haitian-Dominican border was not as porous as it appears today. From this simple element of the military hierarchy and in its most informal aspect (the object, by the way, of numerous abuses of authority), the state managed to maintain a fragile social cohesion in the most far-flung places in the country and throughout the most tight-knit networks of Haitian society.

This upheaval that we have observed in the historical trajectory of Duvalierism, does not seem to be particular to Haiti, but can be found in most countries marked at some point of their existence by a totalitarian power. It seems, however, that countries such as Germany, Italy, or Spain, to cite countries that differ from ours by their nature or structure, or on the other hand, countries closer to us by their social profile, like the Dominican Republic or Paraguay, were more successful with their emergence from totalitarianism thanks to a democratic transition more adapted to their personality.

It is most likely due to not having grasped what is a true democratic transition, nor having fully measured the havoc Duvalierism caused in people's minds, that the Haitian authorities, aided by foreign partners, full of certainty and utterly lacking in humility, wanted to radically change this country. They thought to transform it by imposing a new legal/political model such as during colonial times, but without those brutal procedures. In applying this model, they attempted to build a new Haiti by rejecting the institutions which preceded Duvalierism or by systematically ignoring those that could still be of use. By imposing an extremely complex constitution in terms of its application methods and new rules poorly adapted to its sociological universe on this country, they contributed to neutralizing an already weak state, rendering it inoperative and inefficient in its main function, maintaining the unity of the social body.

Since the December 1990 elections, the United Nations and several other international organizations can be found on Haitian soil. In 2004, they reinforced this presence by an official mandate, as they have done for other countries in crisis. It's been twenty years since these institutions have taken charge of Haitians' destiny to accompany them on the road to democracy—

twenty years in which the social situation has hardly improved. And the terrible events of 12 January clearly showed the limits of this presence. All of the institutional scaffolding built during this long period brought practically no appropriate response to the population's despair.

In striving to guide this society on the laudable path of formal democracy, these organizations did not sufficiently account for the true needs of the population. In advocating the great principles of the philosophy of Rights of Man and democratic norms, they did not sufficiently measure that fictive and formal equality before the voting urn could not compensate for the lack of real equality. The viability of putting into practice in a lucid and rational way, as well as respecting the Rights of Man, absolutely necessitates first meeting the population's most basic needs. Thus, if we must reestablish something in this battered country, it would be best to reformulate, even to rethink the strategic foundations of this democratic transition. Twenty years of presence on this soil, almost the span of a generation for so few results. If the United Nations does not change the terms of its mission, it risks staying for another fifty years, or even a century. It would need, to avoid such a failure, to appreciate more, and with much humility, the country's historical and anthropological reality in order to help Haitians overcome one of the most acute crises of their history, that of the crumbling of the state. Then, and only at that moment, will it be able to stop this process of social regression and downward spiral. There is still time.

Translated by Nadève Ménard

Suggestions for Further Reading and Viewing

The literature on Haiti is vast. What follows is a necessarily partial list of books and films we recommend, largely focused on English-language works.

General Works

Averill, Gage. *A Day for the Hunter, a Day for the Prey: Popular Music and Power in Haiti.* Chicago: University of Chicago Press, 1997.

Beaubrun, Mimerose P. *Nan Dòmi: An Initiate's Journey into Haitian Vodou.* San Francisco: City Lights, 2013.

Bellegarde-Smith, Patrick, and Claudine Michel, eds. *Haitian Vodou: Spirit, Myth, Reality.* Bloomington: Indiana University Press, 2006.

Benson, LeGrace. *Arts and Religions of Haiti.* Kingston, Jamaica: Ian Randle, 2015.

Bouchereau, Madeleine Sylvain. *Haïti et ses femmes: Une étude d'évolution culturelle* [Haiti and its women: A study of cultural evolution]. Port-au-Prince: Les Éditions Fardin, 1957.

Brown, Karen McCarthy. *Mama Lola: A Haitian Vodou Priestess in Brooklyn.* Berkeley: University of California Press, 2011.

Casey, Matthew. *Empire's Guestworkers: Haitian Migrants in Cuba during the Age of US Occupation.* Cambridge: Cambridge University Press, 2017.

Chapman, Dasha A., Erin L. Durban-Albrecht, and Mario LaMothe. "Nou Mache Ansanm (We Walk Together): Queer Haitian Performance and Affiliation." Special issue, *Women and Performance: a journal of feminist theory* 27, no. 2 (2017).

Dalembert, Louis-Philippe, and Lyonel Trouillot. *Haïti: Une traversée littéraire* [Haiti: A literary journey]. Paris and Port-au-Prince: Philippe Rey and Presses Nationales d'Haïti, 2010.

Dash, J. Michael. *Haiti and the United States: National Stereotypes and the Literary Imagination.* New York: Palgrave, 1996.

Dejean, Yves. "Yon lekòl tèt anba nan yon peyi tèt anba" [An upside down school system in an upside down country]. Port-au-Prince: Fokal, 2006.

Desmangles, Leslie. *Faces of the Gods: Vodou and Roman Catholicism.* Chapel Hill: University of North Carolina Press, 1992.

Dubois, Laurent. *Haiti: The Aftershocks of History.* New York: Metropolitan Books, 2012.

Haiti: An Island Luminous. http://islandluminous.fiu.edu/.

Jackson, Régine O., ed. *Geographies of the Haitian Diaspora*. New York: Routledge, 2011.

Lerebours, Michel-Philippe. *Bref regard sur deux siècles de peinture haïtienne (1804–2004) / Brief overview of two centuries of Haitian painting (1804–2004)*. Port-au-Prince: Éditions de l'Université d'État d'Haïti, 2018.

"Littérature haïtienne." Île en île, http://ile-en-ile.org/lit-haitienne/.

Maguire, Robert, and Scott Freeman, eds. *Who Owns Haiti? People, Power, and Sovereignty*. Gainesville: University Press of Florida, 2017.

Nicholls, David. *From Dessalines to Duvalier: Race, Colour and National Independence in Haiti*. New Brunswick, NJ: Rutgers University Press, 1996.

Plummer, Brenda Gayle. *Haiti and the United States: The Psychological Moment*. Athens: University of Georgia Press, 1992.

Polyné, Millery. *From Douglass to Duvalier: U.S. African Americans, Haiti, and Pan Americanism*. Gainesville: University Press of Florida, 2010.

Trouillot, Michel Rolph. *Silencing the Past: Power and the Production of History*. Boston: Beacon, 1996.

Part I

Daut, Marlene. *Baron de Vastey and the Origins of Black Atlantic Humanism*. New York: Palgrave Macmillan, 2017.

Dayan, Colin (Joan). *Haiti, History, and the Gods*. Berkeley: University of California Press, 1998.

Dubois, Laurent. *Avengers of the New World: The Story of the Haitian Revolution*. Cambridge, MA: Harvard University Press, 2004.

Fick, Carolyn. *The Making of Haiti: The Saint Domingue Revolution from Below*. Knoxville: University of Tennessee Press, 1990.

Gaffield, Julia. *Haitian Connections in the Atlantic World: Recognition after Revolution*. Chapel Hill: University of North Carolina Press, 2015.

James, C. L. R. *The Black Jacobins: Toussaint Louverture and the San Domingo Revolution*. New York: Vintage, 1989.

Part II

Eller, Anne. *We Dream Together: Dominican Independence, Haiti and the Fight for Freedom*. Durham, NC: Duke University Press, 2016.

Hector, Michel, and Laënnec Hurbon, eds. *Genèse de l'état Haïtien (1804–1859)* [The genesis of the Haitian state (1804–1859)]. Port-au-Prince: Editions Presse Nationales d'Haïti, 2009.

Ramsey, Kate. *The Spirits and the Law: Vodou and Power in Haiti*. Chicago: University of Chicago Press, 2015.

Sheller, Mimi. *Democracy after Slavery: Black Publics and Peasant Radicalism in Haiti and Jamaica*. Gainesville: University Press of Florida, 2000.

Smith, Matthew J. *Liberty, Fraternity, Exile: Haiti and Jamaica after Emancipation*. Chapel Hill: University of North Carolina Press, 2014.

Parts III and IV

Bellegarde-Smith, Patrick. *In the Shadow of Powers: Dantès Bellegarde in Haitian Social Thought*. Atlantic Highlands, NJ: Humanities Press International, 1985.

Castor, Suzy. *L'occupation américaine d'Haïti*. Port-au-Prince: Société haïtienne d'histoire, 1988.

Corvington, Georges. *Port-au-Prince au cours des ans: La capitale d'Haïti sous l'occupation, 1915–1922* [Port-au-Prince over the years: The capital of Haiti under occupation, 1915–1922]. Port-au-Prince: Deschamps, 1984.

Corvington, Georges. *Port-au-Prince au cours des ans: La capitale d'Haïti sous l'occupation, 1922–1934* [Port-au-Prince over the years: The capital of Haiti under occupation, 1922–1934]. Port-au-Prince: Deschamps, 1987.

Gaillard-Pourchet, Gusti. *L'experience Haïtienne de la dette exterieure (ou) production cafeiere pillee, 1875–1915* [The Haitian experience of foreign debt or coffee production pillaged]. Port-au-Prince: Imprimerie Henri Deschamps, 2001.

Manigat, Leslie. "La substitution de la prépondérance américaine à la prépondérance française en Haïti au début du XXe siècle: La conjoncture de 1910–1911" [The substitution of the supremacy of the United States of America for the supremacy of France at the start of the twentieth century: The context of 1910–1911]. *Revue d'histoire moderne et contemporaine* 14 (October–December 1967): 321–55; reprinted in Leslie Manigat, *Eventail d'histoire vivant d'Haïti*, vol. 3. Port-au-Prince: CHUDAC, 2001.

Plummer, Brenda Gayle. *Haiti and the Great Powers, 1902–1915*. Baton Rouge: Louisiana State University Press, 1988.

Renda, Mary A. *Taking Haiti: Military Occupation and the Culture of U.S. Imperialism, 1915–1940*. Chapel Hill: University of North Carolina Press, 2001.

Schmidt, Hans. *The United States Occupation of Haiti, 1915–1934*. New Brunswick, NJ: Rutgers University Press, 1995.

Shannon, Magdaline. *Jean Price-Mars, the Haitian Elite and the American Occupation, 1915–35*. New York: Palgrave Macmillan, 1997.

Part V

Dunham, Katherine. *Island Possessed*. Chicago: University of Chicago Press, 1994.

Fowler, Carolyn. *A Knot in the Thread: The Life and Work of Jacques Roumain*. Washington, DC: Howard University Press, 1980.

Paulino, Edouardo. *Dividing Hispaniola: The Dominican Republic's Border Campaign against Haiti, 1930–1961*. Pittsburgh: University of Pittsburgh Press, 2016.

Philoctète, René. *Massacre River*. Translated by Linda Coverdale. New York: New Directions, 2008.

Roumain, Jacques. *Masters of the Dew*. Translated by Langston Hughes. London: Heinemann, 1987.

Smith, Matthew J. *Red and Black in Haiti: Radicalism, Conflict, and Political Change, 1934–1957*. Chapel Hill: University of North Carolina Press, 2009.

Verna, Chantalle F. *Haiti and the Uses of America: Post-U.S. Occupation Promises*. New Brunswick, NJ: Rutgers University Press, 2017.

Part VI

Arthus, Wien Weibert. *Duvalier à l'ombre de la guerre froide: Les dessous de la politique étrangère d'Haïti (1957–1963)* [Duvalier in the shadow of the Cold War: The underside of Haitian foreign policy]. Port-au-Prince: L'Imprimeur, 2014.

Danticat, Edwidge. *The Dew Breaker*. New York: Knopf, 2004.

Diederich, Bernard. *Haiti and Its Dictator*. Princeton, NJ: Markus Weiner, 1998.

Glover, Kaiama L. *Haiti Unbound: A Spiralist Challenge to the Postcolonial Canon*. Liverpool: Liverpool University Press, 2010.

Trouillot, Michel Rolph. *State against Nation: The Origins and Legacies of Duvalierism*. New York: Monthly Review Press, 1990.

Vieux-Chauvet, Marie. *Love, Anger, Madness: A Haitian Triptych*. Translated by Rose-Marie Réjouis and Val Vinokur. New York: Modern Library, 2010.

Part VII

Dupuy, Alex. *The Prophet and Power: Jean-Bertrand Aristide, the International Community, and Haiti*. Lanham, MD: Rowman & Littlefield, 2007.

Farmer, Paul. *AIDS and Accusation: Haiti and the Geography of Blame*. Berkeley: University of California, 2006.

Fatton, Robert. *Haiti's Predatory Republic: The Unending Transition to Democracy*. Boulder, CO: Lynne Rienner, 2002.

Fleurimond, Wiener Kerns. *Haïti de la Crise à l'occupation: Histoire d'un chaos, 2000–2004*. Paris: L'Harmattan, 2009.

James, Erica Caple. *Democratic Insecurities: Violence, Trauma, and Intervention in Haiti*. Berkeley: University of California Press, 2010.

Richman, Karen E. *Migration and Vodou*. Gainesville: University Press of Florida, 2008.

Smith, Jenny M. *When the Hands Are Many: Community Organization and Social Change in Rural Haiti*. Ithaca, NY: Cornell University Press, 2001.

Part VIII

Buteau, Pierre, Rodney St. Éloi, and Lyonel Trouillot, eds. *Refonder Haïti?* [New foundations for Haiti?]. Montreal: Mémoire d'encrier, 2011.

Danticat, Edwidge. *Brother I'm Dying*. New York: Vintage, 2007.

Dumas, Reginald. *An Encounter with Haiti: Notes of a Special Advisor*. Port of Spain, Trinidad: Medianet, 2008.

Katz, Jonathan. *The Big Truck That Went By: How the World Came to Save Haiti and Left Behind a Disaster*. New York: Saint Martin's, 2013.

Ménard, Nadève. *Écrits d'Haïti: Perspectives sur la littérature haïtienne contemporaine (1986–2006)* [Writings of Haiti: Perspectives on contemporary Haitian literature]. Paris: Karthala, 2011.

Polyné, Millery, ed. *The Idea of Haiti: Rethinking Crisis and Development*. Minneapolis: University of Minnesota Press, 2013.

Schuller, Mark, and Pablo Morales. *Tectonic Shifts: Haiti since the Earthquake*. Sterling, VA: Kumarian Press, 2012.

Ulysse, Gina. *Why Haiti Needs New Narratives: A Post-earthquake Chronicle.* Middletown, CT: Wesleyan University Press, 2015.

Films

Antonin, Arnold. https://arnoldantoninfilms.com/.

Asté, Patricia, dir. *Égalité for All: Human Rights and the Haitian Revolution.* PBS Home Video, 2009.

Benoit, Patricia. *Stones in the Sun.* Lotbo Films, 2012.

Bergan, Renée, and Mark Schuller, dir. *Poto Mitan: Haitian Women, Pillars of the Global Economy.* Documentary Educational Resources, 2009.

Blouin, Eve, and Raynald Leconte, dir. *In the Eye of the Spiral.* 2014.

Delatour, Mario, dir. *Storming Papa Doc.* 2014.

Demme, Jonathan, dir. *The Agronomist.* Clinica Estetico, 2005.

Hillel, Joseph, dir. *Ayiti Toma, in the Land of the Living.* Fun Film Distribution, 2012.

Lescot, Anne, and Laurence Magloire. *Of Men and Gods.* 2002.

Magloire, Rachel, dir. *Deported.* Velvet Films, 2012.

Peck, Raoul, dir. *Fatal Assistance.* Velvet Films, 2013.

Salnave, Rachelle, dir. *La Belle Vie: The Good Life.* 2015.

Acknowledgment of Copyrights and Sources

Part I: Foundations

"An Account of the Antiquities of the Indians," by Ramón Pané, from *An Account of the Antiquities of the Indians* (Durham, NC: Duke University Press, 2002), 3–6, 13–14, 17–21.

"Sou lanmè," a Haitian folksong, original author unknown, transcribed and translated by Laurent Dubois and Erol Josué, 13 March 2005.

"Account of a Conspiracy Organized by the Negros, 1758," by an anonymous author, previously published as "Relation d'une conspiration tramée par les nègres dans l'îsle de S. Domingue (1758)," from Digital Library of the Caribbean, http://www .dloc.com/UF00095960/.

"The Infamous Rosalie," by Évelyne Trouillot, from *The Infamous Rosalie* (Lincoln: University of Nebraska Press, 2013), 3–7. Translated into English by M. A. Salvodon. Originally published in French as *Rosalie l'infâme*, copyright 2003 by Éditions Dapper, Paris. English translation copyright 2013 by M. A. Salvodon. Reprinted courtesy of University of Nebraska Press.

"The Declaration of Independence," by Jean-Jacques Dessalines, originally from the British National Archives, CO 137/111, 113ff, included in *Slave Revolution in the Caribbean 1789–1804: A Brief History with Documents*, by Laurent Dubois and John Garrigus (New York: Macmillan, 2006).

"Haitian Hymn," originally included in Dessalines's *Journal de campagne*, from the British National Archives, CO 137/111, BNA.

"Writings," by Jean-Jacques Dessalines: proclamation, Gouverneur General aux Habitants d'Hayti, 28 April 1804; letter, Jean-Jacques Dessalines to George Nugent, May 1804, National Library of Jamaica, MS72, box 2, 628N.

"A Woman's Quest for Freedom in a Land of Re-enslavement," Notarial Act in Favor of the Freedom of Marie Melie, 18 March 1808, from the Archives Nationales d'Outre-Mer (ANOM), Aix-en-Provence, France, Dépôt des Papiers Publics des Colonies, Notariat de Saint-Domingue 1700.

"An Exchange of Letters," by Alexandre Pétion and Simón Bolívar, from *Alexandre Pétion devant l'humanité: Alexandre Pétion et Simón Bolívar. Haïti et l'Amérique latine* by François Dalencour (Port-au-Prince, 1929), 125, 139.

"The Code Henry," by King Henry Christophe, previously published as "Loi concernant la culture," from *Code Henry* (Cap-Henry [Cap-Haïtien]: Chez P. Roux, Imprimeur du Roi, 1812), 5–8.

"Henry Christophe and the English Abolitionists," by King Henry Christophe: article excerpt from *Gazette Royal d'Hayti* (17 October 1816), copy from the Danish National Archives; letters to Clarkson and the Emperor Alexander, from *Henry Christophe and Thomas Clarkson: A Correspondence*, ed. and trans. Earl Leslie Griggs and Clifford H. Prator (Berkeley: University of California Press, 1952), 91–93, 128–31. Reprinted by permission of University of California Press.

"The Colonial System Unveiled," by Baron de Vastey, from *The Colonial System Unveiled*, trans. Chris Bongie (Liverpool: Liverpool University Press, 2014), 108–11, 123–26. Reprinted by permission of Liverpool University Press.

"Hymn to Liberty," by Antoine Dupré, from *Panorama de la poésie haïtienne*, edited by Carlos St-Louis and Maurice A. Lubin (Port-au-Prince: Éditions Henri Deschamps, 1950), 1.

"The King's Hunting Party," by Juste Chanlatte, from *La partie de chasse du roi, opéra, en trois actes. Paroles de Son Excellence M. le Comte de Rosiers, Musique de M. Cassian, haytien* (Sans-Souci: De l'Imprimerie Royale, 1820).

"Voyage to the North of Haiti," by Hérard Dumesle, from *Voyages dans le nord d'Hayti, ou, Révélation des lieux et des movements historiques* (Aux Cayes, 1823).

"On the Origins of the Counter-plantation System," by Jean Casimir, from an unpublished paper titled "The Sovereign People of Haiti during the Eighteenth and Nineteenth Centuries," 2013. Printed courtesy of Jean Casimir.

Part II: The Second Generation

"The Indemnity: French Royal Ordinance of 1825," by King Charles X of France, from *Bulletin des lois de la République française* 58, 1798 (1825), 185. Bibliothèque Nationale de France.

"Hymn to Independence," by Jean-Baptiste Romane, from *Histoire de la littérature haïtienne ou l'ame noire*, by Duraciné Vaval (Port-au-Prince: Imp. Héraux, 1933), 22.

"Boyer's Rural Code," by President Jean-Pierre Boyer, from *Code Rural d'Haïti* (Port-au-Prince: Imprimerie du Gouvernement, 1826), 2, 7–8, 11–15, 18–19.

"Le lambi," by Ignace Nau, from *L'Union, Recueil Commercial et Littéraire* (Port-au-Prince, 20 April 1837), 2–3.

"An Experimental Farm," by Victor Schoelcher, from *Colonies étrangères et Haiti: Résultats de l'emancipation anglaise* (Paris: Pagnerre, 1843), 261–66, 268–70, 273–74.

"The 1842 Earthquake," by Démesvar Delorme, from *1842 au Cap tremblement de terre* (Cap-Haïtien: Imprimerie du Progrès), 2–9, 13–15, 16–17, 23–24.

"Acaau and the Piquet Rebellion of 1843," by Gustave d'Alaux, originally published as *Soulouque and His Empire. From the French of Gustave d'Alaux*, translated and edited by John H. Parkhill (Richmond: J. W. Randolph, 1861), 74–75, 134–39. Originally published as *L'empereur Soulouque et son empire* by Gustave d'Alaux (Paris: Michel Levy Freres, 1856).

"The Separation of Haiti and the Dominican Republic," by Thomas Madiou, originally published in *Histoire d'Haïti, Tome VIII: de 1843 à 1846* (Port-au-Prince: Editions Henri Deshamps, 1985), 106–15, 103–4.

"President Geffrard Protests the Spanish Annexation of the Dominican Republic," by Fabre Geffrard, originally published in *Anexión y guerra de Santo Domingo (Vol. 1)* by José de la Gándara (Madrid: Imprenta de Correo Militar, 1884), 417–21.

"*Stella*, the First Haitian Novel," by Émeric Bergeaud, originally published as *Stella* (Paris: E. Dentu, 1859), translated by Lesley Curtis and Christen Mucher (New York: New York University Press, 2015), 171–75.

"*Haiti and Its Visitors* and 'Le vieux piquet,'" by Louis Joseph Janvier, originally published as *La République d'Haïti et ses visiteurs (1840–1882)* (Paris: Mappon et Flammarion, 1883), xiv–xvi, 510–13, 518–21, 523–25.

"Atlas critique d'Haïti," by Georges Anglade, from *Atlas critique d'Haïti* (Montréal: Groupe d'études et de recherches critiques d'espace, UQAM, 1982), 20–23, 37–38.

Part III: The Birth of Modern-Day Haiti

"Nineteenth-Century Haiti by the Numbers," by Louis Gentil Tippenhauer, previously published in *The Island of Haiti* (Leipzig, 1893), 355, 422–23.

"My Panama Hat Fell Off," anonymous folksong, originally published as "Panama m tonbe" in *Chansons d'enfants en français et créole, Children Songs in French and Creole, Chante Timoun* (Coconut Creek, FL: EducaVision, ca. 2000), 80.

"God, Work, and Liberty!," by Oswald Durand, previously published as "Chant national" in *Rires et pleurs* (Corbeil: Imprimerie É. Crété, 1896; repr., Port-au-Prince: Editions Presses Nationales d'Haiti, 2005), 177–80.

"The National Anthem, 'La Dessalinienne,'" by Justin Lhérisson and Nicolas Geffrard, originally published as *La Dessalinienne, hymne national* (Port-au-Prince: Impr. A. A. Heraux, 1906). English translation by Martin Shaw (with Diccon Shaw and Mary Elizabeth Shaw for first verse).

"Trial about the Consolidation of Debt," by various authors, from *L'affaire de la consolidation: Documents et pièces judiciaires* (Port-au-Prince: Fardin, 1979), 7, 199–200, 546–47.

"The Execution of the Coicou Brothers," by Nord Alexis and Anténor Firmin: Nord Alexis's version, from letter in *Le Nouvelliste*, 16 March 1908; Anténor Firmin's reaction, from Firmin, *Lettres de Saint Thomas: Études sociologiques, historiques et littéraires* (Paris: V. Girard & E. Brière, 1910).

"The Luders Affair," by Solon Ménos, from *L'affaire Luders* (Port-au-Prince: Verrollot, 1893), 65–67, 78–79, 87, 134–35.

"Anti-Syrian Legislation," by the Haitian Legislature, originally published as "Loi du 10 Août, 1903," in *Le Moniteur*, no. 46 (8 June 1904).

"Choucoune," by Oswald Durand, from *Rires et pleurs, poésies* (Imprimerie É. Crété, 1896; repr., Nendeln, Liechtenstein: Kraus Reprint, 1970).

"Bouqui's Bath," by Suzanne Comhaire-Sylvain, from *Le roman de Bouqui* (Impr. du Collège Vertières, 1940; repr., Québec: Léméac, 1973), 19–21.

"Zoune at Her Godmother's," by Justin Lhérisson, from *Zoune chez sa ninnainne* (Port-au-Prince: Editions Presses Nationales d'Haiti, 2005).

"The Haytian Question," by Hannibal Price, from *The Haytian Question* (New York: Weiss & Co., 1891), 9–13.

"African Americans Defend Haiti," by Ebenezer Don Carlos Bassett, originally published as "Should Haiti Be Annexed to the United States?," in *The Voice of the Negro* 1 (May 1904), 191–97.

"On the Caribbean Confederation," by Anténor Firmin, originally published as "Haiti et la Confederation Antillienne," in *Lettres de Saint-Thomas: Études sociologiques, historiques et littéraires* (Port-au-Prince: Fardin, 1986).

Part IV: Occupied Haiti (1915–1934)

"1915 Treaty between the United States and Haiti," by Robert Beale Davis Jr. and Louis Borno, from *Treaty between the United States and Haiti: Finances, Development and Economic Tranquility of Haiti* (Washington, DC: Government Printing Office, 1922).

"The Patriotic Union of Haiti Protests the U.S. Occupation," by the Delegates to the U.S. of the Union Patriotique d'Haiti, from "Memoir on the Political, Economic and Financial Conditions Existing in the Republic of Haiti under the American Occupation," 1 May 1921 (Washington, DC: Columbus Memorial Library).

"Memories of Corvée Labor and the Caco Revolt," by Roger Gaillard, from *Hinche mise en croix* (Port-au-Prince: Imprimerie Le Natal, 1982), 215–16, 224, 179–80.

"My Dear Charlemagne," by Widow Massena Péralte, ca. 1915–17, from the John H. Russell Jr., Personal Papers, box 2, Haiti, folder 8, History & Museums Division Headquarters, U.S. Marine Corps, Quantico, VA.

"La vocation de l'élite," by Jean Price-Mars, from *La vocation de l'élite* (Port-au-Prince: Imprimerie Edmond Chenet, 1919), i–iv, 1, 16, 58–66, 68–69.

"Dix années de lutte pour la liberté," by Georges Sylvain, from *Dix années de lutte pour la liberté, 1915–1925* (Port-au-Prince: Editions H. Deschamps, 1927). Vol. 1: 4–5, 88–89. Vol. 2: 67–69, 88–92, 193–97, 183–86.

"Les simulacres," by Fernand Hibbert, from *Les simulacres: L'aventure de M. Hellénus Caton* (1923; repr., Port-au-Prince: Fardin, 1976).

"La Revue Indigène: The Project," by Normil Sylvain, from *La Revue Indigène: Anthologie de la poésie haïtienne "indigène"* (Nendeln, Liechtenstein: Kraus Reprint, 1971), 1–6, 9–10; originally published as "Chronique—Programme" in *La Revue Indigène*, no. 1 (July 1927): 1–6, 9–10.

"La Revue Indigène: The Poetry," by various authors: "Subway," by André Liautaud, from *La Revue Indigène: Anthologie de la poésie haïtienne "indigène"* (Nendeln, Liechtenstein: Kraus Reprint, 1971); first collected in *Anthologie de la Poésie haïtienne "indigène"* (Port-au-Prince: Imprimerie modèle, 1928), 28. "Grand'Rue" and "Prends l'élégance et tords-lui de corps," by Philippe Thoby-Marcelin, from *La Revue Indigène: Anthologie de la poésie haïtienne "indigène"* (Nendeln, Liechtenstein: Kraus Reprint, 1971); first collected in *Anthologie de la Poésie haïtienne "indigène"* (Port-au-Prince: Imprimerie modèle, 1928), 61–62. "Poème," by Daniel Heurtelou, from *La Revue Indigène: Anthologie de la poésie haïtienne "indigène"* (Nendeln, Liechtenstein: Kraus Reprint, 1971); originally published in *La Revue Indigène* no. 3 (September 1927), 119. "Nostalgia [Nostalgie]," "Nous," and "Vous," by Carl Brouard, from *La Revue Indigène: Anthologie de la poésie haïtienne "indigène"* (Nendeln, Liechtenstein: Kraus Reprint, 1971); first collected in *Pages Retrouvées: Œuvres en prose et en vers* (Port-au-Prince: Editions Panorama, 1963), 15, 19–21. "O Loulouse," by Carl Brouard, from *La Revue Indigène: Anthologie de la poésie haïtienne "indigène"* (Nendeln, Liechtenstein: Kraus Reprint, 1971); first collected in *Anthologie de la Poésie haïtienne "indigène"* (Port-au-Prince: Imprimerie modèle, 1928), 5.

"La blanche négresse," by Cléante Valcin, from *La blanche négresse* (Port-au-Prince: Presses Nationales, 2007), 57–58, 114–16, 119, 170–71.

"Souvenir d'Haïti," by Othello Bayard, originally published as "Souvni d'Ayiti" in *Chansons d'enfants en français et créole, Children Songs in French and Creole, Chante Timoun* (Coconut Creek, FL: EducaVision, ca. 2000), 107–9.

"Veneer of Modernization," by Suzy Castor, from *L'occupation américaine d'Haïti* (Port-au-Prince: Imprimerie Henri Deschamps, 1988), 215–20.

Part V: Second Independence

"Proud Haiti," by Edouard A. Tardieu, originally published as *Fière Haiti* (patriotic song), 1937. Available at https://web.archive.org/web/20160415025532/http://www .ayitihistory.com/index.htm#patriotic_songs.htm.

"Color Prejudice," by Jacques Roumain, from *Analyse schématique* (Port-au-Prince: V. Valcin, 1934).

"Migration to Cuba," by Maurice Casséus and Jacques Roumain: Casséus, excerpt from *Viejo* (Port-au-Prince: Éditions La Presse, 1935; repr., Nendeln, Liechtenstein: Kraus Reprints, 1970]), 42–43; Roumain, excerpt from *Gouverneurs de la rosée* (Imprimerie de l'État, 1944; repr., Montreal: Mémoire d'Encrier, 2004), 59.

"Anti-superstition Laws," by President Sténio Vincent, originally published as "Décret-loi," 5 September 1935, in *Bulletin des lois et actes: Année 1935* (Port-au-Prince: Imprimerie de l'Etat, 1935), 351–52.

"An Oral History of a Massacre," by Isil Nicolas Cour, from interview with Cour conducted by Lauren Derby and Richard Turits, Dosmon, Ouanaminthe, Haiti, 1988, with the assistance of Édouard-Jean Baptiste and Ciprián Soler.

"Massacre River," by René Philoctète, from *Massacre River*, translated by Linda Coverdale (New York: New Directions, 2005), 31–34, 46–47; originally published as *Le peuple des terres mêlées* (Port-au Prince: H. Deschamps, 1989).

"On the 1937 Massacre," by Esther Dartigue, from Esther Dartigue and John Dartigue, *Forging Ahead: Recollections of the Life and Times of Esther Dartigue* (North Charleston, SC: CreateSpace Independent Publishing Platform, 2013), 176–79, 202.

"Official Communiqué on 'Incidents' in the Dominican Republic," by the Governments of Haiti and the Dominican Republic, originally published as "Communiqué" in *Le Nouvelliste*, 16 October 1937.

"Vyewo," by Jean-Claude Martineau (Koralen), from *Flè dizè* (New York: Marika Roumain, 1982).

"Nedjé," by Roussan Camille, from *The Poetry of the Negro, 1746–1949*, ed. Langston Hughes, trans. Mercer Cook (New York: Doubleday, 1951), 366–68.

"Dyakout," by Félix Morisseau-Leroy, from *Dyakout 1, 2, 3, 4* (New York: Haitiana Publications, 1990), 20–21, 24–28.

"On *The Voice of Women*," by Madeleine Sylvain Bouchereau, originally published as "Nous revoici" in *La Voix des Femmes* 9, no. 1 (11 January 1947).

"On Women's Emancipation," by Marie-Thérèse Colimon-Hall, originally published as "L'émancipation de la jeune fille (êtes-vous pour ou contre?)" in *Premier Congres National Des Femmes Haïtiennes*, by La Ligue Feminine d'Action Sociale (Port-au-Prince, 1950).

"On the 1946 Revolution," by Matthew J. Smith, from *Red and Black in Haiti: Radicalism, Conflict, and Political Change, 1934–1957* (Chapel Hill: University of North Carolina Press, 2009), 71–81.

"O My Country," by Anthony Phelps, from *Mon pays que voici* (Port-au-Prince: Mémoire d'encrier, 2007), 26–28, 31–35, 36–47, 49–52.

"General Sun, My Brother," by Jacques Stephen Alexis, from *General Sun, My Brother*, trans. Carrol F. Coates (Charlottesville: University of Virginia Press, 1999), 15–16; originally published as *Compère Général Soleil* (Paris: Gallimard, 1955).

"Flicker of an Eyelid," by Jacques Stephen Alexis, from *In the Flicker of an Eyelid*, trans. Carrol F. Coates and Edwidge Danticat (Charlottesville: University of Virginia Press, 2002), 218–19; originally published as *L'espace d'un cillement* (Paris: Editions Gallimard, 1959).

"The Trade Union Movement," by Daniel Fignolé and Jacques Brutus: Fignolé, from *Contribution à l'histoire du mouvement syndical en Haïti* (Port-au-Prince, 1954); Brutus, "Le syndicalisme haïtien hier et aujourd'hui," *Rond Point* 7 (May 1963).

"Speech by the 'Leader of the Revolution,'" by François Duvalier, speech previously published as "Improvisation du Chef de la Révolution à l'Occasion de la Grande Parade du 22 Mai 1964 des VSN des 9 Départements," in *Œuvres essentielles*, 3rd ed., vol. 4 (Port-au-Prince: Collections, 1970), 389–90.

"The Haitian Fighter," by Le Combattant Haïtien, previously published as "L'ésprit de *Le Combattant*," 30 June 1966.

"Atibon-Legba," by René Depestre, from *A Rainbow for the Christian West*, trans. Joan (Colin) Dayan (Amherst: University of Massachusetts Press, 1977), 123–25; originally published as *Un arc-en-ciel pour l'occident chrétien* (Paris: Présence Africaine, 1967).

"The Festival of the Greasy Pole," by René Depestre, from *The Festival of the Greasy Pole*, trans. Carrol F. Coates (Charlottesville: University Press of Virginia, 1979), 26–29; originally published as *Le mât de cocagne* (Paris: Gallimard, 1979).

"Dance on the Volcano," by Marie Chauvet, from Marie Vieux-Chauvet, *Dance on the Volcano*, trans. Kaiama L. Glover (New York: Archipelago Books, 2016), 225–28; originally published as *La danse sur le volcan* (Paris: Plon, 1957).

"Interview of Jean-Claude Duvalier: Duvalier's 'Liberal' Agenda," interview by Jon-Blaise Alima, previously published as "L'interview accordée par le Président Duvalier à Jon-Blaise Alima de *Jeune Afrique*" in *Le Petit Samedi Soir*, 22 April 1978.

"On the Saut-d'Eau Pilgrimage," by Jean Dominique, previously published as "Inter-Actualités Magazine: Saut-d'Eau, Ville Bonheur. Saut-d'Eau, Ville Mystère; Saut-d'Eau, Ville Misère," July 1976, Radio Haiti Collection, RL10059RR0077, David M. Rubenstein Rare Book & Manuscript Library, Duke University, http://library .duke.edu/rubenstein/findingaids/radiohaiti/; "Jean Dominique on the Saut-d'Eau Pilgrimage," by Jean Dominique, previously published as "History of Radio Haiti, Special 56th Anniversary Broadcast, Jean L. Dominique," 19 September 1976, Radio Haiti Collection, RL10059RR1224, David M. Rubenstein Rare Book & Manuscript Library, Duke University, http://library.duke.edu/rubenstein/findingaids /radiohaiti/.

"Dreams of Exile and Novelistic Intent," by Jean-Claude Fignolé, from *Vœu de voyage et intention romanesque* (Port-au-Prince: Fardin, 1978), 54–56.

"Dezafi," by Franképienne, from *Dezafi* (Port-au-Prince: Fardin, 1975).

"And the Good Lord Laughs," by Edris Saint-Amand, from *Bon Dieu rit* (Paris: Hâtier, 1988), 131–36.

"Letter to the Haitian Refugee Project," by various imprisoned Haitian refugee women, from letter to the Haitian Refugee Project, 2 April 1982, box 23, folder 4, Ira Gollobin Haitian Refugee Collection, Schomburg Center for Research in Black Culture, New York Public Library.

"Immigration," by Tanbou Libète, from *4 chabon dife* (New York, 1974).

"Gender and Politics in Contemporary Haiti," by Carolle Charles, from "Gender and Politics in Contemporary Haiti: The Duvalierist State, Transnationalism, and the Emergence of a New Feminism (1980–1990)," *Feminist Studies* 21, no. 1 (Spring 1995): 135–64, 138–41.

Part VII: Overthrow and Aftermath of Duvalier

"Four Poems," by Georges Castera: "Prolètè" and "Bisuit léta," from *Bisuit léta* (Port-au-Prince: Idées nouvelles, idées prolétariennes, 1978), 30, 37; "San," from *Pye Pou Pye* (Port-au-Prince: Idées nouvelles, Idées prolétariennes, 1986), 38; "Lari Pòtoprens," from *Gate Priyè* (Haiti: Editions à Contre-Courant, 1990); "Lanmè Pòtoprens," from *Rèl* (Haiti: Editions à Contre-Courant, 1995).

"Liberation Theology," by Conférence Épiscopale d'Haïti, from *Conférence Épiscopale d'Haïti, Présence de l'Église en Haïti: Messages et documents de l'épiscopat, 1980–1988* (Paris: Éditions S.O.S., 1988), 51–65.

"On the Movement against Duvalier," by Jean Dominique, from "La fin du marronage haïtien: Éléments pour une étude des mouvements de contestation populaire en Haïti," *Collectif Paroles* 32 (December 1985): 39–46.

"Interview with a Young Market Woman," by Magalie St. Louis and Nadine Andre, from "Interview with Magalie St. Louis, a young market-woman, December 6, 1987," box 1, folder 3, Haiti Dechoukaj Collection, Schomburg Center for Research in Black Culture, New York Public Library.

"Nou vle," by Ansy Dérose, from *Ansy Dérose, Nou vle*, Productions Artistiques YA 001, 1987.

"The Constitution of 1987," by the Government of Haiti, available from the Political Database of the Americas, Georgetown University, http://pdba.georgetown.edu/Constitutions/Haiti/haiti1987fr.html.

"*Rara* Songs of Political Protest," by various groups, from *Zap Zap Forever*.

"The Peasants' Movement," by Tèt Kole: "Peasants' Movement Holds News Conference," Radio Métropole, 17 July 1990, FBIS Daily Reports, FBIS-LAT-90-139, Foreign Broadcast Information Service, 19 July, 1990; "Further on Peasants' Position," Radio Soleil, 18 July 1990, FBIS Daily Reports. FBIS-LAT-90-139, Foreign Broadcast Information Service, 19 July 1990.

"Aristide and the Popular Movement," by Jean-Bertrand Aristide, from *Theology and Politics* (Montreal: CIDHICA, 1995), 79–87.

"My Heart Does Not Leap," by Boukman Eksperyans: "Kè m pa sote," by Boukman Eksperyans, from *Vodou Adjae*, Mango Records 16253 9899-1, 1991.

"On Theology and Politics," by Jean-Bertrand Aristide, from *Theology and Politics* (Montreal: Centre International de Documentation et d'Information Haïtienne, Caribéenne et Afro-canadienne, 1995), 79–87.

"Street of Lost Footsteps," by Lyonel Trouillot, from *Street of Lost Footsteps*, trans. Linda Coverdale (Lincoln: University of Nebraska Press, 2004), 29–31.

Part VIII: Haiti in the New Millennium

"The Agronomist," by Kettly Mars, previously published as "L'agronome" in *Mirage-Hôtel* (Port-au-Prince: Imprimerie Caraïbe, 2002), 9–13.

"Poverty Does Not Come from the Sky," by *AlterPresse*, from "Catastrophe en Haïti: La misère ne vient pas du ciel," 27 September 2004, http://www.alterpresse.org /spip.php?article1731, previously published by *Convergences Révolutionnaires*.

"Pòtoprens," by BIC, from *Wow!*, Nouvel Jenerasyon Records NJCD-172, 2005.

"Political Music from Bel Air," by Rara M No Limit, Bèlè Masif, and Blaze One: Rara M No Limit, "Lepolis" and "Untitled," from *Rara M No Limit* (2004); Bèlè Masif, "Stil Bèlèlè" [Bel Air style] and "Nan mas la" [In the masses], 2006; Blaze One, "Gran dosye" [Grand rap sheet] and "Istwa Baghdad" [Story of Baghdad], 2011 and 2012.

"Strange Story," by Bélo, from *Lakou Trankil* (Solèy Sounds, 2005).

"Faults," by Yanick Lahens, from *Failles* (Port-au-Prince: Lune, 2010), 42–43, 75–76, 77–79, 96–100.

"Everything Is Moving around Me," by Dany Laferrière, from *Tout bouge autour de moi* (Paris: Bernard Grasset, 2011), 26–27, 33, 77–79, 92–93.

"We Are Wozo," by Edwidge Danticat, previously published as "Edwidge Danticat Speaks on Mac McLelland Essay" in *Essence*, 10 July 2011.

"The Cholera Outbreak," by Roberson Alphonse, previously published as "Sur tra décces du premier décès" in *Le Nouvelliste*, 3 November 2010.

"On the Politics of Haitian Creole," by various authors: interview with Emmanuel W. Védrine conducted by Gotson Pierre, previously published as "Interview with Haitian Linguist Emmanuel W. Védrine on the Occasion of His Ten Years of Research on the Kreyòl Language," translated by Emmanuel W. Védrine, available at http:// www.potomitan.info/vedrine/sicrad.pdf; open letter to President Michel Martelly by Jacques Pierre, previously published as "Ayiti: Respekte dwa lengwistik pèp ayisyen an 'tèt kale': Lèt tou louvri Jacques Pierre pou prezidan eli Michel Martelly" [Haiti: Honor the linguistic rights of the Haitian people "tèt kale": An Open Letter from Jacques Pierre for President-elect Michel Martelly] on *AlterPresse*, 10 May 2011, http://www.alterpresse.org/spip.php?article11015; excerpts from the law establishing the Haitian Creole Academy, from "Chapter II Status and Mission of the Academy" (in French), *Le Moniteur*, 7 April 2014.

"Stayle," by Brothers Posse.

"To Reestablish Haiti?," by Lemète Zéphyr and Pierre Buteau: Lemète Zéphyr, "Let's Build a Leadership That Can Live Up to Our Challenges!," previously published as "Forgeons un leadership à la hauteur de nos défis!" in *Refonder Haiti?*, ed. Pierre Buteau, Lyonel Trouillot, and Rodney St. Eloi (Montreal: Mémoire d'encrier, 2010), 376–79, 381–86; Pierre Buteau, "Why Re-establish?," previously published as "Pourquoi refonder?" in Buteau, Trouillot, and St. Eloi, *Refonder Haiti?*, 64–68.

Every reasonable effort has been made to obtain permission. We invite copyright holders to inform us of any oversights.

Index